FLORIDA STATE
UNIVERSITY LIBRARIES

SEP 19 2000

TALLAHASSEE, FLORIDA

ROYAL HISTORICAL SOCIETY
STUDIES IN HISTORY
SERIES
No. 47

REFORM AND REVIVAL
English Government in Ireland, 1470-1534

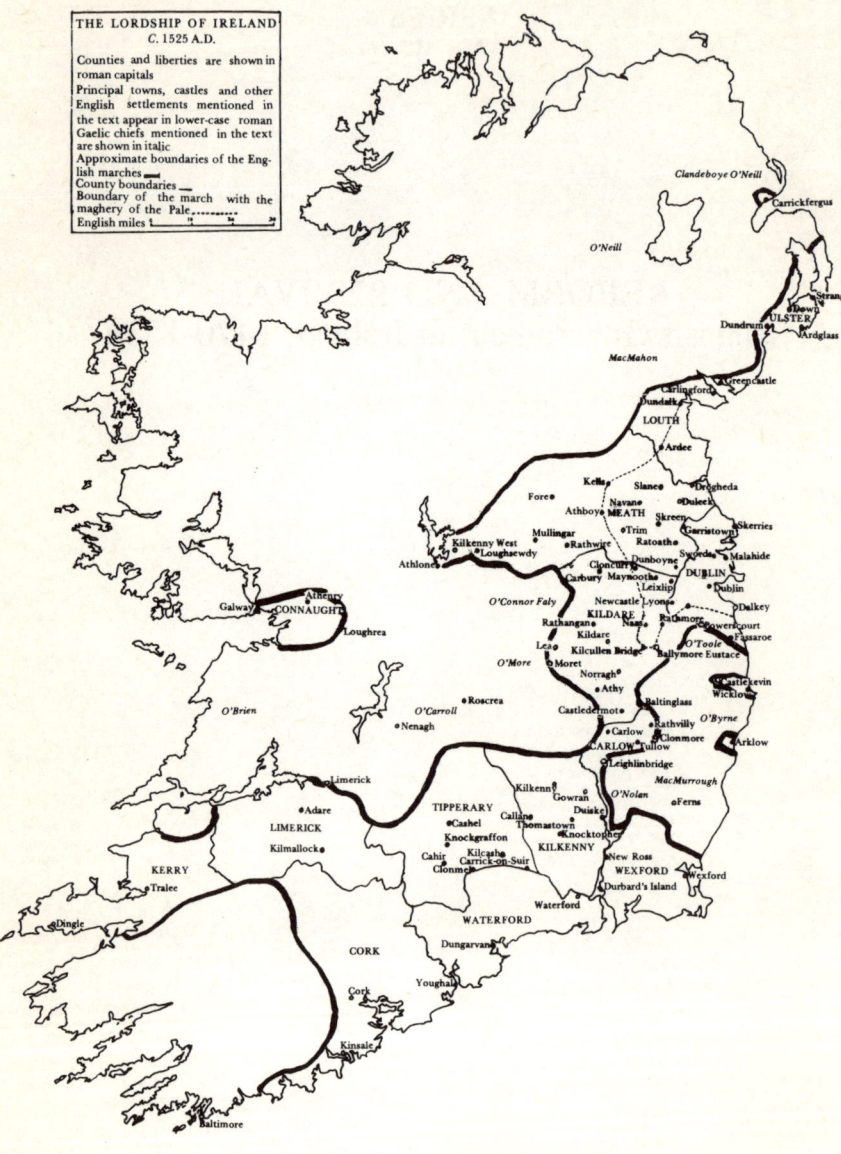

REFORM AND REVIVAL
English Government in Ireland, 1470-1534

Steven G. Ellis

ROYAL HISTORICAL SOCIETY
THE BOYDELL PRESS · WOODBRIDGE
ST MARTIN'S PRESS · NEW YORK

© Steven G. Ellis 1986

First published 1986

Published by
The Boydell Press
an imprint of Boydell & Brewer Ltd
PO Box 9 Woodbridge Suffolk IP12 3DF
and St Martin's Press Inc
175 Fifth Avenue New York NY10010
for
The Royal Historical Society
University College London WC1

UK ISBN 0 86193 204 8
US ISBN 0 312 66751 5

Printed in Great Britain by Short Run Press Ltd, Exeter

CONTENTS

		Page
Preface		ix
Abbreviations		xi
Introduction		1
1	The Executive	12
2	Defence	49
3	Revenue and Collection	67
4	Lawyers, Litigation and the Common Law	106
5	Legislation and the Prerogative Courts	143
6	The Seals and Secretariat	165
7	Local Government	181
Conclusion		206
Appendix		216
Bibliography		226
Index		237

ILLUSTRATIONS

The Lordship of Ireland c.1525 A.D. *Frontispiece*
Fifteenth-century sketch of the Irish exchequer *facing p. 88*

TO MY PARENTS

The Society records its gratitude to the following whose generosity made possible the initiation of this series: The British Academy; The Pilgrim Trust; The Twenty-Seven Foundation; The United States Embassy's Bicentennial funds; The Wolfson Trust; several private donors.

PREFACE

In recent years historians have devoted much attention to the problem of what exactly Tudor governments were trying to do in Ireland and why the reduction of that country took so long. This book originated in an attempt to clarify the problem in two ways; to analyse how the government operated in practice at the end of the middle ages and to discover how much of the medieval lordship survived into the sixteenth century to serve as a foundation for the 'Tudor reconquest'. Before long, however, I began to think that in many respects Henry VIII and his children did not so much solve the crown's traditional Irish problem as create and partially solve a new one. Of course many of the ingredients were the same, but it appeared that previous historians had done less than justice to the work of the Dublin government in the late medieval period, and this led me to redirect my inquiry backwards rather than to pursue the problem after 1534. The result is, I hope, a study which will serve to alter and broaden perspectives on the English lordship of Ireland and its transformation in the sixteenth century.

Very few original rolls and records of the Yorkist and early Tudor period survived the destruction of the Irish Public Record Office in 1922, and for the most part the historian must rely on transcripts, extracts and calendars to supply the gap. For this reason I have adopted a very full system of reference for records emanating from the central courts in Ireland, citing both the original roll (where identifiable) and the form in which it now survives. In part the difficulties of the source material account for the frequent employment of descriptive analysis where in other circumstances the argument might have been presented more succinctly. I also felt, however, that the advantages of including a full account of government in the lordship outweighed the greater clarity of argument or the savings in space which might occasionally have been achieved by concentrating more on the political reinterpretation of the period.

The debts which I have accumulated in the seven years spent on the book are immense, though space precludes me from acknowledging them all individually. My interest in the Tudor period was forged by Chris Haigh while I was an undergraduate. He supervised my M.A. dissertation and since then has continued to advise and encourage me in my work. My researches in administrative history have been guided and sustained by Geoffrey Elton, who watched over the progress of the present work with his customary kindness. Their help has been invaluable. The pioneering studies of David Quinn in the late medieval lordship have been a frequent source of stimulation, and besides discussing aspects of my research with me he very kindly allowed me to consult his forthcoming contribution to the second volume of the *New history of Ireland*. This book grew out of a Ph.D. dissertation submitted to the Queen's University of Belfast in 1978. It was prepared under the benevolent guidance of John Bossy, J.C. Beckett and the late E.R.R. Green and was greatly facilitated by the award of a research fellowship at the Institute of Irish Studies for the sessions 1974-6. I have also profited from the comments and criticisms made by the examiners of the dissertation, M.L. Bush and James Lydon. More recently, the whole work has been read in draft by Art Cosgrove, Nicholas Canny, Geoffrey Elton and Chris Haigh who suggested some important alterations as well as saving me from many errors. I should in conclusion acknowledge the continued support of my wife who has borne with this project far more patiently than I had any right to expect.

I have modernised the punctuation of quotations and silently extended abbreviations. Moneys are normally expressed in pounds Irish which until 1460 had parity with sterling; thereafter one pound Irish was generally worth one mark sterling. Where the meaning might otherwise be unclear, I have followed the editors of the *New history of Ireland* in describing the descendants of the Anglo-Norman colonists in Ireland as 'Old English' to distinguish them from the indigenous Gaelic population. This is perhaps less misleading than the term 'Anglo-Irish' which has other usages.

I am grateful to the Publications Fund of the National University of Ireland whose grant made possible the inclusion of the illustration from the Red Book of the Irish Exchequer.

S.G.E.
December 1984

ABBREVIATIONS

Acts privy council, Ire., 1556-71 — 'Acts of the privy council in Ireland, 1556-71'. Ed. J.T. Gilbert. In *H.M.C. rep.15,* app. iii. London, 1897.

Alen's reg. — *Calendar of Archbishop Alen's register, c. 1172-1534.* Ed. C. McNeill. Dublin, 1950.

Anal. Hib. — *Analecta Hibernica*

Ball, *Judges* — F.E. Ball, *The judges in Ireland, 1221-1921* (2 vols., London, 1926).

Bodl. — Bodleian Library, Oxford.

Cal. Carew MSS, 1515-74 [etc.] — *Calendar of the Carew manuscripts preserved in the archiepiscopal library at Lambeth, 1515-74* [etc.]. 6 vols., London, 1867-73.

Cal. pat. rolls, 1232-47[etc.] — *Calendar of the patent rolls, 1232-47* [etc.]. London, 1906-

Cal. pat. rolls Ire., Hen. VIII-Eliz. — *Calendar of patent and close rolls of chancery in Ireland, Henry VIII to 18th Elizabeth.* Ed. J. Morrin. Dublin, 1861.

Christ Church deeds — 'Calendar to Christ Church deeds, 1174-1684'. Ed. M.J. McEnery. In *P.R.I. rep. D.K. 20* (1888), *23* (1891), *24* (1892), *27* (1895).

Dowdall deeds — *Dowdall deeds.* Ed. C. McNeill & A.J. Otway-Ruthven. Dublin, 1960.

E.H.R. — *English Historical Review*

Ellis, 'Admin. Ire.' — S.G. Ellis, 'The administration of the lordship of Ireland under the early Tudors' (Ph.D. thesis, Belfast, 1979).

Facs. nat. MSS Ire. — *Facsimiles of the national manuscripts of Ireland.* Ed. J.T. Gilbert. 4 vols., Dublin, 1874-84.

Fiants Ire., Hen. VIII	'Calendar to fiants of the reign of Henry VIII'. In *P.R.I. rep. D.K. 7-22*. Dublin, 1875-90.
Gilbert, *Viceroys*	J.T. Gilbert, *History of the viceroys of Ireland* (Dublin, 1865).
Handbook Brit. chron.	F.M. Powicke & E.B. Fryde (eds.), *Handbook of British chronology* (2nd ed., London, 1961).
Hand, *Eng. law in Ire.*	G.J. Hand, *English law in Ireland, 1290-1324* (Cambridge, 1967).
Hist. Jn.	*The Historical Journal*
H.M.C. rep. 1[etc.]	*Historical Manuscripts Commission First report* [etc.]. London, 1870-
Holdsworth, *Hist. Eng. law*	Sir William Holdsworth, *A history of English law* (7th ed., 13 vols., London, 1922-52).
Holinshed, *Chronicles*	R. Holinshed, *The . . . chronicles of England, Scotlande and Irelande*. Ed. H. Ellis. 6 vols., London, 1807-8.
Hore & Graves, *Southern & eastern counties*	*The social state of the southern and eastern counties of Ireland in the sixteenth century*. Ed. H.F. Hore & J. Graves. Dublin, 1870.
I.H.R. Bull.	*Bulletin of the Institute of Historical Research*
I.H.S.	*Irish Historical Studies*
L. & P. Hen. VIII	*Letters and papers, foreign and domestic, Henry VIII*. 21 vols., London, 1862-1932.
L. & P. Ric. III & Hen. VII	*Letters and papers illustrative of the reigns of Richard III and Henry VII*. Ed. J. Gairdner. 2 vols., London, 1861-3.
Liber mun. pub. Hib.	*Liber munerum publicorum Hiberniae*. Ed. R. Lascelles. 2 vols., London, 1852.

Lydon, *Lordship*	J.F. Lydon, *The lordship of Ireland in the middle ages* (Dublin, 1972).
New hist. Ire.	T.W. Moody, F.X. Martin & F.J. Byrne (eds.), *A new history of Ireland,* ii (Oxford, forthcoming), iii (Oxford, 1976), ix (Oxford, 1984).
N.L.I.	National Library of Ireland.
Ormond deeds, 1172-1350 [etc.]	*Calendar of Ormond deeds, 1172-1350* [etc.] Ed. E. Curtis. 6 vols., Dublin 1932-43.
Otway-Ruthven, *Med. Ire.*	A.J. Otway-Ruthven, *A history of medieval Ireland* (London, 1968).
P.R.O.	Public Record Office, London
Proc. king's council Ire., 1392-3	*A roll of the proceedings of the king's council in Ireland for a portion of the sixteenth year of the reign of Richard II, 1392-3.* Ed. J. Graves. London, 1877.
P.R.O.I.	Public Record Office of Ireland, Dublin.
Quinn, *Guide finan. rec.*	D.B. Quinn, 'Guide to English financial records for Irish history, 1461-1558 with illustrative extracts, 1461-1509' *Anal. Hib.*, x (1941).
Rec. comm. Ire. rep., 1811-15 [etc.]	*Reports of the commissioners appointed . . . respecting the public records of Ireland.* 3 vols., [London, 1815-25].
Red Bk Kildare	*The Red Book of the earls of Kildare.* Ed. G. Mac Niocaill. Dublin, 1964.
R. Hist. Soc. Trans.	*Transactions of the Royal Historical Society*
R.I.A.	Royal Irish Academy, Dublin.
R.I.A. Proc.	*Proceedings of the Royal Irish Academy* (Section C)

Richardson & Sayles, *Admin. Ire.*	H.G. Richardson & G.O. Sayles, *The administration of Ireland, 1172-1377* (Dublin, 1963).
Richardson & Sayles, *Ir. parl. in middle ages*	H.G. Richardson & G.O. Sayles, *The Irish parliament in the middle ages* (Philadelphia, 1952).
Rot. pat. Hib.	*Rotulorum patentium et clausorum cancellariae Hiberniae calendarium.* Dublin, 1828.
R.S.A.I. Jn.	*Journal of the Royal Society of Antiquaries of Ireland*
Rymer, *Foedera*	*Foedera, conventiones, litterae et cujuscunque generis acta publica.* Ed. T. Rymer. London, 1740-1.
S.P. Hen. VIII	*State papers, Henry VIII.* 11 vols., London, 1830-52.
S.P.W.	St. Peter's College, Wexford.
Stat. Ire.	*The statutes at large passed in the parliaments held in Ireland.* 20 vols., Dublin, 1786-1801.
Stat. Ire., Edw. IV	*Statute rolls of the parliament of Ireland . . . reign of King Edward IV.* Ed. H.F. Berry & J.F. Morrissey. 2 vols., Dublin, 1914-39.
Stat. Ire., Hen. VI	*Statute rolls of the parliament of Ireland, reign of King Henry VI.* Ed. H.F. Berry. Dublin, 1910.
Stat. Ire., Hen. VII & VIII	'The bills and statutes of the Irish parliaments of Henry VII and Henry VIII'. Ed. D.B. Quinn. In *Anal. Hib.*, x (1941).
Stat. Ire., John-Hen. V	*Statutes and ordinances, and acts of the parliament of Ireland, King John to Henry V.* Ed. H.F. Berry. Dublin, 1907.
T.C.D.	Trinity College, Dublin.
Wood, *Public records of Ireland*	H. Wood, *A guide to the records deposited in the Public Record Office of Ireland* (Dublin, 1919).

INTRODUCTION

This study has two main aims, first, to analyse how the English lordship of Ireland was administered in the late middle ages and, second, to suggest that the period witnessed a revival in its fortunes based on a reform of government there. The book addresses the problem of the government's strength, efficiency and effective range in the years before crown policy towards Ireland was transformed, under the impact of the Reformation crisis and the Kildare rebellion, and it explores the similarities and differences between government in Ireland and in other parts of the English state. The lordship's administrative institutions were the product of the one whole-hearted attempt by the English monarchy during the middle ages to adapt the machinery evolved for the government of England to the rule of an overseas territory. And since the kingdom of England was much the most centralized and in many ways the most efficiently governed state of later medieval Europe, the fate of the Irish experiment is of wider relevance concerning the strengths and weaknesses of the common law system and the nature of the Anglo-Norman achievement. No detailed overall study of English government in medieval or early modern Ireland has previously been attempted, but studies of individual institutions have suggested that in the late middle ages they were antiquated, inefficient and unresponsive to changing needs and conditions.[1] By covering in depth a limited period of some sixty years, it is hoped to examine these suggestions more carefully, to evaluate crown policy, and to provide an insight into the general nature of English rule there.

So far as the second of its aims is concerned, this book attempts to demolish the view that the lordship experienced a period of continuous decline throughout the later medieval period, which was only halted by Henry VIII's decision in the mid-1530s to maintain an English governor and permanent garrison there. On the contrary, it is argued that from the 1470s the lordship enjoyed over half a century of relative stability after the disasters of Lancastrian rule, in which a series of modest administrative reforms brought about a perceptible revival in its fortunes and a strengthening of royal authority.

Traditionally, though for different reasons, historians have emphasised the failings and feebleness of government there and its increasing state of dissolution and decay. Medievalists have seen this

---

[1] For example, *New hist. Ire.*, iii (Oxford, 1976), 20-5, based on earlier, more specialized studies by D.B. Quinn.

as the logical culmination of processes which were already at work in Anglo-Norman society and government by 1300, whilst early modernists have in this way traced the need for the programme of reform which was implemented under the Tudors.[2] Thus it has been plausibly argued that by 1500 the English lordship had retreated to a small coastal strip between Dublin and Drogheda and a few walled towns beyond, and had to be rescued from oblivion by massive subventions in men and money from 1534 onwards. Certainly, Henry VIII's later years witnessed a renewed effort to exercise close supervision of his Irish administration, in contrast to the preceding period in which royal control was noticeably slacker than it had been in the best days of the medieval lordship. The weakness of royal authority in the later middle ages had also both allowed and compelled the colonists to forge closer ties with the Gaelic Irish: but whether, as has been suggested, the origins of Irish nationalism may be pushed back into a period in which relations between Gaelic and Old English were comparatively good and when the lordship's administration was mainly in the hands of those of Irish birth is another matter.[3] In fact, a political perspective which reaches from the coming of the Normans to the accession of the Tudors or thereabouts, or from the Kildare ascendancy to the treaty of Limerick, does not afford much opportunity for a detailed study of Yorkist and early-Tudor Ireland, although it is in this context that the period has hitherto been considered.[4] But perhaps the most basic reason why historians have failed to detect the revival in government which characterized the years after 1470 is the excessive reliance previously placed on the views of self-appointed critics of government in the state papers, whereas the actual products of that government, the court rolls, have been largely neglected.

There are also more particular reasons for believing that the existing interpretation of the political history of the period is inadequate. I have tried to show elsewhere that the ultimate establishment of a permanent garrison in Tudor Ireland was not the result of long-term policy but the only expedient available, and that initially at least this strategy was less successful in preserving the lordship than the previous policy of aristocratic delegation.[5] If this has served to

[2] Lydon, *Lordship,* p. 81; Otway-Ruthven, *Med. Ire.,* p. 270; Brendan Bradshaw, *The Irish constitutional revolution of the sixteenth century* (Cambridge, 1979), ch. 1, and *The dissolution of the religious orders in Ireland under Henry VIII* (Cambridge, 1974), chs. 1-2.

[3] Lydon, *Lordship,* pp. 262-3, ch. 10.

[4] For example, Otway-Ruthven, *Med. Ire.; New hist. Ire.,* iii.

[5] S.G. Ellis, 'Tudor policy and the Kildare ascendancy in the lordship of Ireland, 1496-1534', *I.H.S.,* xx (1976-7), 235-71, and 'Thomas Cromwell and Ireland, 1532-40', *Hist. Jn.,* xxiii (1980), 497-519.

emphasise the Kildare rebellion as marking a watershed in Anglo-Irish relations, the deputyship of Sir Edward Poynings (1494-5), which was the first occasion on which the Tudors set aside aristocratic delegation and which also saw important reforms in government, is on balance less convincing as such.[6] There are in fact good grounds for believing that the years 1470-1534 form a distinct period in the history of the medieval lordship.

Between 1470 and 1534 the acting chief governor of Ireland was for all but nine years a principal magnate of the region known as the English Pale. In comparison, the first seventy years of the fifteenth century had seen Pale landowners occupying the governorship for just under thirty of them, and for the remainder of the Tudor period the governor was almost invariably English-born.[7] This contrast reflects the crown's policy in the intervening period of cutting its losses in Ireland and concentrating on the defence of the Pale. At its height, the king's lordship had embraced rather more than half of the island, but for most of the fourteenth and fifteenth centuries royal authority was in decline. Since 1361 the crown had checked the growth of semi-autonomous lordships in the English districts and defended them from the Gaelic chiefs beyond only by large subventions of men and money from England. Under the Lancastrians, the size of these subventions had gradually been limited to the provision and payment of a force of betwen 300 and 500 archers for the governor, a force which had long been regarded as adequate to maintain the *status quo*. Even so, the English exchequer frequently defaulted on payments, and royal control in consequence diminished. Suitable candidates for office were increasingly difficult to find because of the liabilities and small rewards, and the Dublin administration had gradually to limit the normal scope of its military operations to the defence of the four counties which became the English Pale. The political centre of the lordship thus shifted during the middle years of the fifteenth century from the south midland territories of the earl of Ormond to Dublin, and the outlying English districts were left to fend for themselves. During Henry VI's personal rule, this strategy finally collapsed. From most of the lordship, the king received scant loyalty or revenue, and out of the remainder Richard of York built a Yorkist stronghold from which he made his attempt on the throne in 1460.

The fortuitous accession of Richard's son as Edward IV in 1461 strengthened the position of the crown. The new king was able to

---

[6]See S.G. Ellis, 'Henry VII and Ireland, 1491-6' in J.F. Lydon (ed.), *Anglo-Irish relations in the later middle ages* (Dublin, 1981), pp. 237-54.
[7]Calculated from *New hist. Ire.,* ix (Oxford, 1984), 478-87.

capitalize on previous support for the house of York as well as traditional loyalty to the crown. In general, Edward and his successors concentrated on keeping the Pale loyal and English, but Edward himself made two serious attempts during his first reign to extend royal authority in Ireland. In 1463, he appointed the principal Old English magnate of the south-west, the earl of Desmond, as deputy-lieutenant, and in 1467 he reverted to the earlier policy of appointing a trusted councillor, financed from England, and replaced Desmond by the earl of Worcester with a force of 700 archers. Worcester, however, perished in the Lancastrian restoration of 1470-1.[8] Thereafter, the conditions for a major departure in royal policy towards Ireland did not recur until the Kildare rebellion. The revolt of 1534 and the changes in England during the 1530s both necessitated increased control and, together with the recovery in royal finances, also provided the means and opportunity.[9] Thus during the years 1470 to 1534, the king normally acquiesced in the restraints on his control imposed by the employment, for the sake of economy, of a Pale landowner, and tried to ensure that this system worked to his best advantage.

Viewed from Westminster, this period was one in which kings of England treated the lordship's problems much as they treated those in outlying areas of England proper. In both Ireland and the north, for example, the extent to which the king subsidized the defence of the marches was gradually reduced during the fifteenth century, and both areas effectively ceased to be a charge on the English revenue from the end of Edward IV's reign.[10] In both areas, the tendency was to appoint a magnate whose social standing and numerous tenantry in the locality enabled him to defend the region more effectively and at less cost, but kings also showed themselves aware of the possible dangers inherent in delegating too much power in this way. Again, the involvement of the customary ruling magnates in major rebellions in the 1530s, the Kildare rebellion and the Pilgrimage of Grace, forced Henry VIII to experiment with new forms of government. In particular, the council in the north and the council of Ireland were reorganized in terms of personnel, and their powers were increased at

---

[8] Art Cosgrove, 'The execution of the earl of Desmond, 1468', *Journal of the Kerry Archaeological and Historical Society,* viii (1975), 11-27; Otway-Ruthven, *Med. Ire.,* pp. 389-95.

[9] Above, note 6; S.G. Ellis, 'The Kildare rebellion and the early Henrician Reformation', *Hist. Jn.,* xix (1976), 807-30.

[10] Below, chs. 1-2; R.L., Storey, 'The wardens of the marches of England towards Scotland, 1377-1489', *E.H.R.,* lxxii (1957), 593-615.

the expense of the local magnates. And in both areas the experiments were, in the short term at least, not particularly successful.[11]

Perhaps because of the survival of an independent Celtic society in much of the island and the greater isolation from England, the government generally attempted in Ireland to obliterate native law and custom and to build and preserve English institutions, whereas in Wales after 1282 it also tolerated a large measure of Welsh law and custom among the native population. This has tended to focus attention in Ireland on the extent to which external pressures forced the government and colonists to tolerate or accept divergence from English norms. By the later fifteenth century, therefore, the lordship of Ireland effectively comprised the four counties of the English Pale over which central government control remained fairly continuous plus a much larger and more fluctuating area beyond which was less amenable to control. The Normans had colonized most heavily the low-lying areas of Munster and Leinster and these remained the heart of the English lordship. They contained nearly all the towns, 'the sheet anchors of the state',[12] which distinguished the English from the Gaelic districts, although Galway in Connaught and Carrickfergus in Ulster were important outposts. The larger towns and cities were situated on the coast or the lower stretches of navigable rivers and most had strong trading links with English ports. Inland towns were most numerous in the Pale and the south midland territories of the earl of Ormond where they probably helped to resist the pressures by Gaelic society on the lordship.[13] The towns were primarily entrepôts for the surrounding countryside and were perhaps little different in function and size from those in many parts of England. There is almost no evidence from which reliable estimates of population may be made, but a recent rough calculation has put the population of the lordship's administrative capital, Dublin, at *c.* 8,000 in 1540, about the size of a major English provincial town.[14] English observers also considered Drogheda, Waterford, Cork, Limerick and Galway important, and among the secondary settlements the unwalled town of

---

[11]M.L. Bush, 'The problem of the far north: a study of the crisis of 1537 and its consequences', *Northern History*, vi (1971), 40-63; R.R. Reid, *The king's council in the north* (London, 1921), pp. 152-3; above, note 5.

[12]Quoted in Lydon, *Lordship*, p. 241.

[13]*New hist. Ire.*, iii, ch. 1.

[14]Gearóid Mac Niocaill, 'Socio-economic problems of the late medieval Irish town' in D.W. Harkness & M. O'Dowd (eds.), *The town in Ireland: Historical Studies XIII* (Belfast, 1981), pp. 18-19; W.G. Hoskins, *The age of plunder: the England of Henry VIII, 1500-47* (London, 1976), p. 89.

Wexford claimed 500 adult males in 1536.[15] The lordship was probably as little urbanized as contemporary England, although the commercial interests of the towns found substantial expression in parliament and the government frequently enlisted their support in its efforts to control the surrounding countryside.[16]

In large parts of the south and east a distinctively English manorial economy survived, though in the Gaelic areas and some marchlands conditions were quite exceptional by European standards. By 1500, to judge by their names, the small tenantry of the lordship was mainly Gaelic in origin, although this generalization conceals wide regional variations. Substantial freeholders were almost invariably of English descent, but where lists survive of the lower ranks of the peasantry there were often few English names. In 1510 of fifty-three small farmers and cottiers on lands held by a Meath gentleman, Christopher Cusack of Gerardstown, twenty-nine had English names, and on three Dublin manors of the earl of Ormond in the late 1470s only a quarter of the customary tenants and cottiers had retained Gaelic names.[17] This was the usual position in the more sheltered parts of the Pale and on some manors in Wexford, Kilkenny and Tipperary.[18] These areas were also predominantly English-speaking, although even the Pale gentry could also speak Gaelic.[19] On the earl of Kildare's manor of Maynooth in 1518, however, less than forty per cent of the cottiers were English, and just over a third of the husbandmen on the lands of Sir Roland FitzEustace in the Kildare marches near Ballymore Eustace in 1479.[20] In other shires the peasantry was predominantly or exclusively Gaelic.

Where a substantial peasant population of English origin survived, and with it the traditional manorial economy, social structures were

[15] P.R.O., S.P. 60/4/30 (printed in P.H. Hore, *History of the town and county of Wexford* (6 vols., London, 1900-11), v, 141); N.P. Canny, *The Elizabethan conquest of Ireland: a pattern established 1565-76* (Hassocks, 1976), p. 4; R.A. Butlin (ed.), *The development of the Irish town* (London, 1977), pp. 62-77.

[16] *Stat. Ire., Hen. VII & VIII, passim;* V.W. Treadwell, 'The Irish parliament of 1569-71', *R.I.A. Proc.,* lxv (1966), 60.

[17] T.C.D., MS 594, ff 23-4v; *Ormond deeds, 1413-1509,* no. 245.

[18] C.A. Empey, 'The Butler lordship', *Journal of the Butler Society,* i (1970-1), 184. For this and what follows, see generally the extents made by royal commissioners in 1540-41 in P.R.O., S.C. 11/934-5, S.P. 65/3/2; N.B. White (ed.), *Extents of Irish monastic possessions 1540-41* (Dublin, 1943), *passim.* See also *New hist. Ire.,* iii, ch. 1; K.W. Nicholls, *Gaelic and gaelicised Ireland in the middle ages* (Dublin, 1972), pp. 17-20.

[19] Empey, 'Butler lordship', pp. 184-5; *New hist. Ire.,* iii, 28.

[20] B.L., Harleian MS 3756, ff 31v-32; Parliament roll, 19 & 20 Edward IV c. 9 (*Stat. Ire., Edw. IV,* ii, 702-10).

diversified, unlike the rigid division between landowners and peasant cultivators which obtained in Gaelic Ireland.[21] Few manorial tenants were still personally unfree, but the peasantry ranged from landless labourers and poor cottiers and farmers holding two or three acres or less to prosperous husbandmen and yeomen who could afford to sue their landlords in the king's courts.[22] Labour services were frequently demanded, though they were far less onerous than in either Gaelic Ireland or medieval England: at Kells in 1510 fifteen days' work at harvest time was required of some tenants instead of rent, but normally no more than six days a year was demanded.[23] A comparatively low money rent was usually the chief burden on the tenant and though many farmers were nominally tenants at will, until the inflationary pressures of the mid-Tudor period forced landlords to raise rents and shorten leases, tenants enjoyed a fair measure of protection from arbitrary eviction and rack-renting since they were in short supply.[24] In Gaelic and some border areas, however, rent was in kind, frequently cattle or a proportion of the crop, and the lord might impose additional exactions at his discretion.[25]

The Gaelic recovery of the period c.1300-1460 had swept away many of the manorial settlements in areas which had been less heavily settled, and in general the more disturbed conditions and the related population decline stimulated a changeover from arable to pasture farming, especially in border areas.[26] But where, despite the raids, Anglo-Norman landlords managed to hang on to their lands, English land tenures remained the norm among the gentry, even where the acceptance of Gaelic tenants at will and the proximity of the frontier meant that culturally society was more Gaelic than English.[27] The gentry comprised a very miscellaneous group of landowners, ranging from thriving yeomen, parvenu merchants and royal officers and judges to wealthy and influential knights like the ninth earl of

---

[21]Cf. Canny, *Elizabethan conquest*, ch. 1; Nicholls, *Gaelic and gaelicised Ireland*, ch. 4.

[22]For this and what follows, see especially A.J. Otway-Ruthven, 'The organization of Anglo-Irish agriculture in the middle ages', *R.S.A.I. Jn.*, lxxxi (1951), 1-13. See also the entries of attorneys in suits pending in the Dublin bench, 1479-80; P.R.O.I., CB 1/10.

[23]T.C.D., MS 594, f. 23.

[24]*New hist. Ire.*, iii, 4-5. Cf. Canny, *Elizabethan conquest*, ch. 1.

[25]Nicholls, *Gaelic and gaelicised Ireland*, pp. 20, 31-32.

[26]*Ibid.*, pp. 17-20; Lydon, *Lordship*, esp. pp. 101-2.

[27]For example, Hore & Graves, *Southern & eastern counties*, passim.

Kildare's brother, Sir Thomas Fitzgerald, with an annual income of 400 marks from lands in Ireland and England.[28]

It is fashionable to emphasise the growth of separatist sentiments in the fifteenth century among colonists who were supposedly isolated from their cultural homeland,[29] but men like Fitzgerald were clearly regarded as part of the English political nation. Despite the tendency in the later fourteenth century for those resident in England to sell their Irish landholdings, before 1536 twelve English monasteries and lay landowners still held Irish lands worth almost £700 a year and at least six Irish peers and one or two others held or claimed lands in England and Wales.[30] And since there were no universities or Inns of Court in Ireland, merchants and gentry in pursuit of a higher education and legal training were accustomed to spend a few years in England.[31] With a common law, language, ancestry, culture, and structure of government, and with strong trading links with English towns and cities, the lordship was comparatively resistant to the pressures exerted on it by the utterly different form of society which existed in other parts of Ireland and Scotland.[32] In the short term at least, the unification of Ireland was more likely to come about through the conquest of one or other of the two communities by its rival than by the fusion of Gaelic and English into an Irish civilization. Certainly the clash of cultures did produce some interesting hybrid forms, but for the most part regions such as the Pale and the south midlands remained highly anglicized and parts of the north and west were largely uninfluenced by the Normans. Between these two extremes were an infinite number of local variations, but there is no real evidence that in the late middle ages a distinctive Hiberno-Norman civilization was gradually emerging.[33]

[28] *S.P. Hen. VIII,* ii, 175; Ball, *Judges,* i, 100-17; Mac Niocaill, 'Late medieval Irish town', pp. 13-15; Canny, *Elizabethan conquest,* pp. 17-20.

[29] Perhaps the most plausible account from this school is in Lydon, *Lordship,* chs. 9, 10.

[30] P.R.O., S.P. 65/1/2; *Alen's reg.,* pp. 286, 307-12; *Calendar of the close rolls, 1500-9* (London, 1963), no. 243; *L. & P. Ric. III & Hen. VII,* i, 75; *L. & P. Hen. VIII,* i (1st ed.), nos. 1299, 4254, ii, no. 1277, iv, no. 6135 (26); J. Mills & M.J. McEnery (eds.) *Calendar of the Gormanston register* (Dublin, 1916), pp. 87-110, 165-8; Parliament rolls, 16 & 17 Edward IV c. 8, 19 & 20 Edward IV c. 50 (*Stat. Ire., Edw. IV,* ii, 468, 812); J.A. Guy, *The Cardinal's court* (Hassocks, 1977), pp. 128-30; Gearóid Mac Niocaill, *Na Buirgéisí* (2 vols., Dublin, 1964), ii. 485-6n; Ellis, 'Thomas Cromwell and Ireland', pp. 507-8.

[31] Ball, *Judges,* i, 163-228 *passim;* N.P. Canny, *The formation of the Old English Elite in Ireland* (Dublin, 1975), pp. 9-10, 13-14.

[32] Cf. Otway-Ruthven, *Med. Ire.,* chs. 3, 5; Nicholls, *Gaelic and gaelicised Ireland,* pt. i.

[33] Cf. R.D. Edwards, *Ireland in the age of the Tudors: the destruction of Hiberno-Norman civilization* (London, 1977).

The survival of an independent Gaelic polity in many parts of the island posed some difficult problems for government. Gaelic Ireland comprised a series of autonomous lordships each with its own politics. The lordships of the midlands and the Leinster mountains almost bisected the main English districts, while in the north-east the expansion of the Clandeboye O'Neills had reduced the earldom of Ulster to a small coastal strip in Co. Down and in the west Co. Connaught now comprised only an isolated area around Galway and Athenry.[34] Ireland was therefore a land of many marches each with its own problems which had usually to be solved by the local community: the governor could not be in two places at once and the distances involved were quite considerable. To an extent self-reliance fostered local particularism and the governor aimed to promote cooperation and mutual assistance among the king's subjects and to prevent his English rebels and Irish enemies from exploiting internal dissensions.[35] Nevertheless, the lordship's problems were far from insuperable, and in the fifteenth century the difficulties of the Dublin administration sprang more from royal neglect than from the challenge mounted by Gaelic Ireland. If there were often serious feuds among the Old English magnates,[36] among the Gaelic chiefs there was almost no political cohesion at all, except when a few chiefs were briefly united by self-interest. The Elizabethans compared the wild Irish with American Indians, though Gaelic society was in fact the more advanced. In terms of material culture, however, it fell far short of the standards generally obtaining in western Europe. Militarily its weapons were outmoded, though the tactics of its chiefs were well-suited to the defence of the heavily-wooded, marshy or mountainous territory in which many of the Irish lived. From here they preyed on the wealthier colonists and some clans perhaps survived largely on the booty thus obtained.[37] Nevertheless, most of the border chieftaincies were weak, their raids were on a small scale, did little damage and were largely concentrated on a campaigning season which lasted from Easter to Michaelmas.[38] Each sought to exploit weaknesses and

---

[34]Frontispiece; *New hist. Ire.,* iii, ch. 1.

[35]See especially, Robin Frame, 'Power and society in the lordship of Ireland, 1272-1377', *Past & Present,* no. 76 (Aug. 1977), 3-33.

[36]M.C. Griffith, 'The Talbot-Ormond struggle for control of the Anglo-Irish government, 1414-47', *I.H.S.,* ii (1940-41), 376-97.

[37]Nicholls, *Gaelic and gaelicised Ireland,* pt. i; K. Simms, 'Warfare in the medieval Gaelic lordships', *Irish Sword,* xii (1976), 98-108; Canny, *Elizabethan conquest* pp. 160-3.

[38]*Ibid.,* Liam Price, 'Armed forces of the Irish chiefs in the early sixteenth century', *R.S.A.I. Jn.,* lxii (1932), 201-7.

dissension among the colonists, but since they rarely combined the threat was easily contained even if effective counter-measures were usually beyond the resources of the governor.

In these circumstances, despite misgovernment, plague and the trade slump in the fourteenth century, all of which had hit the comparatively sophisticated economy of the lordship much harder than it had Gaelic Ireland, the colonists had traditionally exercised an influence in Irish politics which was out of all proportion to their declining numbers; and this influence had been sustained after 1361 by substantial financial and military support from England. But under the Lancastrians, the lordship became a much lower priority and with fewer resources available this exacerbated the perennial problem of how to maintain royal control of a distant border region and yet ensure that government there was cheap and effective without being tyrannical. From Henry VI the Dublin administration received neither effective leadership, because of the king's incapacity, nor money and men which were largely diverted towards the support of a losing war in France. It was thrown back on its own resources which were inadequate to maintain the tenuous hold of the colonists on areas which had not been well settled. In consequence the already seriously weakened control exercised by government in many areas collapsed as the colonists abandoned their lands or reached such accommodation with their Gaelic neighbours as reflected the realities of the situation.[39]

Yet because the Gaelic chiefs were primarily exploiting a situation which was not of their own making, they failed to sustain the challenge when under Edward IV circumstances altered. To an extent certain new factors which then began to operate have been noted by historians, though hitherto considered insufficient to arrest the lordship's decline. Renewed building activity in the fifteenth century has been rightly regarded as evidence of an economic upswing and the establishment of a new stability and prosperity, but it has been thought that the government was by then too weak to profit from this.[40] The Hundred Years War was followed by the Wars of the Roses, but the disruption caused by the latter is easily exaggerated and both Edward IV and Henry VII were far more capable of effective intervention in Ireland than Henry VI had been. Finally, on the face of it, the reversal of population decline in England and the greater stability in Ireland should have created conditions more favourable to the efforts of the

---

[39]For all this, see Lydon, *Lordship*, chs. 6-9.
[40]*Ibid.*, p. 242.

Dublin administration to arrest the emigration of peasants of English descent to England.[41]

Since the principal problems encountered in governing the lordship were in fact ones which also affected other areas of crown rule or which sprang from general weaknesses of English government especially in border areas, they remained largely intelligible to the king and his council despite the complications posed by Gaelic Ireland. There is really no justification for the practice of discussing Wales and the north of England as particularly acute manifestations of the problems faced by Edward IV and his successors in restoring royal authority while virtually excluding the lordship on the grounds that society and government there were totally different.[42] Certainly some differences existed and this study aims to isolate them, but the fact that under Elizabeth the country was treated differently and reduced by military conquest and colonization instead of by the strategies employed in the north or Wales has perhaps been allowed to colour our appreciation of the state of the late medieval lordship. It is just conceivable that the problems of governing Ireland were so intractable that they defied conventional solutions. Yet there is good reason to question whether perhaps it was not the state of Ireland in 1534 but the government's switch to a more coercive strategy after 1547, in a bid to bring about a quick solution to the problem, which narrowed its options and suggested the need for a military conquest. By exacerbating difficulties it created at least some of the special circumstances which demanded a departure from tried and tested policies.[43] Had the lordship been close to extinction in 1534 it would certainly have constituted a special case, but it is the contention of the present study that the problems of English government in Ireland, though serious, were by 1500 neither so severe nor so unique as historians of the period have suggested.

---

[41] See below, pp. 130-1.

[42] Cf. P. Williams, *The Tudor regime* (Oxford, 1979), p. vii.

[43] These points are developed in S.G. Ellis, 'Parliament and community in Yorkist and Tudor Ireland' in A. Cosgrove & J.I. McGuire (eds.), *Parliament and community: Historical Studies XIV* (Belfast, 1983), pp. 43-68.

1

THE EXECUTIVE

The Chief governor[1]

The chief problem facing the king in his choice of governor lay in striking a balance between control and economy. As was illustrated on a number of occasions by the political events of the period 1450-1500, an unreliable governor could use his office to mount a serious challenge to the throne. On the other hand, to maintain an outsider was normally too expensive. The king therefore strove to limit as far as possible the opportunities for misconduct without denying to the governor the powers which he needed to govern. Although standards of government remained far from high, by 1500 governors had been persuaded to safeguard the king's vital interests, and for the most part to apply their energies in directions of mutual benefit.

Except briefly in the winter of 1506-7, when Henry VII thought of making 'a viage personall in his moste noble persoun', and then thought better of it,[2] there was never any likelihood in this period that the king might take personal charge of his Irish administration. The king was therefore represented by a governor who supervised the administration of the land and generally executed those functions which would have been performed by the king himself if he was present. Such governors were appointed with varying titles and powers, of which that of lieutenant, originating in the fourteenth century, was the highest and most honourable. In contrast with the position under the Lancastrians, when the earl of Ormond, several English barons and even a commoner had been appointed lieutenant, the Yorkists and early Tudors almost always reserved the office for princes of the blood. As a result, the office recovered somewhat in prestige. During the fifteenth century, however, the lieutenant tended increasingly to delegate the actual government of the lordship to a deputy. The lieutenancy thus became increasingly an honorary office, with the king supervising the deputy directly, so that when Prince Henry, titular lieutenant since 1494, acceded to the throne in 1509, the office was left vacant and the earl of Kildare governed as king's

---

[1] The term '(chief) governor' is here used in a general sense to denote any officer, whatever his actual title, who had charge of the administration at a particular time in place of the king, even though he might merely be deputising for another officer.

[2] C.G. Bayne & W.H. Dunham Jr. (eds.), *Select cases in the council of Henry VII* (Seldon Soc. 75, London, 1968), p. 46.

deputy instead of deputy-lieutenant.³ Only in 1520, when the earl of Surrey was given the more honourable title almost as an afterthought and spent nearly two years in the lordship, did a lieutenant exercise his office in person under the Yorkists and early Tudors,⁴ and even then his powers were generally no greater than those of the deputies who preceded and followed him.

The powers and conditions of appointment of a governor were laid down in his commission and the indenture which most of them made with the king. Since the fourteenth century these commissions had become increasingly elaborate, now granting and defining powers which had long been exercised by the governor.⁵ The provisions were frequently altered and their interpretation was occasionally ambiguous. It became the rule that any power not explicitly granted was reserved to the king. Thus soon after his arrival in Ireland in 1520, Surrey discovered that although he had asked Wolsey for the same powers as the marquis of Dorset had had in Spain in 1512-13, or he himself had as lord admiral, his commission did not even grant all the powers normally enjoyed by a lieutenant. After he had uncovered a plot by some of his retinue to seize a boat and turn pirate, the king's legal counsel informed him, after scrutinising his commission, that he was only empowered to administer capital punishment in accordance with the common law, which did not regard intention as a capital offence. This was a significant omission, Surrey wrote, 'for if I shuld make a proclamasion upon peyne of deth, as it shalbe nedefull many tymes to doo, I have none auctoritie to put any of theym to deth that shall breke the same'. He received in response a commission enlarging his powers against criminals, and also one authorising him to confer knighthoods; but a year later some pirates were captured at Cork and Surrey had again to refer the matter, asking for a commission to execute them and a general commission to execute or pardon pirates.⁶

When the king's brother, George, duke of Clarence, was reappointed in 1472, his previous wide powers were all confirmed. He was granted the office for twenty years with powers to appoint a deputy as he wished. He was to keep the king's peace and the laws and customs of

---

³See, however, below, p. 24.

⁴John Tiptoft, earl of Worcester, was promoted to lieutenant after his recall in 1470 and, but for the readeption of Henry VI, Edward IV perhaps intended that he should return to Ireland.

⁵A.J. Otway-Ruthven, 'The chief governors of mediaeval Ireland', *R.S.A.I. Jn.*, xcv (1965), 228-30.

⁶*S.P. Hen. VII,* ii, 42, 55, 76-7. Proclamations of course did not extend to life and limb by the common law: Surrey was looking for power to proclaim martial law.

Ireland, to do justice, punish offenders, fine rebels and grant pardons, to go with the king's forces against those who would not submit and to make peace with them, to grant lands recovered from Irish enemies or English rebels or otherwise forfeit, to grant lands in mortmain, to inquire concerning royal rights withheld from the king, to confer all ecclesiastical benefices, to receive fealties and renunciations of bishops and archbishops and to restore temporalities, to receive the homage of the king's tenants and grant livery, to levy purveyance for his household and retinue in accordance with the statutes of purveyors, to appoint to all offices during pleasure, in fee or for life, and to remove unsuitable officers by the advice of the king's council there, to hold parliaments and councils, to levy the revenues and spend them in the defence of the land without account, and to call all officers to account; all this subject only to correction by the king's council of England should his actions be contrary to the law.[7]

With certain important exceptions, these powers continued to be exercised by all governors throughout the period, regardless of their particular title. Their powers, therefore, were little short of those exercised by the king personally in England, and considerably superior to those granted to principal officers in other outlying parts, in Wales or the north. This was in part necessarily so, for communications with Ireland were slower and less certain. But the governor of Ireland was both head of an entire, though subordinate, civil administration and also military commander of a turbulent border area with a sizeable standing force and full control over the military resources of the lordship. Even an officer who was both warden of the marches towards Scotland and king's lieutenant in the north parts lacked powers normally enjoyed by the governor, and in any case the king usually kept these offices in separate hands.[8]

After the attainder of Clarence, however, Edward IV and his successors began to reserve to themselves certain of the more profitable powers or those most open to abuse, or to grant them only to especially favoured governors. The power to appoint to offices in the Irish administration was permanently curtailed by an act of 1494-5, which stipulated that judges and officers accountable in the exchequer should hold during the king's pleasure only, though the king himself sometimes excepted individual officers from its terms.[9] In fact, Prince

---

[7] P.R.O., C. 66/529 mm 14-13 *(Cal. pat. rolls, 1467-76,* pp. 335-6).

[8] Reid, *The king's council in the north,* pt. i; P. Williams, *The council in the marches of Wales under Elizabeth I* (Cardiff, 1958), ch. 1.

[9] Statute roll, 10 Henry VII c. 6 (*Stat. Ire.,* i, 42-3).

Henry, appointed lieutenant in 1494, and Poynings as his deputy lacked explicit power to appoint to any office, although by the custom of Ireland, accepted by the king, any governor might appoint someone to discharge a vacant office until the king's pleasure were known. This reservation, however, was exceptional and otherwise confined to temporary governors with the title of justiciar which are discussed below.[10] Under the Yorkists, the seventh earl of Kildare as deputy had granted for life important offices carrying with them a seat on the council and had then had these grants confirmed by parliament.[11] As late as 1485 the eighth earl, anticipating Henry Tudor's invasion of England, had safeguarded his control of government by having parliament confirm councillors in their offices for life, even though Richard III had specifically reserved to himself in 1484 the nomination to six chief offices. This practice of reserved appointments had in fact normally operated for the chancellorship and treasurership, and during Henry VI's reign had frequently been extended further in a bid to curb faction in the Irish council.[12] It was revived by Edward IV in 1479, and in commissions of 1479, 1480 and 1484 appointments to six offices were reserved for the king – the chancellor, treasurer, the two chief justices, chief baron (all *ex officio* of council), and the master of the mint. And Henry VII, in appointing Bedford as lieutenant in 1486, withheld the nomination of the first five officers. Similarly, the nomination of bishops and archbishops was, from 1478 onwards,

---

[10] Richardson & Sayles, *Ir. parl. in middle ages*, app. x. Bishop Deane, appointed deputy and justiciar in 1496, also had no power to appoint to offices. To save repetition, references are only given in the following section to factual remarks not based on governor's commissions. The principal references to commissions for the following section are (name of governor and year of appointment first): Clarence, 1471 (*Liber mun. pub. Hib.*, i, pt. iv, 97-8); Clarence, 1472 (P.R.O., C. 66/529 mm 14-13; *Cal. pat. rolls, 1467-76*, pp. 335-6); George Plantagenet, 1478 (P.R.O., C. 66/543 m. 28; *Cal. pat. rolls, 1477-85*, p. 118); York, 1479 (*Cal. pat. rolls, 1477-85*, p. 153); 1480 (*ibid.*, p. 210); Gormanston, 1479 (Rymer, *Foedera* (ed. 1740-1), v, pt. ii, 102); Lincoln, 1484 (P.R.O., C. 66/557 m. 12; *Cal. pat. rolls, 1477-85*, p. 477); Bedford, 1486 (*Cal. pat. rolls, 1485-94*, p. 84); York & Poynings, 1494 (P.R.O., C. 66/576 mm 18-19; *Liber mun. pub. Hib.*, i, pt. iv, 100-1; *Cal. pat. rolls, 1494-1509*, p. 12); Deane, 1496 (P.R.O., C. 66/578 m. 19; *Cal. pat. rolls, 1494-1509*, p.65); Kildare, 1496 (P.R.O., C. 66/578 m. 12; *Cal. pat. rolls, 1494-1509*, p. 62); 1510 (*L. & P. Hen. VIII*, i (2nd ed.), no. 632 (22)); 1513 (*ibid.*, no. 2535 (3)); 1516 (P.R.O., C. 66/626 m. 24; *ibid.*, ii, no. 1704); Surrey, 1520 (Memoranda roll, 12 Henry VIII m. ? (P.R.O.I., Ferguson coll., iv, f. 61)); Ormond, 1522 (P.R.O., C. 66/637 m. 11; *Ormond deeds, 1509-47*, no. 80; *Liber mun. pub. Hib.*, i, pt. iv, 103); Kildare, 1524 (*Ormond deeds, 1509-47*, no. 100); Skeffington, 1530 (P.R.O., C. 66/656 m. 5; *L. & P. Hen. VIII*, iv, no. 6490 (22)); Kildare, 1532 (P.R.O., C. 66/661 m. 33; *L. & P. Hen. VIII*, v, no. 1207 (16)); Skeffington, 1534 (P.R.O.I., 1A 52 f. 32).

[11] Parliament rolls, 11 & 12 Edward IV cc 12, 13, 12 & 13 Edward IV cc 7, 13, 30, 15 & 16 Edward IV c. 38 (*Stat. Ire., Edw. IV*, i, 732-6, ii, 12, 22-4, 60, 340). Cf. Richardson & Sayles, *Ir. parl. in middle ages*, p. 169.

[12] Richardson & Sayles, *Ir. parl. in middle ages*, pp. 170, 330-1; Otway-Ruthven, 'Chief governors', p. 229; Griffith, 'Talbot-Ormond struggle', pp. 378-9.

always reserved, and until 1486, the heads of religious houses too.

Poynings's statute, requiring appointments to the principal offices to be at the king's pleasure only, lessened the need for reserved appointments. Kildare's patent of 1496, which remained in force until 1509, excluded only the chancellorship, but in practice after 1494 an officer holding by English patent could not be dismissed by the deputy.[13] During Poynings's deputyship the king was conducting a reformation of the central government, but from a peak in the years 1494-6, appointments under the English great seal almost ceased after Kildare's restoration.[14] From 1510 the office of chief justice was additionally reserved; and in 1520 Surrey's commission reserved the nomination of the treasurer too, though there was an obvious reason for this. Throughout the period, Irish-born governors had power to receive and spend the Irish revenues without account, so the treasurership was only of importance to the king when an English governor was appointed and maintained, in part, from the English revenues.[15] Nevertheless, Surrey's successor, the earl of Ormond, could not appoint to nine offices: by the 1520s Henry VIII was using the system of reserved appointments in an attempt to curb the Geraldine-Butler feud, and Kildare's patents of 1524 and 1532 were the same as Ormond's in this respect. Skeffington's commission in 1530 reserved only five offices, but these now included the under-treasurer, who was by then rapidly replacing the treasurer as the man in actual charge of the revenue; and after the prominent role played by William Bath, Kildare's undertreasurer, 1532-4, in the 1534 rebellion, this became the norm. From 1534, the deputy did however recover the power to appoint the puisne judges.[16]

One significant alteration in the deputy's powers touched the terms on which he was empowered to appoint to offices. Under Henry VIII, in consequence of the statute of 1494, his patent usually included a clause giving him 'plenam potestatem & auctoritatem faciendi deputandi & constituendi quoscumque officiarios nostros infra terram nostram predictam durante beneplacito nostro duraturos'.[17]

---

[13] See below, pp. 17, 179.

[14] *Cal. pat. rolls, 1485-94, 1494-1509, passim.*

[15] In consequence, English governors were not normally empowered to call the treasurer or, later, the undertreasurer to account either.

[16] The nine offices reserved in 1522 were the chancellor, treasurer, justices of both benches, barons of the exchequer and the clerk of the rolls. In 1530, they comprised the chancellor, treasurer, undertreasurer and both chief justices.

[17] E.g. Memoranda roll, 12 Henry VIII m. ? (P.R.O.I., Ferguson coll., iv, f. 61).

In practice, this clause was interpreted as allowing the governor to appoint to all offices vacant and not reserved to the king, but not to remove appointees under the great seal of England: otherwise there would have been no point in Surrey's request of 1520 that the chief baron, whom he had recently appointed under the great seal of Ireland, be granted a patent under the great seal of England as the chief justice had.[18] In the Kildare patents of 1496, 1510 and 1513, however, and in those of Old English deputies from 1522 until, probably, 1529, this clause was somewhat surprisingly altered to 'durante beneplacito suo', and in consequence appointments were made during the king's pleasure and that of his deputy.[19] One effect of this was a wholesale redistribution of offices each time a new deputy was appointed, and this probably assisted the growth of faction in the administration in the 1520s. The practice probably originated because the patent of 1496 granted Kildare the deputyship for ten years and then during pleasure, but deputies were appointed subsequently during pleasure only. The ninth earl of Kildare, however, apparently interpreted the clause as giving him full control over offices not specifically reserved during the period of his deputyship. In fact, the clause reverted permanently to 'durante beneplacito nostro' in 1530, but Kildare failed to notice this after his reappointment in 1532, and when Cromwell got the king to appoint to the chancellorship of the Irish exchequer and then threatened to do likewise with the office of chief remembrancer, the earl complained to the earl of Wiltshire that the offices were 'in my gift by my patent of deputacion'.[20]

Frequently, the king would impose conditions on the deputy's power to grant a royal pardon: treasons touching the king's person or counterfeiting the coinage were invariably excepted after 1494, but Poynings and Deane had no power to pardon treasons of any sort. Kildare undertook in 1524 'that he shall not graunte pardons for heynous offences... but onely by the advise of the lordes of the kinges counsaill'.[21] From 1420 until 1494, a lieutenant's patent explicitly empowered him to hold parliaments and great councils. The chief

---

[18] *S.P. Hen. VIII*, ii, 63. Cf. Ellis, 'Tudor policy and Kildare ascendancy', p. 253 and n. 57.

[19] E.g., Patent rolls, 22-3 Henry VIII (printed in translation in J.R. O'Flanagan, *The lives of the lord chancellors and keepers of the great seal of Ireland* (2 vols., London, 1870), i, 164); 24-5 Henry VIII (P.R.O.I., Lodge MSS 'Acta regia', i. f. 10); Memoranda roll, 22 Henry VIII m. 13 (P.R.O.I., Ferguson coll., iv, f. 146).

[20] *Cal. pat. rolls Ire., Hen. VIII-Eliz.*, pp. 2-14; *Liber mun. pub. Hib.*, i, pt. iv, 112; Ellis, 'Tudor policy and Kildare ascendancy', pp. 246-8, 253 and the references there cited.

[21] *S.P. Hen. VIII*, ii, 116; P.R.O., S.P. 60/3/168 (*L. & P. Hen. VIII*, xi, no. 932).

governor had however always enjoyed this power and even a justiciar sometimes held them, even though not explicitly empowered to do so.[22] Nevertheless, a parliament held by Viscount Gormanston in 1494 was subsequently declared invalid because, *inter alia,* 'the said deputie had no maner power by his commission to keep parliament'. His successor, Poynings, received power to summon only one parliament, to be dissolved before Easter 1495 (19 April), and thereafter, in accordance with Poynings' Law, governors had to apply for a licence to hold parliament and to submit all bills for the king's prior approval.[23]

Throughout the period, the king steadily reduced the powers of the governor in other ways. Until the later fifteenth century, lieutenants were normally appointed for a term of years, though they also had power to appoint a deputy with the result that this did not ensure as much continuity as was hoped. After Clarence's execution in 1478, however, a succession of absentee lieutenants, most of them children, were appointed for short terms of between one and three years. Latterly Bedford's patent was renewed in 1488 for one year and then during pleasure, and thereafter lieutenants were appointed during pleasure only.[24] From 1478, therefore, the king effectively chose the deputy-lieutenant, initially because the next three lieutenants were all minors. Traditionally, the lieutenant had exercised a fair measure of autonomy in his choice of deputy, particularly if he were in Ireland; although even in the 1460s Clarence's responsibility for the lordship was more apparent than real. The lieutenant had of course always been responsible for the conduct of his deputy, and theoretically remained so, but in 1479 Richard of York appointed Gormanston 'by thadvice and commaundement of our said souerain lord', and none of his successors can be shown to have exercised any real influence over the king's choice of a deputy.[25] The king tended increasingly to

[22] Richardson & Sayles, *Ir. parl. in middle ages,* pp. 32n, 260, 327, 331; Otway-Ruthven, 'Chief governors', p. 230.

[23] Statute roll, 10 Henry VII cc 9, 40 (*Stat. Ire.,* i, 44, 57).

[24] *Cal. pat. rolls, 1467-76, p.* 235; *1477-85,* pp. 118, 153, 403, 477; *1494-1509,* p. 12; Otway-Ruthven, 'Chief governors', p. 231. An exception was the extension in 1480 for a further twelve years of Richard of York's appointment in 1479 for two years; but he was only four years old when appointed: *Cal. pat. rolls, 1477-85,* pp. 153, 210.

[25] P.R.O., E. 28/92 no. 2. Cf. Gilbert, *Viceroys,* p. 600. After Clarence's appointment as lieutenant in 1462, Edward continued to deal with the lordship directly, appointing Desmond as deputy-lieutenant by privy seal warrant: see Cosgrove, 'Execution of the earl of Desmond', pp. 11-27 esp. p. 16. Clarence also overrode his deputies, presumably on the king's instructions: e.g. *Cal. pat. rolls, 1467-76,* pp. 391, 438, 461, 466, 468, 583, 598. Cf. Parliament roll, 18 Edward IV (I) c. 11 (*Stat. Ire., Edw. IV,* ii, 596: parliament ordered by the king's letters under his privy seal and by the lieutenant under his signet to repeal an act of a previous parliament); *Ormond deeds, 1413-1509,* no. 222 (privy seals to be sent by the king and lieutenant to the deputy, *c.* 1465).

appoint the deputy during pleasure only: Kildare was appointed deputy for term of four years in 1480 and probably for ten years by Richard III in 1484, but until 1496 all Henry VII's deputies held during pleasure. Kildare's patent of 1496 was for ten years and then during pleasure, but this was the last appointment of its kind and thereafter the governor invariably held during pleasure.[26] It is probably significant that the eighth earl's second period of office (1496-1513) was easily the most successful deputyship, so far as both king and colonists were concerned, in the late medieval period. Though other factors were certainly involved, it might seem that the more secure in his office the governor was, the less likely were critical reports about his conduct to be sent to the king. In 1534, in consequence of the Geraldine-Butler feud and the frequent changes of governor since 1519, there was a strong demand among the Palesmen that an English-born deputy be appointed for life or term of years.[27] After 1534 the king's deputy was always English born, but he continued to hold office during pleasure only.

The lieutenant had very often in the fifteenth century granted his deputy power to appoint a deputy of his own if he came to England, and over a vice-deputy the king had much less control. The last deputy definitely known to have received this power in his commission was Gormanston in 1479. Gormanston had himself been vice-deputy, in 1477 and early in 1479, but in 1477 the deputy-lieutenant, having no power to appoint a deputy, had had parliament pass an act empowering him to do so, and Desmond had done likewise in 1463.[28] Almost certainly, Bedford's deputies also had this power: during Gormanston's absence in 1493-4, his son acted as his deputy.[29] From 1494, however, this power was invariably withheld from a deputy, and not even Surrey as lieutenant in 1520 received it. Instead, when recalling a deputy for talks, the king might or might not send him a special commission to appoint a deputy, and the receipt of such a commission was apparently regarded as a mark of royal favour.[30] The change was

---

[26] Gilbert, *Viceroys,* p. 600; *L. & P. Ric. III & Hen. VII,* i, 91-3.

[27] *S.P. Hen. VIII,* ii, 163, 165, 169-70, 182-3. For the more general remarks, see the chapters by D.B. Quinn in *New hist. Ire.,* ii (forthcoming); Ellis, 'Tudor policy and Kildare ascendancy', *passim.*

[28] Rymer, *Foedera,* v, pt. ii, 102; Parliament rolls, 3 Edward IV c. 5, 16 & 17 Edward IV cc 5, 45, 18 Edward IV (II) c. 9 (*Stat. Ire., Edw. IV,* i, 42-4, 266-8, ii, 464, 548-52, 658-60); *Christ Church deeds,* no. 1014.

[29] *New hist. Ire.,* ix (Oxford, 1984).

[30] *S.P. Hen. VIII,* ii, 89; *L. & P. Hen. VIII,* iii, no. 1719. In 1533-4, the earl of Kildare was coaxed to England by the issue of such a commission: Ellis, 'Tudor policy and Kildare ascendancy', p. 255.

important because, as in the case of a lieutenant or other official, his patent lapsed if he left the country without appointing a deputy,[31] or if his deputy died in office or resigned. In such circumstances, as also if a governor's patent were voided by the king's death, an ancient custom known as the Statute of Henry fitz Empress allowed the election of a justiciar until the king's pleasure were known. This office had originated in twelfth-century England, but in the fifteenth and early sixteenth centuries the title was reserved for a temporary, elected governor.[32] To this end, the chancellor was empowered to issue writs to convoke the council for the election, and the justiciar was then appointed under the Irish great seal.[33] Although he might have no power to appoint a deputy, however, there seems to have been nothing to prevent a powerful personality like the earl of Kildare from presiding over the council to secure the election of his own candidate: in 1515 the election was held before the deputy went to England, although this was not the case when a deputy was recalled after 1534. After 1534, however, Henry VIII always notified the council of his candidate in such circumstances.[34]

Even after 1494, when a lieutenant or deputy required the king's licence to appoint his own deputy during his absence, the king's control over such an officer was minimal. Except in the case of Surrey in 1521, when Henry VIII had the earl of Ormond appointed as deputy-lieutenant in order to test his suitability to succeed Surrey as king's deputy,[35] the choice of a deputy seems to have been left entirely to the acting governor. The terms of the deputy's appointment and regulations for his conduct were set down in an indenture with the governor, although the formal commission might withhold some of the powers enjoyed by the governor himself. Regulations concerning Ormond's taking of coign and livery in the Pale for his retinue formed part of his indenture with Surrey in 1521, and were no doubt little different from those in Kildare's indenture of 1524 with the king: they

---

[31] A statute of 1467 empowered the governor to go to any island annexed to the land of Ireland without his patent being voided: Parliament roll, 7 & 8 Edward IV c. 22 (*Stat. Ire., Edw. IV,* i, 468-70).

[32] Otway-Ruthven, 'Chief governors', p. 227.

[33] Statute roll, 33 Henry VIII, sess. II, c. 3 (*Stat. Ire.,* i 207-9); *Facs. nat. MSS Ire.,* iii, app. viii; Parliament rolls, 18 Edward IV (II) c. 9 (*Stat. Ire., Edw. IV,* ii, 658-60); Richardson & Sayles, *Ir. parl. in middle ages,* pp. 324-31; Otway-Ruthven, 'Chief governors', p. 232. For the form of the writ in 1571, see *Anal. Hib.,* vi (1934), pp. 365-6.

[34] Patent roll, 6 Henry VIII (P.R.O.I., Lodge MSS 'Acta regia', i, f. 1); *Liber mun. pub. Hib.,* i, pt. ii, 1-2.

[35] *S.P. Hen. VIII,* ii, 72, 89-90; *L. & P. Hen. VIII,* iii, no. 1646.

had formed the basis of a renewed attempt to curtail this exaction by a royal commission in 1523.³⁶ Ormond's powers as deputy-lieutenant compared very unfavourably with those previously enjoyed by Kildare and, in reappointing him as king's deputy in 1522, Henry VIII was afraid that if he were not granted reasonably comparable powers, he might refuse to serve – to the king's dishonour.³⁷ Temporary deputies were probably restrained from interfering unnecessarily with appointments to offices, although no doubt they were empowered, in accordance with custom, to make appointments during the king's pleasure if vacancies occurred.³⁸ In 1519-20, however, Sir Maurice Fitzgerald was clearly granted wide powers of pardon as vice-deputy.³⁹ The subordination and responsibility of a governor's deputy to his superior seems to have been particularly marked with regard to finance. In 1519-20, Kildare's officers and receivers continued to levy the royal revenues up to the time that Surrey took his oath of office, which suggests that Kildare had agreed upon a salary with Fitzgerald. In 1521-2, Surrey apparently did likewise; though in his arrangement with Delvin in 1527-8, Kildare seems merely to have reserved to himself the profits of certain farms of land, leaving the vice-deputy to manage as best he could on what remained.⁴⁰

The previously wide powers granted to lieutenants and their deputies of alienating the landed rights of the crown and granting licences in mortmain were qualified from 1478 by the proviso that grants should be made only for the defence of the land by the advice of the king and his council. From 1494, they were withdrawn entirely, and instead a clause in the commission of Irish-born deputies alone granted to them in tail any lands which they might recover from the king's Irish enemies. And though Irish-born deputies continued to enjoy the revenues without account, the treasurer's control over lands in the king's hands and being administered by the exchequer was strengthened by a statute of 1494.⁴¹

A governor was in office and responsible for the government of the

---

³⁶*Ormond deeds, 1509-47*, no. 93. Cf. *ibid., 1413-1509*, no. 161; *S.P. Hen. VIII*, ii, 114-18.

³⁷*L. &. P. Hen. VIII*, iv, no. 81; *S.P. Hen. VIII*, ii, 92. The only recorded instance of a governor actually refusing to serve occurred in 1372: Richardson & Sayles, *Ir. parl. in middle ages*, p. 83.

³⁸Cf. *Ormond deeds, 1413-1509*, no. 159 (p. 143).

³⁹*Ormond deeds, 1509-47*, no.61.

⁴⁰*S.P. Hen. VIII*, ii, 90, 95, 126, 137; *L. & P. Hen. VIII*, iv, nos. 81, 4562. Cf. *Ormond deeds, 1413-1509*, no. 161.

⁴¹Statute roll, 10 Henry VII c. 5 (*Stat. Ire.*, i, 41-2).

lordship from the time he took his oath on receiving the sword of state until the time he relinquished the sword.[42] In 1515, Kildare continued to act as deputy until he left for England, even though a justiciar had already been elected to succeed him and his patent sealed. Judging from practice later in the century, Kildare would have surrendered the sword immediately before his departure, and in fact Viscount Gormanston was not sworn until almost a month after the date of his appointment.[43] The delivery of the sword had become, by Elizabeth's reign, an essential part of the ceremony, although it is not clear how old this practice then was. In a record concerning an admission to office in 1423, there is no mention of the sword of state nor of an oath of office, though the latter had certainly existed for over two centuries. But in 1534 Lord Offaly surrendered the sword in token of his resignation, and in 1580 Lord Grey de Wilton was prevented from taking office for nearly a month because Lord Justice Pelham was on campaign in Munster and had the sword with him.[44] Mid-Tudor practice concerning a change of governor can be deduced from entries on the chancery rolls after 1534 (before then the evidence is insufficient).[45] The new governor exhibited his commission to the retiring governor who summoned the council. In the presence of the council, the master of the rolls read out the commission; the chancellor administered the oath to the new governor kneeling; and finally the retiring governor surrendered the sword to his successor. If, as sometimes happened, one governor left the country before his successor had arrived or been admitted to office, he surrendered the sword to the chancellor before departure. In such circumstances, as also if the land for any other reason had no governor, the chancellor had temporary charge of the administration.

Although the distinction has not always been kept by antiquaries

[42] Richardson & Sayles, *Ir. parl. in middle ages*, app. vii in printing a record of the council concerning the refusal of the justiciar and council to admit a new deputy-lieutenant to office in 1423, suggest that the justiciar's office technically lapsed on the appointment of a lieutenant. Nevertheless, the document itself shows that the justiciar continued in office, despite this appointment, until the arrival of the deputy-lieutenant and that he only ceased to act on receipt, by the deputy's hands, of the king's letters ordering him to do so. Even then, he continued in charge of the government in his capacity as chancellor until the deputy was admitted to office in council.

[43] Memoranda roll, 8-9 Henry VIII m. 17d (B.L., Add. MS 4791, f. 198); *Cal. pat. rolls Ire., Hen. VIII-Eliz.*, p. 1; P.R.O.I., Lodge MSS 'Acta regia', f. 1; Christ Church deed (Bodl., Rawl. MS B. 484, f. 76. Cf. *Christ Church deeds*, no. 403); *Liber mun. pub. Hib.*, i, pt. ii, 4. See below, ch. 6, for chancery practice concerning the dating of patents.

[44] Richardson & Sayles, *Ir. parl. in middle ages*, app. vii; T.C.D., MS 543/2 *sub anno* 1534; Cyril Falls, *Elizabeth's Irish wars* (London, 1950), p. 134; *Liber mun. pub. Hib.*, i, pt. ii, 4; Otway-Ruthven, 'Chief governors', p. 228.

[45] Conveniently collected in *Liber mun. pub. Hib.*, i, pt. ii, 1-4.

and historians, contemporaries were well aware of the difference in their powers and mode of appointment between a justiciar and deputy or vice-deputy. This fact can be illustrated by the response of the council to two emergencies affecting the governorship. In winter 1533-4, Kildare was commissioned to appoint a deputy 'pro quo nobis respondere volueritis' and appointed his son, Lord Offaly. When Offaly resigned in June, Kildare's patent automatically lapsed and the council, with Lord Chancellor Cromer in charge, elected Lord Delvin as justiciar.[46] In contrast were the events which followed Kildare's summons to England in 1526. The earl initially appointed his brother, Sir Thomas Fitzgerald, as vice-deputy, but later substituted Lord Delvin, apparently under pressure at court. Delvin, however, was captured by O'Connor Faly on 12 May 1528 and held prisoner, and on the 15th the council elected Fitzgerald as 'captain' to take charge of the military situation. Nevertheless, Delvin had not resigned nor left the country, so, although he was obviously incapable of acting, he continued in office. Likewise Kildare remained deputy, even though it was intended to replace him, and in England the king discussed with his councillors whether it were better to replace Delvin by Lord Butler as Kildare's deputy, so that the earl would remain responsible for government and the less inclined to create trouble, or whether to appoint the earl of Ossory as king's deputy.[47]

A curious misconception concerning governors is that justiciars, deputies and lieutenants were somehow transformed into *lords justices*, deputies and lieutenants around the year 1509.[48] In fact all governors were properly addressed as 'my lord justice/deputy/ lieutenant', whether or not they were peers and despite the fact that 'my lord deputy' might be the king's deputy, deputy-lieutenant or merely vice-deputy. So far as the justiciar was concerned, however, in fifteenth and sixteenth-century English, 'justice' was borrowed from Norman-French in preference to the Latin loan-word now preferred by medievalists. Nevertheless, justiciars were called 'justice' in the few surviving English documents long before 1509 and 'justiciarius' in Latin commissions long after.[49]

Until 1534, a justiciar was invariably appointed under the great seal of Ireland, although thereafter Henry VIII sometimes appointed

---

[46] Ellis, 'Tudor policy and Kildare ascendancy', pp. 255-6, 260 and the references there cited.

[47] *S.P. Hen. VIII*, ii, 127-39; *L. & P. Hen. VIII*, iv, nos. 4510, 4562.

[48] E.g. Herbert Wood, 'The office of chief governor of Ireland, 1172-1509', *R.I.A. Proc.*, xxxv (1923), sect. C, 211.

[49] E.g., *I.H.S.*, ii (1940-1), p. 396; *Acts privy council, Ire., 1556-71*, pp. 48-9.

him directly under the English great seal on recalling the deputy. There was, however, some confusion about the correct mode of appointing a deputy. Lieutenants and king's deputies were appointed under the great seal of England, although there was presumably no reason why the king should not direct a privy seal to the Irish chancellor to make out the patent: certainly justiciars were later so appointed.[50] In the case of deputy-lieutenants, however, a commission under the lieutenant's privy seal, backed if necessary by the lieutenant's own commission, had earlier sufficed; although in 1423 the chancellor and council had made difficulties about accepting such an appointment. Perhaps in consequence, lieutenants' commissions of the 1470s specified that deputies should be appointed under the great seal of England or of Ireland. Thus in 1478, the chancellor refused to accept the appointment of Lord Grey as deputy, apparently on the grounds that it had been made under the king's privy seal.[51] Edward IV, however, later overruled these objections, and in 1479 Viscount Gormanston was successfully appointed in the same manner.[52] After 1494, the king invariably appointed a deputy under the English great seal, and even though a nominal lieutenant was sometimes appointed and acted by deputy, the deputy so appointed was styled king's deputy as well as deputy-lieutenant. Thus after doubts had arisen about whether the Irish Reformation Parliament had been invalidated by the death of the lieutenant in July 1536, it was argued that the parliament was valid because his deputy was also king's deputy, although in the event an act of confirmation was also passed by the 1541 parliament.[53] If a lieutenant or deputy appointed a deputy while in Ireland, the commission had normally been under the Irish great seal, but in 1519 Kildare was commissioned to appoint a deputy 'per litteras vestras patentes sigillo vestro sigillandas'. Presumably similar commissions in 1503, 1521, 1526 and 1533 contained the same clause, and this may reflect earlier doubts about the correct mode of appointment.[54]

[50]*Liber mun. pub. Hib.*, i, pt. ii, 1-4, pt. iv, 100-3. In 1535, when there was a proposal to recall Skeffington and appoint Grey as deputy, the keeper of the Irish great seal offered to seal, on receipt of the king's warrant, a patent 'according the forme of this deputies patent': *S.P. Hen. VIII*, ii, 271.

[51] Probably by letters patent in the lieutenant's name: Parliament roll, 18 Edward IV (II) c. 9 (*Stat. Ire., Edw. IV*, ii, 658-60); P.R.O., E.28/92, nos. 1-2. Cf. Gilbert, *Viceroys*, p. 404; Otway-Ruthven, 'Chief governors', p. 232; Richardson & Sayles, *Ir. parl. in middle ages*, pp. 311-17.

[52] P.R.O., E. 28/92, nos. 1-2; Rymer, *Foedera*, v, pt. ii, 102; Richardson & Sayles, *Ir. parl. in middle ages*, p. 265. Cf. Gilbert, *Viceroys*, pp. 600-1.

[53]*S.P. Hen. VIII*, ii, 366-7; *L. & P. Hen. VIII*, xi, no. 382; *Stat. Ire., Hen. VII & VIII*, pp. 158, 160-1.

[54] Otway-Ruthven, 'Chief governors', p. 232; *Red Bk Kildare*, pp. 188-9; *L. & P. Hen. VIII*, iii, no. 1719.

The governor's salary and the perquisites of office varied considerably in accordance with his status and the terms of his appointment. The salary of a justiciar continued, until 1431 at least, to be the £500 per annum at which it had been fixed since 1228, and out of this he was traditionally obliged to maintain a retinue of twenty men-at-arms.[55] In 1499, however, when the custom known as the Statute of Henry fitz Empress was restored, the justiciar was empowered, in lieu of a salary to levy all revenues due or outstanding and to apply them to the defence of the land.[56] This act may merely have reestablished practice prior to 1494, for in 1463 the earl of Kildare's election as justiciar in 1461 had been confirmed by parliament, Kildare, it was said, having discharged the office 'a sez graundez custages & em[por]table chargez'. Since the purpose of the act was clearly to indemnify Kildare against the crown, even though the financial aspects of the justiciarship were not mentioned, this suggests that the earl had received the revenues in lieu of a salary.[57] After 1534, the justiciar was granted a salary of 100 marks a month, an arrangement which lasted until 1552.[58]

Since the mid-fourteenth century, a governor appointed by the king had normally entered into an indenture by which he agreed to maintain additional troops in return for an increased salary. But when, under Edward IV, this system was effectively abandoned, the deputy's salary was little more than a justiciar's. Kildare was apparently granted 1,000 marks a year as deputy, 1472-5, Viscount Gormanston was paid at the annual rate of 1,190 marks for four months in 1479, and Kildare served for £600 per annum from 1481, although in 1479 and 1481 at least the deputy agreed to maintain a retinue rather in excess of the traditional twenty men-at-arms – an additional forty mounted archers in 1479, and eighty mounted archers and forty horse (spears) in 1481.[59] These sums were payable by the Irish exchequer in the first instance, with the exception of *c*. £270 for the first two months of Gormanston's deputyship. From 1379, governors were commonly granted in addition any surplus on the Irish revenues without account, plus anything which could be levied by way of taxation in the lordship,

---

[55] P.R.O., E. 101/248/8; Otway-Ruthven, *Med. Ire.*, p. 147.

[56] *Facs. nat. MSS Ire.*, iii, app. viii; Statute roll, 33 Henry VIII, sess. II, c. 3 (*Stat. Ire.*, i, 207-9); Otway-Ruthven, 'Chief governors', p. 230.

[57] Parliament roll, 3 Edward IV c. 4 (*Stat. Ire., Edw. IV*, i, 42); A. Conway, *Henry VII's relations with Scotland and Ireland, 1485-98* (Cambridge, 1932), pp. 212-13.

[58] *Liber mun. pub. Hib.*, i, pt. ii, 2.

[59] *Rec. comm. Ire. rep., 1811-15,* p. 54; P.R.O., E. 28/92, no. 2; Gilbert, *Viceroys,* pp. 600-11; Quinn, *Guide finan. rec.*, pp. 38-9, 48-9.

but by this time the revenue would scarcely bear the ordinary charges.[60] In fact, from 1479 a clause in the indentures aimed to ensure that the deputy would at least receive his full salary. The balance of Gormanston's salary was payable from the Irish revenues 'if it soo be that the same revenues woll stretche therto', but otherwise, upon certificate to the king, the remainder was to be supplied from England. In practice, the level of subvention was apparently fixed at the round sum of £100 per annum from 1481, a figure which suggests that no attempt was made to draw up an accurate balance of account for the Irish revenues.[61] As deputy to Henry VII's uncle, Jasper Tudor, Kildare petitioned for £1,000 a year. Henry seems to have promised an increase on condition that Kildare came to court and brought a view of account with him.[62] But short of appointing a reliable servant to replace Kildare's father-in-law as treasurer, the king could hardly prevent him from cooking exchequer accounts so as to increase the subvention from England, and this, together with the difficulty in controlling the deputy, may explain why the earl apparently received nothing after 1483. The inadequacies of this system probably prompted the Tudors to confine any financial commitments from England after 1494 to periods when an English-born governor was in office. On his restoration in 1496, Kildare and all Irish-born deputies after him received as a salary the profits from the Irish revenues without account, but nothing from England; and it is probably significant too that there is no sign that any of them were bound by indenture to maintain specified members of English troops.[63] After 1494, the governor designate continued to agree terms by indenture, but the indenture was now chiefly used to regulate the governor's conduct.[64]

Lord Grey of Codnor indented in 1478 to serve with 300 archers for two years in return for a salary of £2,000 for the first year and £1,825 for the second, although in fact he remained in Ireland for only three months.[65] This indenture was the last of its kind: of the later

[60] Richardson & Sayles, *Ir. parl. in middle ages*, ch. 15 and *Admin. Ire.*, p. 13; Otway-Ruthven, *Med. Ire.*, pp. 165-6.

[61] P.R.O., E. 28/92, no. 2; Gilbert, *Viceroys*, pp. 600-11; Quinn, *Guide finan. rec.*, pp. 32, 50.

[62] *L. & P. Ric. III & Hen. VIII*, i, 92. Two views of c. 1483-4 and 1491-2 survive, but there is no reliable evidence that Kildare met Henry VII before his dismissal in 1492. See P.R.O., E. 101/248/17, C. 47/10/31 (printed, Quinn, *Guide finan. rec.*, pp. 17-28).

[63] See above, note 10. Cf. *S.P. Hen. VIII*, ii, 114-18.

[64] *S.P. Hen. VIII*, ii, 114-18; *Ormond deeds, 1509-47*, no. 93.

[65] Quinn, *Guide finan. rec.*, pp. 48-9; *Christ Church deeds*, no. 1014.

English governors, Poynings's salary was £500 per annum, and his troops were a direct charge on the king, being paid through the Irish exchequer.[66] Under Surrey, an attempt was made to resurrect in part the indenture system and to bind him to serve with fifty spears, fifty foot, one hundred Irish horse and three hundred kerne, in addition to troops raised and paid by the king through the undertreasurer, in return for an agreed salary. Surrey, however, refused to agree to more than 200 Irish troops and asked instead that all his troops be put in wages and, as was normal in other theatres of war, that he be granted a reasonable sum for his expenses. It looks as if his request was ignored: his salary was fixed at £3,000 per year out of which he was obliged by indenture to maintain troops to a number which cannot now be ascertained.[67] In 1530, Skeffington was granted 1,000 marks per annum as deputy, with his retinue in wages, and this arrangement was invariably followed after 1534.[68]

The financial outlay which the Yorkists and early Tudors were prepared to make on the governor, and the low priority which the lordship generally received as a theatre of war in this period cannot have made the office a very popular one. Clearly it conferred considerable distinction on its holder,[69] and for this reason the largely nominal lieutenancy was regarded as a great honour generally reserved for royal princes. The comparatively small rewards and the heavy financial commitments of the man actually in charge of the administration, however, probably narrowed the field of suitable aspirants to the governorship to a handful. After 1534 comparatively large sums out of the English revenues were diverted to Ireland and the country's standing as a theatre of war also rose, so that under Elizabeth the governorship became a coveted office, but even then its military nature still made it a considerable risk.[70] Between 1470 and 1534 all four of the English-born governors who served were

---

[66] Conway, *Henry VII's relations*, p. 187.

[67] *L. & P. Hen. VIII*, ii, no. 889, xi, no. 709; *S.P. Hen. VIII*, ii, 79, 85-7, 91, 95-7; P.R.O., E. 101/248/21. *S.P. Hen. VIII*, ii, 87 implies that Surrey may have signed the original indenture devised by Wolsey under protest. The undertreasurer's account contains no allowances for the lieutenant or his retinue, which perhaps appeared in the treasurer-at-war's account and does not survive (cf. Quinn, *Guide finan. rec.*, p. 15: B.L., Cotton MS, Otho E IX, no. 79 (*L. & P. Hen. VIII*, iv, no. 974 (4)) appears to be part of an English account for hire of shipping, including shipping to Ireland, 1520-21). Kerne were Irish footmen equipped with either a sword, a small bow or javelins: Nicholls, *Gaelic and gaelicised Ireland*, pp. 85-6.

[68] Memoranda roll, 24 Henry VIII m. 15 (S.P.W., Hore MS I, pp. 1177-80); *L. & P. Hen. VIII*, v, p. 320; *Liber mun. pub. Hib.*, i, pt. ii, 1.

[69] E.g. *L. & P. Hen. VIII*, ii, no. 411.

[70] See Canny, *Elizabethan conquest*, esp. pp. 45-6.

primarily military commanders, and both in 1529, when he served as royal commissioner, and again in 1534, when he was reappointed deputy, Skeffington seems to have got the job because there was no-one else suitable and willing to serve.[71] Among the Old English, only the three earls could command sufficient support and were at the same time sufficiently respected by the Gaelic Irish to undertake the government of the lordship on a regular basis without military and financial support from England. In the 1460s, Edward IV had taken a calculated risk and employed the earl of Desmond with some success despite his 'degeneration' from English ways, but after his attainder and execution in 1468 his successors were never considered reliable enough for the post.[72] The seventh earl of Ormond (1477-1515) was essentially a courtier and an almost-permanent absentee from Ireland, although, as a result of good service to Surrey, the eighth earl, Sir Piers Butler, head of the Polestown branch of the family, provided an acceptable alternative to the Kildares, who had established a virtual monopoly of the office after 1478.[73]

Before 1478, William Sherwood, the English-born bishop of Meath had, despite considerable friction with the seventh earl of Kildare, successfully governed for two-and-a-half years at less charge to the king than had been customary;[74] but in 1491-2, when Kildare's unreliability against Yorkist pretenders necessitated his replacement, a similar series of experiments was less successful. Henry VII eventually appointed two governors in a bid to offset Kildare's influence in the lordship. Walter FitzSimons, archbishop of Dublin succeeded as deputy-lieutenant on 20 May 1492 with authority over the Pale, and soon after Sir James Butler alias Ormond, the earl of Ormond's deputy in Ireland, was appointed king's governor of Ireland with authority over the area beyond. The experiment apparently increased government control over the English areas beyond the Pale but, so far as Henry's fear of possible invasion by Perkin Warbeck was concerned, this benefit was negated by a renewed outbreak of the Geraldine-Butler feud. And the experiment failed because FitzSimons lacked the resources to maintain order in the Pale. Viscount Gormanston

---

[71] E.F. Jacob, *The fifteenth century* (Oxford, 1961), p. 340; D.B. Quinn, 'Henry VIII and Ireland, 1509-34', *I.H.S.*, xii (1960-1), 338, 341-2; *L. & P. Hen. VIII*, vii, no. 1014.

[72] Cosgrove, 'Execution of the earl of Desmond', pp. 16-17. Cf. Richardson & Sayles, *Ir. parl. in middle ages*, p. 165.

[73] Ellis, 'Tudor policy and Kildare ascendancy', pp. 240-2.

[74] Richardson & Sayles, *Ir. parl. in middle ages*, pp. 263-4; Quinn, *Guide finan. rec.*, pp. 30-1, 46-9; *Cal. pat. rolls, 1477-85*, pp. 71, 79.

was therefore put in charge of a caretaker administration in September 1493 and the magnates summoned to court to devise a more permanent solution to the lordship's problems. The upshot was Poynings's expedition which, however, convinced Henry that closer supervision through an English-born deputy and troops aimed at the gradual conquest of Ireland would, in the short term at least, involve a sizeable charge on his English revenues. He concluded that, unless some special effort were necessary, the lordship could be governed more effectively at less cost by the appointment of the most powerful Old English magnate, the earl of Kildare.[75]

Thus, in view of the liabilities of the office and the king's reluctance to subsidise the lordship's defence, the governorship was normally an attractive proposition only to a local magnate like Kildare. Only Kildare had a sufficient land-base in the Pale to maintain order in this, the political centre of the lordship, through the network of relationships built up with the Old English lords and gentry and neighbouring Gaelic chiefs. Only Kildare could exploit the office effectively for his own ends as well as those of king and community in general. And when, occasionally, the Dublin administration did run into difficulties in this period, in 1492-3 or 1527-9 for example, this usually arose from the earl's temporary replacement by a lesser noble. Because the Irish revenues were so small, the maximisation of the profits of office was important if the governor was to avoid a heavy financial loss in taking office. This was one reason why the system of reserved appointments, and indeed close supervision in general, was unpopular with governors. In 1522, Ormond pointed out that, because the revenues were so small, he would have to reward good service with offices instead of wages, and requested the king not to appoint absentees or to alienate further the revenues.[76] In 1534 the deputy designate, Skeffington, complained that the fiants drafted for offices in Ireland 'sholde be moche to the discommoditie of my romith. For after souch fashion, I shall nether have proffite, strength, love nor thanke.' And in 1533 Kildare reacted strongly to attempts by Cromwell to place his own supporters in office.[77]

It would be impossible to calculate from the scanty surviving evidence the value of the profits and perquisites of the governorship. No doubt they fluctuated widely from year to year, but that they were

[75] See Ellis, 'Henry VII and Ireland', pp. 237-54.

[76] *L. & P. Hen. VIII*, iv, no. 81. The petition was not entirely successful: see *ibid.*, iii, no. 3677 (8). Cf. Parliament roll, 3 Edward IV c. 68 (*Stat. Ire., Edw. IV*, i, 183, 187: a similar petition on behalf of Desmond, 1464).

[77] *S.P. Hen. VIII*, ii, 198; Ellis, 'Tudor policy and Kildare ascendancy', pp. 252-9.

considerable is suggested by the fact that Gormanston was in effect allowed no more than forty marks a quarter in 1479 after deductions for the wages of his troops. And Kildare's indenture in 1480, if his troops received the same wages as Gormanston's, would in fact have involved him in a net loss of £45 a year.[78] The largest profits were apparently made from the grant of offices in the governor's gift and from making peace and war with the Irish,[79] but some idea of their extent is conveyed by a letter to the king in 1536 in which Lord Leonard Grey contrasted his own meagre powers and allowances with those of former deputies.[80] Previous deputies, he observed, had had

> the order, setting and letting of your graces maners, landes customes and other revenues, or at the leaste the same hath ben done by theire goodwilles and assentes... [They used] to grante liveryes of landes, sell custodies of the wardeschipes thereof and graunte pardons for all maner offences (treason vnto your parson onely excepted), gyue licences, placardes and all other thinges that here belong vnto your graces auctoritie.

Grey, however, although he had 'by your graces letters patentes the same auctoritie that others hath had', had 'noo intromedling accordingly'; and therefore 'I haue but the name onely of your deputie'. 'The seruice and obedience of your subiectes that sholde grow vnto me' by such powers would be 'in the stede of one hunderith men'. Grey referred to the fines levied by the deputy for fiants to chancery when 'the revenues were in your owne handes', and not to periods when they were granted to the deputy. Thus a principal legitimate source of profit had apparently been curtailed since 1534.

Sizeable parts of what in England would have been considered the king's revenue were evidently regarded in Ireland as perquisites of the deputy. Understandably, booty from raids on the Irish was in part so deemed, but in 1530 Skeffington agreed that profits from raids by troops in the king's pay and under the deputy's command should be answered in the Irish exchequer. If commanded by Kildare, however, he should receive half, and any troops not in wages should likewise receive a portion.[81] The *Ordinances* of 1534 decreed that fines from Irishmen in compensation for raids on the king's subjects should, if

---

[78] P.R.O., E. 28/92, no. 2; Gilbert, *Viceroys,* pp. 600-1.

[79] *Ormond deeds, 1413-1509,* no. 161.

[80] P.R.O., S.P. 60/3/168 (*L. & P. Hen. VIII,* xi, no. 932).

[81] *S.P. Hen. VIII,* ii, 150. The ordinances of 1534 laid down that fines for pardons, liveries of lands, restitutions of temporalities and for riots '&c.' should be paid into the hanaper and accounted for by the clerk: *ibid.,* ii, 209.

they resulted from the deputy's intervention, be divided between the deputy and subjects so injured. In 1537, however, the deputy and council were instructed that such fines were to go firstly to recompense subjects and the balance to be divided between king and deputy. Profits of fines for pardon of treason and misprision should be the king's, but the deputy should receive a half of those for felonies. Evidently the deputy had previously received more: in 1506, a pardon for alienation of land without licence was granted for a fine paid to the deputy.[82]

Until 1534, these perquisites must have increased considerably the attractiveness of the governorship. But there were additional profits to be made by less scrupulous deputies. Kildare received sizeable sums in cash or in kind from extending his protection to the Irish, and in retainers from Old English gentry. He also did a brisk trade in setting and taking lands to farm.[83] Much of this business was explicitly stated to be conditional on the earl retaining the deputyship, but clearly the earl could in any case profit effectively only if he controlled the government. Skeffington was charged by the chief justice and treasurer in 1532 with more blatant malpractices: he had fined the town of Athboy 100 marks and appropriated the money, and did likewise with other offenders. He exported wool to England for his own profit, in contempt of the statutes, and licensed others to export corn and wool. He had abused his right of purveyance to obtain corn at less than half the market price. Finally, when mustered, his retinue was found to be thirty men and fifty horses below strength.[84] Until royal control over the Dublin administration was tightened up after 1534, there was in fact little but the council to prevent a strong governor from exploiting his office in undesirable ways. This was a defect of the system: unless the king was prepared to pay for good government, he had to allow his governor considerable latitude in devising means to recoup his expenses.

The king's council

The evidence is for the most part lacking which would explain the composition, functions and institutional development of the king's

---

[82]*L. & P. Hen. VIII,* xii (i), no. 503; *S.P. Hen. VIII,* ii, 214; *Christ Church deeds,* no. 384; *Rot. pat. Hib.,* p. 272 no. 8. Cf. *S.P. Hen. VIII,* ii, 369.

[83]B.L. Harl. MS 3756 (discussed in S.G. Ellis, 'The Kildare rebellion, 1534' (M.A. thesis, Manchester, 1974), pp. 1-6, 10-12, 182). Cf. *S.P. Hen. VIII,* ii, 126: 'therll of Kildair coude help hym self in taking advantaige of Irishemen better then any other here'.

[84]*L. & P. Hen. VIII,* v, no. 1061.

council of Ireland in this period. Nevertheless, the decline in royal control over the Dublin administration during Henry VI's reign, and his successors' policy of allowing governors considerable latitude in their conduct might suggest that the council went through a period of comparative eclipse after 1470, and chance references to its activities would support this view. It was of course an important function of the council to inform the king and his council in England of the state of the lordship, independently, if need be, of the deputy. This duty might also extend to restraining the deputy from pursuing his own interests at the king's expense. Thus the system of reservations was important as a means of ensuring conciliar independence of the deputy, although in practice probably not very effectively used by the king. Before the 1520s, the relationship between governor and council must remain largely conjectural, but until the reorganisation of the council which accompanied Henry VII's initiatives in Ireland, 1491-6, Kildare's supporters were continued in the top posts of the administration which they had occupied since the 1470s, and from 1496 Kildare was appointed for ten years with power to nominate all officers except the chancellor.[85] Thus it is unlikely that the council was capable of sustained opposition.

During the early years of Henry VIII's reign, the office of chief justice was additionally reserved.[86] Nevertheless, the circumstances surrounding the first surviving hint of opposition in council, to the ninth earl, are obscure. The deputy was summoned to court in 1515 and Irish affairs were debated by the English council, with Kildare apparently in attendance. An important item on the agenda was a set of articles put in by Sir William Darcy concerning the gaelicization of the English districts and complaining of 'wilful war made by the king's deputy without the assent of the lords and king's council'.[87] Unfortunately it is unclear which, if any, of the Irish council were present at this session, though some councillors were certainly in England later in the year.[88] Until Lord Slane's appointment as treasurer in January

[85] Above, pp. 15-16 Chief Justice Topcliffe was, however, confirmed in office by English patent in 1504: *Cal. pat. roll, 1494-1509*, pp. 60, 64, 354. Chief Baron Cornewalshe was deprived of office for insulting the deputy in council in 1472, and about the same time appealed the king's messenger before the deputy and lords in parliament of bringing forged letters from the king. Edward summoned him to court, the matter was settled and Cornewalshe restored. He had been first appointed in 1441 and this incident seems to be something of a throwback to a previous age: Parliament roll, 12 & 13 Edward IV cc 6, 28, 61 (*Stat. Ire. Edw. IV*, ii, 8-12, 54-8, 136-8); Memoranda roll, 12 Edward IV m. 13d (S.P.W., Hore MS I, pp. 1130-1).

[86] *L. & P. Hen. VIII,* i (2nd ed.), nos. 632 (22), 2535 (3), ii, no. 1704.

[87] Printed *in extenso* in *Cal. Carew MSS, 1515-74*, pp. 6-8.

[88] *L. & P. Hen. VIII,* ii, no. 1153 (*ibid.,* ii, no. 1269 is misplaced: cf. Quinn, 'Henry VIII and Ireland', p. 321). *L. & P. Hen. VIII,* ii, no. 411, suggesting that Kildare was in

1514, Darcy had been deputy-treasurer,[89] but Sir Bartholomew Dillon replaced him shortly afterwards, and Kildare also excluded him from his private council.[90] Moreover, if Darcy was of the king's council in 1515, no evidence of this survives. Thus he may not have been the informed and impartial observer which he appears and we do not know whether Kildare's summons to court arose directly out of opposition to him in council.

Even in the 1520s when, it would seem, a strong, independently-minded council would have been useful in curbing the Kildare-Ormond feud, there is little sign of such opposition to Kildare in council. It was later objected that in sending reports to England Kildare had used to 'geve his matter ower partially, and then serten of the cownssell wyche in all thenges wher at his commandment sholde fyrste pwtte to their names, by resson wher of the other of the cownsselle, watt for fere and watt for laber and fayre wordes, wolde be browrt to dowe the same'. The earl could thereby 'keppe alle matters of Yerlland dercke from the counselle of Yngland, sawyng seche as plessyd hym selfe'.[91] If the king hoped to build a strong council, the reservation of appointments was an obvious means, and indeed the increase in this practice during the 1520s might be so interpreted. In fact, however, Henry made little effective use of his powers. In consequence of the Geraldine-Butler feud, the Old English gentry was split between supporters and opponents of Kildare; and since the administration was increasingly centred on Dublin, Pale families, who were usually pro-Kildare, predominated there. Henry VIII made little attempt to increase English representation on the council before 1534, but English-born officials were in any case often little more impartial. Lord Chancellor Alen was dismissed in 1532 because Kildare could not work with him, but his successor, another Englishman, Primate George Cromer, was denounced in 1533 'for his opyn parcialitie in all therle[s]. . procedinges'.[92] Earlier, during Surrey's

England by 3 May is unreliable. Kildare attested in Ireland on 5 May: Memoranda roll, 8-9 Henry VIII m. 17d (B.L., Add. MS 4791, f. 198).

[89]Memoranda roll, 4-5 Henry VIII m. 24 (P.R.O.I., Ferguson coll., iv, f. 19; B.L., Add. MS 4791, f. 196). Darcy had been reappointed in Oct. 1508: Memoranda roll, 24 Henry VII m. 2 (B.L., Add. MS 4793, f. 154v).

[90]Memoranda roll, 7-8 Henry VIII m. 12 (P.R.O.I., Ferguson repertory, iv, 99) m. 23d (B.L., Add. MS 4791, f. 197v); N.L.I., D. 15963-4. (*Dowdall deeds,* nos. 519-20); *Cal. Carew MSS, Book of Howth,* pp. 192-3 (the story about Robert Cowley's complaints against Kildare before the English council after his exclusion, along with Darcy, from the earl's private council should probably also be assigned to 1515).

[91]P.R.O., S.P. 1/104/158 (*L. & P. Hen. VIII,* x, no. 1102). Cf. *S.P. Hen. VIII,* ii, 179.

[92]*S.P. Hen. VIII,* ii, 168; A Gwynn, *The medieval province of Armagh, 1470-1545* (Dundalk, 1946), p. 64.

lieutenancy, only two of the eight justices had retained their offices — Patrick Bermingham and Richard Delahide, the chief justices — though Patrick Finglas, J.C.P., was promoted to chief baron. Their replacements, however, were all acceptable to Kildare, and included the former justice of his liberty. On Ormond's appointment all eight offices were reserved, and with the exception of the clerk of the rolls, those then in office retained them until 1528 at least. Lord Trimbleston, J.K.B. until 1519, was reappointed by Kildare in 1524 as his undertreasurer, an office held until 1520 by Sir Bartholomew Dillon, a notorious Kildare supporter who became J.K.B. in 1520. Of the others, only Finglas became an opponent of Kildare.[93] Early in 1529, Ormond tried unsuccessfully to have Delahide and Dillon dismissed because they incited other councillors to oppose his policies and undermined his authority by spreading rumours that Kildare would shortly be restored.[94] The overall effect of the reserved appointments, therefore, was to maintain Kildare's supporters in office when the earl was in disgrace.

Not surprisingly, therefore, the council exercised little effective restraint on Kildare's conduct as deputy. In 1525, Ormond complained that Kildare got councillors to write to the king against him, whereby 'ye may perceive the parcialitie of theym that so certified, being ordred and conducted therin as the deputie wolde have theym': when Ormond had been deputy, 'they never certified any of therl of Kyldares apparaunt mysorder or transgression in any maner'.[95] When Kildare left for England in 1526, he took an oath from each councillor, unknown to each other, to write in his favour, and as late as 1533, his opponents complained that the council was 'partely corruptid with affection' toward him, and 'partely in soche dreade of him that either they will not or dare not do any thing that shuld be displeasante to him'.[96] It appears, therefore, that such opposition in council as manifested itself after 1520 stemmed as much from the influence of faction as from the emergence of a strong council with royal support.

Throughout the period, deputies were frequently accused of acting without consulting the council, but they were not always able to do this with impunity,[97] and in certain matters, such as the making of peace or

---

[93] Appendix; Ellis, 'Tudor policy and Kildare ascendancy', pp. 247-8.

[94] *L. & P. Hen. VIII*, iv, no. 5349.

[95] *S.P. Hen. VIII*, ii, 118; *L. & P. Hen. VIII*, iv, no. 1352.

[96] *L. & P. Hen. VIII*, iv, no. 3698; *S.P. Hen. VIII*, ii, 168, 179.

[97] E.g. *S.P. Hen. VIII*, ii, 100, 102, 192; *Cal. Carew MSS, 1515-74*, pp. 6-8; *L. & P. Hen. VIII*, iv, no. 1352, v, no. 1061.

war with the Irish, they were particularly expected to obtain its advice. There was of course a general obligation on the deputy so to govern, although a clause to this effect was only occasionally inserted in his commission.[98] A proviso was however normally inserted that he should grant pardons only by their advice.[99] Occasionally, other matters were to be transacted specifically with the consent of the council: in 1520, Surrey had to consult the council before discharging English soldiers and enlisting Irish ones and in 1524 Kildare was ordered not to proceed against Ormond, Darcy or Delvin nor to appoint to important offices or impose coign and livery except by their advice.[100]

The value of the council both as a body to which the governor might turn for assistance and expert advice and as a means by which the king could bridle a wayward viceroy might also vary in accordance with its composition. The Irish council was entirely distinct from the council in England: members of one might be appointed to the other, but they were not automatically members.[101] Irish councillors were normally unpaid, and this may account in part for the predominance, even by English standards, of office-holders and especially lawyers in the fifteenth-century council. After the 1460s this tendency perhaps became even more pronounced. Under English-born governors, their councillors were sometimes admitted to the king's council even though they might hold no high office in the administration: Irish peers also attended, and from time to time one or two of them were retained of the council with fees, latterly £10 a year. With the departure of the earl of Worcester in 1470, however, the government became almost exclusively Old English and the practice of retaining peers, which had continued throughout the 1460s, seems to have lapsed.[102] Thereafter

---

[98] *S.P. Hen. VIII,* ii, 115, 207; N.L.I., D. 2096 (*Ormond deeds, 1509-47,* no. 93). Surrey's commission of 1520 contained such a clause. Cf. Otway-Ruthven, 'Chief governors', p. 235.

[99] Cf. *S.P. Hen. VIII,* ii, 116. In consequence, fiants to the great seal in these two categories were signed, additionally, by councillors: *Fiants Ire., Henry VIII,* pp. 27-8 (the copy in the Public Record Office of Northern Ireland contains pencilled marginalia confirming this point by someone who had evidently seen the originals, destroyed in 1922).

[100] *S.P. Hen. VIII,* ii, 55, 58, 113, 117.

[101] John Estrete, king's serjeant and councillor in Ireland, was sworn a councillor in England, c. 1487: *Cal. pat. rolls, 1485-94,* pp. 158, 169; P.R.O., E. 101/248/17 (Quinn, *Guide finan. rec.,* p. 27). Cf. S.B. Chrimes, *Henry VII* (London, 1972), pp. 97-8.

[102] Richardson & Sayles, *Ir. parl. in middle ages,* pp. 164-8; appendix. The bishop of Kildare was appointed to the council in 1468 with a fee of £10 p.a.: Memoranda roll, 8 Edward IV m. 11d (B.L., Add. MS 4793, f. 156). Cf. J.R. Lander, *Crown and nobility, 1450-1509* (London, 1976), pp. 204-19. The king's serjeant-at-law received £5 p.a.

an inner circle, comprising the chancellor, treasurer, the chief justices and chief baron, the keeper of the rolls and the king's serjeant, took charge of day-to-day administration, and others ceased to attend regularly. A statute of 1478, quashed the following year, enacted that a justiciar should be elected by 'le counseill du roy entierment', afforced by other magnates of the Pale, instead of by 'vij persons del counseill le roy' as had sometimes been the case.[103] This act was clearly the result of a reaction to recent developments, but in 1479, when this and other problems were referred to the king, Edward IV laid down that nothing should be taken as an 'act of consele, unless the kyngs lieytennant or his deputie give his assent therunto by the advis of the more part of the kyngs consell there', 'the more part' being defined as these seven ministers.[104] A statute of 1485, confirming the Statute of Henry fitz Empress, also mentioned a council of these seven; but when, about the same time, the council examined a view of account of the Irish revenue to be sent to the king, the two puisne judges were also present.[105]

The decision to summon the council was traditionally a matter for the governor, and summonses issued under his privy seal.[106] Thus it may be that a powerful deputy such as Kildare had been able to influence proceedings unduly by introducing his retainers, and perhaps by excluding known opponents. For the discharge of one of its more important functions, therefore, the act of 1478 may be interpreted as an attempt to secure a more representative council. And Edward's instructions of 1479, viewed in conjunction with his reservation of the nomination of five of the seven councillors by right of their offices, appear as a more general application of this initiative, aimed at securing a council more independent of the earl's influence. Nevertheless, the establishment of a distinct 'privy council' did not occur until Henry VIII's reign. Although historians have used the term of the later medieval period to denote an inner circle of ministers in charge of daily administration,[107] throughout the fifteenth century

for his attendance at councils, great councils and parliaments: Parliament roll, 16 & 17 Edward IV c. 30 (*Stat. Ire. Edw. IV*, ii, 506-10).

[103] Parliament roll, 18 Edward IV (II) c. 10 (*Stat. Ire., Edw. IV*, ii 660-2); Richardson & Sayles, *Ir. parl. in middle ages*, pp. 168-9.

[104] Close roll, 19 Edward IV m. 7d (printed in Gilbert, *Viceroys*, p. 599, with corrections in *P.R.I. rep. D.K. 62*, p. 569).

[105] Richardson & Sayles, *Ir. parl. in middle ages*, app. x; Quinn, *Guide finan. rec.*, pp. 17-27.

[106] Below, pp. 174-7.

[107] Richardson & Sayles, *Ir. parl. in middle ages*, ch. 12. The term 'privy council' was, however, occasionally used to distinguish the continual council from a great

the king's council was undifferentiated; and regardless of whether the attendance at a particular session was large or small, a special status was not accorded to this inner circle until 1479. It is, however, true that the Tudor privy council approximated in composition to this inner circle: by 1547, the date of the first full surviving list of privy councillors, one of the puisne judges had replaced the king's serjeant, the undertreasurer had ousted his, by then, nominal superior, and the archbishop of Dublin and bishop of Meath were also included, but otherwise the two groups were similar.[108]

The council was, as in England, served by a clerk whose status and importance probably reflected his relationship with the governor at any particular time. Down to the mid-fifteenth century the clerk was normally drawn from among the chancery clerks, but sometime after 1472 this connection ceased and between 1495 and 1513 the clerk's salary was increased from the customary ten marks to £10 per annum.[109] During the years 1513 to 1520, Lord Deputy Kildare's secretary and keeper of his privy seal, William Delahide, was at times doubling as clerk of the council, though in 1529 at least, the clerk was elected to office by the council.[110] This situation presumably created little difficulty so long as the council was normally attendant on the deputy and under his control. Under Surrey, however, Robert Cowley, a fairly prominent Irish-born administrator, occupied the office; and for fourteen years from 1529, it was held by an Englishman, John Alen, subsequently also master of the rolls and then chancellor. Alen had accompanied his namesake, the archbishop of Dublin, to Ireland.[111] Both got on badly with Kildare, and the connection between the two offices was probably broken about this time, although as late as 1537 the earlier association hindered the determination of the proper duties of the clerk's office, particularly as to whether he should attend upon the deputy or the council.[112]

council: Parliament roll, 16 & 17 Edward IV c. 30 (*Stat. Ire., Edw. IV,* ii, 506-10); above, n. 102 (the bishop of Kildare appointed 'unus de privato consilio domini regis').

[108]B.L., Add. MS 4801, f. 222v.

[109]Parliament rolls, 7 & 8 Edward IV c. 48, 12 & 13 Edward IV c. 28 (*Stat. Ire., Edw. IV,* i, 540, ii 56); B.L., Royal MS 18C, XIV, f. 25v; Memoranda roll, 3-4 Henry VIII n.23 (P.R.O.I., Ferguson repertory, iv, 97); Otway-Ruthven, *Med. Ire.,* pp. 150-1.

[110]Memoranda rolls, 3-4 Henry VIII m. 23 (P.R.O.I., Ferguson repertory, iv, 97), 8 Henry VIII m. 23d (B.L., Add. MS 4791, f. 197v); *Alen's reg.,* p. 262; *S.P. Hen. VIII,* ii, 44, 104, 497. Delahide was probably a kinsman of Kildare's receiver-general, Sir Walter Delahide: *ibid.,* ii, 145; *L. & P. Hen. VIII,* iv, no. 4302. He died in England: *ibid.,* iv, no. 6125 (n.d.).

[111]P.R.O., E. 101/248/21; *S.P. Hen. VIII,* ii, 104: *Cal. pat. rolls Ire., Hen. VIII-Eliz.,* plate I, pp. 11, 96.

[112]*S.P. Hen. VIII,* ii, 497.

The clerk later kept a register of the council's proceedings, and in 1576 Lord Deputy Sidney called the register known as the Red Book, begun in 1542-3, of which a repertory survives, 'the eldest councell booke that ever was made here'.[113] In fact this statement seems to have been based on no more than a surmise that it somehow represented, as the earliest register then available, a new departure in conciliar development: there is no other evidence to suggest that the year 1542-3 was important in this context. No original council records have survived prior to a register for the years 1556-71 with the exception of a roll of petitions to the council, together with its replies, dating from 1392-3.[114] Nevertheless this roll is clearly a specialised record of only a part of the council's business, the rest of which must have been entered either on the patent or close roll, or perhaps kept on file. It may be that the severance of the connection between chancery clerks and the council provided the initial stimulus towards keeping a register. Despite Sidney's remark, there are occasional references to early Tudor council books, although it is also clear that many records were appropriated by the governor or chancellor. Sir James Ware, the seventeenth-century antiquary, alluded to a memorandum of 2 February 1486, recording the arrival of the king's messenger with news of his marriage, which was 'taken out of the records of the councel-book, being the first year of the reign of Henry the 7th'; and other data exclusive to his *Annals* — for instance that the new archbishop of Cashel was made one of the king's privy council in 1527 — may also have been extracted from lost council registers.[115] Sir John Davies, James I's attorney-general, also refers to documents entered in lost registers: 'the counsell booke of Ireland, 16.H.8.' contained an undated report of late 1533 to the king, the original of which survives among the state papers; and in 'the counsell booke of Ireland 28.H.8.' were a series of submissions by Gaelic chiefs during Grey's deputyship (1536-40).[116] Moreover, Alen's register, compiled at a time when John Alen was both clerk of the council and the archbishop's secretary, contains a copy of a petition of 1514 to the council with its endorsement and reply, and also copies of proceedings in four cases before the council in the 1520s: very probably these were

---

[113] D.B. Quinn (ed.), 'Calendar of the Irish council book, 1581-6', *Anal. Hib.,* xxiv (1967), 98.

[114] *Proc. king's council Ire., 1392-3, passim.*

[115] Sir James Ware, *The antiquities and history of Ireland* (ed. R. Ware, Dublin, 1705), sect. ii, pp. 3, 33, 81 and *passim; S.P. Hen. VIII,* ii, 494. See also below, ch. 6.

[116] Sir John Davies, *A discovery of the true causes why Ireland was never entirely subdued* (facsimile reprint of 1st ed., London, 1612; Shannon, 1969), pp. 237, 239, 241. Davies's dates evidently refer to the commencement of the council books.

extracted from the council register. Delahide endorsed the petition of 1514,

> this matier is remittid to the Iustice Bermynghame, the Iustice Delahyde and to the chief baron to be examined and fully determyned by them. Written at Trim, the xviijth day of Octobr., anno H. octaui sexto.   Willm. Delahyde.

Almost two years later, the three judges determined the matter, apparently entering their decision on the original petition, since they refer in it to 'this bill of complaynt'.[117] This may perhaps be taken as an indication of the undeveloped organization of the king's council during the period.

Nevertheless, if registers were kept throughout the early Tudor period, council business which it was thought particularly important to record — the admission of Gaelic chiefs to the king's peace, or of a new governor to office, or the proceedings of afforced councils — might also be entered on the chancery rolls, which suggests that the register had not yet attained the formality of the traditional court rolls.[118] Even the register of 1556-71 is a considerably less full record than its English counterpart. It recorded only the more formal administrative decisions, whether taken by an afforced or the privy council, together with the signatures (subscribed) of councillors present and normally the place and date. By no means all sessions are recorded and there is otherwise no record of the work done.[119]

It has been suggested, again on the basis of the commencement of a register, that the privy council emerged as a 'definitely constituted body' about 1542.[120] This, however, is certainly too extreme a view of the position. It may well be that the privy council was more organized and, as the burden of government increased, met on a more regular basis in the 1540s, but the key changes appear to have occurred rather earlier. From 1520, it is apparent that two sorts of councils were meeting to transact ordinary business. For example, an arbitration

---

[117]'Liber niger Alani', f. 157v (on loan to T.C.D.; *Alen's reg.*, p. 262). Cf. *Alen's reg.*, pp. 266, 271-3.

[118]E.g. Richardson & Sayles, *Ir. parl. in middle ages,* app. vii; *Proc. king's council, Ire., 1392-3,* pp. 276-84, 288-313; *Stat. Ire., Hen VII & VIII,* pp. 88-91; *Cal. pat. rolls Ire., Hen. VIII-Eliz.,* passim.

[119]*Acts privy council, Ire., 1556-71, passim;* Quinn, 'Ir. council bk', pp. 97-105; G.R. Elton, *Studies in Tudor and Stuart politics and government* (2 vols. Cambridge, 1974), i, esp. pp. 310, 330-5.

[120]D.B. Quinn, 'The early interpretation of Poynings' Law, 1494-1534', *I.H.S.,* ii, (1940-1), 244.

between Ormond and Kildare was drawn up in 1524 by three royal commissioners from England 'by the consent and advise of the hole counsaill of this lande', but difficulties arising were to be resolved 'by the lorde chauncellour and the kinges privey counsaill of this lande'.[121] This document leaves no doubt that two manifestations of the king's council existed, known as the privy council and, perhaps, the general council. It was signed by the commissioners, the two earls, five lords of the Pale including the treasurer, and four more ministers, who apparently constituted the general council, or such of its members as attended. References to a privy council, so styled, survive in the state papers from 1520 onwards,[122] and in October 1534 Cromwell remodelled it, appointing the new chancellor Lord Trimbleston, the earl of Ossory, Lord Delvin, some of the captains of the king's army and others to membership.[123] The distinction between the two councils is clearly brought out in a letter of November 1536 by the deputy and privy council in answer to the charge that there were dissensions among councillors; as might be surmised, so the council feared, because letters to the king and Cromwell were sometimes signed only by a few of them. The council therefore noted that

> except it be for a urgent affaire, thole generall counsaill cannot assemble contynually togethers: and over that, the mater sometyme may be soche as peradventure it is necessary that none shalbe prevay therunto but the prevay counsaill, of which number been therle of Ossorie and his sonne, being but seldome present in theis parties.

Clearly the general council was envisaged as a true governing council and not just a body which met occasionally to ratify some important decision. The primary purpose of the privy council was evidently to allow a more secret discussion of confidential matters. To this end, it had been the custom 'whan matters touched contrary the appetites of the Butlers or Geraldines' to exclude even the two earls.[124] Nevertheless, by 1532 the customary injunction in the deputy's commission not to grant pardons except by the council's advice had been revised to read 'nisi ex assensu priuati consilii nostri. . vel ex consensu minoris [*sic* for 'majoris'] partis eorundem'.[125]

---

[121]*S.P. Hen. VIII*, ii, 34, 41, 104-8; *Alen's reg.*, p. 271. See also *S.P. Hen. VIII*, ii, 35-8, where 'the counsaill of the land' is contrasted with 'your gracis privey counsaill'.

[122]*L. & P. Hen. VIII*, iii, no. 670; *S.P. Hen. VIII*, ii, 33, 106, 131, 133, 156, 158. T.C.D., MS 543/2, a contemporary (at this point) Dublin chronicle, refers to the privy council in June 1534.

[123]*S.P. Hen. VIII*, ii, 206-7, 224.

[124]*Ibid.*, ii, 395. Cf. *ibid.*, ii, 37.

[125]P.R.O., C. 66/661 m. 33 (*L. & P. Hen. VIII*, v, no. 1207 (16)).

It is difficult to determine precisely how far the appearance of the term 'privy council' reflects a development in the council's functions, in its composition, or merely a change in nomenclature. Probably Edward IV's instructions of 1479 conferred formality on an existing, working division of councillors into a ministerial inner circle and the others. But whereas the ministerial circle had hitherto predominated largely, no doubt, because of its professional expertise and more assiduous attendance, Edward effectively introduced a qualitative distinction between a fixed, inner group of seven, the consent of the majority of whom was necessary for any important decision, and the remaining, lesser councillors. In this way, expression was given to the need to associate, as far as possible, the leading magnates and gentry with government, while not restricting royal control and that of the governor over policy and the council. Certainly, the association of parliamentary peers with the council continued. In 1491, fifteen lords of parliament wrote to the king, the letter being subscribed: 'by your true and feithfull subjectes, the lordes spirituels and temporels and your counseillours of your land of Irland in playne parlement ther assembled'.[126] All the signatories, however, were parliamentary peers. Similarly, Kildare agreed as deputy in 1524 not to make peace or war 'withoute assent of the lordes and the kinges counsaill', nor to grant pardons 'but onely by the advise of the lordes of the kinges counsaill'; manifestly, these references were to the same body.[127] Similar juxtapositions survive in a patent of 1516, a letter of 1528 and in the *Ordinances* of 1534.[128]

Thus, to an extent, the emergence of a general and a privy council was an institutional development along the lines of Edward's earlier differentiation of councillors. Very probably, the Tudor privy council was first constituted, through the work of Thomas Wolsey, upon the arrival of Surrey in 1520. A set of memoranda relating to preparations for his expedition recommended that councillors be appointed of the deputy's privy council, three of them to be Englishmen then resident in England, and that Surrey should act only by its advice.[129] Though all governors, like any magnate, had their own privy councils, distinct from the king's council and appointed by themselves,[130] the context

---

[126] *L. & P. Ric. III & Hen. VII,* i, 377-8. Cf. *S.P. Hen. VIII,* ii, 64, 184.

[127] *S.P. Hen. VIII,* ii, 115, 116.

[128] *Ibid.,* ii, 137, 207, 209, 213; *Cal. pat. rolls Ire., Hen. VIII-Eliz.,* p. 1

[129] *L. & P. Hen. VIII,* iii, no. 670. Surrey's appointment was originally intended to be as king's deputy.

[130] For references to the governor's private council, see *Cal. Carew MSS, Book of Howth,* pp. 192-3; P.R.O., S.P. 60/6/60 (printed in J.T. Gilbert (ed.), *Chartul aries of St. Mary's Abbey, Dublin,* (2 vols., London, 1884-6), ii, p. xxviii); *S.P. Hen. VIII,* ii, 174; *L. & P. Hen. VIII,* iv, no. 1352.

shows that it is a royal council which was meant in this case, and indeed Surrey referred to 'your gracis privey counsaill here' shortly after his arrival.[131]

There was, however, a functional difference between the Tudor privy council and its Yorkist predecessor. With the exception of its judicial functions, the late medieval council appears to have been primarily an advisory body. From the 1520s onwards, however, it was apparently capable of acting in an executive capacity independently of the deputy. At the same time, the chancellor, following his English counterpart, emerged as president of the council, a development of his function as residual head of the administration, in the governor's absence. On Surrey's departure in December 1521, the bishop of Meath, probably then lord keeper and appointed chancellor soon after, presided in council;[132] but much of the evidence is indirect, such as indentures in which the possibility of independent action by the council is envisaged. For instance, in 1524, Lord Deputy Kildare undertook for himself and his household to appear before the chancellor, treasurer, the chief justices and chief baron, or any three of them 'uppon reasonable monition by write, letter missife, or private sealle' to make restitution 'as shalbe determyned by them' for offences not amounting to a felony.[133] That summer, the council adjudged Ormond to pay 200 marks damages to Kildare for a raid by his servants on Kildare's lands and tenants.[134] For the period when Lord Delvin was vice-deputy, there is more positive evidence. On 14 September 1527, Sir James Fitzgerald received a farm of two royal manors, the patent being attested, by virtue of a signed bill from the king, by the chancellor (not the governor, as was normal until 1534) and witnessed by other councillors.[135] On 15 November, the council wrote to Wolsey about the urgent need to attend to the lordship's defence.[136] On the 18th and 22nd, four and three councillors respectively witnessed exemplifications, attested by Delahide C.J.C.P., of two enrolments in the bench which were probably required in England in connection with the settlement of the Ormond inheritance being negotiated between Sir Peter Butler and the Boleyns.[137] On 23

---

[131]*S.P. Hen. VIII*, ii, 37.

[132]*ibid.*, ii, 91-2; *L. & P. Hen. VIII*, iii, no. 2088.

[133]*S.P. Hen. VIII*, ii, 113. Cf. *ibid.*, ii, 91-2, 111; *L. & P. Hen. VIII*, iv, no. 4933.

[134]*S.P. Hen. VIII*, ii, 122.

[135]N.L.I., D. 2146 (*Ormond deeds, 1509-47*, no. 130); below, p. 173.

[136]*L. & P. Hen. VIII*, iv, no. 4933 (misplaced in 1528).

[137]N.L.I., D. 1820, 2149 (*Ormond deeds, 1413-1509*, no. 243, *1509-47*, no. 133). Cf. *ibid., 1509-47*, nos. 115, 136.

February, the chancellor and chief justice repeated the council's previous warning about the lordship's defence, adding that the vice-deputy was inadequate for the task.[138] And finally, after Delvin had been kidnapped by O'Connor Faly on 12 May, the chancellor and council had full responsibility for the government until alternative provision could be made.[139] The council acted independently at other times too, organising purveyance for Lord Deputy Skeffington's retinue on his arrival in 1530, examining two merchants on matters which had serious implications concerning Lord Deputy Kildare's conduct in 1533, and at the end of that year an afforced council reported to the king concerning the general state of the lordship.[140] Although isolated examples survive of the council meeting in the governor's absence at an earlier date — the chancellor, for example, presided at sessions in July 1495 when the deputy was campaigning in Munster[141] — circumstances were clearly exceptional. Sessions so held from the 1520s were less unusual and seemingly arose from the establishment of a privy council.

Among the factors which account for the increasing role of the council in government during the 1520s the coincidence of the final stage in the long-term process whereby Dublin became the administrative capital of the lordship with a period of rapid turnover of governors — particularly Ormond's two deputyships (1522-4, 1528-9) when he was often outside the Pale for long periods — may be accounted of some importance. It was only in the early Tudor period that the chancery and king's bench ceased finally to itinerate,[142] and at the same time the council was ceasing to be always in attendance on the deputy and coming to regard Dublin as its normal meeting place. As late as 1514 the council could assemble at Trim in term time, apparently to transact ordinary business,[143] but surviving references to sessions in the 1520s were usually to Dublin as the place of assembly. Probably the centralisation of the courts there, in view of

---

[138]*S.P. Hen. VIII*, ii, 126-7. Cf. *L & P. Hen. VIII*, iv, no. 4277, referring to a letter from the chancellor to Norfolk, *c.* April 1528.

[139]*S.P. Hen. VIII*, ii, 127-34; *L. & P. Hen. VIII*, iv, nos. 4264, 4302. Ossory wrote sometimes to the chancellor and sometimes to the privy council at this time: *S.P. Hen. VIII*, ii, 132-3.

[140]*L. & P. Hen. VIII*, v, no. 1061; P.R.O., S.P. 2/0/3 (*L. & P. Hen. VIII*, vi, no. 567); *S.P. Hen. VIII*, ii, 162-6.

[141]B.L., Royal MS 18C, XIV, f. 14. Cf. Richardson & Sayles, *Ir. parl. in middle ages*, pp. 26, 312.

[142]Below, pp. 112, 173-5.

[143]*Alen's reg.*, p. 262.

the ministerial composition of the council, meant that the council could assemble outside Dublin during term only with great inconvenience. When, for instance, the lieutenant and council wrote to Wolsey from Clonmel on 6 October 1520, none of the common law judges was present.[144] And by 1533 a report to Cromwell was suggesting that some of the lords of the Munster shires should be appointed to the council and should sit with a president as a regional council for the south 'because that Dublin, where the kinges counsaile doo sytt, is soo far from the said counties'.[145] The importance of the council in general after 1520 is well illustrated by an award between Kildare and Ormond. In November 1523, on receipt of the king's instructions by the archbishop of Armagh, the two earls chose the archbishop, the chancellor, treasurer and chief justice to arbitrate between them. Neither earl, awarded the arbitrators, should 'in anywyse maike in seuerall bandes seuerall warre ne seuerall peax with Englisshe or Irisshmen without licence of the kinges grace or consent of his deputy and counsaill, and in thabsens of the deputy, the counsaill here'. Kildare was, in Ormond's absence, to take charge of the military situation in the Pale and to lead such raids on the Irish as should be 'thought mete by the counsaille and necessarye to bee doen for the comon welthe'. The earls were to discipline their kinsmen or surrender them to the deputy and council, and in particular Kildare was to arrest Sir Gerald MacShane and his son and to bring them for examination 'befoire the kinges deputie and counsaill at Dublyn... or in the deputies absens befoire the counsaill theire'. Nevertheless, the deputy was not to pardon them of offences determinable within the liberty of Kildare, but to deliver them 'aftir such examynacion had, yf the counsaill think it so expedient, to the saied erle'.[146] In what was probably a reflection of the council's increasing importance as an executive body, the king experimented in 1529-30 with the appointment of a secret council of the chancellor, treasurer and chief justice to govern the lordship in the name of a titular lieutenant in place of a deputy.[147]

Because of the loss of its registers, attendance at and the composition of the early Tudor council can now be only partially

---

[144]*S.P. Hen. VIII*, ii, 51.

[145]*Ibid.*, ii, 173. Cf. *L. & P. Hen. VIII*, iv, no. 2405.

[146]N.L.I., D. 2096 (*Ormond deeds, 1509-47*, no. 93). Sir Gerald Mac Shane was of Kildare's privy council: *L. & P. Hen. VIII*, iv, no. 1352.

[147]D.B. Quinn, 'Henry Fitzroy, duke of Richmond, and his connexion with Ireland, 1529-30', *I.H.R. Bull.*, xii (1934-5), 175-7.

determined, chiefly from signatures on council letters. The privy council of 1520 probably varied little in composition from the ministerial group of 1479 or the privy council nominated in 1547, but since privy councillors are indistinguishable from others in letters, this must remain a presumption based on the survival of documents emanating from a succession of councils so composed. Thus a council which met on 6 September 1530, apparently to consider defence measures, comprised the deputy, chancellor, treasurer, both chief justices and the chief baron, the second justice K.B., the earls of Kildare and Ormond, and Lord Trimbleston, who was perhaps auditor at this time.[148] Four days later, at a session with a much thinner attendance, the archbishop of Armagh was also present.[149] A session on 20 October 1532 was attended by the deputy, chancellor, chief justice C.P., the chief baron, second justice K.B., the bishop of Meath and Lord Trimbleston.[150] More usually, however, the attendance was much smaller: extant letters and proceedings of the council, 1520-34, were usually signed by the deputy and three or four councillors.[151] Occasionally a session might be held by the chancellor and only one other councillor, though this was perhaps sometimes a council committee.[152] The chancellor was apparently the most assiduous in his attendance, no doubt because he presided in the deputy's absence, but until his death late in 1532 Bermingham C.J. attended as regularly, though the other councillors were much less regular in their attendance.[153]

Clearly much depended on the governor. Throughout the period, he probably admitted to the council additional advisers as he saw fit, but until 1478 he had apparently been able to control its composition by not summoning opponents. His powers were probably more extensive in this respect, for in 1520 Surrey excluded Lord Howth

---

[148] Memoranda roll, 22 Henry VIII m. 20d (B.L., Add. MS 4791, f. 203; S.P.W., Hore MS I, p. 1173); Patent roll, 16 Henry VIII (T.C.D., MS 1731, f. 75).

[149] *Fiants Ire., Henry VIII*, pp. 28, 35.

[150] Memoranda rolls, 24 Henry VIII m. 15 (S.P.W., Hore MS I pp. 1176-80).

[151] E.g. *S.P. Hen. VIII*, ii, 40-41, 47-8, 50-51, 121n; *L. & P. Hen. VIII*, iii, no. 971, iv, no. 5392. This was true also of the mid-Tudor period: *Acts privy council, Ire., 1556-71, passim*.

[152] P.R.O., S.P. 2/0/3 (*L. & P. Hen. VIII*, vi, no. 567: examination before 'the lorde chancellour and othere the kinges counsaill in Irland', signed by the chancellor and second justice K.B.). Cf. *S.P. Hen. VIII*, ii, 126-7, 129-30; B.L., Royal MS 18C, XIV, f. 90v (warrant signed by Lord Deputy Poynings and Sir Henry Wyatt, commissioner and auditor, Kilkenny, 1495).

[153] This statement is based on surviving references to attendance at sessions, mainly to signatures on state papers noted above.

altogether for a time.[154] Nevertheless, Henry VII and his son were not content, as Edward IV had apparently been in 1479, to preserve the council's independence of the deputy by utilizing the system of reserved appointments. Both made appointments to the council from outside the circle of top ministers: in 1494, Henry VII appointed two of his chaplains, both prominent Irish-born clerks, to be councillors and masters in chancery;[155] and in 1512 Henry VIII appointed the new prior of St. John's, who had then no office at all, to the council.[156] This latter appointment was reminiscent of the earlier retainder of peers as councillors, but there is no record of payment for this service in the Tudor period.

In composition, the general council of the post-1520 period was probably indistinguishable from the afforced councils of the previous half-century or so of Elizabeth's reign,[157] and it seems likely that particular problems of government in Henry VIII's later years led to a temporary extension in the activities of such councils. Certainly, councils which met to consider business earlier discharged in afforced councils are indistinguishable in composition from sessions of the general council.[158]

The period 1520-34, it appears, saw a marked increase in the activity and importance of the council, although its assertion of authority vis-à-vis the deputy was to some extent retarded by Kildare's continuing influence in council. The evidence for an independent executive role by the council together with the emergence of a distinct privy council in 1520 strongly suggest that it was at this date that a council was established in Ireland, organized and institutional in the same way as the privy council later set up in England by Thomas Cromwell.[159] The possibility that the usage of the term privy council denoted a fluctuating group of close advisers — such as was meant by references to the king's privy councillors in England from the fourteenth century onwards — may be discounted. The evidence shows that some more precisely defined body was in question and it is, moreover, unlikely that such an amorphous group could have survived the frequent changes of deputy in these years, and

---

[154] *Cal. Carew MSS, Book of Howth*, p. 191.

[155] *Cal. pat. rolls, 1485-94*, pp. 472-3, *1494-1509*, p.7.

[156] Memoranda roll, 4 Henry VIII m. 16 (B.L., Add. MS 4791, ff 195-5v).

[157] Cf. *S.P. Hen. VIII*, ii, 91-2, 92-3, 104-6, 162-6.

[158] Cf. Memoranda roll, 20 Henry VIII m. 18d (B.L., Add. MS 4791, f. 202v; S.P.W., Hore MS I, pp. 1169-70); *S.P. Hen. VIII*, ii, 91-2.

[159] See G.R. Elton, *The Tudor revolution in government* (Cambridge, 1953), ch. 5.

particularly the reforms projected and implemented by Cromwell from 1533. Indeed, the fact that, despite the survival of a detailed series of ordinances concerning the administration, we learn nothing of fundamental changes initiated by Cromwell for the council, beyond a reshuffle in its membership, suggests that the chief minister was satisfied with the role previously mapped out for it in the administration of the lordship.

Responsibility for the establishment of the privy council thus appears to rest with Thomas Wolsey: no doubt the reorganization in Ireland helped to inspire Wolsey's reforms of the councils in the north and in the marches of Wales in 1525, but in fact circumstances were not entirely similar. In Ireland, the council had no connection with the governor's household, and the increase and remodelling of its powers were achieved, not by further delegation of duties previously discharged from Westminster, but by the redistribution at the governor's expense of power long vested in the Dublin administration.[160] In the lordship, the king had perforce to delegate most of his executive powers to a deputy and, as we have seen, these might in certain circumstances devolve on the chancellor. Thus the fact that bureaucratization of the Irish council should have preceded its English counterpart is understandable, for it was its executive functions which distinguished the Tudor privy council from its counterparts in other national monarchies of Western Europe.[161] Moreover, even before this, attempts were being made to reduce the independence of the deputy. Sometimes this was accomplished by reducing his executive powers and substituting an advisory role only, as by Poynings' Law or the system of reserved appointments; sometimes he was ordered to act only by the advice of the council. By diminishing the deputy's powers in this way and increasing, to a lesser degree, the council's the king gradually acquired greater control over government in the lordship and reserved to himself some of the patronage available.

Cromwell's contribution to the development of the council was seemingly confined to ensuring that previous arrangements for the exercise of executive functions by deputy and council were adhered to by Skeffington and Grey. At the same time, however, the Dublin administration fell victim to his policy of erecting the unitary realm of England on the foundations of the feudal lordship over Ireland

---

[160] Williams, *Council in the marches of Wales,* pp. 11-14; Reid, *King's council in the north,* pp. 101-7.

[161] See G.R. Elton, 'Tudor government: the points of contact. II. The council', *R. Hist. Soc. Trans.,* 5th ser., xxv (1975), 197.

previously exercised by its kings: thereafter 'the Irish government was not allowed any real independence, being — like that of Calais — firmly controlled by Cromwell and the English Privy Council'.[162] As Cromwell's papers clearly show, from 1534 all important decisions were taken in England after consultation which was not confined to the Irish council and in which the deputy's views were by no means automatically accepted. And even in more routine matters, Henry and Cromwell were increasingly sensitive to suggestions that the deputy was not governing by the council's advice.[163] While Kildare survived his influence concealed the full extent of the changes, but in reality executive power in Ireland had come to lie more nearly with the deputy and council jointly, 'and in thabsens of the deputy, the counsaill here'.

---

[162] G.R. Elton, *Reform and reformation: England 1509-58* (London, 1977), p. 209, also pp. 201, 207-11, 302, 392.

[163] E.g. *S.P. Hen. VIII,* ii, 395.

2

DEFENCE

More so than contemporary England, the Yorkist lordship was a society organized for war. The overriding administrative problem was the defence of the English districts against those officially described as 'the king's rebels and Irish enemies', who comprised not merely the Gaelic Irish, although they were the principal and underlying source of disorder, but also at times almost any Old English magnate and his connection who could pose a serious challenge to good order and government in his locality. And since no governor in the period 1470-1534 commanded resources which allowed him to take the offensive or to ignore the Irish except for short periods, Old English society probably appeared the more violent as Henry VII and his son were able to strengthen central government control over England south of the Trent. To the king, therefore, the lordship must have appeared increasingly like those other areas where disorder was endemic, the marches of Wales where another Celtic society challenged the dominance of English law and customs, or the north where the kingdom of the Scots constituted a serious military treat to the peace and stability of that border: it is no coincidence that Henry VIII tended to recruit from these marchlands when English troops were required for service in Ireland.[1] But even if good government was not established in Ireland to the extent which occurred in England under Edward IV and Henry VII, conditions in the more heavily settled parts of the lordship certainly improved. And in large measure, this improvement sprang from a reorganization of the arrangements for the lordship's defence.

The governor's own retinue provided the nucleus of almost every substantial force raised for the king's service in Ireland; and without such a body of household troops to reinforce his authority, no governor could have served effectively. During the later fifteenth century important changes were made in the arrangements to maintain a standing force at the governor's disposal, and an effective distinction was thereby introduced between English and Irish-born governors. Under the Lancastrians, the governor's indenture of service had customarily specified the number of troops with which he should serve, frequently a force of between 300 and 500 archers; and his salary, charged on the English exchequer, was augmented to cover

---

[1] *S.P. Hen. VIII*, ii, 32-3; P.R.O., S.P.65/1/1 (*L. & P. Hen. VIII*, xi, no. 934).

the costs of this retinue: but arrangements for their recruitment and pay were usually left to the governor.[2] After 1478, however, Irish-born governors served with greatly reduced retinues and for much smaller salaries which were charged on the Irish exchequer. In fact, from the outset Edward IV normally assigned money specifically for those troops provided as a retinue, so leaving the governor's salary as a separate item to be met by the Irish exchequer. Moreover, Irish deputies could no longer count on financial and military assistance from England: Desmond received a mere £500 towards his costs in 1463 and an annuity of £100 from 1464; and Kildare apparently received neither troops nor money until 1474. And when, in 1480, the eighth earl of Kildare agreed to maintain 120 horsemen in return for £600, charged on the Irish exchequer in the first instance, the king had effectively transferred the entire burden for the defence of the land onto the lordship. With few exceptions, this remained the position until 1534.[3]

Not surprisingly, therefore, the period saw various efforts to ensure both that a sufficient force was available for the defence of the land and that defence costs were borne more evenly by the whole community. In consequence, responsibility for defence came to lie, even more so than before, on unpaid local levies, since the deputy could no longer afford to maintain even the 300 archers which had been considered an acceptable minimum for most of the fifteenth century. These changes reinforced the earlier *de facto* division of the lordship into the Pale and the outlying shires. Principally, the reform of parliamentary taxation, discussed in a later chapter, greatly increased its yield within the Pale but exonerated the outlying shires from their subsidy quotas (rarely paid in any case). Since the Dublin administration had long since ceased to provide a standing force for defence and to maintain public order in the outlying shires, this was understandable, while worthwhile sums were now levied from the Pale to offset the costs of its defence.

The fifteenth-century English Pale was not, however, quite as small as historians have supposed, and though it had shrunk in size during the Lancastrian period, it expanded thereafter and the principal development of the period following was that its extent and significance were increasingly defined. The earliest surviving reference to the term Pale dates from 1446, but the four shires already existed as a separate

---

[2] See Richardson & Sayles, *Ir. parl. in middle ages*, pp. 152-4, 227-8.

[3] Quinn, *Guide finan. rec.*, pp. 28-68 *passim;* Cal. pat. rolls, 1461-7, p. 340; above, pp. 25-7.

administrative unit long before this, and by 1428 had been vaguely divided into 'la terre de pees, appelle Maghery' and the marches.[4] The marches lay open to raids by the Irish, but successive parliaments offered subsidies to those who would build castles and ordered the construction of dykes and the fortification of key bridges. Thus the maghery (*Irish* machaire = a plain) was gradually enclosed by ditches, and piles and small castles erected for its defence. A tract of 1515 equated the maghery with the Pale, but normally the march was also included. This change, if it be one, seemingly reflects an increasingly evident distinction between march and maghery in terms of defence rather than any obvious decline in control over the marches. Throughout the period, though conditions in the marches were more unsettled, all but its frontiers remained amenable to government control.[5] By 1477 the boundaries of march and maghery had been precisely delineated and were then confirmed by statute. They are known from a statute of 1488, called the Act of Marches and Maghery, which it has been supposed defined the boundaries of the Pale, the well-known coastal strip, twenty miles deep, stretching from Dundalk to Dalkey: its real purpose, however, was to modify previous legislation which had prohibited coign and livery except by consent. Henceforward, taking coign and livery within the maghery as laid down by the statute was a felony, but it could be imposed by lords on their own tenants in the marches.[6] The marches of each county were organized into captainries under the authority of a captain or warden chosen by the deputy and council in association with the local gentry.[7] Finally, in 1495 Poynings's parliament required inhabitants of the marches to build a double rampart and ditch six feet high on the boundary of march with maghery and further ditches 'in the wastes or fasaghe landes' between the marches and the Irishry.[8]

In 1533 it was claimed that only in a region twenty miles wide were the king's laws obeyed and English customs used. Nevertheless such reports, intended to convince the king of the need for substantial intervention in Ireland, merit little credence: they hardly differed from

---

[4]Parliament roll, 8 Henry VI c. 13 (*Stat. Ire., Hen. VI*, pp. 34-6); Lydon, *Lordship*, pp. 260-1.

[5]*S.P. Hen. VIII*, ii, 22; *L. & P. Hen. VIII*, iv, no. 2405; Lydon, *Lordship*, pp. 260-1.

[6]*Stat. Ire., Hen. VII & VIII*, p. 84; S.G. Ellis, 'Parliaments and great councils, 1483-99: addenda et corrigenda', *Anal. Hib.*, xxix (1980), 104-5; Hore & Graves, *Southern & eastern counties*, p. 167; P.R.O., E.30/1548, f. 18 (Conway, *Henry VII's relations*, pp. 215-16).

[7]*S.P. Hen. VIII*, ii, 86, 211, 225; *Cal. pat. rolls Ire., Hen. VIII-Eliz.*, p. 26.

[8]P.R.O., E.30/1548, f. 18 (Conway, *Henry VII's relations*, pp. 215-16).

complaints of 1428 and 1435 that 'the Englisshe grounde... obeying to the kingis laue' amounted to less than 'on schir in Englande' and that there were 'scarcely thirty miles in length and twenty miles in breadth thereas a man may surely ride or go... to answer to the king's writs and to his commandments'.[9] In fact, far from an inexorably shrinking Pale, the period actually saw an increasing differentiation of the region into waste land 'in frontura marchie', the march proper and the maghery, in an on-the-whole successful attempt to build up a system of standing defences for the Pale. There were complaints in the 1520s that the principal lords of the maghery kept 'little ordinary houses, as they were in a land of peace' and left the defence of the Pale to the marchers.[10]

The establishment of a locally paid and recruited defence force to replace the troops formerly provided and financed from England dates from the 1470s. The earl of Desmond seems to have maintained a retinue as deputy (1463-7) largely by imposing coign and livery on the Pale, a practice which was not new but was probably more widely employed by the earl: charges of this nature apparently lay behind his dismissal and execution.[11] His successor, Worcester (1467-70), was provided with English troops and money, but after his departure Irish raids became more menacing, particularly in Co. Dublin where the commons granted a subsidy for the defence of the march. From January 1472, therefore, parliament agreed to retain a force of eighty archers for three months for the Pale's defence, to be paid for jointly by Lord Justice Kildare, by virtue of his obligation to maintain a force of twenty men-at-arms or its equivalent out of his salary, and by subsidy of £40 levied on the four shires.[12] Militarily, this force was the precursor of the Brotherhood of Arms established after consultation with royal commissioners in 1474: evidence of complete continuity is lacking, but in March 1473, when the war season approached, a larger force of 160 archers and 63 spears was retained for three months, to be maintained by a subsidy of 160 marks on the Pale and £42 13s. 4d. from the Irish revenues out of the deputy's fee. And since these monies would not fully cover the force's wages, permission was

---

[9] Sir William Betham, *The origin and history of the constitution of England and early parliaments of Ireland* (Dublin, 1834), p. 361; D.A. Chart (ed.), *The register of Primate John Swayne* (Belfast, 1935), p. 108; *L. & P. Hen. VIII*, iv, no. 2405; *S.P. Hen. VIII*, ii, 22, 162.

[10] *L. & P. Hen. VIII*, iv, no. 2405.

[11] See Cosgrove, 'Execution of the earl of Desmond', pp. 11-27.

[12] Parliament rolls, 10 Edward IV cc 9, 12-14, 16, 29, 30, 11 & 12 Edward IV cc 15, 16, 23, 43, 48-9 (*Stat. Ire., Edw. IV*, i, 664-810 *passim*).

granted in certain circumstances to quarter them on the country, a partial toleration of coign and livery. Finally, a year later, a Brotherhood of thirteen magnates was created from whom a captain would be elected annually on St. George's Day. A force of 120 archers and forty horse was to be at the Brotherhood's disposal, to be maintained by the extension to Ireland of poundage, $12d$. in the pound on goods entering or leaving the land. In fact, the cost of this force in wages was over £1,200 a year, far more than the value of poundage, which suggests that the balance would again be recouped by imposing coign and livery.[13]

Since the members of the Brotherhood were mostly supporters of Kildare, on whom as deputy ultimate responsibility for defence lay, it probably did not long survive his replacement by the bishop of Meath in July 1475. English subventions had in fact already been resumed, a force varying between 300 and 500 archers according to season being maintained for a year from September 1474, plus an additional 100 archers for the year from May 1475. Poundage was abolished from February 1476 on the grounds that it was prejudicial to trade, but it is probably significant that the following year saw unprecedentedly high taxation on the Pale through parliamentary subsidies. From June 1477 until the deputy's supersession the following February, 200 archers were maintained from England and Lord Deputy Grey had a retinue of 300 for a few months in winter 1478-9.[14] Soon after, however, subventions from England ceased, and in December 1479, when the eighth earl of Kildare was deputy, the Brotherhood and poundage were restored, although on this occasion troops were to be maintained only to the extent that the revenue from poundage permitted.[15] In this form, the Brotherhood lasted into the 1490s to be formally abolished by Lord Deputy Poynings when poundage was consolidated into the king's customs revenue.[16]

At need, troops raised by the deputy continued to be paid for by parliamentary subsidy, in 1477 and 1485 for example, but subsidies were in fact normally granted to the deputy to offset the costs of defence, and earlier they had been granted on the express condition

---

[13] Parliament rolls, 12 & 13 Edward IV c. 60, 14 Edward IV c. 3 (*Stat. Ire., Edw. IV*, ii, 130-36, 188-94).

[14] Quinn, *Guide finan. rec.*, pp. 30-2, 38-9, 46-7; *Cal. pat. rolls, 1476-85*, p. 79; Parliament roll, 16 & 17 Edward IV c. 14 (*Stat. Ire., Edw. IV*, ii, 478-80); above, p. 26.

[15] Parliament roll, 19 & 20 Edward IV c. 27 (*Stat. Ire., Edw. IV*, ii, 740-6).

[16] Davies, *Discovery*, p. 64; below, pp. 72-4.

that coign and livery should not be imposed.[17] In 1494 a subsidy was again granted on this condition, but after Kildare's restoration the clause disappeared and did not recur until 1531, when parliament apparently threw out a bill granting a subsidy in return for reducing the level of coign and livery, and 1533, when a subsidy was granted in return for its abolition.[18] In fact after 1496, the subsidy, supplemented by coign and livery, provided the financial basis for the deputy's retinue. Obviously, the burden of coign and livery varied with the size of the deputy's retinue, but the eighth and ninth earls generally limited its incidence to Kildare and the Pale marches. Until 1527, they imposed it in the maghery of the other three shires only for a night in one area when travelling through. This was increased to two nights during Delvin's vice-deputyship and to four under Ossory in 1528-9, but was reduced to two after Kildare's restoration in 1532.[19] An additional burden on the Palesmen was the governor's right to purvey supplies for the maintenance of his household, a right usually termed 'cess' in Ireland although other impositions also went by that name. Purveyance extended to the governor's retinue, but since this rarely exceeded three hundred before 1534, and since the king's price remained broadly in line with the market price, it did not constitute the grievance which it later became.[20]

From c.1500, Kildare's retinue normally consisted of 120 galloglass and 120 kerne, built up over the preceding period and quartered mainly on Kildare, with Carlow and Westmeath, for their defence. In addition, twenty horsemen were maintained in Kildare by the earl's creation – in an interesting reversion to the military arrangements of an earlier age – of new military tenures-at-will, holdings of sixty acres let in return for military service.[21] By 1518, however, the ninth earl had lightened the burden on Kildare by cessing most of the

---

[17] Parliament rolls, 16 & 17 Edward IV cc 4, 45, 18 Edward IV (III) c. 15, 19 & 20 Edward IV cc 4, 21 (*Stat. Ire., Edw. IV,* ii, 460-4, 548-52, 672, 682-4, 730), 2 & 3 Richard III cc 14, 17 (P.R.O.I., transcript); Richardson & Sayles, *Ir. parl. in middle ages,* pp. 232-3.

[18] Statute roll, 10 Henry VII cc 4, 27, 35 (Conway, *Henry VII's relations,* pp. 202-4, 213; *Stat. Ire.,* i, 54; Davies, *Discovery,* pp. 191-2); *Stat. Ire., Hen. VII & VIII,* pp. 105-6, 110, 114-15, 126-7, 137.

[19] *S.P. Hen. VIII,* ii, 503.

[20] *L. & P. Hen. VIII,* v, no. 1061; Parliament roll, 15 & 16 Edward IV c. 25 (*Stat. Ire., Edw. IV,* ii, 300); S.G. Ellis, 'Taxation and defence in late medieval Ireland: the survival of scutage', *R.S.A.I. Jn.,* cvii (1977), pp. 18-19.

[21] P.R.O., S.P.65/3/2; Hore & Graves, *Southern & eastern counties,* p. 161; *S.P. Hen. VIII,* ii, 503. Irish military groupings are explained in Nicholls, *Gaelic and gaelicised Ireland,* pp. 84-90.

galloglass on neighbouring Irishmen.[22] These arrangements reflected Kildare's usual responsibilities as governor in the period, but except for their scale they mirrored the military arrangements of other magnates for the defence of their own lands. A statute of 1460 required landlords to maintain one mounted archer with an English longbow for each twenty librates of land which they possessed, on the grounds that these weapons gave 'le trespluis graunt resistance & paoure dascun hablement de guere vse en la dit terre'. The statute's immediate significance probably lay in the weapon prescribed, but this additional military obligation was in fact continued throughout the period, although the obligation to arms was otherwise as in England.[23]

The mainstay of the Pale's defences continued to be English bills and bows supplied by the towns and the magnates who traditionally kept retinues of English yeomen. These were regarded as superior to the usual Irish weapons, but by the 1520s many of the border chiefs had obtained supplies of handguns and light artillery.[24] At the same time there was concern that the influx of Gaelic tenants, unskilled in English weapons, and the reliance of many marcher lords on kerne and galloglass were undermining the Pale's defences. These changes were attributed to the greed of the magnates who expelled English husbandmen so as to increase their rents by letting lands to hardier Irish tenants.[25] In practice, however, lands cultivated by Irish tenants usually had to be defended by kerne and galloglass maintained by coign and livery, whereas the more substantial English husbandmen defended the marches themselves: and since the charge of coign and livery was deducted from the rents, the lords were in fact no better off.[26] It is noticeable that in Newcastle barony the traditional military arrangements survived in the relatively stable Dublin march, whereas kerne and galloglass were more prevalent in the principal areas of Geraldine expansion, Kildare and Westmeath. And since there was undoubtedly a severe shortage of English tenants, the magnates had

---

[22]*S.P. Hen. VIII*, ii, 214, 503; B.L. Harleian MS 3756, f. 4v.

[23]Parliament roll, 38 Henry VI c. 7 (*Stat. Ire., Hen. VI*, pp. 646-8); *S.P. Hen. VIII*, ii, 12, 163, 212-13, 434-5; *Stat. Ire., Hen. VII & VIII*, p. 141; Patent roll, 14 Henry VII (*Rot. pat. Hib.*, p. 272 no. 15; P.R.O.I., Lodge MSS 'Articles', i, f. 221); R.F. Frame, 'The judicial powers of the medieval Irish keepers of the peace', *Irish Jurist*, n.s. ii (1967), 310-14.

[24]*S.P. Hen. VIII*, ii, 19-20, 159, 163, 213; *Cal. Carew MSS 1515-74*, p. 5; T.C.D., MS 543/2 s.a. 1521, 1523; S.G. Ellis, 'An indenture concerning the king's munitions in Ireland, 1532', *Irish Sword*, xiv (1980-1), 100-3.

[25]*S.P. Hen. VIII*, ii, 163, 449, 497.

[26]*Ibid.*, ii, 12, 507; *L. & P. Hen. VIII*, iii, no. 670ii.

perforce to take Irish tenants in these highly exposed areas.[27] Thus in the early sixteenth century, Pale levies generally comprised a mixture of English and Irish troops. And while some commentators lamented the decline of English weapons for their superiority in open country, others recognised that kerne and galloglass were more expendable and suitable for raids into the Irishry. Likewise, the crown's near monopoly of field and siege artillery tipped the military balance further in favour of the colonists.[28]

At need, the governor could raise a substantial force of 1,000 men or more by proclaiming a hosting. In the fourteenth century, hostings had applied to all free tenants and county levies raised in this way were paid once they moved outside the county. Evidently the *posse comitatus* continued to play an important role into the Tudor period, but by the mid-fifteenth century hostings were usually unpaid: magnates served with their customary quotas of troops, but were sometimes excused this service.[29] Thereafter the obligation began to be assessed more precisely on the basis of landed income: it became compulsory within the Pale and Co. Carlow and by 1485 amercements were being inflicted for absence.[30] Presumably these amercements were used to hire additional troops and the greater landowners could in any case be expected to exceed their quotas.

The most important of the various roads, journeys and hostings which the deputy organized to secure the Pale borders was the general hosting. It was customarily agreed in an afforced council, where the date of commencement, its duration and the amount of cartage required would be fixed, to be followed by chancery writs ordering its proclamation throughout the Pale, although some governors had ordered hostings without obtaining the consent of the lords and council. Cartage was the obligation to provide for the carriage of victuals at a hosting: commonly the rate was four ploughlands per cart, which in 1510 produced 71 carts from Co. Meath.[31] General

---

[27] *Ibid.; S.P. Hen. VIII*, ii, 502-4. Cf. Canny, *Old English Élite in Ireland*, pp. 5-9.

[28] *L. & P. Hen. VIII*, iii, no. 670ii; Donough Bryan, *Gerald Fitzgerald, the Great Earl of Kildare, 1456-1513* (Dublin, 1933), pp. 245-6; G.A. Hayes-McCoy, 'The early history of guns in Ireland', *Journal of the Galway Archaeological and Historical Society*, xviii (1938-9), 43-65.

[29] W.G.H. Quigley & E.F.D. Roberts (eds.) *Registrum Iohannis Mey, The Register of John Mey Archbishop of Armagh, 1443-1456* (Belfast, 1972) nos. 141, 174-5; T.C.D., MS 557, xi, 1339-40; Frame, 'Medieval Irish keepers of the peace', pp. 310-14; Patent roll, 14 Henry VII (P.R.O.I., Lodge MSS 'Articles', i, f. 221).

[30] Hore & Graves, *Southern & eastern counties*, p. 162. For this and the following, see Ellis, 'Taxation and defence', pp. 5-19.

[31] T.C.D., MS 594, f. 9; Bodl., Rawl. MS C. 168, f. 110; *S.P. Hen. VIII*, ii, 13, 35, 77-82, 492.

hostings, it appears, were usually proclaimed only once or twice a year, for a maximum of forty days. Occasionally, a scutage, or royal service as it was known in Ireland, was levied at the same time, no doubt to raise additional troops. Other hostings ('sodden rodes and jorneys'), however, might last a week or less and would be assembled by writ of the governor's privy seal.[32] Additionally, or at other times when the defence of the marches required it, the governor might proclaim a holding by which anything up to 400 kerne were quartered on the Pale. In 1495-6 when the exchequer paid the costs of two holdings of 24 horsemen and 80 kerne, and 20 horsemen for six weeks each, they amounted to £16 and 10 marks respectively.[33]

While the governor's retinue and the hosting came to be associated primarily with the Pale's defence, they could also be applied to the defence of the outlying shires. Nevertheless, the towns and magnates beyond the Pale did not normally supply contingents to a hosting except when one into Munster or South Leinster was proclaimed.[34] In these areas, primary responsibility for defence rested with the chief captain and the local magnates, though the governor intervened from time to time: between 1495 and 1510, for example, visits to Carlow, Carrickfergus, Cork, Galway and Athenry, Kilkenny, Limerick, and Waterford occurred in connection with hostings.[35] Little evidence has survived concerning the ordinary arrangements for the defence of these shires, but those for Kilkenny and Tipperary were probably not untypical. The freeholders, both within and beyond the Ormond palatinate, placed themselves under the earl's protection and agreed to bear the charges of his kerne and horsemen maintained for their defence. A series of local ordinances throughout the fifteenth and sixteenth centuries reiterated that coign and livery was to be imposed only by the earl and with the freeholders' consent, and tried to prohibit its illicit imposition by others.[36] Thus within the Ormond lordship, the incidence of coign and livery was similar to that in the Pale, although in both areas weak government (notably, in the Ormond lordship, an absentee earl from 1452 to 1515) aided the spread of illegal exactions. The *posse comitatus* could at need supplement the lord's retinue, and in Kilkenny, Tipperary and

---

[32] T.C.D., MS 557, xi, 1339-40; *Registrum Iohannis Mey*, nos. 174-5.

[33] *S.P. Hen. VIII*, ii, 213, 265, 492; B.L., Royal MS 18C, XIV, ff 30, 46.

[34] *Ibid.*, ii, 35, 156, 213; *L. & P. Hen. VIII*, iv, no. 2405.

[35] Conway, *Henry VII's relations*, pp. 85, 232-4; Bryan, *Great Earl of Kildare*, pp. 226, 234, 250, 256-7; *Liber primus Kilkenn.*, p. 156.

[36] C.A. Empey & K. Simms, 'The ordinances of the White Earl and the problem of coign in the later middle ages', *R.I.A. Proc.*, lxxv (1975), sect. C, 162-78.

Waterford the two were led by a specially appointed captain whose functions in defending the marches probably approximated to the later lords lieutenant in England.[37] Additionally, the liberty court of Tipperary granted the earl subsidies of thirty or sixty marks for defence at the annual plenary sessions.[38]

In Kildare and Carlow too coign and livery had been imposed by the earls of Kildare with the freeholders' consent for their defence, and the earl of Desmond's arrangements for Cork, Kerry and Limerick had probably originated in the same way.[39] In Wexford, however, coign and livery was almost unknown, although the earl of Shrewsbury sometimes retained English archers for the defence of his palatinate.[40] The contrast between Wexford on the one hand and the oppressive burden of Desmond's military exactions in west Munster was probably shaped largely by three factors: the proximity or otherwise of English rebels and Irish enemies – Wexford was comparatively easily defended – the government's ability to intervene, which in part declined in proportion to the distance from Dublin, and the extent and density of the English settlement. In the Ormond lordship, for example, a substantial class of gentry and freeholders vigorously resisted the abuse of coign and livery and the oppressions which were practised in the Desmond lordship.

Basic to the good government of the lordship was the containment of the Gaelic chiefs of the Leinster mountains and the midlands. Even Dublin was vulnerable to their raids and the supervision of the English districts of Munster and south Leinster largely depended on the security of the southern marches of the Pale, which had long been a priority, and the control of the major overland route south via the Barrow valley. By the end of the fourteenth century, the town of Gowran lay 'in frontura hibernicorum inimicorum McMorgh et O'Nolan' and the section of the king's highway from there northwards

---

[37] *Ibid.*, p. 171; Hore & Graves, *Southern & eastern counties,* pp. 98, 185, 232; *Liber primus Kilkenn.,* pp. 156-8. Cf. G.R. Elton, *The Tudor constitution* (Cambridge, 1960), pp. 451-2.

[38] *Ibid.,* pp. 171-2. There seems, however, to be a parallel between this subsidy and the composition (larger but payable over a longer period) granted in the Welsh marcher lordships for discontinuing the sessions, since both were closely modelled on the old eyre: cf. T.B. Pugh, *The Marcher Lordships of South Wales 1415-1536* (Cardiff, 1963), pp. 36-48; Carole Rawcliffe, *The Staffords, earls of Stafford and dukes of Buckingham, 1394-1521* (Cambridge, 1978), pp. 113, 132, 155.

[39] Hore & Graves, *Southern & eastern counties,* p. 160; Nicholls, *Gaelic and gaelicised Ireland,* pp. 35-8, 163; Empey & Simms, 'The ordinances of the White Earl' pp. 170, 177.

[40] Hore & Graves, *Southern & eastern counties*, pp. 39-74; *L. & P. Hen. VIII,* ii, no. 430.

to Carlow was passable only with an armed escort.[41] Under the Lancastrians, the position deteriorated still further, with the loss of Tullow castle sometime after 1435 and the destruction of Castledermot c. 1443 as the Irish took advantage of the abeyance in the earldom of Kildare (1432-c. 55) to push into south Kildare. Of Co. Carlow, there remained only Carlow castle itself and Baltinglass abbey.[42] To the north-west, the O'Connors of Offaly were reconquering the original Fitzgerald patrimony as lords of Offaly and had recently retaken Rathangan, and on the Meath-Kildare border the Berminghams of Carbury had long been uncontrollable and hindered joint action by the two shires. These difficulties were later compounded by a dispute between the Butlers and Fitzgeralds over the manors of Maynooth and Rathmore and by 1454 the two communities were being terrorized and their lands wasted.[43] Under the Yorkists and early Tudors, however, this process was reversed; firstly by Geraldine expansion southwards from Kildare and later by Butler penetration northwards from Kilkenny. In Kildare, the seventh earl soon reestablished his authority and a series of fortifications was erected, particularly at key points on the frontiers, to strengthen the marches: towers were built at Norragh in 1465, at Lackagh in 1484, and at Kilcullen bridge in 1468, followed by the walling of the town there in 1478; Kildare castle was strengthened in 1484 and the town, together with Athy, received a very generous royal charter of incorporation at the earl's instance in 1515.[44] In the west, the important castles and manors of Rathangan, Lea and Moret were recovered and the Berminghams of Carbury reduced, and in the south Leighlin castle was recovered in 1480. A substantial castle at Castledermot, building in 1485, promised 'la vray readepcion de toutz lez terrez gastez del counte de Cathirlagh'.[45] A parliament at Limerick in 1483 vested in the earl all waste lands between Calverstown and Leighlinbridge, unless their owners occupied them within six years, on the grounds that Kildare had recovered them from the Irish. And between 1467 and 1480 at least

---

[41] Empey, 'The Butler lordship', pp. 179-81.

[42] Otway-Ruthven, *Med. Ire.*, p. 369; *Ormond deeds, 1413-1509*, no. 320(3); *I.H.S.*, ii (1940-1), p. 396.

[43] Otway-Ruthven, *Med. Ire.*, pp. 296 n.43, 297, 354, 363, 380, 385-6; Nicholls, *Gaelic and gaelicised Ireland*, pp. 174-5.

[44] Parliament rolls, 5 Edward IV cc 47, 62, 7 & 8 Edward IV c. 66, 18 Edward IV (I) cc 18, 19 (*Stat. Ire., Edw. IV*, i, 368, 396, 608-10, ii, 614), 1 Richard III cc 4, 18 (P.R.O.I., RC 13/8); *Red Bk Kildare*, nos. 196-7.

[45] *New hist. Ire.*, iii, 20; R. Butler (ed.), *The annals of Ireland* (Dublin, 1849), p. 46 (annals of Ross); Parliament roll, 2 & 3 Richard III c. 15 (P.R.O.I., transcript); below, p. 185. Cf. Hore & Graves, *Southern & eastern counties*, p. 70n.

three major hostings, for which scutage was levied, assembled at Kildare, and the earl also began to use Carlow as a place of assembly.[46]

Leighlinbridge marked the effective southerly limit of Kildare lordship, although the eighth earl further contained the Leinster Irish by buying up old titles to land and ejecting the Irish occupants – on the south-east marches of Co. Dublin, where he recovered Castlekevin and Fassaroe and had built Powerscourt castle by 1500, and in Co. Carlow, where he maintained castles at Rathvilly, Clonmore and Clonogan, and on the northern marches of the liberty of Wexford, where by 1533 McMurrough was farmer of the castle and manor of Ferns rendering twenty marks per annum at the exchequer.[47] Piers Butler of Polestown recovered Tullow castle between 1505 and 1515 and Arklow in 1525.[48] This expansion owed much to marriage alliances between the McMurroughs and Butlers and Fitzgeralds. In 1522, the McMurrough abbot of Duiske, intruded by his father, a former chief, even found it expedient to purchase a charter of denization during Ormond's deputyship, and in 1531 Kildare secured the election of his own candidate as chief. Thus by the 1520s the Leinster Irish, it was considered, were 'but feeble in regard of the strength they have been in of former time'.[49] The threat to the Barrow valley route had been progressively reduced and a chain of castles, fortified bridges and walled towns erected on its more exposed sections. Raids and robberies by the Irish remained a problem of course, and the Kildare-Ormond feud posed a new one, but a substantial trade developed between the towns of Kilkenny and New Ross, and Carlow, Castledermot and Athy, on which the constables of Leighlin and Athy illegally levied customs, as, ironically, did McMurrough on river traffic north of New Ross.[50]

This phenomenon of colonial expansion in Leinster illustrates an important problem of government in the late medieval lordship. The

---

[46]*Stat. Ire., Hen. VII & VIII*, pp. 132-4; Ellis, 'Taxation and defence', pp. 7, 28; T.C.D., MS 557, xi, 1339-40.

[47]*S.P. Hen. VIII*, ii, 184, 264; *Cal. Carew MSS, 1515-74*, p. 6; B.L., Harleian MS 3756, ff 84v-86; *L. & P. Hen. VIII*, iv, no 2405; P.R.O., S.P.65/1/2; *New hist. Ire.*, iii, 7; *I.H.R. Bull.,* li (1978), p. 194.

[48]*Ormond deeds, 1413-1509*, no. 320 (3); *1509-47*, nos. 118, 192; *S.P. Hen. VIII*, ii, 153-4.

[49]*Cal. Carew MS 1515-74*, p. 5; T.C.D., MS 578, f. 7; Nicholls, *Gaelic and gaelicised Ireland*, pp. 171-2; *New hist. Ire.*, ii (forthcoming); *L. & P. Hen. VIII*, iv, no. 2405; Harris (ed.), *Hibernica*, p. 44.

[50]Hore & Graves, *Southern & eastern counties*, pp. 67-9, 71, 108, 130; *S.P. Hen. VIII*, ii, 157-8; Holinshed, *Chronicles* (ed. 1807-8), vi, 280.

activities of the Kildares have been seen as essentially independent of crown rule and their establishment of a supremacy over the border chieftaincies as potentially inimical to royal interests, since they allowed the earls to govern without reference to the wishes of the king or the Palesmen.[51] On this assumption, what was reviving was not royal government but Kildare power. Even in lowland England, however, the king's authority depended in large measure on the cooperation of the local magnate, and in fact the interests of king and earl were in large measure the same. Though historians have tended to concentrate on conflict between the two, Kildare needed the support of the government in order to legitimise the consolidation of his power in the Pale marches and this in turn created the necessary conditions for the growth of stable government. Conversely, when at times in the 1520s Henry VIII tried to rule the lordship independently of the Kildare interest, this quickly affected the security of the Pale, but the earl was also hard put to maintain his standing both among the gentry there and the chieftains of the borders.[52] In fact councillors in Ireland were well aware that the 'quietie and restfullnes' of the king's subjects in Ireland 'standith in the vnitie and concord of the noblis of the sayme'.[53] Alone, the Dublin administration lacked the resources to maintain a satisfactory level of public order. Thus the stability of these years was built on the cooperation of the magnates – each in his own sphere of influence – and the Dublin government to the mutual benefit of crown and subject.

In other areas too, the lordship was being consolidated through the efforts of the magnates. The revival of Butler power in the south midlands after 1500 helped to strengthen the northern marches of Kilkenny and Tipperary where Piers Butler had recovered the ancestral castle of Nenagh by 1505.[54] In western Meath the Nugents, barons of Delvin, and the Kildares were expanding, and after 1496 the king encouraged the recovery of a part of the old earldom of Ulster by a series of grants to the Kildares of lands along the Down coast.[55] Nevertheless, the contribution of the government itself to this recovery was far from negligible. Throughout it found the money for arms and artillery and to maintain a number of important castles. Dublin was the most important of these and also acted as the principal

[51] Cf. Bryan, *Great Earl of Kildare*.
[52] Ellis, 'Tudor policy and Kildare ascendancy', pp. 238-50.
[53] N.L.I., D.2096 (*Ormond deeds, 1509-47*, no. 93).
[54] *Ormond deeds, 1509-47*, no. 192.
[55] *New hist. Ire.*, iii, 4, 18, 19.

armoury, although by the 1520s Carlow and Waterford had joined Drogheda as alternative arms stores. When Kildare was reappointed deputy in 1532, he received custody of 460 bills, eighteen bows, seven demilances, fourteen handguns, eighteen serpentines, three sakers, a curtall and a culverin, plus large stocks of arrows, bowstrings, powder and shot.[56] Many small castles were entrusted to constables assigned by sheriffs or the governor, with lands or other perquisites attached in lieu of a salary.[57] The constables of the more important castles, however, Carrickfergus, Carlingford with Greencastle on the far side of the lough, Trim, Dublin, Wicklow and Limerick, were all appointed by letters patent with salaries, usually £10 or 20 marks, attached. The constable of Carlingford received the town's feefarm, and customs and rents, worth altogether £16 a year, as his salary, and at Limerick the salary of £10 was charged on the feefarm. The constableships of Carrickfergus, 'le cliest del borient', and Wicklow had earlier attracted more, however, reflecting their exposed positions. Wicklow was worth £50 under the Yorkists, which even Kildare found attractive, and Carrickfergus yielded between 60 and 85 marks. By 1534 the salary for Wicklow castle had been reduced to 20 marks, and at Carrickfergus after 1496 the constable received only certain local profits. These economies saved the exchequer c. £80 a year, but the fact that they could be made suggests a growing stability in the outlying parts of the lordship.[58]

Other arrangements for the lordship's defence were more traditional. The government tried to ensure that none 'in anywyse maike in seuerall bandes seuerall warre ne seuerall peax with Englisshe or Irisshmen without licence of the kinges grace or consent of his deputy and counsaill'.[59] Disorders among the Old English were dealt with by the courts, but the governor aimed to elicit at the conclusion of a successful military campaign against a Gaelic chief an undertaking that he would be the king's faithful liege, maintaining the king's peace and the king's war against others, that he would make fine for damages caused to the king's subjects, delivering pledges for its payment, and

---

[56] Ellis, 'King's munitions in Ireland', pp. 100-3.

[57] Parliament rolls, 2 Edward IV c. 13, 7 & 8 Edward IV c. 78, 16 & 17 Edward IV c. 19 (*Stat. Ire., Edw. IV,* i, 32, 626, ii, 488).

[58] P.R.O., E.101/248/21, S.P.65/1/2, P.S.O.1/42/2192, 1/44/2291; *Cal. pat. rolls, 1467-76,* pp. 162, 598, *1477-85,* pp. 160-1, 339, *1485-94,* pp. 232, 464, *1494-1509,* p. 44; *L. & P. Ric. III & Hen. VII,* i, 93; *L. & P. Hen. VIII,* iii, no. 1351; Memoranda roll, 16 Henry VIII m. 38 (P.R.O.I., Ferguson repertory, iv, 114); D.B. Quinn, 'Anglo-Irish Ulster in the early sixteenth century', *Proceedings and Reports of the Belfast Natural History and Philosophical Society,* (1934), 56-78.

[59] N.L.I., D.2096 (*Ormond deeds, 1509-47,* no. 93).

would also deliver hostages for the maintenance of the peace.[60] The complicated system of diplomacy engaged in by the governor to establish and maintain peace with the Leinster chiefs who were the government's principal concern has been well described elsewhere on the basis of the much fuller evidence available in surviving exchequer records of the fourteenth century.[61] Rarely does the evidence survive which would illustrate the operation of the system in the later period, although there are many incidental references to it: for example, a suit in Star Chamber brought by Robert Suttell against the eighth earl of Kildare's executors concerning goods taken from his ship by the constable of Wicklow and apparently seized by O'Byrne. The deputy had compelled O'Byrne to deliver his son as pledge for restitution and on the strength of this had offered Suttell £103 in full satisfaction. Suttell declined, but O'Byrne then died and his son, without lands or goods, was worthless as a pledge against the newly elected chief. Rather than continue to pay for his maintenance, Kildare released the son, but the case apparently turned on whether he had previously received some of the actual compensation and the status of two of the gentry of the country also held as pledges or hostages.[62]

A more general exception to the veil drawn over this aspect of the government's work is provided by Undertreasurer Hattecliffe's day-book for 1495-6. The exchequer made a series of disbursements for the purchase of items given in reward to various chiefs – six rolls of fine cloth, two rolls of velvet and five of Camelot for O'Brien, his wife, Bishop O'Brien and two others; 5½ rolls of fine cloth and one of velvet for McWilliam and his wife; 1½ rolls of green kersey for 'Arteboye'; saffron for McMahon, a barrell of wine for O'Byrne, and a pipe of wine for an English marcher, Edmund Harrold.[63] Small rewards were given to messengers and servants of O'Byrne, O'Neill, McMurrough and O'Carroll with letters to or from the governor;[64] Fr. John received 2s. for spying in O'Byrne's country '& alibi iuxta march. anglicorum', and Arthur O'Toole received his diets in O'Toole's chamber in Dublin castle.[65] The exchequer paid some traditional annual black-rents, £40 each to O'Neill and O'Connor and 80 marks to McMurrough,

---

[60] Conway, *Henry VII's relations*, pp. 232-5; *Cal. Carew MSS, 1515-74*, nos. 34, 56, 71-2, 76-7, 80, 82.

[61] Robin Frame, 'English officials and Irish chiefs in the fourteenth century', *E.H.R.*, xc (1975), 748-77.

[62] *L. & P. Hen. VIII*, Add., no. 297 iii, iv.

[63] B.L., Royal MS 18C, XIV, ff 51, 56v, 102v, 137.

[64] *Ibid.*, ff 47, 55v, 61v, 63v.

[65] *Ibid.*, ff 14, 19v, 27v.

although O'Connor elected to receive a butt of Romney (? wine), transported to Cloncurry for him, out of his rent.[66] The costs of O'Byrne and Bishop O'Brien visiting Dublin were paid and, finally, William McMahon and three horsemen were taken into pay for three months.[67] These payments therefore illustrate most of the traditional devices employed by the government to maintain peace in the marches.

At the end of the middle ages, as three centuries before, the foundation and ultimate sanction of lordship in Ireland was power and armed might, and apart from the most heavily colonized areas, this was perhaps more transparently and immediately true than of any other part of the English state. The English law courts were tolerably successful in adjudicating between conflicting titles to land among the king's subjects,[68] but even in the Irishry 'tenants-at-will' tended to convert themselves into 'freeholders' (to use common law terminology) over several generations and secure title was no real defence against military force.[69] In the marches, therefore, where conflict between common law tenure and Gaelic ownership was most evident, power and possession frequently established title to land. It is significant, however, that English land titles remained important even in areas where Gaelic law predominated in other matters, and that magnates like Kildare troubled to buy up titles to land in Irish possession.[70] While coign and livery might enhance the military capacity of marcher lords, the adoption of other Gaelic customs was no defence against the encroachment of the clans.

Recent work on the sixteenth century has stressed the extent to which social barriers between English and Irish were being broken down and the emergence of an integrated economy.[71] Nevertheless, the underlying conflict between the king's subjects and Irish enemies still survived, particularly with regard to land; and as the balance of

---

[66]*Ibid.,* ff 29, 29v, 31, 37, 40v, 41, 57v. For blackrents, see D.B. Quinn, 'The Irish parliamentary subsidy in the fifteenth and sixteenth centuries', *R.I.A. Proc.,* xlii (1935), sect. C, 223-4, 231.

[67]*Ibid.,* ff 29v, 40, 41, 46v, 100.

[68]Below, chs. 4-5.

[69]Nicholls, *Gaelic and gaelicised Ireland*, pp. 57-8.

[70]*New hist. Ire.,* iii, 7, 8-9, 20.

[71]Especially Canny, *Elizabethan conquest,* ch 1. In another area of English colonization, the Welsh marches, society and the economy also gradually became less divided than contemporary, quasi-legal, classifications into settler and native would suggest, but nonetheless these remained important: R.R. Davies, *Lordship and Society in the March of Wales 1282-1400* (Oxford, 1978), pt. iv.

power shifted again in favour of the lordship, the differences formed the basis of a colonial supremacy gradually built up in Leinster and parts of Munster and Ulster. The Old English earls exacted tribute and military service from Gaelic chiefs and were at the same time encroaching on their possessions in border areas.[72] Concurrently, the reorganization of the lordship's defences under the stimulus of declining military and financial support from England facilitated the complete withdrawal of these subventions, so that for the first time in over a century the lordship was militarily self-sufficient. By the early sixteenth century, so successfully was the defence of the Pale being conducted that the ascendancy of the nobles was drawing complaints from independently-minded gentry who regarded Gaelic Ireland more as an opportunity than a threat.[73] Critics of overmighty subjects like Kildare could compose satirical arguments in support of his activities, but even they could be unintentionally revealing:

> Some sayeth also that the kinges subgetes hadde never better pease with ther enymyes in 300 yere then they have nowe, and that the Iryshe enymyes was never more adred of the kinges deputye then they be nowe, and that Englishe mennes landd was never better tyllyd in this hundred yere then nowe; and all this coulde not be don wythoute myght and strayngeyth of the deputyes armye and retynue, whiche he coulde not holde wyth hym wythoute the said extortions.[74]

More to the point was a Gaelic annalist who remarked in his obit of the eighth earl that 'in power, fame and estimation, he exceeded all the Galls, conquered more territory from the Gaels, built more castles for the Galls, rased more castles of the Gaels and kept better justice and law'.[75]

The fall of the Fitzgeralds in 1534 and the subsequent changes in crown policy towards Ireland had a destabilizing effect on government in the lordship. The claims of government on the king's subjects increased, but in general the resources of the Dublin administration did not increase in full proportion to its additional commitments. For example, the garrison of 340 troops maintained in the years 1537-40

---

[72] Cf. *S.P. Hen. VIII*, ii, 16, 187, 190.

[73] Bradshaw, *Constitutional revolution*, ch. 2.

[74] *S.P. Hen. VIII*, ii, 16.

[75] An t-en macgoill dob' ferr 7 bud mo nert 7 clú 7 oirrdercus 7 is mó do rinde do ghabhaltus ar Gaídealaibh 7 is lía do cumdaigh do chaislenaibh do Ghallaibh 7 do bris do chaislenaibh Goidhel 7 dob' ferr recht 7 riagail: B. MacCarthy (ed.), *Annála Uladh Annals of Ulster*, iii (Dublin, 1895), 506 (my translation).

did not adequately perform the function previously discharged by Kildare's retinue and connection in defending the Pale, and the Gaelic chiefs of the borders were frequently able to exploit dissensions created or exacerbated by the discontinuities of policy which characterized the mid-Tudor period.[76] In many ways, therefore, the years 1470 to 1534 marked a period of peace and prosperity such as was not to recur until after the completion of the Tudor conquest.

---

[76] See especially, Ellis, 'Thomas Cromwell and Ireland', pp. 505-19.

3

REVENUE AND COLLECTION

The king's Irish revenues were tiny in comparison with their English counterpart, nominally *c.* £1,600 in most years, which just covered the costs of government. The reality, however, was more satisfactory, particularly in comparison with the Lancastrian period when the revenue had declined almost constantly, when the English exchequer had been expected to subsidize the lordship to the tune of *c.* £2,000 a year, and when large debts to ministers, soldiers and ordinary subjects had been run up, many of which remained unpaid.[1] The subsequent recovery was made possible by a rigorous pruning of expenses and a modest increase in the revenue, almost to the levels of the late fourteenth century. In many respects it was characterized by the same strategies that the Yorkists and Henry VII pursued in England, an increase in crown lands and their more efficient exploitation, a growth in customs revenue, and a more careful regard for the financial possibilities of the crown's prerogative rights. Additionally, however, the period saw a reorganization of parliamentary taxation.

The parliamentary subsidy

Unlike the standard, late-medieval English tax of tenths and fifteenths on moveable goods, the Irish parliamentary subsidy which developed in the fourteenth century was primarily a tax on arable land. Its basis, a carucage *alias* the danegeld based upon the ploughland or hide, can be traced back to Anglo-Saxon England, although taxes on chattels and tenths on the spiritualties of the clergy were sometimes collected in addition. And even in a period of heavy taxation like that between 1369 and 1371 the actual yield never exceeded £1,500 a year. By 1420 the governor could expect at most £400 a year from this source and usually received much less, and the yield certainly declined still further in the years following. There persisted throughout the fifteenth century, however, a tradition of local taxation on a scale unknown in England, and until the 1470s worth at times as much to the government as a parliamentary subsidy. Between 1408 and 1450, moreover, at least ten scutages were levied, worth perhaps £300 each.[2]

[1]For example, Richardson & Sayles, *Ir. parl. in middle ages*, pp. 152-3, 227-32; J.F. Lydon, *Ireland in the later middle ages* (Dublin, 1972), pp. 125-30.

[2]Richardson & Sayles, *Ir. parl. in middle ages*, pp. 80-1, 111-14, 233-43; *Parliaments and councils of mediaeval Ireland,* i (Dublin, 1947), xxxii-xxxv; Ellis, 'Taxation and defence', pp. 14-16, 27-8.

Under Henry VI it became established that no more than 700 marks a year should be levied by parliamentary subsidy, but the arrangements for a levy ensured that in practice it was soon worth much less. Of the fourteen counties, the quotas of Meath and Dublin together were fixed at half the total, but if individual counties defaulted on their quotas, as was already true of the most remote ones by 1420, then there was a short-fall in the yield. Moreover, taxation in Ireland was closely linked to the problem of defence: subsidies were granted to the governor rather than the king to help offset his charges in defending the land, and as central government control over the outlying shires slackened, these communities ceased regularly to attend parliament or to contribute to taxation which was no longer being expended on their own defence.[3] By the early 1470s, therefore, the leviable extent of the common subsidy had fallen to no more than £324 11s. 4½d., of which all but £7 7s. 8d. on communities in Wexford and Waterford was charged on the Pale.[4] This total also included the contributions of the clergy, for in Ireland the clerical proctors survived until 1537 as a third house of parliament and clerical consent was obtained in parliament instead of by separate grants agreed in convocation.[5]

With the ending of English subventions, however, it became imperative that the yield from taxation be increased. In January 1477, when no force was being maintained by the English exchequer and the deputy intended to go to England to solicit the king for the relief of the land, parliament agreed to a double subsidy towards his costs. In addition it ratified the grant of a local subsidy of 20s. per ploughland on Co. Meath, and in October a further subsidy was granted towards the payment of troops, raised by the vice-deputy, whose wages were £360 in arrears.[6] Apart from the high level of taxation, a second novelty in these grants (or rather a reversion to fourteenth-century practice) was the determination *in parliament* of new rates per ploughland at which subsidies were to be levied and also the explicit limitation of the subsidies to the Pale (though Wexford at least contributed £80 to some subsidies under Henry VII).[7] No doubt this

---

[3] Richardson & Sayles, *Ir. parl. in middle ages,* pp. 234-7.

[4] B.L., Royal MS 18C, XIV, f. 108. For a discussion and dating of this extent, see Ellis, 'Admin. Ire.', app. iii.

[5] Richardson & Sayles, *Ir. parl. in middle ages*, pp. 183-6.

[6] Parliament roll, 16 & 17 Edward IV cc 4, 45 (*Stat. Ire., Edw. IV,* ii 460-64, 548-52). Two local subsidies in Co. Dublin and Co. Meath were also confirmed in October, but the levies were to be allowed against the general subsidy so that only the balance was payable.

[7] See below, pp. 82, 85.

was the reason for the unwonted entry of this and later subsidy acts on the parliament roll. Subsidies continued to be divided between the lands of the laity, those of the clergy (crosslands), the clergy's spiritualties and the towns in each shire, but the old county quotas towards a lump sum of 700 marks were abandoned: what was now to be fixed was the rate of the levy, not the subsidy's yield, which would depend on the extent of ploughlands drawn up for each county under exchequer supervision, and ultimately on the amount of land under cultivation. Some of the rates were initially fixed at double the common subsidy until new extents could be drawn up and there also survived marked discrepancies in rate between the four shires, but by 1478 the principle had been accepted of an uniform rate per ploughland on county and crossland throughout the Pale.[8]

Fortunately, the extents on which the subsidy of January 1477 was levied have survived, together with the revised 1479 extent for Kildare. With slight modifications prescribed by subsequent acts, they evidently remained in force until 1494 and allow the anticipated yield of the various subsidies to be calculated. Those of the two general subsidies and the local subsidy of 1477 were £803 4s. 8d., £278 10s. 8d., and £276 respectively, a total of £1,357 15s. 4d. collected in taxation within a year, £714 of it from Meath, which was probably without precedent in the fifteenth century.[9] Seemingly local resentment at the burden of taxation provoked Edward IV's well-known instruction of 1479 that 'in noo parliament to be holdyn herafter ther shall no subsidie be axed ne graunted in the same upon the commouns, ne levied, but one in a yere whiche shall not excede the extent of vii^c mark, as haith ben accustumed'.[10] Whatever Edward's intentions, however, his instructions were apparently interpreted as a compromise between the Palesmen and the governor's necessity faced with an empty treasury: subsidies were not to exceed 700 marks, but their yield should approximate to this. Already in November 1478 a subsidy granted to Lord Grey had been at the slightly lower (uniform) rate of 10s. per ploughland: the levy was subsequently stopped and then ratified in December 1479 with slight modifications which according to the extents should have increased the yield by £15 9s. 6d. to £519 15s. 2d. After allowances for

---

[8]Parliament rolls, 18 Edward IV (III) c. 15, 19 & 20 Edward IV c. 4 (*Stat. Ire., Edw. IV*, ii, 672, 682-4), 2 & 3 Richard III c. 17 (P.R.O.I., transcript); Richardson & Sayles, *Ir. parl. in middle* ages, pp. 264-6.

[9]B.L., Royal MS 18C, XIV, ff 105-5v, 107v. For a discussion and dating of these extracts, see Ellis, 'Admin. Ire.', app. iii.

[10]Close roll, 19 Edward IV m. 7d (Gilbert, *Viceroys*, p. 599; *P.R.I. rep. D.K. 57*, p. 569).

collection, the net yield was therefore close enough to the permissible maximum of 700 marks.[11] But together with other aspects of his Irish policy, Edward's orders concerning the subsidy were apparently flouted after his death and a subsidy granted in 1485 was at the uniform rate of 13s. 4d. a ploughland which should have yielded £749 7s.[12]

Thus even before 1494, the Irish parliamentary subsidy had been substantially reorganized: the reforms of Poynings's deputyship did no more than consolidate previous efforts to update the subsidy. The subsidy granted in December 1494 was at double the normal rate, two marks per ploughland in consideration of eschewing coign and livery, and the act stipulated that it should remain in force for five years (i.e. five annual subsidies) instead of the customary single grant. The exchequer was made responsible for its collection, instead of a receiver appointed by and answerable to the governor as previously, and a new extent of ploughlands was drawn up in accordance with a clause in the act which disallowed all previous exemptions from subsidy.[13] In fact the undertreasurer levied £1,503 17s. 3¼d. in the year 1495-6, representing an extent of c. 1,040 ploughlands, or an increase of c. 120 on the extents of the 1470s.[14]

Thereafter, apart from the years 1527 to 1532 inclusive, when the revenues correspondingly failed to cover costs, subsidy acts of normally five or ten years' duration were in force and a subsidy was levied every year until 1576 by which time, after rallying in the 1540s, its yield had been reduced to an average of just over £300 a year since Elizabeth's accession.[15] The level of taxation between 1494 and 1499 was exceptionally high, but until the switch to direct rule in 1534, the subsidy remained the single most important item in the revenue. In

---

[11]Parliament rolls, 18 Edward IV (III) c. 15, 19 & 20 Edward IV c. 4 (*Stat. Ire., Edw. IV,* ii, 672, 682-4). In Meath in ?1508 the collectors were allowed £18 1s. 8d. for their labours in a levy of £192 13s. 4d.: Quinn, 'Irish parliamentary subsidy', pp. 236-7.

[12]Parliament roll, 2 & 3 Richard III c. 17 (P.R.O.I., transcript). Cf. S.G. Ellis, 'The struggle for control of the Irish mint, 1460-c.1506', *R.I.A. Proc.,* lxxviii (1978), sect. C, 27-9.

[13]Statute roll, 10 Henry VII c. 4 (Conway, *Henry VII's relations*, pp. 202-4; Davies, *Discovery*, pp. 191-2); Quinn, 'Irish parliamentary subsidy', pp. 222, 226.

[14]Calculated from B.L., Royal MS 18C, XIV, ff 22-89v, 105-5v, 107v (this total is rather higher than that given by Quinn, 'Irish parliamentary subsidy', p. 230). The undertreasurer's estimate of £1,275 11s. as the likely yield is based on old extents and not those of 1494-5 which do not survive: cf. Conway, *Henry VII's relations*, pp. 72-3.

[15]*S.P. Hen. VIII,* ii, 126; *L. & P. Hen. VIII,* iv, no. 5349; Quinn, 'Irish parliamentary subsidy', p. 231; *Stat. Ire.,* i, 313-16.

1499 or soon after, the extent was reduced to just under 850 ploughlands, but fragmentary evidence for the years 1501-2, 1520-2 and 1533-4 suggests that the subsidy should still have yielded c.£600, £607 5s. 7d., and £632 17s. 6¾d. per annum respectively, although disturbances reduced the actual yield to £470 17s. 10½d., £507 11s. 11d. and £516 6s. 4d. in 1520-1, 1521-2 and 1533-4 respectively.[16] Thus from being an occasional grant to the governor to help him meet his expenses, the subsidy was progressively transformed between 1477 and 1494 into 'the substaunce of the kynges revenuous without the which the. . . lond may not be defended'.[17] Its total yield did not of course compare with the English subsidy, but because subsidies were levied more frequently in Ireland, from 1494 at least the Pale was taxed more heavily than some of the poorer English shires; and if the outlying counties no longer paid parliamentary taxation, neither did Wales and the Marches, and the six northern counties of England were also excused in return for military service against the Scots.[18]

Apart from the parliamentary subsidy, the feudal levy of scutage survived into the Tudor period, in the more disturbed conditions of the lordship, as a second form of taxation: between 1467 and 1531 it was levied six times.[19] It was usually imposed with the consent of a parliament or an afforced council in connection with a general hosting, although strictly a feudal incident. In the fourteenth century a scutage had yielded c. £400, but like the subsidy its incidence was gradually confined to the Pale as the Dublin administration ceased to provide for the daily defence of the outlying shires. Small sums at least were received from Co. Kilkenny in 1467 when the earldom of Ormond was in the king's hands, and as late as 1480 scutage was being levied in Co. Wexford. Thereafter, however, the scutage owed amounted to no more than £269 15s. 4d. for the Pale, although it had theoretically been worth £850 for the lordship as a whole two centuries before; but at least £175 of this was actually received for the service of 1531. Between 1415 and 1442 scutages had been levied comparatively frequently, no doubt because the yield was not far

---

[16]N.L.I., MS 761, pp. 328-32 (cf. Quinn, 'Irish parliamentary subsidy', pp. 234-9); P.R.O., E.101/248/21, S.P.65/1/2.

[17]*Stat. Ire., Hen. VII & VIII*, p. 110; Quinn, 'Irish parliamentary subsidy', p. 226; Richardson & Sayles, *Ir. parl. in middle ages*, pp. 156, 236-7.

[18]Cf. J.R. Lander, *Government and community: England 1450-1509* (London, 1980), pp. 80-1, 84-5; Hoskins, *Age of plunder*, pp. 17-18, 214-16, 245; Pugh, *Marcher Lordships of South Wales*, p. 148.

[19]See Ellis, 'Taxation and defence', pp. 5-28 for this paragraph.

short of that available from a parliamentary subsidy and the burden fell on substantial freeholders who could afford to pay. Thereafter, however its incidence tailed off progressively and after 1494 it was no substitute for the regular and more substantial revenue available from the subsidy.

The customs

Ordinary taxation in the form of customs duties likewise yielded more in the later fifteenth century.[20] This was partly achieved by a concentration of effort on the Pale ports, where the increase in revenue more than offset the value of customs from other ports alienated for murage, although the government no doubt also benefited from the upswing in European trade which must have begun to affect Ireland by 1450. The evidence is unfortunately fragmentary and until 1494, when it was converted into a royal tax and accounted for in the exchequer, the Irish customs revenue did not include poundage, estimated in 1520 to be worth 100 marks a year. In Edward I's early years the great custom had been worth £1,400 per annum, but it had fallen to less than half this by the end of the reign and to c. £360 a year by 1344.[21] In 1420-1 the customs realized only £168 15s. 1d. and, though this may have been a bad year, by 1443 probably even less.[22] By the 1460s, however, a recovery had set in: the customs of Dublin and Drogheda alone rose in value from £175 2s. 10d. a year in 1465-6 to c. £285 in 1483-4, and further assignments of between twenty and forty marks on the customs of Dundalk, Ardglass and Carrickfergus were made to the constable of Carrickfergus throughout Edward IV's reign.[23] Thereafter, down to 1534 and beyond, the government was assured of at least £300 a year from this source and at times got substantially more. Until 1532 the exchequer normally administered the customs directly, appointing customers and controllers: after that date they were farmed, at rents which tended to decline even in nominal value.

Renewed exchequer activity in enforcing collection accounts for the remarkable increase in receipts from Dublin and Drogheda in this period which is illustrated by the accompanying table. It culminated

[20]Except where otherwise stated, the following paragraphs are based on S.G. Ellis, 'The Irish customs administration under the early Tudors', *I.H.S.*, xx (1980-1), 271-7; PRO; S.P.60/1/146 (L.&.P. Hen. VIII, v, no. 676).

[21]Lydon, *Ireland in the later middle ages*, pp. 12, 63; Mac Niocaill, *Na Buirgéisí*, ii, 523-8, 533.

[22]Cf. Richardson & Sayles, *Ir. parl. in middle ages*, p. 236 n. 64.

[23]*Cal. pat. rolls, 1467-77*, p. 162, *1477-85*, pp. 161, 339.

Customs Receipts, Ports of Dublin and Drogheda, 1344-1534

Dublin		Drogheda	
Period	Receipts	Period	Receipts
10 1 1345 – 25 2 1351	£313 9s. 9d.	23 10 1344 – 24 2 1351	£336 8s. 2d.
20 1 1396 – 25 6 1397	£143 0s. 11½d.[24]		
27 11 1420 – 26 11 1421	£52 14s. 2d.	27 11 1420 – 26 11 1421	£90 5s. 7d.
12 1 1427 – 3 10 1427	£55 13s. 0½d.	12 1 1427 – 3 10 1427	£120 6s. 8d.
31 7 1465 – 16 7 1466	*(Dublin and Drogheda)*		*£175 2s. 10d.*
16 8 1483 – 31 1 1485	£200	22 7 1483 – 31 12 1483	£56 11s. 1d.
30 9 1494 – 29 9 1495	£205 2s. 2d.	30 9 1494 – 29 9 1495	£150 8s. 7d.
30 9 1495 – 29 9 1496	£272 4s. 1d.		
30 9 1496 – 29 9 1497	£309 7s. 4d.		
5 years, c. 1498 – 1503	£1,282 7s. 9½d.		
12 4 1504 – 25 9 1505	£369 12s. 9½d.		
10 3 1520 – 25 3 1522	£272 8s. 5d.	10 3 1520 – 25 3 1522*	£277 13s. 0d.
24 8 1532 farm per ann.	£146 13s. 4d.	24 8 1532 farm per ann.	£138 6s. 8d.

*including Dundalk

[24] Pipe roll, 22 Richard II (N.L.I., MS 761, p. 262).

in the reforms of Poynings's deputyship when a searcher and separate controllers for Dublin and Drogheda were appointed. English customs regulations were enforced and by 1496 the undertreasurer thought that the customs were 'in moche bettir ordir than hath ben in tyme past'.[25] Customs revenue reached a peak about 1497, but there was a perceptible decline between 1505 and 1520 which the administration attributed to changing patterns of trade as 'merchauntes strangers' forsook the Pale ports where they paid customs for others.[26] Nevertheless, receipts remained substantially higher than in the Lancastrian period. Elsewhere in the Pale, the customs of Dundalk were farmed for £22 in 1532, those of Carlingford for £12 in 1530, and the small inland towns of Trim, Naas and Fore together contributed £12 in 1533-4. After the acts of resumption in 1493 and 1494, the earls of Kildare as deputy seemingly also extracted some revenue from ports beyond the Pale, from Limerick, Cork, Youghal and Baltimore in Munster, and from Carlingford, Ardglass, Strangford and Carrickfergus in Ulster, although the amounts were probably not large – the ninth earl farmed the customs and feefarm of Limerick for £20 a year in 1518 and the customs of Strangford and Ardglass for £4 shortly before. Thus under the early Tudors, the customs revenue probably averaged $c.$ £350 a year and constituted a significantly larger item in a larger revenue than under Henry VI.

The crown lands

The crown lands in Ireland at this date effectively consisted of twenty manors in and on the borders of the Pale, plus a few outlying lands and rights and some feefarm rents mainly on towns and cities. Disregarding certain lands long since recovered by the Irish, or from which the government had small prospect of levying any revenue, a maximum of $c.$ £540 per annum was leviable from the manors, plus a further $c.$ £125 from lands and rights, chiefly in Westmeath and Ulster, which more normally yielded nothing. Certain small farms, rents in kind from tenants holding by petit sergeanty, and fixed chief rents in the Pale, most of which were normally levied by the sheriffs, were nominally worth $c.$ £144 in 1495-6 but extents and evidence elsewhere suggest that much was unleviable and that of the rest all but $c.$ £40 was normally allowed for minor expenses by the sheriffs. Finally, the feefarm rents of Dublin, Drogheda, Waterford, Limerick and Cork

---

[25] *Stat. Ire., Hen. VII & VIII*, p. 112.
[26] *L. & P. Ric. III & Hen. VII*, ii, 69.

(considered separately below) were valued at 590 marks.²⁷ In all, therefore, the crown lands might have been made to yield £1,200 a year, but as in England they were regarded primarily as a source of patronage. Probably for political reasons, Edward IV was especially lavish in his grants, whilst Henry VII was much less generous after the early years. In this way, the bulk of the feefarm rents were remitted to the towns for murage, many of the manors were granted to magnates and ministers for life or in tail male, and others were farmed for less than half their real value. Moreover, most royal manors were subject to raids by the Irish and other disturbances which greatly affected their yields.

Nevertheless, some effort was made to increase the farms of manors remaining in the king's hands, although as in England the principal changes arose from the acquisition of additional lands, most notably the Mortimer inheritance in 1461. The ancient royal demesne had been small and by the fifteenth century the Gaelic resurgence had reduced it still further, both in extent and value, to four manors in the Dublin marches. Between the 1340s and 1420s the farms of these manors had been reduced from £203 17s. 0¼d. to just £100,²⁸ but they were farmed at £152 19s. 9¾d. a year between 1483 and 1492 and a minimum of £123 per annum down to 1534. And despite large grants by Edward IV, the farms of the Mortimer lands in Meath and Ulster also rose, by c. £80 a year to c. £185 between 1492 and 1534, notably for the manor of Trim, increased from £25 in 1492 to £58 by 1501.²⁹ The king's manors were usually farmed in this period, but receivers were occasionally appointed, as at Newcastle Lyons and Crumlin in 1533-4, and in 1500 when the deputy suspected that lands and rents in the manor of Esker were being concealed an inquisition was ordered.³⁰

---

[27] Except where otherwise stated, this section is based on two extents of the revenue for 1483-4 (compiled in spring 1485) and ?1491-2 in P.R.O., E.101/248/17 and C.47/10/31 (printed in Quinn, *Guide finan. rec.,* pp. 17-28); Undertreasurer Hattecliffe's journal of receipts and payments, 1495-6, and estimates for 1495-6, in B.L., Royal MS 18C, XIV, ff 18-89v, 105-20, 148-51; extracts from Sir William Darcy's enrolled account as receiver-general, 1501-2, Pipe roll, 18 Henry VII (N.L.I., MS 761, pp. 327-32); Undertreasurer Stile's declared account, 1520-22 in P.R.O., E.101/248/21; and Undertreasurer Brabazon's audited account, 1533-7 in P.R.O., S.P.65/1/2.

[28] P.R.O., E.101/248/1; *P.R.I. rep. D.K. 42*, pp. 26-7, 33, 54-5, 54, pp. 40-64. Cf. Otway-Ruthven, *Med. Ire.,* pp. 122, 165.

[29] See also, S.G. Ellis, 'Ioncam na hÉireann, 1384-1534', *Studia Hibernica*, xxi (1985), and the references there cited; Quinn, 'Anglo-Irish Ulster in the early sixteenth century', pp. 56-78.

[30] Memoranda roll, 15 Henry VII m. 21 (P.R.O.I., RC 8/43, p. 201); P.R.O., S.P.65/1/2.

During his reign, Edward IV alienated for life or longer lands and rents which had yielded at least £267 to the exchequer.[31] Thus major increases in revenue from crown lands could be achieved by reversions and resumptions, which swelled the profits of royal manors and chief rents from £216 6s. 5½d. by extent in 1483 to at least £398 10s. 2½d. actually received during 1495-6 (based on an estimate of c.£470 leviable compiled in late 1495). Two acts of 1493 and 1494 resumed lands formerly worth £144 13s. 4d. and £107 6s. 8d. respectively, but manors worth £63 6s. 8d. were regranted to Sir James Ormond in September 1494 and only reverted to the crown on his death in 1497.[32] Additionally, there was a net increase of £10 11s. 4d. in rents from lands formerly waste: for example, in 1466 the exchequer had been pursuing £115 18s. 4d. arrears of £6 15s. chief rent from 760 acres of land in the Dublin marches which were listed as waste in the 1484 and 1492 extents, though charged with £6 10s. in 1495-6 and subsequently.[33] Nevertheless, the prinicipal farms were greatly reduced in 1495-6 because of renewed war in the marches.

By 1501-2, the individual farms of manors had been increased to their highest recorded level in this period, although the evidence is unfortunately incomplete: manors which yielded £302 12s. 10d. in 1501-2 were extended at £279 13s. 1¾d. in 1484 and 1492, £240 13s. 4d. in 1495 and £283 2s. 7d. in 1533. By 1534, however, the total yield from crown lands had declined slightly to £318 8s. 3½d., although the actual charge was nearer £430 and £85 2s. 8d. could not be levied because of the Kildare rebellion. These figures, however, conceal substantial fluctuations in the revenue between 1520 and 1532. Until 1520, apparently, reversions more than offset the crown's alienation of its manors,[34] but the disruptions which followed Surrey's arrival as lieutenant soon affected the farms and between 1523 and

---

[31] P.R.O., E.101/248/17; Parliament rolls, Edward IV, *passim* (*Stat. Ire., Edw. IV*, i, ii).

[32] *Ibid.*; B.L., Royal MS 18C, XIV, ff 106, 111, 148v; Parliament roll, 9 Henry VII c. 20 (P.R.O.I., RC 13/9); Statute roll, 10 Henry VII c. 11 (*Stat. Ire., Hen. VII & VIII*, pp. 93-6, and see Ellis, 'Parliaments and great councils', pp. 109-10 and the references there cited); Conway, *Henry VII's relations*, pp. 110-12, 239, 241; Bryan, *Great Earl of Kildare*, pp. 213-17; *Cal. pat. rolls, 1494-1509*, p. 8.

[33] Memoranda roll, 6 Edward IV mm 16-21 (P.R.O.I., RC 8/41, pp. 96-138 *passim*: one of the tenants eventually appeared and exhibited a pardon of arrears); B.L., Royal MS 18C, XIV f. 116v.

[34] These changes can be followed in *Cal. pat. rolls, 1494-1509*, pp. 109, 169; *L. & P. Hen. VIII*, i (1st ed.), no. 1314, ii, no. 999; Memoranda rolls, 7 & 8 Henry VIII m. ? (P.R.O.I., Ferguson coll., iv, f. 2), 17 & 18 Henry VIII m. 10 (*Ibid.*, Ferguson repertory, iv, 108).

1529 the king alienated land worth *c*. £130 a year.³⁵ To a large extent these losses were subsequently offset by the reversion to the crown in 1532 of lands, chiefly within the earldom of Ulster, granted for life to Sir Thomas Fitzgerald of Leixlip. These yielded *c*. £125 a year, and together with rents of £34 from *le Annall* and Fartullagh within the old manor of Loughsewdy and 20 marks from the manor of Ferns, were mainly the product of forty years of activity by the Fitzgeralds in making something of a reality out of crown titles which had been usurped by the Irish.³⁶

Although theoretically worth 590 marks per annum, the feefarms of the major towns and cities in fact yielded only *c*. £144 for much of the period, chiefly because of allowances for murage, and much of the remainder was charged with payments of annuities. The allowances for murage of Dublin and Drogheda crept up from £19 6*s*. 8*d*. and £13 6*s*. 8*d*. a year respectively in 1467 to £69 6*s*. 8*s*. and £33 6*s*. 8*s*. by 1494.³⁷ By 1443 Cork and Limerick were refusing to account for their feefarms, though in 1466 Waterford was still making proffers twice a year for the feefarm and other debts. In 1465 the feefarm rent of Cork was remitted *in toto* and in 1474 after additional annuities had been charged on the Waterford feefarm that city was exonerated for the time being from accounting at the exchequer in Dublin.³⁸ Nevertheless the exchequer disputed Limerick's claim to exemption from the feefarm and at least 20*s*. was in fact paid *c*. 1477: from 1494 £10 a year was levied and by 1520 £15 a year was charged and paid, although the account was frequently in arrears.³⁹ The act of 1494 also resumed £49 6*s*. 8*d*. in allowances from the Dublin feefarm, and Cork's charter was forfeited at this time for rebellion. Henry VII

---

³⁵*S.P. Hen. VIII*, ii, 40, 78, 85, 95, 169; *L. & P. Hen. VIII*, iii, no. 3677 (8), iv, no. 2610; *Fiants Ire., Hen. VIII*, nos. 13, 20, 26; *Calendar of ancient deeds and muniments preserved in the Pembroke estate office, Dublin* (Dublin, 1891) nos. 216-17 (cf. P.R.O., S.P.65/1/2); Memoranda roll, 17 & 18 Henry VIII m. 10 (P.R.O.I., Ferguson repertory, iv, 108).

³⁶P.R.O., S.P.65/1/2; *S.P. Hen. VIII*, ii, 169.

³⁷P.R.O., E.30/1548, ff 5-8, E.101/248/17.

³⁸Memoranda rolls, 5 Edward IV m. 11 (P.R.O.I., Ferguson coll., iii, f. 223), 6 Edward IV mm 2, 5 (*Ibid.*, RC 8/41, pp. 25, 32); P.R.O., E.101/248/17; *Cal. pat. rolls, 1467-76*, pp. 459, 466; Richardson & Sayles, *Ir. parl. in middle ages*, p. 236 nn 64, 66. An annuity of £10 to the earl of Ormond was temporarily resumed in 1494 and £20 assigned on the Waterford feefarm in 1495-6: B.L., Royal MS 18C XIV, ff 72, 72v, 84; *Ormond deeds, 1413-1509*, no. 288.

³⁹Counter-roll of receipts, 14-18 Edward IV (P.R.O.I., Ferguson coll., ii, f. 47); P.R.O., E.101/248, nos. 17, 21, SP.65/1/2; *Cal. pat. rolls, 1485-94*, p. 464; *Ormond deeds, 1413-1509*, nos. 261, 292; B.L., Add. MS 19865, ff 1v-2, Harleian MS 3756, ff 4, 7v; Memoranda roll, 29 Henry VIII m. 29d (P.R.O.I., Ferguson coll., iv, f. 205).

confirmed the charter and pardoned arrears of the Cork feefarm in 1500, but some revenues were certainly collected, though in Dublin from 1506 new grants for murage gradually nullified the effect of the resumption on the Dublin feefarm there.[40]

Thus, although alienations and allowances by Edward IV had lowered the value of the crown lands to c. £360 a year at the end of his reign, they yielded nearly £600 a year after Poynings's act of resumption. In fact, the average between 1461 and 1534 was probably over £500. From 1534, however, attainders, resumptions and the monastic dissolutions transformed the crown lands: the yield increased to c. £1,200 a year in 1534-5, to c. £1,650 the following year and c. £2,650 by Michaelmas 1537.[41]

Prerogative rights

These 'casualties' included fines for homage, livery of lands and reliefs, wardships, escheats and episcopal temporalities during vacancies. Necessarily, they fluctuated considerably in value from year to year, and in Ireland the exploitation of feudal incidents was generally geared to quick profits rather than to extracting every last farthing. Partly this was because the exchequer could not efficiently administer additional lands in outlying counties far from the Pale in which the bulk of the crown lands lay, partly because Old English governors could not afford to alienate local support and also, under Henry VIII, because governors held office at the king's pleasure, receiving the profits of the revenue instead of a salary. Certainly after 1534 new English officials thought that the Dublin administration had been lax in this matter: wardships were sold for more and royal commissioners sent to Ireland in 1537 were instructed to examine feoffments to see that they were not 'fraudulent', but it was also acknowledged that the non-application of English legislation against enfeoffments to use had hindered the full exploitation of the king's feudal rights.[42] Yet the profits of temporalities and wardships were considerable. By far the richest see in Ireland was the archbishopric of Dublin whose lands

---

[40]Close roll, 10-15 Henry VII (B.L., Add. MS 4787, f. 52v); *Rot. pat. Hib.*, p. 272 no. 13; *Ormond deeds, 1413-1509*, no. 261; *Cal. pat. rolls, 1494-1509*, pp. 204-5, 262; Conway, *Henry VII's relations*, pp. 52, 91, 221-5; Memoranda roll, 14 Henry VII mm 14 26 (P.R.O.I., RC 8/43, pp. 124, 148-9); Statute roll, 10 Henry VII c. 11 (see Ellis, 'Parliaments and great councils', pp. 109-110).

[41]P.R.O., S.P.65/1/2; *Cal. Carew MSS, 1515-74*, no 111.

[42]*L. & P. Hen. VIII*, xii (i), nos. 684-5, 1027, xii (ii), no. 382. Cf. J.M.W. Bean, *The decline of English feudalism, 1215-1540* (Manchester, 1968), chs. 4-6. See also below, ch. 4, for the exchequer's efforts to enforce the king's feudal rights.

yielded £528 5s. 5½d. net to the exchequer for 1½ years to Michaelmas 1535. Others, however, were much less profitable: a farm of a portion of Armagh temporalities yielded £5 for six months in 1474-5 and £9 12s. arrears were charged for the vacancy of three months in 1521; and in 1496 the bishop of Ossory paid £10 for the restitution of his temporalities.[43] In 1495-6 there were six wards worth £110 a year, one of whom, worth £3 a year, was sold for £106 13s. 4d. with his marriage: the exchequer also levied an £80 fine for alienation of land without licence.[44] For the two years 1520-2, the profits of four wards amounted to at least £250, a fifth wardship was sold for £200 and fines for livery of eight tenants-in-chief whose wardships had earlier been sold amounted to £174 14s. 4d.[45] Again in 1534, there were seven wards whose lands yielded £74 9s. 4d. net per annum.[46] Additionally, many tenants preferred to make fine for respite of homage from year to year and these profits, recorded on the memoranda roll, averaged c. £6 a year. Escheats were worth £115 6s. 8d. in 1495-6, although all but £22 of this accrued from three ships captured from Perkin Warbeck, and the £13 4s. 4d. received from this source for 1534-5 was probably more typical.[47]

Other revenue

The only other considerable sources of revenue were the profits of justice, of the hanaper, and of the mints which operated periodically between 1460 and c. 1506, plus the king's rights, based on the Statute of Absentees passed by the Westminster Parliament of 1380, to two-thirds of the profits of lands held by persons absent from the land to offset the costs of their defence (a right which was peculiar to the lordship). The profits of justice fluctuated greatly from year to year, £156 2s. 5d. in 1483-4, £198 4s. 10d. in 1494-5, £344 6s. 11d. in 1495-6, and £511 12s. 2d. for two years 1520-2, of which the exchequer usually contributed the bulk; but they were only a shadow of their value under Edward I and had long since ceased to cover the salaries of the judges and clerks who staffed the courts.[48] The profits of the hanaper

---

[43]Counter-roll of receipts, 14-18 Edward IV (P.R.O.I., Ferguson coll., ii, 47); B.L., Royal MS 18C, XIV, ff 71v, 86v; P.R.O., E.101/248/21, S.P.65/1/2; *Handbook Brit. chron.*, pp. 308-9, 342. Cf. Art Cosgrove, 'Irish episcopal temporalities in the thirteenth century', *Archivium Hibernicum*, xxxii (1974), 67-8.

[44]B.L., Royal MS 18C, XIV, ff 13-89v, 106v, 121.

[45]P.R.O., E.101/248/21 (torn).

[46]P.R.O., S.P.65/1/2.

[47]*Ibid.*; B.L., Royal MS 18C, XIV, ff 17, 19, 32, 85v.

[48]P.R.O., E.101/248, nos. 17, 21; B.L., Royal MS 18C, XIV, ff 13-89v, 106v, 149.

were estimated to be worth 40 marks and £40 a year in 1485 and 1495 respectively, sums which tally with the £108 12s. 4d. received for 2¼ years to 1537, but until 1534 apparently only the balance after deductions for the chancellor's diets was normally available to the exchequer and this was often nil.[49]

The chief profit from absentees derived from Ormond's lands within the Pale (worth £80 17s 10½d. to the exchequer in 1483-4), but smaller sums were regularly received from Irish lands held by English monasteries, Furness abbey (worth £20 in 1495-6), Cartmel priory and Tintern abbey, together with those of Patrick Bellew of Roche who also held property in England.[50] And since the exchequer frequently initiated proceedings upon information for casual absences without licence of the king or governor,[51] probably over £150 was received in good years from this source. Nevertheless, the king was often generous with licences of absence, particularly for the duke of Norfolk and earl of Shrewsbury, and from 1505 Kildare as governor made separate arrangements with Ormond for his prise wines as chief butler (which yielded £93 1s. 1d. when temporarily resumed in 1495-6) and for lands in the south midlands.[52] Chance survivals of evidence show that the profits of the mints could be quite considerable when they were operating: they amounted to £238 7s. 1d. from 8 December 1460 to 3 February 1463, £94 15s. 9½d. from 1 September 1483 to 8 March 1485 and £125 5s. 1d. from 25 July 1495 to 4 March 1497.[53]

Expenditure[54]

Since the governor was expected to maintain his household out of his salary and since the Dublin administration was not called upon in this period to help with the costs of royal diplomacy and war outside Ireland, the two major items of expenditure were internal defence costs and ministers' salaries and rewards. By 1483-4 assignments for

---

[49]*Ibid.;* P.R.O., S.P.65/1/2; see below, ch. 6.

[50]*Ibid.;* Pipe roll, 18 Henry VII (N.L.I., MS 761, p. 328). Cf. Guy, *Cardinal's court,* pp. 113, 128-30.

[51]Below, ch. 4.

[52]For example, *Rot. pat. Hib.,* p. 268 nos. 32-4; *Cal. pat. rolls, 1477-85,* pp. 487, 539, *1485-94,* pp. 56, 178, 196-7; B.L., Royal MS 18C, XIV, ff 13-89v *passim*; *Ormond deeds, 1413-1509,* nos. 316, 320, 322-3.

[53]Pipe roll, 2 Edward IV (N.L.I., MS 761, pp. 324-5; R.I.A., MS 12 D 10, p. 199); P.R.O., E.101/248/17; Memoranda roll, 12 Henry VII m. 24 (R.I.A., MS 24 H 17, p. 209).

[54]In general, the documents listed at n.27 above provide the documentation for this section.

the payment of annuities had risen to £141 11s. a year, but the resumptions of 1493 and 1494 recovered £123 14s. 4d. of this, and even by 1534 this item had only increased to £51 13s. 4d. again. There were fewer than forty officers in receipt of a regular salary by exchequer assignment at this time, though others received occasional rewards; and by reducing some comparatively large salaries, raising others and in general paying officials far less than their English counterparts, the administration was able to keep wage costs to c.£650 a year (excluding the governor's salary) down to 1534. The extent of 1484 included assignments of £491 6s. 2¾d. for this item, but at least sixteen officers were excluded and three others assigned only part of their salary: if we add the usual salaries and rewards, this figure should be increased to slightly over £650. For 1495-6, when some comparatively well-paid, English-born administrators held office, Undertreasurer Hattecliffe estimated expenditure at £948 0s. 7d., plus £500 for the deputy's salary, but in practice this total was kept to less than £1,200 because the chancellor doubled as justiciar after Poynings's departure in December 1495 and the treasurership was vacant from November.[55] Undertreasurer Stile's declared account shows assignments of £509 5s. 4d. per annum for ministers' salaries 1520-2, but again some salaries and rewards are omitted which would have added at least £100 a year, and for the year to Michaelmas 1534 expenditure on this count amounted to £654 8s. 4d.

The financial balance

Unfortunately details of military expediture survive only for the period 1494-6 which the presence of an English army rendered highly untypical. The exchequer, however, was primarily interested in the balance available after the ordinary administrative costs, excluding the governor's salary, had been met. The governor was normally expected to meet the costs of defence out of his own salary. Nevertheless, as under the Lancastrians, it was sometimes necessary to remind governors that other costs had to be met before they received payment: in 1524 Kildare agreed that the king's judges should be 'trewly and yerely payed their fees and wages', and to lay out £40 in the first year and 40 marks annually on repairs to the king's castles and manors.[56] Because most governors received the balance of the revenues without account, or could expect no assistance from England, there was small incentive to strike a realistic balance on

---

[55] See also S.G. Ellis, 'Henry VII and Ireland', pp. 245-6.
[56] *S.P. Hen. VIII,* ii, 117. Cf. Richardson & Sayles, *Ir. parl. in middle ages,* p. 230.

account, provided this was in credit. From *c.* 1500 the earls of Kildare began to levy some of the revenue directly (as in effect had occurred with the parliamentary subsidy and poundage earlier), very often moneys accruing from the outlying shires which were more difficult for the exchequer to collect, rather than wait for assignments to be made on what was available at the end of each term. For example, the ninth earl's rental records that in 1514 he farmed 'the kinges castell and iland of Lymerik' to one of the citizens 'paing yerely x *libri* sterling at Michelmas, and if any other wil yeve any more fore the same he to yeve asmoch, and to haue the same to ferme aslong as the said erl haue right therto'.[57] The receipt roll for Hilary 1505 recorded that

> nothing is expressed in this roll except the parcels above included... because all such fees, fee-farms, customs, coketts, poundage, issues and rents, & the said subsidies of the said counties of Kildare & Wexford therefrom arising have been received by the hands of Lord Gerald Earl of Kildare, the deputy lieutenant of the lord the king of his land of Ireland, and by his assigns.[58]

So long as there was a credit balance and governors received the profits of the revenue without account, this system worked well and no doubt helped to mitigate exchequer inefficiency in certain areas. For most of Henry VI's reign, however, there had been an adverse balance of payments. The revenue had declined from an average of over £2,000 a year under Richard II to less than £1,300, excluding subsidies, in the years 1420-7 when figures are next available; and despite a slight rally to 1431, this decline continued to 1446 at least, when our sources again fail, with an average of less than £900 a year over the last seven years. The treasurer accounted for a mere £1,288 6s. 2d. for the two years to Easter 1446.[59] Other evidence suggests that this trend was not reversed before 1461.[60] Nevertheless, ministers' salaries certainly cost more than in the early Tudor period,[61] and by the 1430s the revenue only just covered ordinary expenditure. As late as 1427, the exchequer made assignments of £979 10s. 8d. to the justiciar out of £1,831 4s. 7¾d. collected over a period of ten months, but both assignments and receipts seem to reflect a maximum effort. Sir

---

[57] B.L., Harleian MS 3756, f. 4.
[58] Receipt roll, 18-22 Henry VII (R.I.A., MS 12 D 19, p. 189).
[59] See Ellis, 'Ioncam na hÉireann'.
[60] E.g. Otway-Ruthven, *Med. Ire.,* pp. 370, 373, 382, 384.
[61] Cf. P.R.O., E.101/248/8.

Thomas Stanley, lieutenant 1431-7, received only £73 10s. in six terms, but even this much was achieved by issuing bad tallies for officers' salaries, and in 1440-1 a very high adverse balance of £1,456 18s. 1d. was recorded.[62] In Hilary 1476, however, the deputy apparently received at least three assignments worth £250, and a *liberate* of March 1502 ordered the payment of £333 11s. 2d. to the deputy.[63]

The extent of 1484 shows a total of just over £960 in revenue accounted for in the exchequer, excluding the parliamentary subsidy and poundage. This figure, however, is certainly too low, for it takes no account of the king's prerogative rights, the customs of Dundalk, most of the lands of the earldom of Ulster, a scutage of 1480 which was still being collected, and the profits of all but one absentee.[64] Thus the real balance of ordinary revenue over non-military expenditure was probably slightly above the £300 suggested by the extent on the basis of under-estimates of both revenue and expenditure. And since the increasing yields from the subsidy, customs and farms of crown lands during Edward's reign apparently offset the losses through alienations of land, allowances for murage and annuities, the balance available to the governor must have remained fairly stable from 1461 at c. £900 a year including taxation, an increase of perhaps £400 on what had been available in Henry VI's later years.

The resumptions of 1493 and 1494 were a response to a decline in revenue in Henry VII's early years. Although no figures are available, the decline was evidently substantial and caused by a temporary fall in customs revenue, alienations of land, licences of absence and the cessation of mint activity c. 1491.[65] In 1495-6, however, the exchequer received no less than £3,055 15s. 7¾d. from internal sources including the subsidy, a sum which exceeded Hattecliffe's estimates by more than £350.[66] And down to Michaelmas 1499, when the subsidy was reduced by c. £900 a year, this total was probably bettered in some years because of improved farms of the king's

---

[62]P.R.O., E.101/248/1; Otway-Ruthven, *Med. Ire.,* p. 373; Lydon, *Ireland in the later middle ages*, pp. 129-30; *Rot. pat. Hib.,* pp. 264-5.

[63]Counter-roll of receipts, 14-18 Edward IV (R.I.A., MS 12 D 19, p. 175); *Anal. Hib.,* ii, 200-1.

[64]P.R.O., E.101/248/17; *Anal. Hib.,* ii, 287-9 (extracts from Receipt roll, 22 Edward IV relating to scutage: at least £27 3s. 6½d. was received); Ellis, 'Taxation and defence', pp. 15, 28.

[65]Cf. P.R.O., E.101/248/17, C.47/10/31; *Cal. pat. rolls, 1485-94,* pp. 56, 64, 178, 197, 368; Ellis, 'Struggle for control of the mint', pp. 30-2.

[66]B.L., Royal MS 18C, XIV, ff 13-89v, 148-51.

manors and the reversion to the crown in 1497 of lands and an annuity worth nearly £200.[67] Against this, the exchequer disbursed £3,855 6s. 3d. for both defence costs and ordinary administration, making a deficit of £800 on the year; but this balance was in fact somewhat artificial because the English army had been reduced in size by the end of 1495 and was totally disbanded in July 1496.[68] Nevertheless, there should have been a balance of revenue over non-military expenditure of nearly £1,900, sufficient to pay for a retinue of 250 archers had the king continued with an English governor and troops in 1496.[69] No wonder then that Kildare's position as deputy and the influence of the Dublin administration were so strong in the years immediately after the earl's restoration, for with the replacement of the English administrators by Irish-born officials paid the traditional salaries, Kildare must have had a balance of c. £2,500 available from the revenues. Early in 1498, he even petitioned the king for an army of 300 archers and sixty gunners 'to bee wagid at the charge of me and other of my frendes in this contray' the better to resist raids by O'Brien of Thomond into Co. Kilkenny and Co. Tipperary.[70]

For the year 1501-2, however, Sir William Darcy accounted for only £1,587 3s. 3d.[71] This total is suspiciously low, although the surviving extracts omit details about individual sources. But by correlating the information about royal manors, the subsidy, wards and absentees with that available elsewhere, particularly concerning the customs and feefarms, it would appear that the deputy had levied at least £200 directly for which Darcy did not account. Thus despite the closure of the mint, increased murages and complaints about the fall in customs revenue in the years following, Sir John Stile declared a revenue of £3,536 17s. 8d. in his account for the two years to Easter 1522 during which a full account had to be rendered of the profits. This total, it is true, included £511 6s. 1d. in arrears, much of which was still outstanding in 1538, but the subsidy of Kildare had had to be remitted for the entire second year.[72] And in 1521 Stile had complained that because of 'the contynewell warres, death and derthe' the revenues had not reached £1,400 per annum, and that

[67] *Cal. pat. rolls, 1485-94*, p. 464, *1494-1509*, p. 8. Two fines of 800 marks and ?£500 had been imposed by Poynings, but only 200 marks was actually levied in 1495-6: Ellis, 'Henry VII and Ireland', p. 245 and n. 49.

[68] B.L., Royal MS 18C, XIV, ff 13-89v; Ellis, 'Henry VII and Ireland', pp. 243-6.

[69] Cf. Ellis, 'Henry VII and Ireland', p. 246.

[70] P.R.O., S.C.1/51/164 (Conway, *Henry VII's relations*, p. 241).

[71] Pipe roll, 18 Henry VII (N.L.I., MS 761, pp. 327-32). Cf. *S.P. Hen. VIII*, ii, 77-8.

[72] P.R.O., E.101/248/21; *L. & P. Hen. VIII*, xiii (i), no. 641.

although Darcy and others had assured the king that the revenue exceeded ordinary expenses by 2,000 marks a year, his own accounts enrolled on the pipe rolls for 18 and 20 Henry VII (1502-3, 1504-5) showed that the total revenue was no more than £1,587 13s. 3¼d. a year, of which subsidies of £80 each on Co. Kildare and Co. Wexford could not now be levied. Evidently much of the balance had earlier been levied directly by the deputy.[73]

Stile's work in levying only c. £1,500 a year was considered disappointing, but again in 1533-4 only c. £1,600 was levied, although c. £50 was allowed for waste caused by rebellion in Trinity 1534.[74] Even this, however, was a substantial improvement on the decade 1522-32 which had evidently witnessed a slump induced by the king's politically unrealistic politics and consequent weak government.[75] The king ignored a warning against renewed grants of the revenues or licences of absence, and when the subsidy ran out in 1527 the revenues barely sufficed to cover ordinary costs of government. By 1529 the deputy was complaining that there was a deficit of 200 marks a year and ministers' fees were falling into arrears, a phenomenon which had not occurred on any scale since the Yorkist period.[76] A biproduct of the Geraldine-Butler feud, renewed in the 1520s, was that deputies kept the salaries of political opponents in arrears, but by 1532 Lord Chancellor Alen's salary was 2½ years in arrears and he was also owed for repairs to Dublin castle and the chancery. And in his account to Michaelmas 1537 Sir William Brabazon was allowed £116 paid in arrears of salaries due between Michaelmas 1532 and Easter 1534.[77]

The period thus ended on a disappointing note, but with the expectation of better times and with the finances of the Dublin government still in substantially better shape than under Henry VI. A report of 1533 claimed that 'the kingis revenues there is nighe trebill somoche as it was whan Sir William Skeffington was there by reason of a subsydie yerely for 3 yeris lately graunted, and also the Banne, the lordship of Rathwyre, Carlingforde, Rathtouth and other lordships. . . whiche be revertid to his grace.' And the council advised that if an act

---

[73]*S.P. Hen. VIII*, ii, 77-8, 85.

[74]Calculated from P.R.O., S.P.65/1/2.

[75]Ellis, 'Tudor policy and Kildare ascendancy', pp. 240-6.

[76]*S.P. Hen. VIII*, ii, 126, 128, 129-30; *l. & P. Hen. VIII*, iv, nos. 81, 5349; P.R.O., E.101/248/17.

[77]P.R.O., S.P.1/67, f. 34v (*L. & P. Hen. VIII*, v, no. 398), S.P.65/1/2; *L. & P. Hen. VIII*, v, no. 399, Add. no. 486; *S.P. Hen. VIII*, ii, 118, 159.

of resumption were passed, the revenue would suffice to support an English deputy and retinue.[78] Ironically, the Kildare rebellion which broke out the following year precipitated Henry VIII into just this course of action, but in much less favourable circumstances which eventually forced the king to acquiesce in Ireland as a continuing charge on the English revenues and so undid the achievements of Edward IV and Henry VII.[79]

The initial increases in revenue under Edward IV were apparently due chiefly to the acquisition of new sources, the Mortimer inheritance and the mint, but thereafter the more effective exploitation of existing sources, the subsidy, customs and crown lands, was responsible for its continued growth until 1500. In part this revival reflects the administration's concentration on maximising revenue within the Pale, which was less costly to govern directly, and under Edward IV there was a tendency to write off certain feefarm rents and customs beyond the Pale which were troublesome to collect. The Pale thus came to provide the largest and an increasing proportion of the revenue: the combination of stronger government and growing stability allowed increased taxation and farms of land in a more prosperous Pale, although small sums were regularly received from beyond. Besides those sources already mentioned and others on which expenses and annuities were regularly assigned, the exchequer received £40 by farm from the manor of Kilkenny West near Loughsewdy and £10 for licence to fish at Athlone in 1478; £6 7s. 8d. in Easter 1466, twenty marks in 1484-5 and £6 in Michaelmas 1499 were assigned on the bailiwick of Cork and £4 in Easter 1466 and £3 6s. 8d. in Michaelmas 1499 on that of Limerick; and from June 1525, 10s. a year or more was received from a mill and licence to fish in Galway.[80]

The machinery of collection

In large measure ultimate responsibility for the buoyant revenue of the period must rest with the machinery for its collection. In Ireland the principal treasury and place of audit remained the exchequer: there was no parallel to the experiments in England with chamber finance

---

[78]*S.P. Hen. VIII*, ii, 165, 169-70.

[79]See Ellis, 'Thomas Cromwell and Ireland', pp. 497-519 *passim*.

[80]Counter-roll of Receipts, 14-18 Edward IV (Bodl., Laud MS 613, f. 308); Memoranda rolls, 6 Edward IV mm 33-3d, 2-3 Richard III mm 32-3, 15 Henry VII m. 11 (P.R.O.I., RC 8/41, pp. 12-17, RC 8/43, pp. 176-7), 22 Henry VIII m. 13 (*Ibid.,* Ferguson coll., iv, f. 146); T.C.D., MS 569, f. 13; *Cal pat. rolls Ire., Hen. VIII-Eliz.,* p. 5; P.R.O., S.P.65/1/2.

and, in the later 1530s, the establishment of new revenue courts. Indeed the tendencies were precisely the reverse: responsibility for the collection of the parliamentary subsidy and poundage was entrusted to the exchequer from 1494, where previously *ad hoc* receivers appointed by and accountable to the governor had been employed; and at the same time exchequer control over sheriffs and escheators was increased.[81] Yet, since the fact of a rising revenue has remained unrecognised, there has hitherto been no reason to question the traditional view that the procedures of the Dublin exchequer, more so even than those of its English counterpart, were inefficient and archaic.[82] Whether this was so can now only be ascertained by a general description of its operation because the nature of the evidence precludes any attempt at selective analysis over an extended period. This method is the less satisfactory because of the comparative dearth of evidence for the years *c.* 1430-65 and because the surviving rolls and accounts for the period from *c.* 1370 have not yet been fully investigated. Nevertheless, some changes can certainly be dated to the post-1470 period, and if it can also be shown that other changes had occurred since *c.* 1370 and that the procedures of the Dublin exchequer were more flexible and its structures less elaborate than those of the English exchequer, the case for its leading role in the revival of the revenue must be overwhelming.

The exchequer was the best-staffed and administratively the most important court of the late medieval lordship. Its primary task was to organize the levy and disbursement of the king's revenue, although in Ireland it had important functions as a court which are described in the next chapter. Apart from receivers of subsidy and poundage before 1494, ministers who received money from England and those governors who were granted the profits of the revenue, all financial officials were accountable to it. This account was still theoretically divided as in the fourteenth century into the proffer, view, sum and final view, though practice was by now somewhat different.[83] Details of the proffer were entered on the memoranda rolls under the headings *amerciamenta* and *proffra* which usually headed the entries of

---

[81] See below, p. 89.

[82] See especially, D.B. Quinn, 'Agenda for Irish history. II. Ireland from 1461 to 1603', *I.H.S.,* iv (1944-5), 259; 'Anglo-Irish local government, 1485-1534', *ibid.*, i (1938-9), 355; D.B. Quinn and K.W. Nicholls, 'Ireland in 1534', *New hist. Ire.,* iii, 23.

[83] Cf. M.H. Mills, '"Adventus vicecomitum", 1272-1307', *E.H.R.,* xxxviii (1923), 331-54; J.F. Lydon, 'A survey of the memoranda rolls of the Irish exchequer, 1294-1509', *Anal. Hib.,* xxiii (1966), 51-70 (mainly on fourteenth-century practice).

Michaelmas and Easter terms: twice a year all accountants were traditionally required to attend the exchequer and make a payment of the issues so far collected. Throughout the fifteenth century, however, only sheriffs, seneschals, escheators and five towns and cities made proffers and these had become standardized in multiples and fractions of 6s. 8d. The total revenue from this source never exceeded £20 in the Yorkist and early Tudor period and might be less than £2, but payment was more usually in cash than tallies of assignment.[84] Moreover, treasurers' accounts show that the proffers now formed a separate item of revenue and were no longer a prepayment for which the accountant would later receive allowance.[85] The sheriffs had formerly paid farms for the pleas and perquisites of the county,[86] but there is no sign of this in the later period. Probably with the decline of this customary revenue, it had been commuted to a nominal sum represented by the proffer and the fine for release from account noted below in a bid to make more attractive an office which by the late medieval period was regarded as a distinct liability.

In contrast to English practice, sheriffs and escheators were until 1494 elected annually in the county courts, though for this purpose special meetings might be held before the barons.[87] For the Pale counties, the election was subject to confirmation by the treasurer, the commission issued *quamdiu nobis placuerit* under the exchequer seal, and the sheriff was then sworn in before the barons.[88] Beyond the Pale, the system of election certainly survived in the 1450s and probably under Edward IV, but in 1487 and 1489 sheriffs of Kilkenny were appointed under the great seal, and in 1488 after the Simnel conspiracy the king intervened and appointed Lord Roche as sheriff of Co. Cork directly under the English great seal.[89] The system of

---

[84] P.R.O., E.101/247/8, 248/1; B.L., Royal MS 18C, XIV, ff 13-70v; Irish Record Commissioners' calendars of memoranda rolls, P.R.O.I., RC 8/33, 8/41, 8/43 passim. Cf. Lydon, 'A survey of memoranda rolls' p. 55. See also Quinn, 'Anglo-Irish local government', pp. 355-6.

[85] P.R.O., E.101/248/21, S.P.65/1/2; Lydon, 'A survey of memoranda rolls', p. 55. Hattecliffe vainly recommended in 1496 that English practice be restored: *L. & P. Ric. III & Hen. VII*, ii, 64.

[86] A.J. Otway-Ruthven, 'Anglo-Irish shire government in the thirteenth century', *I.H.S.*, v (1946-7), 13-14.

[87] E.g. Memoranda roll, 10 Edward IV m. 10 (P.R.O.I., RC 8/41, p. 236). Cf. H.M. Jewell, *English local administration in the middle ages* (Newton Abbot, 1972), pp. 193-4.

[88] Memoranda rolls, 2 Richard III m. 3, 9 Henry VII mm 2-3 (P.R.O.I., RC 8/33, p. 395, 8/43, pp. 53-4).

[89] *Cal. pat. rolls, 1485-94*, p. 232; N.L.I., D.1857; *Ormond deeds, 1413-1509*, nos. 272, 274; Memoranda roll, 35 Henry VI mm 4, ? (P.R.O.I., Ferguson coll., iii, f. 208v; S.P.W., Hore MS I, pp. 1103-4: commissions to elect sheriffs for the crosses of

Fifteenth-century sketch of the Irish exchequer, in the Red Book of the Irish Exchequer (from *Facs. nat. MSS Ire.*, **pt. iii, plate 37).**

election was clearly more open to abuse in outlying districts under the control of the magnates, and by statute of 1494 power of appointment to all shrievalties and escheatorships was vested in the treasurer.[90]

This change seemingly followed the acceptance of a distinction for purposes of account between sheriffs from the Pale and others, exemplified by the terms of their commissions. Exchequer commissions invariably required the sheriff to account annually for the rents, issues and profits of the county, though in practice the frequency was less.[91] In the two extant commissions for Kilkenny, however, general clauses reserving the issues to the king replaced the specific injunction to account annually at the exchequer.[92] The lists of proffers clearly reflect this distinction among accountants. Within the Pale proffers were made twice-yearly, but beyond only at intervals of a few years. For example, no proffers were received from beyond the Pale for Michaelmas and Easter terms 1484-5, 1495-6, 1499-1500, 1507-8, 1508-9 or for Michaelmas 1498. For Michaelmas 1493 and Easter terms 1494 and 1499, however, proffers were received additionally from the sheriffs of Kilkenny, Carlow, Waterford, Limerick, Connaught and the crosses of Kerry and Tipperary, from the seneschals of the liberties of Kerry and Wexford and the cities of Limerick, Cork and Waterford.[93] These extreme fluctuations in attendance evidently arose from deliberate policy rather than directly from the weakness of exchequer control over local officials, as has been suggested.[94] In 1495-6, for example, the undertreasurer made payments to Waterford city and also assignments on the feefarm and prise wines there, but no proffer was received from the city and it was not called to account.[95] The distinction made in the sheriffs' terms of appointment indicates an

---

Tipperary and Wexford); Parliament roll, 16 & 17 Edward IV c. 48 (*Stat. Ire., Edw. IV*, ii, 558-62). Cf. Otway-Ruthven, *Med. Ire.,* pp. 176-7.

[90]*Stat. Ire.,* i, 42-3; Parliament roll, 16 & 17 Edward IV c. 48 (*Stat. Ire., Edw. IV,* ii, 558-62).

[91]N.L.I., D.15963-4, 15974 (*Dowdall deeds*, nos. 519-20, 530); Memoranda rolls, 1 Henry VIII m. 11 d. (B.L., Add. MS 4791, f. 194), 9-10 Henry VIII m. ? (P.R.O.I., Ferguson coll., iv, f. 53); T.C.D., MS 594, ff 9-9v; Pipe roll, 20 Henry VII (N.L.I., MS 761, pp. 335-6).

[92]N.L.I., D.1857; *Ormond deeds, 1413-1509,* nos. 272, 274. Occasionally Pale sheriffs were appointed under the great seal: *Rot. pat. Hib.,* p. 272a no 1; Memoranda roll, 15 Henry VII mm 6, 13 (P.R.O.I., RC 8/43, pp. 171, 179).

[93]The sheriff of Cork also made a proffer at Easter 1499, whereas earlier he had probably been implicated in Warbeck's conspiracy: cf. Conway, *Henry VII's relations*, p. 52.

[94]Quinn, 'Anglo-Irish local government', pp. 355-6.

[95]B.L., Royal MS 18C, XIV, ff 50, 52, 55, 72, 72v, 83, 84, 151v-2v.

attempt by the administration to come to terms with the difficulties of controlling outlying districts. Clearly local conditions and the distance from Dublin inhibited full control, but accountants evidently answered summonses to account provided they were not too frequent.

In theory, the accountant attended on the first day of the new term to make his proffer: if he failed to appear or subsequently to pay his proffer, he was amerced by the barons, often in the amount he would normally have proffered, and the amercement recorded under the heading *amerciamenta* on the memoranda roll. In practice, accountants may not have appeared in person, and they paid proffers at the receipt at any time during that term, even though they might in the interim have been superseded.[96] Liberties and franchises appointing their own officials certified their names into chancery for the issue of a patent and then had to register them with the exchequer on the first day of term: '30 Septembris anno 10 H. 7, cives & communitas civitatis Dublin. venerunt coram baronibus [hujus] scaccarij & presentauerunt Patricium fitz Leones in majorem civitatis predicti pro anno proximo futuro.'[97] By comparison, the entries for Waterford, Cork and Limerick cities under *proffra* show that accountants from the outlying districts not only failed to make bi-ennial proffers but did not appear at all: whereas the remembrancer could enter the names of sheriffs year by year by referring to their patents, he did not usually know the names of the city officials.[98]

An accountant was more commonly amerced 'quia non venit primo die ad proffrum suum faciendum', although an alternative reason was 'quia non solvit proffra'.[99] Under Edward IV, Pale sheriffs were not markedly less prone to default than others, though this position subsequently changed. At least two sheriffs defaulted in six out of seven years 1465-6 and 1478-82, and one in 1481, but very few under Henry VII: beyond the Pale, however, although all the sheriffs were amerced for the two terms 1484-5 – a continuation of previous practice – and probably most at Michaelmas 1486, Easter 1491 and Michaelmas 1504 also, none were amerced for the ten terms of Henry VII's reign for which calendars of the memoranda rolls survive, even though they made no proffer in seven of them. Moreover, whereas

---

[96]*Ibid.*, ff 22v, 23v, 24, 26, 30: proffers made on 30 Sept. 1495 were actually paid between 8 Oct. and 18 Dec.

[97]Memoranda roll, 10 Henry VII m. 1 (B.L., Add. MS 4793, f. 150).

[98]Cf. Quinn, 'Anglo-Irish local government', p. 356.

[99]E.g. Memoranda roll, 2 Richard III mm 1, 5 (P.R.O.I., RC 8/33, pp. 391-2, 400-1).

under the Yorkists *amerciamenta* were regularly included in the memoranda rolls and this source might be worth up to £15 a year, under Henry VII they became intermittent and apparently disappeared after 1504-5.[100] Unfortunately the evidence does not survive which would establish this point fully, but it appears that about 1485, in a bid to reform accounting procedure, the exchequer began to insist on regular proffers by Pale sheriffs, but other sheriffs were discharged from this duty and only summoned every few years when their accounts were actually audited. *Amerciamenta* thus ceased to be a regular feature of the rolls, although their occasional appearance suggests that the exchequer was only partially successful in operating the new system.

A further change was apparently made about 1516 and regular proffers again required. In 1511 proffers had also been made by the sheriffs of Cork and Connaught and probably others, but between 1512 and 1516 only by the sheriffs of Dublin, Meath and Louth.[101] In 1515, however, the deputy was summoned to England to answer charges of misgovernment by a former deputy treasurer, and this may have prompted the issue of new commissions enjoining annual accounts. At Easter 1517 the sheriffs of Kilkenny, Waterford and the cross of Tipperary also made proffers and by April 1518, when a new sheriff of Kilkenny was appointed, commissions for the outlying counties were again issuing under the exchequer seal and enjoining annual accounts.[102] Between 1517 and 1532 surviving evidence indicates that up to five sheriffs outside the Pale made proffers per term and that proffers were received from the sheriffs of Kilkenny (at least seven times), Waterford (6x), Limerick (4x), Cork (4x), Carlow (3x) and the cross of Tipperary (3x). This position was much more satisfactory than in the years following: until Easter 1543 there was no evidence that any of the more distant sheriffs made proffers except

---

[100]*Rec. comm. Ire. rep., 1816-20*, pp. 535-41 (includes a repertory of the first two items of each memoranda roll, usually *amerciamenta* under the Yorkists); Irish Record Commissioners' calendars, as in no. 84 above. On the membranes of *amerciamenta* and *proffra,* the accountants appeared in the same order, commencing with the Pale sheriffs and followed by those of Kilkenny and Carlow. The repertory includes only the names of officials, but these can normally be associated with counties, thus indicating from which counties proffers were received.

[101]H.F. Berry, 'Sheriffs of the county Cork – Henry III to 1660', *R.S.A.I. Jn.,* xxxv (1905), 46; Memoranda roll, 3 Henry VIII m. 6*d.* (B.L., Add. MS 4791, f. 194v).

[102]Memoranda rolls, 9-10 Henry VIII m. ?, 20 Henry VIII m. 17d, 23 Henry VIII m. 18, 35 Henry VIII m. 21 (P.R.O.I., Ferguson coll., iv, ff 53, 136, 152, 284); Quinn, 'Henry VIII and Ireland', p. 321. Certain 'articles for [the] lord lieutenant' were enrolled on Memoranda roll, 8-9 Henry VIII m. 17 (P.R.O.I., Ferguson coll., iv, f. 2v).

for the cross of Wexford, to which a separate sheriff was probably reappointed in 1535.[103]

Only within the Pale then did sheriffs make proffers at Easter and Michaelmas as in England. The second stage of the account, the view, also saw differences from exchequer procedure in England. Earlier a view had been made twice a year to provide 'a rough estimate of each accountant's receipts and expenditure before the actual audit was begun'[104] and so speed the payment of moneys for which no allowances were claimed, but by the later fifteenth century it had been discontinued: c. 1495 motion was made 'that every accomptaunt may make a due avieue of their accompt at Estir and that [the treasurer] calle for suche mony as shalbe than founde due in theire handes'.[105] The memoranda rolls continued to include membranes headed *status et visus compotorum,* but these now contained only audits of account.[106] In practice, therefore, the exchequer proceeded directly to account, a note of the summons being commonly entered on the memoranda rolls under *dies dati*.[107] A description of his account was left by Christopher Cusack of Gerardstown, sheriff of Meath, 1510-11:

> Memorandum that this is the order of the account of the ?sheriffship. First, ye shall deliver all your books unto the chief baron in a 'mall' [= a bag]. Then ye shall come to your account and ye shall have your ?'tu^{n}st' part, and first ye shall pay the fine for your court, then ye shall come to for the barons, the engrosser & the summamster; & there all your receipts ye shall *tot*, and all the amercements you shall *nint* and all that ye may not receive, otherwise leave ye shall say '*tot a viscount*'. This all done, the engrosser shall leave you and then shall ye know what is your charges. That done, the said barons will bring forth the indentures whereupon all men were assigned: then must the sheriff bring forth his discharges, that is to say, tallies for fees, *mandamus* and [ac]quittance for rewards. This done, the

---

[103] J.F. Ferguson's extracts and notes from the memoranda rolls P.R.O.I., Ferguson coll., iv, ff 38-222 *passim*.

[104] Lydon, 'Memoranda rolls', p. 65; Mills, '"Adventus vicecomitum"', p. 333.

[105] *L. & P. Ric. III & Hen. VII,* ii, 65.

[106] *Visus compotorum* for 1495 by Treasurer Conway and Undertreasurer Hattecliffe survive, but these officers were not accountable to the Irish exchequer: B.L., Royal 18C, XIV, ff 141-7v.

[107] E.g. Memoranda rolls, 14 Henry VII m. 27, 23 Henry VII mm 6, 22 (P.R.O.I., RC 8/43, pp. 150, 219, 251). Cf. Memoranda roll, 12 Henry VII m. 29 (P.R.O.I., Ferguson coll., iii, f. 337): chancery writ ordering the mayor and bailiffs of Waterford to account.

engrosser will make up his account and give him *quietus est* with that [i.e. provided] that ye pay well your fee etc.[108]

Upon his appearance with the 'books', the accountant was sworn to render faithful account and received a day to close his account.[109] In the sheriff's case, the books consisted of the lists of farms to be collected for the process of the pipe and the 'green-wax books' – issues, fines and amercements estreated by the courts into the exchequer and sorted by the clerk of the estreats into the respective counties for levy. They were then sent to the sheriff under the exchequer seal (appended in green wax) with orders for their levy.[110] From these the summamster and chief engrosser compiled the charge, though a note of sums leviable in each book was retained by the exchequer as a check and in case, as sometimes happened, the book got lost or destroyed.[111] Hattecliffe implies that the books were sent out annually, though his accounts show that they were sent out up to twice a term for each of the four courts.[112] For example, upon his account in 1495-6 the sheriff of Louth was charged with £28 1s. 10d. arrears of estreats, noted by the undertreasurer as comprising seven totals, all under £2, covering nine terms between Michaelmas 1491 and Hilary 1495.[113] The small farms, the other principal item of the charge, were mainly rents of small parcels of land, plus profits of local hereditary offices, all in the king's hand through escheat, forfeiture or outlawry: they were too small for collection directly from receivers or farmers. In 1495-6 a total of £135 18s. 2d. per annum was charged on six accountants, all within the Pale, of which the sheriffs of Meath and Kildare owed nearly £95.[114] Between 1480 and 1542, when the western half was erected into the separate shire of Westmeath, the issues of Meath were usually the largest of the shrievalties, £82 11s. 8d. *in toto* for the year 1510-11, although they amounted to only £27 14s. for thirteen months in 1544-6. For seventeen months in 1468-70 Co. Dublin yielded £63 19s. 2d.[115]

[108] T.C.D., MS 594, f. 32 (spelling modernised).

[109] E.g. Memoranda roll, 23 Henry VII m. 7 (P.R.O.I., RC 8/43, pp. 223, 225).

[110] Cf. *L. & P. Ric. III & Hen. VII*, ii, 64-7; Memoranda roll, 13-14 Elizabeth mm 14, 36 (P.R.O.I., Ferguson coll., vi, ff 192-5).

[111] E.g. Memoranda roll, 13-14 Elizabeth m. 36 (P.R.O.I., Ferguson coll., vi, ff 194-5: letter by the deputy and council granting a sheriff's petition that he should receive as a reward the amount of a green-wax book burned by rebels).

[112] Cf. B.L., Royal MS 18C, XIV, ff 115, 152, 180v, 231.

[113] *Ibid.*, ff 152, 180v.

[114] *Ibid.*, ff 116v-19v.

[115] T.C.D., MS 594, ff 9-10; P.R.O.I., M.3072; Memoranda roll, 10 Edward IV m. 41d (P.R.O.I., RC 8/41, p. 285); *Stat. Ire., Hen. VII & VIII*, p. 166.

In Cusack's case, his account when audited and engrossed on the pipe roll was in 'superplusage', i.e. his allowances exceeded his charges, and the chief engrosser accordingly issued an acquittance for which a fee was payable, plus another to the chief remembrancer who would normally issue process for any outstanding debts. He then made fine 'tam pro exitibus & proficuis comitatus predicti quam pro compoto suo relaxando'. The amount varied, from 20*d.* to 6*s.* 8*d.* for sheriffs but was apparently standardized at 6*s.* 8*d.* after 1494: escheators made fine at 20*d.* or 40*d.*[116] Commonly, however, the accountant would be found in arrears – 'there was never seen soo sharpe receyvoures and so slowe payers'[117] – in which case further assignments might be levied and he would receive further days to answer until they were paid, when the final view (*facta summa*) was drawn up, or until he was driven to make fine for pardon.[118] Until 1472, accountants were laboriously and fruitlessly opposed at the account on ancient debts incurred from Edward III's reign onwards, but following the changes in the English exchequer in 1464 the terminal date was then altered by statute to 1451, so speeding and simplifying the account.[119]

Thus the procedure for account was in essentials as in England, although much less elaborate.[120] Only pipe and memoranda rolls were regularly compiled in the upper exchequer. The pipe rolls contained all accounts whatever made before the barons in a particular year – there were no separate rolls for subsidies, customs or escheators' accounts – although under Poynings rolls of subsidy assessment were compiled and in the fourteenth century there had been rolls of subsidy and scutages.[121] The roll of 18 Henry VII, for example, contained the accounts of the sheriff of Meath, Drogheda, Dublin, the clerk of the hanaper, the customers of Dublin port and Holmpatrick near Skerries,

---

[116]T.C.D., MS 594, ff 9v-10; Memoranda rolls, 2 Richard III mm 4, 9, 21, 23d (P.R.O.I., RC 8/33, pp. 400, 409, 536, Delafield MSS, M.2675, p. 73), 6-7 Henry VII m. 32 (*Ibid.*, Delafield MSS, M.2675, p. 74), 14 Henry VII mm 1, 8, 16, 20, 23 Henry VII m. 10, 24 Henry VII m. 4 (*Ibid.*, RC 8/43, pp. 90, 111, 128, 140, 232, 272); N.L.I., D.2458 (*Ormond deeds, 1509-47*, no. 346 (2)). Cf. T.C.D., MS 1207, no. 237; B.L., Royal MS 18C, XIV, f. 231, and for examples of the form of the *quietus est*, P.R.O.I., M.3072; N.L.I., D.15994 (*Dowdall deeds*, no. 550).

[117]B.L., Cotton MS, Titus B. XI, f. 401 (*L. & P. Hen. VIII*, xv, no. 849). I am indebted to Professor W.C. Richardson for this reference.

[118]Memoranda rolls, 2 Richard III mm 11, 16, 9 Henry VII mm 8, 9, 19, 23 Henry VII m. 6 (P.R.O.I., RC 8/33, pp. 416, 514-15, 8/43, pp. 65, 67, 84).

[119]Parliament roll, 12 & 13 Edward IV c. 9 (*Stat. Ire., Edw. IV*, ii, 14-16). Cf. Lander, *Government and community*, p. 242.

[120]Cf. Elton, *Tudor revolution in government*, esp. pp. 245-6.

[121]B.L., Royal MS 18C, XIV, f. 138v; Richardson & Sayles, *Admin. Ire.*, pp. 213-14. Cf. Jewell, *English local administration*, pp. 14-15.

and the receiver-general.[122] Dublin and Drogheda normally accounted annually, the sheriffs of the Pale and customers there at intervals varying from less than a year to seven years, and escheators apparently as they left office.[123] From 1494, the treasurer or his deputy, if he was accountable before the barons in Ireland, accounted at intervals of between one and three years: a statute requiring the treasurer to declare his account annually before the barons and the governor's nominees and that the account be subsequently determined before the barons in England was ignored after Poynings's departure.[124] After Sir Roland FitzEustace's celebrated treasurership (1454-92), it was alleged that his accounts had never been closed, although he was certainly summoned to account in 1476. The exchequer was still pursuing the matter in 1497-8 and had amerced him in £40, but FitzEustace had since died and his son pleaded a pardon.[125] Bartholomew Dillon was summoned to account as deputy treasurer for 2½ years to July 1516 in 1516, for which he pleaded a pardon, then as undertreasurer until Michaelmas 1517, and in mid-1526 for the period from Michaelmas 1517 to March 1520. For the third period he also obtained a pardon in May 1526.[126] Under the Lancastrians, some of the accountants from beyond the Pale accounted most infrequently: on Pipe roll, 14 Henry VI (1435-6) were enrolled the accounts of the seneschals of Ulster for the period 1351-1436 and of Tipperary 1399-1436.[127] By and large, however, accounts were rendered and audited promptly after the summons, within a few months of the account being closed: small sums were sometimes outstanding, but the process of account was not allowed to drag on for years as in England. Moreover, the innovations made in the account procedure strongly suggest that the exchequer was responsive to changing conditions in the lordship.

Flexibility of procedure and economy were also evident in other aspects of the exchequer's work. The memoranda rolls were bound up

---

[122]N.L.I., MS 761, pp. 326-32.

[123]E.g. Pipe rolls, 11, 18, 20, 21 Henry VII (B.L., Royal MS 18C, XIV, ff 151v-2v; N.L.I., MS 761, pp. 326-39).

[124]*Stat. Ire.*, i, 42.

[125]Memoranda rolls, 16 Edward IV m. 8d, 13 Henry VII m. 5 (P.R.O.I., Ferguson coll., iii, ff 221v, 222); Parliament roll, 9 Henry VII c. 27 (P.R.O.I., RC 13/9).

[126]Memoranda rolls, 6-7 Henry VIII m. ?, 7-8 Henry VIII m. 12, 17-18 Henry VIII m. 17 (P.R.O.I., Ferguson coll., iii, f. 220, iv, f. 111, repertory, iv, 99). Cf. Pipe roll, 18 Henry VII (N.L.I., MS 761, pp. 326-32).

[127]N.L.I., MS 761, pp. 295, 301.

annually with the different captions of membranes used in each term following in very roughly the same order, but there were exceptions, and the order changed from time to time. Down to 1534 the captions were those employed throughout the fifteenth century, but *brevia retornabilia* was omitted and after 1504 *amerciamenta* also.[128] Apart from a brief attempt under Edward II to conform to the English practice of K.R. and L.T.R. memoranda rolls, only one memoranda roll was compiled each year in the lordship. This usually ran from Michaelmas to Michaelmas, although under Edward IV and Henry VIII rolls ran from Easter to Easter.[129] There were, however, two remembrancers, but the chief remembrancer, charged with compiling the roll, was much the more prominent, receiving a salary of 10 marks a year, increasing to £10 by 1534. The second remembrancer had custody of writs returned to the exchequer, with a mere 50*s*.,[130] and *c*.1502 John Dexcester appears as both second remembrancer and clerk to the chief remembrancer.[131] Both offices were at times held by deputy – Bartholomew Dillon, J.K.B., was also chief remembrancer, 1524-8 – and their clerks were occasionally rewarded by the king.[132] For a time after 1494 there was no regular second remembrancer.[133] By 1545, however, writs countersigned by the chief remembrancer style him king's remembrancer, following English practice, and at a later date the remembrancers and memoranda rolls were organized as in England.[134] By 1545 also, originalia rolls were being compiled.[135] The other principal late medieval classes of records were the various inquisitions and extents ordered by the barons in yearly files, and the 'filacia brevium de Anglia & Hibernia' for each year, though few writs now came direct from England, plus the records subsidiary to accounts.[136]

---

[128] See Lydon, 'Memoranda rolls', pp. 52-4.

[129] *Ibid*., p. 51 n. 1; Hand, *Eng. law in Ire.*, pp. 102-3; *Rec. comm. Ire. rep., 1816-20*, pp. 535-41.

[130] Memoranda roll, 6 Edward IV m. 18 (P.R.O.I., RC 8/41, p. 123); P.R.O., E.101/248/21, S.P.65/1/2.

[131] Pipe roll, 18 Henry VII (N.L.I., MS 761, p. 326).

[132] E.g. Memoranda rolls, 2 Richard III mm 19, 27d, 32, 14 Henry VII mm 6, 18 (P.R.O.I., RC 8/33, pp. 522, 543, 547, 8/43, pp. 105, 138).

[133] Memoranda rolls, 14 Henry VII m. 6, 15 Henry VII m. 11 (P.R.O.I., RC 8/43, pp. 105, 177).

[134] Memoranda roll, 36 Henry VIII m. 7 (P.R.O.I., Ferguson coll., iv, f. 293); N.L.I., D.2458 (*Ormond deeds, 1509-47*), no. 346 (2)); Wood, *Public records of Ireland*, pp. 121-2.

[135] N.L.I., D.2458; Wood, *Public records of Ireland*, p. 123.

[136] E.g. Memoranda roll, 12 Henry VII m. ? (S.P.W., Hore MS I, p. 1148).

The chief engrosser and the summamster, important in connection with the audit, received fees of ten and eight marks respectively. Thomas Sharpe held both offices for most of the Yorkist period and was also joint clerk of the common pleas there and chancellor of the exchequer for part of the time. Later summamsters were often promoted to be chief or second engrosser, the best-documented example being Walter Hussey, in 1495 an obscure clerk rewarded 'pro scriptura rotulorum de assessione... subsidii'.[137] By 1499 he had risen to summamster and he appears as chief engrosser in 1511, remaining there until 1546 (jointly from 1538), though in 1537 he was reputed to be eighty years old.[138] No other office could show anything like the same continuity, and indeed under Poynings some of them, even that of summamster, were effectively suppressed, only expenses being allowed for the clerks exercising them.[139] Moreover, despite the shortage of skilled clerks, with consequent pluralism and underclerks, there was a fairly rapid turnover from the 1520s because the offices were all in the deputy's gift.

The other established exchequer officers were the transcriptor and the janitor and crier (both normally receiving an annual salary of four marks), an usher and at least one messenger. The usher was also responsible for buying paper, parchment and ink for the exchequer and had originally been paid £1 a year, though during this period he received considerably more by way of rewards;[140] and messengers were paid either diets of 1½d. while the exchequer was open or two marks per annum.[141] In Ireland the lone serjeant-at-arms, with a fee of £10 a year, and the marshal, who usually received eight or ten marks, exercised their offices in all four central courts.[142] Additionally, there were a large number of unsalaried clerks who received only rewards, fees and perquisites: some were regular officers, but others must have been employed only on a casual basis at times of pressure.

In the receipt there were two chamberlains, with fees of ten marks each for much of the period, though the chief chamberlain was paid £10 per annum about 1495 and 1534 and the second chamberlain's

---

[137] B.L., Royal MS 18C, XIV, f. 138v.

[138] *Ormond deeds, 1413-1509,* no. 355; T.C.D., MS 594, f. 10; P.R.O., E.101/248/21; *Cal. pat. rolls Ire., Hen. VIII-Eliz.,* pp. 5, 15, 41.

[139] B.L., Royal MS 18C, XIV, f. 148.

[140] *Rot. pat. Hib.,* p. 265 nos. 59-67; *Rec. comm. rep. Ire., 1811-15,* p. 125; Memoranda roll, 2 Richard III m. 9 (P.R.O.I., RC 8/33, p. 407).

[141] *Rec. comm. rep. Ire., 1811-15,* p. 51; P.R.O., E.101/248/21, S.P.65/1/2.

[142] E.g. P.R.O., E.101/248/21, S.P.65/1/2; B.L., Royal MS 18C, XIV, f. 148.

salary was reduced temporarily to £4 *c.* 1495.[143] The traditional issue and receipt rolls continued to be kept, despite their abolition in England, and there was also a separate roll of warrants for payment directed to the treasurer and chamberlains.[144] The Irish equivalent of the undertreasurer who headed the receipt in England was the treasurer's clerk, who, however, remained very much under the treasurer's control. Philip Flatesbury, appointed treasurer's clerk in 1507, received a patent under the great seal,[145] but this was probably exceptional: there was no regular salary attached and the office was probably in the treasurer's gift. From Edward I's reign until 1471 at least, the clerk was allowed 5*d.* a day while the receipt was open – about 220 days a year.[146] The clerk perhaps received a larger salary privately from the treasurer, who recovered the original diets from the king.[147] In addition, he received rewards, often 40*s.* a year in the fifteenth century, rising to £4 by 1534.[148] Under Poynings the salary was £6 15*s.*, while Flatesbury received £12 a year in 1520-2, perhaps in accordance with practice since 1507, but the auditors refused to accept this rate without an inquiry, and by 1534 it had been reduced to £7.[149] All this suggests considerable flexibility in the terms on which the office was granted. The clerk continued to compile issue and receipt rolls, to receive and disburse the revenue, and to strike tallies: there is no sign of any elaborate organization in the Irish receipt, of tellers, writers and strikers of tallies, a clerk of the pells and so on.[150] He had at least two assistants, however: John Fleming, clerk from 1467 until about 1484, was also second remembrancer in 1484. Flatesbury was empowered to act by deputy, and the names of two clerks styled 'unus clericorum receptus scaccarii' have survived.[151]

---

[143]*Ibid.*

[144]*Rec. comm. Ire. rep., 1811-15,* p. 54; P.R.O.I., Ferguson coll., ii, f. 47; R.I.A., MS 12 D 19, pp. 173-7, 189 (all extracts from Issue and Receipt rolls); B.L., Royal MS 18C, XIV, ff 38, 56, 66v; *Rot. pat. Hib.,* pp. 263-5. Cf. H.G. Richardson & G.O. Sayles, 'Irish revenue, 1278-1384', *R.I.A. Proc.,* lxii (1962), 91; Elton, *Tudor revolution in government,* pp. 23-4.

[145]Memoranda roll, 23 Henry VII m. 8 (P.R.O.I., RC 8/43, p. 225).

[146]*Rec. comm. Ire. rep., 1811-15,* p. 54; B.L., Royal MS 18C, XIV, ff 13-70v; P.R.O., E.101/248/8.

[147]See especially, P.R.O., E.101/248/21.

[148]*Rot. pat. Hib.,* pp. 235a no. 5, 268 no. 17; Memoranda roll, 2 Richard III m. 32 (P.R.O.I., RC 8/33, p. 548); P.R.O., S.P.65/1/2.

[149]B.L., Royal MS 18C, XIV, f. 71; P.R.O., E.101/248/21, S.P.65/1/2.

[150]*Rec. comm. Ire. rep., 1811-15,* p. 125. Cf. Elton, *Tudor revolution in government,* p. 20.

[151]Memoranda rolls, 2 Richard III mm 32, 33, 14 Henry VII m. 6 (P.R.O.I., RC 8/33, pp. 547, 551, 8/43, p. 106).

Moreover, a receipt for £20 from a receiver in 1537 was written out in a clerkly hand, signed in a different hand 'per me, Johannem Ryan, clericum Willelmi Brabazon, subthesaurarii', and endorsed in a scrawl, 'Mr Troserd ys aqwytans', which suggests that a degree of bureaucratization had by then occurred.[152]

Procedure at the receipt is in part illustrated by Undertreasurer Hattecliffe's day-book (1495-6).[153] A large part of the volume is in Hattecliffe's hand, but folios 13-70 which comprise the journal of receipts and issues for the first year of his undertreasurership are in a different hand. They were written up or supervised by the treasurer's clerk, Richard Nangle, whose name appears frequently on the pages as having indented with an accountant for a prest. At times, the journal is initialled or signed, seemingly by the recipient of an issue, and it was apparently compiled from day to day in the receipt; but elsewhere issues or receipts over a period of time were covered by one entry, and a second version of small sections survives elsewhere in the day-book. Most of the entries were later scored out, occasionally with references to later entries in the journal, though mostly, it would seem, when the clerk compiled the issue and receipt rolls of which the journal formed the basis. Within the period of the treasurer's account, separate journals were apparently compiled for each exchequer year. An entry of a receipt, for example, was scored out and a marginal note entered, 'quia ponitur in anno sequente'. The journal sometimes formed the basis of process for outstanding debts by the remembrancers: process issued in Michaelmas 1507 and recorded on the memoranda roll was subscribed, 'per librum Willelmi Darcy, subthesaurarii'.[154]

Yet, as the day-book clearly shows, the treasurer rather than his clerk retained responsibility for assignments, and since most of the revenue was anticipated in this way (a point to which I shall turn shortly), he was in no danger of being excluded from supervision of the receipt. Nevertheless, there was a development in the Irish exchequer at this time deceptively similar to that by which the English undertreasurer ousted his nominal superior from control of the exchequer.[155] This development also saw effective control of finances pass, in the period 1495-1534, from the lord treasurer to the

---

[152]T.C.D., MS 1207, no. 222.

[153]B.L., Royal MS 18C, XIV.

[154]*Ibid*., ff 67v, 68; Memoranda roll, 23 Henry VII m. 6 (P.R.O.I., RC 8/43, pp. 219-20).

[155]Cf. J.L. Kirby, 'The rise of the under-treasurer of the exchequer', *E.H.R.*, lxxii (1957), 666-77; Elton, *Tudor revolution in government*, pp. 23-4, 254-6.

undertreasurer. Periodically in the late middle ages, treasurers appointed deputies to act during absences, but these deputy treasurers were in some respects distinguishable from the undertreasurers who began to be appointed in 1495 and who after 1532 replaced the treasurer in his traditional duties. Hattecliffe's assumption of office in June 1495 was a portent of this for he virtually superseded Treasurer Conway who in fact left Ireland in November.[156] Nevertheless the process was reversed after Kildare's restoration, and for a time the official discharging the treasurer's duties might or might not receive that title according to whether or not it was desired to confer upon him the full fees and status pertaining to the office. The powers conferred, it seems, did not vary. The lord treasurer received the comparatively large sum, by Irish standards, of £40 salary per annum plus diets of 6s. 8d. while acting;[157] but as undertreasurer, Hattecliffe received 100 marks a year from the outset, plus diets of 3s. 4d. after Conway's departure, and he presumably continued to receive these wages until his departure sometime after February 1497.[158] Kildare thereafter kept the office vacant and appointed Sir William Darcy as receiver-general with a salary of only £10.[159] This office, with power to levy the revenues, was normally vested in the treasurership, but under Poynings a separate receiver-general of the crown lands and those of wards had been appointed, no doubt to speed the levy of debts.[160] Nevertheless, Darcy was presumably the vice-gerent to whom a warrant for payment was addressed in 1502.[161]

The treasurership was revived for Kildare's son and heir, Gerald Fitzgerald, in 1504, but by 1505 Darcy was acting as his deputy, and when Fitzgerald succeeded his father as deputy, he conferred the treasurership on his supporter, Lord Slane (d. 1517), who again chose to act by deputy. Nevertheless, Fitzgerald exercised the treasurership in person for at least part of the time, for writs of 17 October 1505 and 22 May 1511 attested by him survive.[162] An additional complication is that Darcy was, colloquially at least, also styled undertreasurer,[163]

---

[156] Conway, *Henry VII's relations*, pp. 64-72.

[157] B.L., Royal MS 18C, XIV, f. 135v.

[158] *Ibid.*, f. 67; *Cal. pat. rolls, 1494-1509*, p. 26; Memoranda roll, 12 Henry VII m. 17 (R.I.A., MS 24 H 17, p. 203).

[159] Pipe roll, 18 Henry VII (N.L.I., MS 761, p. 327).

[160] B.L., Royal MS 18C, XIV, ff 24v, 26, 110-0v, 152.

[161] *Anal. Hib.*, ii, 200-1.

[162] Memoranda rolls, 21 Henry VII m. 3, 3 Henry VIII m. 8 (B.L., Add. MSS 4793, f. 153, 4791, f. 194v).

[163] See above, p. 99; T.C.D., MS 594, f. 9v; *S.P. Hen. VIII*, ii, 78.

but that the offices of undertreasurer and deputy treasurer were distinct is clear from the fact that Bartholomew Dillon, Lord Slane's deputy, was in 1516 appointed undertreasurer, and two otherwise identical patents of February and July under the exchequer seal are attested by Dillon as 'deputato thesaurarii nostri' and as 'subthesaurario nostro' respectively.[164] One obvious difference was that a deputy was appointed by the treasurer by virtue of a clause in his patent empowering him to do so, whereas an undertreasurer was appointed by the king or his deputy in Ireland, though both were sworn before the barons on entering office.[165] Moreover, Dillon had to account separately for his two periods of office and the appointment of an undertreasurer evidently voided patents attested by his predecessor.[166]

The decline in the treasurer's powers went a stage further with the resumption of the Geraldine-Butler feud in the 1520s. With the recall of Undertreasurer Stile in 1522, the king again appointed a treasurer, the prior of Kilmainham, and excepted this office from the deputy's control. Since successive deputies were granted the revenues without account at this time, good relations with the treasurer were obviously essential to the deputy. During Ormond's first deputyship (1522-4), an undertreasurer, Darcy again, was acting in October 1523, but whether Rawson had resigned or what was the nature of his relationship with Darcy is obscure. With Kildare's restoration in August 1524 Ormond was appointed treasurer by English patent as a sop, and since Darcy was also on bad terms with Kildare, the earl lost no time in replacing him as undertreasurer with Lord Trimbleston.[167] Writs entered on the memoranda rolls point to the undertreasurer as doing all the work at this time, but the prior was reappointed treasurer in 1528 and both he and an undertreasurer, Dillon again, were apparently active, though perhaps at different times. The earlier problem recurred in 1532 when Kildare was appointed deputy and Lord Butler treasurer. For a time Butler tried to exercise his office, a writ of 24 August being attested by him,[168] but he was the last treasurer to do so and in September Kildare appointed William Bath as undertreasurer, with a salary of £12 a year instead of the £10 hitherto usual for an undertreasurer appointed by the deputy.[169] Butler

---

[164]N.L.I., D.15963-4 (*Dowdall deeds*, nos. 519-20).
[165]Cf. Memoranda roll, 24 Henry VII m. 2 (P.R.O.I., RC 8/43, p. 265).
[166]As in note 126 above.
[167]See Ellis, 'Tudor policy and Kildare ascendancy', pp. 247-8.
[168]Memoranda roll, 24 Henry VIII m. 16 (B.L., Add. MS 4791, f. 203v).
[169]Patent roll, 16 Henry VIII (T.C.D., MS 1731, p. 75); P.R.O., S.P.65/1/2.

continued as treasurer after Bath's supersession and the appointment of William Brabazon as undertreasurer for life in 1534. There is, however, no evidence of Butler acting in the exchequer after August 1532 and some evidence that he did not do so. Kildare's appointment of Bath was manifestly an attempt to recover control of the revenue, and in this he succeeded admirably, for Bath ensured that Butler's salary remained unpaid from Michaelmas 1532 and later followed Kildare into rebellion.[170] This success was acknowledged by the king when he reserved to himself the nomination of the undertreasurer as well from 1534. Brabazon's control of the exchequer is manifest, and when in 1554 an undertreasurer was recalled to answer charges of corruption, it was found necessary to order the treasurer to make payments in his absence.[171]

In conclusion, the overall improvement in the financial position of the Dublin government during this period can be illustrated by the practice of assignment. In Henry VI's later years, the exchequer had been working under a considerable burden of debt, and a large number of bad tallies were issued. The roll of warrants for issue, 1439-41, calendared by the Irish Record Commissioners as Close roll, 20 Henry VI, comprised 67 warrants, of which 31 ordered the payment of arrears totalling £669 14s. 2¾d. mainly on the return of 36 bad tallies dating back to 1419. Stephen Bray, C.J.K.B. intermittently 1397-1435, was owed no less than £487 12s. 2d. on his salary in 1420, and in 1430 Roger Hawkenshaw, J.K.B. 1416-c. 33, was owed £179 4s.: Bray died in 1441 with £280 6s. 2¾d. still owing.[172] In fact there had been a growing tendency to intercept revenue by assignments since Richard II's days, and this process accelerated under Henry V when all but a fraction of the revenue was assigned. On the receipt roll for 1427, for example, all but eleven small items totalling £2 15s. out of a revenue of £1,830 4s. 7¾d. was in fictitious receipts.[173] By then the Irish exchequer had developed a system corresponding to the *sol'* and *pro* marginalia of the English receipt rolls in order to distinguish cash receipts from assignments: in an assignment the entry of the receipt was followed by *per* and the name of the assignee. Earlier, however, assignments were distinguishable only by comparing both receipt and issue rolls entry by entry.[174]

---

[170] P.R.O., S.P.65/1/2; Ellis, 'Tudor policy and Kildare ascendancy', p. 266.

[171] See above, ch. 1, p. 16; P.R.O., S.P.65/1/2; *Acts of the Privy Council*, v, 164.

[172] *Rot. pat. Hib.*, pp. 263-5; Lydon, *Lordship*, p. 259; Ball, *Judges*, i, 170; P.R.O., E.101/248/8.

[173] P.R.O., E.101/248/1; Otway-Ruthven, *Med. Ire.*, p. 165.

[174] P.R.O., E.101/247/8, 248/1; Receipt rolls, 7-8 Edward IV, 14-18 Edward IV

Hattecliffe's journal provides a good indication of practice concerning assignment in 1495-6, although conditions in that year were made somewhat exceptional by the periodic receipt of large sums of money from England, especially in 1495, which greatly increased the number of cash payments. The phrase *per manus* is employed to denote an assignment followed by the name of an accountant or assignee in entries of issues and receipts respectively, but unfortunately it is only a rough guide. Frequently payments by assignment can also be checked by a following entry of an equivalent receipt, but for example one entry which otherwise looks like a cash payment of 40*s*. is scored out with the explanation, 'quia postea folio 29 infra lxxij*s*. sibi assignatos super subsidium baronie de Arde'.[175] Even so, the majority of payments were clearly made by assignment as earlier, except immediately after the receipt of English money, and as a proportion of the total amount disbursed the preponderance of assignments was even larger, because large sums were almost invariably assigned, whereas cash payments tended to be limited to 'minutiis expensis' of a few shillings or less for the exchequer.

In making assignments, the treasurer seemingly tried to make ones convenient for recipients, though pressure on the revenues must at times have made this impossible. Thus in repayment of a loan of £100 from Waterford city, £20 was assigned on the feefarm of the city, 100 marks on the prise wines there, £10 on a fine made by the bishop of Ossory, and £4 on the Dublin customs, making £100 13*s*. 4*d*. for 1495-6 alone and perhaps more later, a discrepancy which suggests that English practice to circumvent usury laws was not unknown.[176] Though somewhat exceptional in that revenue and debts incurred beyond the Pale were usually on a smaller scale, this case illustrates a normal practice: Hattecliffe recommended that the treasurer examine the estreats 'that if eny good summe of mony be in theym, that ye may ordre the assignementes therof as may be most for the kinges prouffithe and youre ease'.[177] So generally assignments were preferred on revenues accruing in the more distant part of the Pale than on, say, the mint in Dublin castle: but assignments on the mint were not uncommon, and when the treasurer was particularly stretched, as was the case in Trinity 1496, he even resorted to the assignment of a

(R.I.A., MS 12 D 19, pp. 173-7); Anthony Steel, *The receipt of the exchequer, 1377-1485* (Cambridge, 1954), pp. ix-x and *passim*, and the review by J.F. Lydon in *I.H.S.*, xi (1958-9), 242-3.

[175]B.L., Royal MS 18C, XIV, f. 35v and *passim*.

[176]*Ibid*., ff 71v, 72, 72v, 84, 86v, 87.

[177]*Ibid*., f. 231 (*L. & P. Ric. III & Hen. VII*, ii, 65).

shilling on the sheriff of Co. Dublin.[178] Most of the rents of crown lands fell due at Michaelmas and Lady Day, but in fact those due at Michaelmas would not actually be leviable until sometime between All Hallowtide and Christmas, and similarly for the second instalment. And since additional revenues were due at Michaelmas this meant that Trinity was the slackest term so far as the receipt was concerned.[179] By c. 1430, moreover, the poverty of the Irish exchequer was notorious and the possibilities of credit in Ireland correspondingly small.[180]

Thus in general, the Irish exchequer was more a court of audit than a treasury, more so even than its English counterpart and in spite of the reforms of Edward IV and Henry VII which diverted the bulk of the English revenue into the king's chamber while gradually abandoning the practice of large-scale assignment.[181] In Ireland assignment remained the norm throughout the late medieval period, although with the rise in revenue from 1461 the opportunity was taken to reform the system. In its necessity, the Lancastrian exchequer had frequently made assignments of ministers' salaries on casual or unreliable sources of revenues, giving priority to the governor for defence costs.[182] Already in 1463, however, the mint-master claimed allowance of only £155 by eleven tallies in accounting for £238 7s. 1d., although reliable sources continued to be fully assigned. On account for £309 7s. 4d. in 1497 the customer of Dublin claimed allowance of £290 11s. 4½d. by nine tallies and the balance for his salary and reward, and in 1511 the sheriff of Meath was allowed £83 14s. paid on assignment against his charge of £82 11s. 8d.[183] Concurrently, an extension took place in the system whereby the principal officers got clauses inserted in their patents specifying the sources on which their salaries should be paid, very often with priority payment specified and confirmation of their patents by parliament.[184] By 1485, as the extent shows, ministers' salaries and diets were

---

[178]*Ibid.*, f. 77. Cf. *L. & P. Ric. III & Hen. VII*, ii, 67-9.

[179]Cf. *L. & P. Ric. III & Hen. VII*, ii 67-9; *L. & P. Hen. VIII*, iv, no. 81; *S.P. Hen. VIII*, ii, 40.

[180]E.g. *S.P. Hen. VIII*, ii, 40-1, 47, 78, 87.

[181]Cf. B.P. Wolffe, *The crown lands 1461-1536* (London, 1970), pp. 38, 41-2, 45, 49, 67, 69-70.

[182]E.g. *Rot. pat. Hib.*, pp. 263-5; P.R.O., E.101/248/1.

[183]Memoranda roll, 12 Henry VII m. 24 (R.I.A., MS 24 H 17, pp. 201, 207, 209); Pipe roll, 2 Edward IV (N.L.I., MS 761, pp. 324-5; R.I.A., MS 12 D 10, p. 199); T.C.D., MS 594, f. 9v.

[184]E.g. Parliament rolls, 7 & 8 Edward IV cc 26, 30, 31, 48, 19 & 20 Edward IV c.

mostly assigned on a semi-permanent basis on reliable sources like the feefarms of Dublin and Drogheda or crown lands, and only £5 from the manor of Trim was available from among the regular sources. Nevertheless, sizeable profits from the mint and Ormond's lands in the Pale were without regular assignments, no doubt because they were not considered certain sources of revenue.[185] In 1466 the exchequer had been busily reassigning rewards granted to clerks there by Henry VI and in 1484 reliable assignments were made for £50 arrears of salary from Easter 1483, but thereafter salaries were regularly paid, until the 1520s, and there is no evidence of bad tallies being issued.[186]

By the later fifteenth century, the exchequer was evidently concentrating on governing the Pale, from which the bulk of its business derived, but its influence beyond the Pale was not negligible and, together with certain special administrative arrangements for these areas which are discussed below,[187] ensured that the government retained substantial control over the outlying English districts. Although the nature of the evidence imposes restrictions on our knowledge of exchequer activities, the court was evidently working fairly efficiently. By comparison with contemporary governments with far greater resources, it was no mean achievement that the Dublin administration was generally solvent in this period and its officers regularly paid. The organization of the Irish exchequer was less elaborate than its English counterpart and its procedures speedier and more flexible. This put it at an advantage: despite the low pay and qualifications of many of its officers, modest reforms aimed at increasing exchequer control ensured that the wasteful duplication of functions and rivalry between exchequer and chamber in England was largely avoided. Thus the Irish exchequer, while no doubt ponderous enough in comparison with the king's chamber, continued to discharge effectively and cheaply the tasks for which it had been created at a time when the English exchequer, notoriously slow and inefficient as it was, appeared to be for most purposes obsolete.

43, 20 Edward IV c. 13, 21 Edward IV c. 1 (*Stat. Ire., Edw. IV,* i, 480-2, 488-92, 528-72, ii, 794-6, 860, 866-88).

[185]P.R.O., E.101/248/17.

[186]*Ibid.*; Memoranda roll, 6 Edward IV mm 9, 12 (P.R.O.I., RC 8/41, pp. 54, 72).

[187]Pp. 134-41.

4

LAWYERS, LITIGATION AND THE COMMON LAW

Under Edward IV, the lordship's legal system was still much as it had been throughout the fourteenth century. By 1534 important changes had brought its structure more closely into line with the legal system in England, and there are indications that the law was administered slightly more impartially. The evidence concerning these changes is thin and difficult to interpret, but points to a gradual improvement under Edward IV culminating in more extensive reforms in the period of direct rule, 1494-6.

The king's legal counsel

The legal establishment in Ireland was modest, there being about ten established posts to which lawyers might aspire. From 1341, there were normally only two judges on each bench and three barons, but under Edward IV a third justice or fourth baron is sometimes encountered.[1] In chancery, the keeper of the rolls gradually became recognized after 1494 as a second judge sitting with the chancellor and, until 1537 when a separate solicitor-general was appointed, the king's legal counsel was completed by a single king's serjeant-at-law and solicitor-general, and the king's attorney.

The king's lawyers were also poorly paid. The fee of the chief justice of king's bench was £100 per annum, but his colleague in common pleas had only £40, and the chief baron received forty marks, increased to £40 from 1521. Puisne barons received twenty marks a year, but the fees of puisne judges varied considerably, from £20 to £50 in king's bench, and from twenty marks to £40 in common pleas. The king's serjeant and attorney received £5 a year each until 1479, but by 1520 this had crept up to twenty marks. Nevertheless, there was as yet no general upward trend in salaries, and at a time when inflation was beginning to bite many offices carried the same fee as they had under Edward I.[2] Some of the lower paid received a reward of 40s. per annum, but all depended heavily on fees from litigants and some more dubious sources of income.

---

[1] Cf. Hand, 'Eng. law in Ire.', p. 409. Much of the first section of this chapter is based on lists of officers and other data, too long for inclusion here, in Ellis, 'Admin. Ire.', ch. 5 and app. i. See also the appendix below; and Ball, *Judges,* i, bk. ii.

[2] Cf. Hand, *Eng. law in Ire.,* p. 9; *Anal. Hib.,* ii (1931), 189-90.

The judges were regularly retained by private parties: Lord Chancellor FitzEustace, for example, received an annuity of ten marks from the archbishop of Armagh for his good counsel, and was offered ten marks to 'labour' the deputy for livery of the earl of Ormond's lands; and William Chevir, J.K.B., received a total of £16 13s. 8d. in annuities from 14 different sources c. 1437-8.[3] Moreover, contemporaries both English and Irish thought that the Irish-born judges were less learned and more corrupt than Englishmen. Throughout the period, there was no lack of criticism about legal standards in Ireland:

> men of this realme [of England] keepe better justice, execute your lawes and favour more the common people there, and ever have done before this tyme, better then ever did any man of that land (the Irish Parliament, 1441);

> here by ryzght fewe well lernid men in the lawe... and thoes that be use grete parcyallyte to ther frynds
> (Undertreasurer Stile, 1521);

> there were but shadowes and showes of justice and iudges, even at the courte at Dublin in terme tyme, moche more in cessions abroad (Lord Chancellor Gerrard, 1577).[4]

More particularly, substantial and specific charges of corruption were levelled against individual justices. In 1463-4, parliament remitted a case for trial in common pleas after allegations of maintenance by the justices of king's bench; and in 1478 Barnaby Barnewall, J.K.B., was ordered to restore £20 levied by wrongful amercement and not recoverable at common law because of Barnewall's 'graund prudence en la ley & plusours & beucoups collours & subtiliteez qil ad en icelle'. Barnewall's excesses eventually drove the Armagh clergy to appeal to the king, complaining that unless they 'please hym with a rewarde othyr an annuel fe or pensyone', he annoyed them with frivolous writs of prohibition and kept juries undischarged for days on end to procure malicious indictments against them.[5] Other parliamentary petitions charged that James Alleyn, C.J.K.B., secretly levied £9 in estreats of the court to his own use; that James Power, J.C.P., upheld a frivolous plaint of trespass there; and that Robert Dowdall, C.J.C.P., had

---

[3]Parliament roll, 20 Edward IV cc 4, 10 (*Stat. Ire., Edw. IV*, ii, 844-6, 856); B.L., Add. MS 4787, f. 105. Cf. *S.P. Hen. VIII*, ii, 187, 372, 499.

[4]*Stat. Ire., Hen. VI*, p. 50; *S.P. Hen. VIII*, ii, 86; *Anal. Hib.*, ii, 114.

[5]Parliament rolls, 3 Edward IV c. 90, 18 Edward IV (I) sess. iii, c. 3 (*Stat. Ire., Edw. IV*, i, 220-2, ii, 632-4); Octavian's register, copy in T.C.D., MS 557, ix, 362-3.

altered the record of a plea in the exchequer concerning his son.[6] Dowdall also connived at offering a speedier, cheaper process in common pleas by allowing plaintiffs to sue bills of privilege as his servants, a practice forbidden by statute in 1449.[7] Other justices augmented their income by acting as chief justices of franchises at the same time — Nicholas Turner, C.J.C.P., and Walter Kerdiff, J.C.P., in the liberty of Tipperary, and possibly Thomas Netterville, J.C.P., in Kildare.[8]

Nevertheless from 1494, if not before, the more specific charges of flagrant corruption disappear, despite the increased evidence available, and this improvement seems to be associated with a reorganization of the judiciary. In the period 1461-94, the level of legal training of the puisne judges seems to have been generally low: at least four of the ten known were clerks who were probably helping out, and the others included the chief baron of the exchequer who sat in common pleas in 1466. Moreover, none progressed further in the legal hierarchy, though Henry Duffe, appointed J.C.P. in 1479, had previously been king's serjeant and chief baron. The two chief justices, however, had usually risen from king's serjeant or other legal post, and from the late 1470s the chief baron was also an experienced lawyer, sometimes advancing to chief justice. In Henry VII's later years there were apparently no regular puisne judges – a king's bench clerk was acting there in 1506 — but under Henry VIII puisne judges were regularly advanced, usually to chief justice by way of chief baron. The king's serjeant could expect promotion to the bench — nine out of thirteen occupants of the post 1463-1532, were so advanced, and another became keeper of the rolls: but as in England, the king's attorney was not originally so promoted, although some attorneys later became puisne barons. The barons, however, were regularly promoted from among the exchequer clerks, being skilled in the *cursus scaccarii* rather than the law; but beginning with Bartholomew Dillon, C.J.K.B. in 1533 and appointed baron in 1507, some attained to judgeship in other courts. From 1471, the king's attorney began to be promoted to the bench, nine out of fourteen attorneys being promoted between 1467 and 1534; but from 1494 serjeants and attorneys normally did a spell as puisne judge before going on to higher things. From 1494 too,

---

[6]Parliament rolls, 35 Henry VI c. 23, 3 Edward IV c. 89, 7 & 8 Edward IV c. 75 (*Stat. Ire., Hen. VI,* p. 466, *Edw. IV,* i, 218-20, 626-8).

[7]Below, pp. 120-1; Parliament rolls, 28 Henry VI c. 9, 3 Edward IV c. 89 (*Stat. Ire., Hen. VI,* pp. 172-4, *Edw. IV,* i, 218-20).

[8]Parliament roll, 8 Henry VII c. 11 (P.R.O.I., RC 13/9); N.L.I., D. 2240 (*Ormond deeds, 1509-47,* no. 210); Plea roll of the liberty of Kildare, 1518-19 (*Rec. comm. Ire. rep., 1816-20,* p. 113; *P.R.I. rep. D.K. 28,* p. 47; T.C.D., MS 1731, p. 60).

the king's judges were usually appointed during pleasure instead of for life, in accordance with a statute of Poynings's parliament.[9] It appears therefore that a single career structure was gradually created for common lawyers, which improved legal standards and eliminated the worst excesses. Finally, after 1494, the top chancery posts were incorporated into this structure. Hitherto the chancellorship had been a political appointment held by English courtiers and Old English magnates, while the keepership of the rolls alternated between common lawyers, courtiers and senior chancery clerks. For the next forty years, a succession of bishops and archbishops held the chancellorship, with common lawyers preponderant from 1534, many of whom had experience on the bench. All the keepers from 1496 to 1530 were senior ecclesiastics, but the first to be promoted to chancellor was John Alen in 1538, and from 1533 common lawyers captured this post too.

In addition to their work in their own courts, most of the king's judges served regularly on commissions where they were assisted by other lawyers. The latter were predominantly men who had or would later be appointed to an established legal post in the central administration or in one of the great liberties. They were most probably the 'pleaders' (*narratores*) who appear from time to time. No distinct order of serjeants-at-law developed in Ireland, but most of the pleaders, of whom two or three were apparently acting at any one time, were later promoted to the bench and must have served regularly on commissions.[10] Turner C.J.C.P., 1492-4, first appears as an assize judge in Kilkenny in 1474;[11] John Wise, chief baron 1492-4, was appointed resident justice in Kilkenny and Waterford in 1493, was commissioned to take two assizes in Kilkenny in 1499, and was described in 1508 as the king's learned councillor;[12] and James Sherlock, Wise's colleague in 1499, was also commissioner in Kilkenny in 1498 and in 1505 justice of the liberty of Tipperary.[13] In

---

[9] Statute roll, 10 Henry VII c. 6 (*Stat. Ire.*, i, 42-3). Cf. *Cal. pat. rolls Ire., Hen. VIII-Eliz., passim*. The remarks in *New hist. Ire.*, iii, 21 are in error.

[10] E.g. Memoranda rolls, 2-3 Richard III m. 17d, 15 Henry VII m. 2, 23 Henry VII mm 4, 8, 23 (P.R.O.I., RC 8/33, p. 517, 8/43, pp. 160, 212, 226, 253), 6-7 Henry VIII m. 10d (P.R.O.I., Ferguson coll., iv, f. 32), 7-8 Henry VIII m. 31d (B.L., Add Ms 4791, f. 198), 9 Henry VIII m.?, 20 Henry VIII m. 4 (P.R.O.I., Ferguson coll., iv, ff 48, 132). Cf J.H. Baker, 'The English legal profession, 1450-1550' in W. Prest (ed.), *Lawyers in early modern Europe and America* (London, 1981), pp. 18-19, 36 n. 12.

[11] *Ormond deeds, 1413-1509*, no. 239.

[12] Parliament roll, 8 Henry VII c. 10 (P.R.O.I., RC 13/9); *Rot. pat. Hib.*, p. 272 no. 16; N.L.I., D. 1893 (*Ormond deeds, 1413-1509*, no. 301 (4)).

[13] *Ormond deeds, 1413-1509*, no. 321; *Liber primus Kilkenn.*, p. 103.

the following generation, much of the work was done by Roger Beg, George Sherlock and Thomas FitzSimons who together served on general commissions in 1522 and 1523 and, excepting FitzSimons who was then king's serjeant, also in 1519. Beg appears as a pleader in 1515 and was speaker of the 1521-2 parliament, Sherlock had apparently been seneschal of the liberty of Tipperary and FitzSimons later became recorder of Dublin.[14] James White, recorder of Waterford, who also served on the 1523 commission, was commissioned to itinerate in Kilkenny, Waterford and Wexford in 1536 and appointed justice of the liberty of Wexford in 1537.[15]

Besides these professional lawyers were others, local dignitaries, chancery clerks or other local lawyers, who afforced commissions from time to time but were generally excluded from the *quorum*. In 1521 the lieutenant asked the king for a special commission of oyer and terminer to deal with pirates captured at Cork and that three bachelors of law, James Cantwell, and two denizized Irishmen, Arthur Magyn and Cormac McRoryk, be included.[16] In the general commissions of 1522 and 1523 blank spaces were left sufficient for five and nine names respectively to be added to the commission. In this way in 1522 two chancery clerks were subsequently added whose primary duties were the issue of writs and process as authorized by the general commissions. In 1532 those of the *quorum* in a general commission were assisted at different times by the bishops of Ossory and Waterford, the mayor of Waterford, and William Wise, constable of Dublin and Limerick castles.[17] The evidence is scanty but suggests that as in England there was a panel of regular justices of assize comprising the king's lawyers and up to half a dozen other professional lawyers who were regularly employed in this work, plus others who assisted in their localities.

The traditional courts

The royal courts in late medieval Ireland continued by and large to be structured on the English model. Irish-born lawyers received their training at the Inns of Court in London and the courts were regarded as subordinate to those in England; but there remained significant

---

[14]N.L.I., D. 1938, 2043, 2080, 2091 (*Ormond deeds, 1413-1509,* no. 331 (4), *1509-47,* nos. 52, 81, 89); P.R.O., E.101/248/21; Memoranda roll, 6-7 Henry VIII m. 10d (P.R.O.I., Ferguson coll., iv, , f. 32).

[15]*Cal. pat. rolls Ire., Hen. VIII-Eliz.,* p. 37; P.R.O., S.P. 65/1/2.

[16]*S.P. Hen. VIII,* ii, 76-7.

[17]*Ormond deeds, 1509-47,* nos. 177, 181.

differences between lordship and kingdom. These differences were normally procedural rather than based on points of substantive law, and frequently arose out of the peculiar conditions of government in Ireland: earlier conflicts between the custom of Ireland and the law of England have left little trace in the late middle ages.

Under the Yorkists, the court of king's bench in Ireland (formerly the justiciar's bench) was considerably busier than the court of common pleas (the Dublin bench), a reversal of the position in England. Its plea rolls, recording cases at issue only, averaged three or four membranes per term as against two or three for common pleas,[18] and in addition the exchequer had, despite repeated injunctions against the hearing of common pleas there, steadily developed as a court for civil suits. By the 1460s it too was busier than common pleas, although during Edward II's reign plea membrances had disappeared as a regular feature of the exchequer memoranda rolls. They reappeared from time to time and were increasingly common on the early Tudor rolls.[19] A more reliable indication of the relative weight of business of the courts, however, is the surviving controlment roll of the estreats of Co. Meath for 1463-8. Those of king's bench for the county, made up annually, cover the first twenty-seven membranes and the thirteen terms from Easter 1465 to Trinity 1468; those of the exchequer for sixteen terms from Trinity 1464 to Easter 1468 form mm 28-49; and those of common pleas, in one continuous roll covering eleven terms between Michaelmas 1463 and Hilary 1468, constitute mm 50-54 of the roll.[20] From Hilary 1496, however, rolls of the Dublin bench average six membranes per term until the end of Henry VIII's reign, whereas during the 1540s king's bench averaged barely more than half this. Likewise in the years 1520-2 and 1534-7 the profits of king's bench amounted to £25 7s. 6d. and £11 7s. a year respectively, whereas those of common pleas were worth £58 8s. 4d. and £36 3s. 4d. per annum and those of exchequer (common pleas) averaged £53 1s. 2½d. a year in 1520-2.[21] In 1465-8, however, the

---

[18]*Rec. Comm. Ire. rep., 1816-20*, pp. 112-14; *P.R.I. rep. D.K. 28*, pp. 43-4; P.R.O.I., Delafield MSS, M. 2675, p. 127; below, p.114.

[19]Lydon, 'Menoranda rolls', p. 53; Hand, *Eng. law in Ire.*, pp. 99-103.

[20]P.R.O.I., EX 3/1, 3/2 (ultra-violet photographs of the original). The roll is badly damaged, but estreats of common pleas for some terms, especially the earlier ones, were apparently never included. The exchequer estreats of course contain a much higher proportion of crown suits. I am indebted to Dr. Philomena Connolly of the P.R.O.I. for her help with this roll.

[21]P.R.O., E. 101/248/21, S.P. 65/1/2; references in note 18. No data are available from the plea side of the exchequer for 1534-7.

sheriff of Meath had collected a total of £67 17s. 8d., or nearly £21 a year in estreats of king's bench from that county alone.[22]

There appear to be three reasons for this recovery of common pleas and for the greater prominence of king's bench under the Yorkists in comparison with its English counterpart. The differentiation of the jurisdictions of the two courts had apparently proceeded less far in Ireland, for at least two of the older personal actions, those of debt and detinue, were being pleaded in king's bench there, although restricted to common pleas in England.[23] King's bench in Ireland also continued to itinerate, but its sessions were by then confined to the Pale and in accordance with a statute of 1410 it spent each term in one location. For example, during Michaelmas 1485 the court was at Dublin, moved to Drogheda for Hilary term, was at Trim during Easter and moved back to Drogheda for Trinity.[24] Thus the court was probably able to cream off the lion's share of the civil litigation which would be attracted to the higher and more accessible court, and it had the additional advantage of a more efficient method of continuation of cases from day to day.[25] By 1520, however, when repairs to Dublin castle necessitated the finding of alternative accommodation for the central courts, king's bench was sedentary.[26] This change cannot be dated precisely, but the years 1494-6 seem most likely. In 1494, as part of his strategy of reforming the administration of justice in the lordship, Henry VII appointed three Englishmen as chancellor and chief justices.[27] And unless the efforts at reform were reflected only in a greater prolixity of the plea rolls, there followed both a redistribution

---

[22] P.R.O.I., EX 3/1, m. 27d. In addition, a total of £80 13s. 4d. was entered as 'pardoned' and a further sum was still owing.

[23] Coram Rege roll, 1 Henry VII m. [2d] (P.R.O.I., RC 8/43, pp 13-17). Cf. Marjorie Blatcher, *The court of king's bench 1450-1550 a study in self-help* (London, 1978), p. 7.

[24] Coram Rege roll, 1 Henry VII (P.R.O.I., RC 8/43, pp. 1-47; Ferguson coll., iii, ff 312-15v; B.L., Add. MS 4793, f. 149); Parliament roll, 11 Henry IV c. 20 (*Stat. Ire., John-Hen. V*, p. 526). By statute of 1467 confirming previous usage, the king or his deputy could order common pleas and the exchequer to sit where he pleased. In 1449 because of the 'ruyne and desolacon of the kinges castle of Dyevelin', common pleas was held 'at a place called Woder is lane' in the city, and in Trinity 1519 and Michaelmas 1525 at Garristown, Co. Dublin: Parliament roll, 7 & 8 Edward IV c. 19 (*Stat. Ire., Edw. IV*, i, 468); De Banco rolls, 27 Henry VI (B.L., Add. MS 4790, f. 67), Trinity 11 Henry VIII (T.C.D., MS 1731, p. 51), 17 Henry VIII (B.L., Add. MS 4784, f. 239).

[25] Cf. Margaret Hastings, *The court of common pleas in fifteenth-century England a study of legal administration and procedure* (Cornell, 1947), pp. 23-7.

[26] P.R.O. E. 101/248/21. Cf. *L. & P. Hen. VIII*, ix, no. 515, xii (ii), no. 729 (4).

[27] Ellis, 'Henry VII and Ireland', p. 243 and n. 34.

of business between king's bench and common pleas and also a significant rise in the total business of the two courts.[28]

Of course king's bench and common pleas under the early Tudors were only a shadow of what they had been two centuries before. Historians have rightly stressed the decline of English law in the lordship in the later middle ages, but for the fifteenth century the picture was not one of unrelieved gloom and the process of change was certainly more complex than has been suggested. In the first place, the well-known statement of Sir William Betham, that the plea rolls shrank in size from 60-90 membranes per term in the fourteenth century, large and well-written, to four smaller and ill-written ones under Henry VI is exaggerated and misleading. In fact, in Edward I's last years, the combined output of the justiciar's court and the Dublin bench exceeded 200 membranes a year: a century later, this figure had fallen to about 90, of which the Dublin bench produced 65. Under the Lancastrians, the size of the rolls of common pleas continued to decline (we lack figures for king's bench at this time), but they still averaged 38 membranes per year during the 1450s. Then in the 1460s, they dropped sharply to less than ten: we shall come back to the reasons for this.[29] The number of cases involving persons from the outlying counties (very often for debts contracted near Dublin) which came before the central courts had similarly been reduced to a trickle: for example in common pleas seven cases from Co. Kilkenny, Co. Wexford and Co. Waterford were pending in Michaelmas 1453, in Easter 1480 at least two actions for debt against a merchant of Kilkenny and a citizen of Waterford, and in Easter 1515 the mayor and bailiffs of Waterford were amerced in 13s. 4d. for not returning a writ directed to the bishop of Waterford and Lismore. In the exchequer two suits were pending against a Waterford merchant in 1466-7, in 1480-1 a plaint of trespass was brought by another Waterford merchant, and in 1499 a plea of debt was pending between a citizen of Waterford and a merchant of Bordeaux.[30] Nevertheless,

---

[28]Evidence concerning the estreats of the courts before and after 1494-6 supports this suggestion: P.R.O., E. 101/248, nos. 17, 21.

[29]Betham, *Const. Eng. & early parl. Ire.*, pp. 350-1; *Rec. comm. Ire. rep., 1816-20*, pp. 104-12; *P.R.I. rep. D.K. 28*, pp. 43-56; Hand, *Eng. law in Ire.*, pp. 227-8, 241-3; and, 'English law in Ireland, 1172-1351', *Northern Ireland Legal Quarterly*, xxiii (1972), 420-1.

[30]De Banco rolls, Michaelmas 32 Henry VI (P.R.O.I., Ferguson coll., iii, ff 199-203v), 19 Edward IV m. 3 (P.R.O.I., CB 1/10), 7 Henry VIII (Bodl., Rawl. MS B. 484, f. 63); Memoranda rolls, 6 Edward IV mm 17-18 (P.R.O.I., RC 8/41, pp. 107, 121), 20 Edward IV mm 8d, 10d, 13d (S.P.W., Hore MS I, p. 1137), 14 Henry VII mm 17, 21 (P.R.O.I., RC 8/43, pp. 132, 144). In Easter 1466, the archbishop of Cashel put in an attorney to answer the king for a contempt in the exchequer: Memoranda roll, 6 Edward IV m. 16 (P.R.O.I., RC 8/41, p. 98).

this development was not new – in Hilary 1414 only one case out of *c*. 120 pending in common pleas originated outside the Pale – and in the later middle ages most of this business would have been dealt with separately by the special commissions discussed below. Moreover, this was a period in which king's bench and common pleas in England were also losing business to the newer court of chancery and to the various manifestations of the king's council.[31] In Ireland, the structure of the law courts developed slightly differently: most obviously, the Irish exchequer had by the mid-fifteenth century attracted considerable business from king's bench and common pleas, although civil litigation in its English counterpart was then small.[32] Yet given the feebleness of government in the lordship, one would expect that the similar tendencies which are apparent there towards a redistribution of business from the traditional to the newer courts might be accentuated. Finally, the Irish plea rolls of the Yorkist period were made up differently both from those of an earlier date and from contemporary English rolls, in a manner which in fact conceals a recovery in the business of the two courts.

In England, the rolls of the court of common pleas averaged 500 membranes per term with perhaps 5,000 entries. However, 3,650 out of the 4,000 entries and 5,100 out of 6,000 on the rolls for the Michaelmas terms 1462 and 1482 respectively recorded merely the issue of process to get defendants into court. And on the civil side of the English king's bench, only twelve out of 958 entries on the roll of Michaelmas 1488 recorded the judgement of the court, and only four out of 499 on that of Michaelmas 1490.[33] By comparison, the Dublin bench roll for Michaelmas 1466, comprising three membranes, has only twelve entries of which eleven were of cases which had been pleaded to issue, and of these between six and eight include the court's judgement. The roll for the four terms of 19 Edward IV (1479-80), which comprises seven membranes, also includes warrants of attorney and a few other memoranda, but again between eight and ten out of 200 entries recorded the court's judgement, and there are also three recognizances enrolled in execution of judgement in separate cases of debt.[34] In neither roll, however, is the issue of mesne process recorded: apparently this began to be recorded separately under

---

[31] P.R.O.I., CB 1/5; Blatcher, *King's bench*, pp. 20-31; E.W. Ives, 'The common lawyers in Pre-Reformation England', *R. Hist. Soc. Trans.*, 5th ser., xviii (1968), 165-70.

[32] Holdsworth, *Hist. Eng. law*, iv, 255.

[33] Hastings, *Common pleas*, p. 183; Blatcher, *King's bench*, p. 59.

[34] P.R.O.I., CB 1/9, 1/10. The ending of two cases on each roll is illegible.

Edward IV – probably to save expensive parchment.[35] In contrast, on the bench roll for Trinity 1308 seven of the twenty-six membranes were of essoins, and even on the rest cases pleaded to judgement were greatly outnumbered by those merely adjourned from term to term, while in general the writing is larger and more widely spaced than on the Yorkist rolls. The roll for Hilary 1414, of fourteen membranes, is broadly similar and none of its 145 entries recorded the court's judgement.[36] And in Michaelmas 1453, when the court's business warranted only thirteen membranes for the longest term, only one of the eighty-seven cases reached judgement. One calendar only of a king's bench roll survives, covering the four terms of 1 Henry VII (1485-6). It was already defective when calendared and the remaining ten membranes dealt mainly with crown pleas, but again, no entries of mesne process are included.[37]

A second indication of the weight of business at this time is provided by the estreats of the courts. To compel appearance in court of the defendant, there were broadly speaking two procedures open to the common law. In criminal cases, process was normally by indictment before a grand jury and arrest leading to outlawry for non-appearance: in civil cases, process was by original writ sued from chancery and by distress infinite until the defendant appeared or, in theory, until his goods were exhausted; or if he had none, then by a milder form of the same arrest procedure leading again to outlawry. Both processes were cumbersome: since all actions had to be brought in the county where the cause of action arose, arrest was easily evaded by moving to another, even if the sheriff bothered to search for the defendant; and distresses were so trivial – normally 6*d*., then 12*d*., and 20*d*. – that any freeholder could afford to ignore the first two or three writs of *distringas*. In fact, the maximum distrained by the sheriff of Meath, 1463-8, and forfeited, was 5*s*., and might be so little as 2*d*., but any sum larger than 2*s*. was rare. Yet for thirteen terms,

---

[35] The first membrane of the common pleas roll for Michaelmas 1466 has a piece cut out of the bottom, about the size of a writ, and there are indications elsewhere that parchment was scarce: e.g. N.L.I., D. 2055 (*Ormond deeds, 1509-47,* no. 61: the great seal appended by a strip cut from a contemporary inquisition *post mortem*). Parchment cost 2*d*. a membrane, or between 16*s*. 8*d*. and 26*s*. 8*d*. a roll according to size: *Rec. comm. Ire. rep., 1810-15,* p. 54; B.L., Royal MS 18C, XIV, ff 38, 50. If mesne process were entered on paper (for which there is no evidence), the annual saving spread over three courts might well have been attractive, given the state of the Irish revenue.

[36] P.R.O.I., CB 1/1, 1/5; De Banco roll, Michaelmas 32 Henry VI (P.R.O.I., Ferguson coll., iii, ff 199-203v). Membrane 3d of the roll for 19 Edward IV was headed *Essonia,* but the contents in fact comprise three memoranda and a pleading: P.R.O.I., CB 1/10.

[37] Coram Rege roll, 1 Henry VII (P.R.O.I., RC 8/43, pp 1-47).

1465-8, the number of distraints in Co. Meath estreated into the exchequer as forfeited (almost all at the suit of a private party) for non-appearance in king's bench totals c. 2,600. Process was normally from term to term, even though in Michaelmas term and in king's bench especially a later day in the same term was often assigned after the defendant's non-appearance. On the other hand, some defendants appeared to answer to the first summons. This total therefore suggests an average of at least 200 cases per term pending in the court from Co. Meath by process of distress alone.[38] For eleven terms, 1463-7, the Meath forfeitures for common pleas total c. 475, or an average of at least forty-three cases per term. And despite a prohibition reimposed by parliament as recently as 1460, the estreats from the exchequer, many of them openly headed 'ad placita communia', total c. 2,300, or an average of at least 143 per term.[39] This large total no doubt explains the repeated efforts in the later middle ages to divert this business elsewhere. After the suppression of the liberty, Meath was much the largest shire in the Pale, but clearly the gentry there were every bit as litigious as those of the Home Counties. In fact, a very rough indication of the business pending in the courts in the mid-1460s can be reached by multiplying the Meath averages by two (to include distraints in other counties), and by one and a half (to include process by *capias* and outlawry). This suggests that there were then 600 civil actions per term pending in king's bench, 425 in the exchequer, and 165 in common pleas.[40] By contrast, an analysis of the common pleas in the justiciar's court during the year from January

---

[38]P.R.O.I., EX 3/1. Cf. Hastings, *Common pleas*, pp. 23-4; Blatcher, *King's bench*, p. 71. Since king's bench sat five of these terms at Kells (Mich. 1466) or Trim (thoughout 1467), it might be expected that the court would attract an unduly large proportion of Meath cases, but this is not borne out by a break-down of forfeitures for each court per term.

[39]*Ibid.;* Parliament roll, 38 Henry VI c. 12 (*Stat. Ire., Hen. VI,* pp. 666-8: this alleged that the business comprised pleas of trespass, contract, debt and account). The estreat roll in badly damaged, particularly the membranes for common pleas. To compensate, the totals for king's bench and exchequer should probably be increased by 5% and those for common pleas by about 30%. Another factor affecting the calculations is the number of defendants in an action: the available evidence suggests that in civil actions there was usually only one defendant, although separate actions were frequently commenced. Cf also Blatcher, *King's bench,* p. 70.

[40]The estreats of the courts of king's bench, common pleas and exchequer (common pleas) amounted to £263 7s. 9d. in the two years 1520-2, of which £152 1s. 10d. were for Meath, £32 13s. 5d. for Dublin, £71 6s. 2d. for Louth and £7 6s. 4d. for Drogheda: P.R.O., E. 101/248/21. If we allow £40 for Kildare which was then a liberty, those of Meath would have amounted to half the total. In Michaelmas 1462, only 14% of actions in common pleas in England proceeded by distraint: Hastings, *Common pleas,* p. 171 n. 10. In Ireland, however, the courts frequently employed distraint against yeomen, merchants and husbandmen who in England would have been arrested: P.R.O.I., EX 3/1. Process by distraint, in fact, seems to have been much the more common.

1306 has shown that there were then 326 actions and enrolments of various sorts, and in the Dublin bench in Easter 1290 a total of 263 (although judging by the length of the rolls, business in this term was exceptionally slack). And in England, king's bench, common pleas and exchequer had about 6,000,600 and perhaps 50 cases respectively pending per term in the Yorkist period.[41]

For process by *capias* and outlawry, the membranes of *attornati* on the bench roll for 19 Edward IV and a comparatively full calendar of those on the exchequer memoranda roll for 6 Edward IV, on which warrants of attorney were entered, also provide some indication of actions pending. Apparently nearly half the plaintiffs in civil cases in the English king's bench abandoned their suits after the first, unavailing writ of summons, no doubt believing that there was little point in throwing good money after bad: less than a quarter proceeded to outlawry. Before proceeding to outlawry, however, or after the defendant had appeared, when pleading began, the attorney had to enter his warrant.[42] The bench roll shows a total of 140 cases which had proceeded to outlawry or had commenced pleading during the course of that year – an average of thirty-five per term and comparable with the thirty-five warrants entered on the roll for Hilary 1414 – suggesting that about 140 cases per term were pending in the court.[43] On the memoranda roll, at least eighty-six separate civil cases and thirty-six crown cases were recorded.[44]

Reference to the kinds of actions being pleaded in the courts at this period illustrates further the reasons for the predominance of king's bench and the exchequer. About 1300, the various real actions of which, assizes apart, the court of common pleas had a monopoly had provided about three-quarters of its business.[45] In 1479-80 not a single real action appeared on the roll and the court was preoccupied

---

[41] Blatcher, *King's bench,* pp. 59, 65; Hastings, *Common pleas,* p. 183; Holdsworth, *Hist. Eng. law,* iv, 255; Hand, *Eng. law in Ire.,* pp. 238-46. For a comparison with Dr. Hand's analysis (bearing in mind the non-enrolment of mesne process), the business of common pleas in the year 1479-80 can be categorized as follows (counting each case once only): 12 at issue, 3 recognizances of debt in execution of the court's judgement, 133 further entries of warrants of attorney, 7 petitions for security of peace (on which one recognizance ensued, and one man was committed to the Marshalsea), 3 entries recording the amercement of sheriffs and a defendant, 5 miscellaneous enrolments of a royal protection under the English great seal, ordinances issued by Edward IV, two writs of error transferring cases into king's bench and the patent of the new second justice of the court; total 163.

[42] Blatcher, *King's bench,* pp. 73-4; Hastings, *Common pleas,* pp. 171-84.

[43] P.R.O.I., CB 1/5, 1/10.

[44] P.R.O.I., RC 8/41, pp. 156-300 (mm 16-19); see also n. 52 below.

[45] Hand, *Eng. law in Ire.,* pp. 97, 244-6.

almost exclusively with actions of debt and the various forms of trespass. This was probably somewhat exceptional, for examples of real actions survive by chance elsewhere: there were, for example, at least two recoveries on writs of entry *sur disseisin* in Michaelmas 1518 and three further, more cryptic references to recoveries between Hilary 1517 and Hilary 1518.[46] Nevertheless, in both Hilary 1414 and Michaelmas 1453 there had been only two real actions pending, and it would appear that already by the end of the fourteenth century litigants were turning elsewhere for a remedy. The possessory assizes likewise were much less used.[47]

Of the 148 actions which can be traced on the roll of 1479-80, eighty-eight were for debt, forty-two for trespass, three for detinue, one for account and three for error. The preponderance of actions for debt was even greater in Michaelmas 1453, exceeding three-quarters of the total.[48] No doubt many of the suits for trespass concealed disputes about title to land (including three on which judgement was given in 1479-80), but a plea determined about Michaelmas 1480, in which the plaintiffs recovered £5 10s. 7d. because the defendant had entered and occupied thirty acres of land from 1470 to 1479, indicates that this action could not as yet be used to recover possession of land, although lawyers in England were beginning to think the contrary.[49] In 1502, however, a suit in the exchequer (which had no jurisdiction in real actions) for lands in Rathmore, Co. Kildare suggests that this development had by then been applied in Ireland.[50] It can hardly have helped common pleas vis-à-vis the other courts, although the substitution of a speedier action no doubt benefited the operation of the common

---

[46] *Alen's reg.*, p. 264; *Christ Church deeds*, no. 407; *Cal. pat. rolls Ire., Hen. VIII-Eliz.*, p. 53; De Banco roll, 9 Henry VIII (Gen. Off., MS 192, p. 402). Incidentally, the limit of legal memory in Ireland at this time ('a principio conquesti Hibernie' in the fourteenth century) was the first crossing of Henry III to Gascony (1230), or rather later than 1189 as current in England until 1540: *Alen's reg.*, p. 264; Hand, *Eng. law in Ire.*, pp. 115, 176; C.R. Cheney (ed.), *Handbook of dates for students of English history* (London, 1970), p. 65.

[47] Seven examples only have been found for this period: *Ormond deeds, 1413-1509*, nos. 239, 332 (novel disseisin, 1474, 1508); B.L., Cotton MSS, Titus B. XI (II), f. 280 (novel disseisin, 1485); *Rot. pat. Hib.*, p. 272 no. 16 (novel disseisin, 1499 – two); T.C.D., MS 594, f. 7. (novel disseisin, 1510-11); *L. & P. Hen. VIII*, xii (ii), no. 763 (order of 1537 to try assize of ?mort d'ancestor before commissioners to secure a fair trial). Cf. Memoranda roll, 6 & 7 Henry VIII m. ? (P.R.O.I., Ferguson coll., iv, f. 1); *Christ Church deeds*, no. 388.

[48] P.R.O.I., CB 1/5, 1/10, Ferguson coll., iii, ff 199-203v. Because of the roll's condition, the remaining eleven actions in 1479-80 are illegible.

[49] *Christ Church deeds*, no. 1029; F.W. Maitland, *The forms of action at common law* (ed. Cambridge, 1965), pp. 56-9.

[50] *Christ Church deeds*, no. 375.

law in general. In part, however, the answer to this problem probably lies in the development of the newer courts which certainly entertained real actions at this time. Moreover, private arbitration was a better remedy concerning disputed title if the parties were willing to settle, and was clearly popular in this period in Ireland as in England. The courts were prepared to enforce any agreement reached, but a recent study of Star Chamber has suggested that even this court was no more successful than the traditional courts in the face of obstruction.[51]

In fact, king's bench, common pleas and the exchequer were largely competing for the same business in the late medieval period. Evidence from warrants of attorney on the king's bench roll of 1485-6 and on the exchequer memoranda rolls confirms that actions of debt and trespass were the staple diet of the common law courts.[52] As in England, there are clear indications of this rivalry on the rolls, and it seems that the overall decline of the common law from *c*. 1300 together with its slightly different evolution in the lordship had combined to precipitate competition between the courts which in England grew fierce only in the Tudor period. For example, a statute of 1449 condemned the practice of suing writs of privilege from the central courts to transfer cases from liberty and lesser courts on the pretence that defendants were officers of the central courts or their servants.[53] Evidently common pleas was having much the worst of this struggle for business. Pleadings on the memoranda rolls show that the development of the writ of *quo minus* formed the basis for successful competition by the exchequer.[54] Its principal advantages as against the writs available to common pleas were procedural, plus the fact that in the older personal actions of debt, detinue and account compurgation was still occasionally allowed in common pleas.[55]

---

[51] Guy, *Cardinal's court,* pp. 56-7; *Christ Church deeds,* nos. 401, 405, 426, 436, 1055, 1130.

[52] Coram Rege roll, 1 Henry VII, Memoranda rolls, 6 Edward IV mm 16-19, 2 Richard III, 9, 14, 15, 23, 24 Henry VII (P.R.O.I., RC 8/41, pp. 96-130, RC 8/33, pp. 391-551, RC 8/43, pp. 1-299). In 1466-7 82 of 86 warrants in civil suits related to debt. The number of warrants of attorney entered on the memoranda rolls was more usually small, up to 25 for three terms from Michaelmas 1508. Apart from stray entries, however, membranes of *attornati* must normally have been bound separately along with the bulk of the plea membranes.

[53] Parliament, 28 Henry VI c. 9 (*Stat. Ire., Hen. VI,* pp. 172-4). Cf. Parliament roll, 38 Henry VI c. 12 (*Ibid.,* pp. 666-8).

[54] See especially, Memoranda rolls, 6 Edward IV m. 19 (P.R.O.I., RC 8/41, pp. 131-6), 15 Henry VIII m. 19d, 24 Henry VIII m. 18 (*ibid.,* Ferguson coll., iv., ff 76-7, 169).

[55] Holdsworth, *Hist. Eng. law,* i, 239-40, 305-8. No examples are known of compurgation in civil suits in Ireland at this time, but by privilege granted in 1475 freemen of Dublin were to be so admitted in appeals of felony and treason: Parliament roll, 15 & 16 Edward IV c. 54 (*Stat. Ire., Edw. IV,* ii, 376). Cf. J.G. Bellamy, *Crime*

Similarly, there are signs that king's bench was already employing a legal fiction analogous to the well-known process by bill of Middlesex and *latitat* developed by its English counterpart.[56] In the early fourteenth century, procedure by bill in the justiciar's court had been more widespread than in the contemporary English king's bench, and although in England it never quite died out it ceased to be regularly available under the Lancastrians as the court ceased to be peripatetic. The continued use in the Tudor period of the special heading, *placita querelarum,* which was peculiar to the Irish court, together with the comparatively greater weight of business there at this time, strongly suggests that this difference survived.[57] And a plaint of debt in Hilary 1486 indicates that this process, already cheaper and more convenient since it obviated the need to purchase an original writ, had developed further: the action arose 'infra ffraunches. de Drogheda', but because the defendant was supposedly 'in custodia marescalli capitalis placee Hibernie existenti', the court had jurisdiction in the suit. Despite this, however, the case was adjourned.[58]

Against the advantages of litigation in king's bench or the exchequer, common pleas had very little to offer. It had begun by 1466 to entertain suits for debt of less than 40s., but these were accepted in the rival courts too.[59] Quite possibly it was behind the fruitless attempt of 1460 to end the use of the exchequer for civil suits, and pressure from this quarter was no doubt an influential factor in the reorganization of 1494-6. Nevertheless, in the Yorkist period the court developed at least one rather dubious legal fiction, condemned by statute in 1449, in its efforts to compete. In nearly all the pleadings on the two surviving rolls, the plaintiff was stated to be a servant (or in one case the chaplain) of the chief justice. In the roll of 1479-80, the only exceptions were a bill of trespass exhibited against a man already in the marshal's custody and a suit for debt by a clerk of the court.

and public order in England in the later middle ages (London, 1973), pp. 142-4; Parliament rolls, 5 Edward IV c. 37, 16 & 17 Edward IV c. 28 (*Stat. Ire., Edw. IV,* i, 364-8, ii, 500-2: archbishop of Dublin admitted to compurgation upon indictments for treason and felony).

[56]Cf. Blatcher, *King's bench,* ch. 7.

[57]*Rec. comm. Ire. rep., 1816-20,* pp. 104-5, 115; Coram Rege roll, 1 Henry VII m. 7 (P.R.O.I., RC 8/43, p. 34); Hand, *Eng. law in Ire.,* pp. 67-79; G.O. Sayles (ed.), *Select cases in the court of king's bench under Richard II, Henry IV and Henry V,* vii (Selden Soc., vol. lxxxviii, 1971), pp. 109, 140, 165, 186, 200, 205.

[58]Coram Rege roll, 1 Henry VII mm 7-7d (P.R.O.I., RC 8/43, p. 34). Cf. Parliament roll, 12 & 13 Edward IV c. 23 (*Stat. Ire., Edw. Iv,* ii, 48-50).

[59]E.g. Parliament roll, 1 Richard III c. 16 (P.R.O.I., RC 13/8); Memoranda rolls, 6 Edward IV m. 19, 23 Henry VII m. 2 (P.R.O.I., RC 8/41, pp. 131-6, RC 8/43, pp. 207-8).

These cases were normal exceptions to the rule that actions should commence by original writ, the only peculiarity being that in the latter case, despite plaintiff's privilege, process against the defendant was still by distraint and not, as in England, by arrest.[60] Clearly the status of servant was temporarily conferred so as to offer a speedier and cheaper remedy which could rival those available in king's bench or the exchequer.

On the crown side, a comparison between the English and Irish courts of king's bench is hampered by the insufficiencies of the only calendar available of an Irish roll which was itself then defective. The workings of the two courts were, however, in some respects dissimilar. Within the Pale, king's bench continued regularly to exercise ordinary criminal jurisdiction in the county in which it was then sitting, and statutes of 1472-3 and 1475 further empowered it to terminate at Drogheda indictments for crimes committed both in Meath and Louth.[61] These powers seem by 1485-6 to have been enlarged, for cases arising in Meath, Louth and Dublin were all tried at the same sessions, and there is no evidence that they were cases which had been referred by an inferior court. Thus the court's ordinary criminal jurisdiction was considerably more extensive than that of king's bench in England. In Michaelmas 1485 and Easter and Trinity terms 1486, four, five and sixteen cases respectively went before a jury, a comparatively large number by English standards. All involved felonies except one case of treason (a breach of an Irish statute of Provisors) and a case in which the servant of an underserjeant had been assaulted and imprisoned when he tried to make an arrest on a plea of debt, and all but four offences had been committed within the previous four years. Procedure was by indictment, except for three appeals, and all the defendants were acquitted, the usual outcome of trials in England at this date too.[62] Two of the cases illustrate one of the court's more important duties, the enforcement of new statute law. In addition, a total of thirty-two, twenty and twenty-three persons in each term found mainprise for their future appearance to answer (unspecified) offences of which they had been indicted, and in Michaelmas term six persons made fine in small sums ranging from

---

[60]Parliament rolls, 28 Henry VI c. 9, 3 Edward IV c. 89 (*Stat. Ire., Edw. IV* i, 218-20); Hastings, *Common pleas,* p. 17. Cf Baker, 'English legal profession', p. 22.

[66]Parliament rolls, 12 & 13 Edward IV c. 23, 15 & 16 Edward IV c. 36 (*Stat. Ire., Edw. IV* ii, 48-50, 338).

[62]Viz. larceny 18 cases, harbouring felons two, homicide one, attempted homicide one, breach of statute concerning fishing one. Cf. Blatcher, *King's bench,* ch. 4; C. Ross, *Edward IV* (London, 1974), pp. 388-9; Bellamy, *Crime and public order,* pp. 157-8.

6*d*. to 3*s*. 4*d*. to avoid standing trial for lesser offences.⁶³ The entries of fines for other terms seem to be missing – warrants of attorney, likewise, appear only for Michaelmas (twenty entries) and Trinity (one) – and again there are no entries of mesne process. Altogether the court was in a position to proceed in thirty-nine cases in Michaelmas 1485 and in sixty-six cases for the three terms, but others must have been at an earlier stage of process. These figures hardly suggest that the criminal law was well enforced, but they are reasonably comparable with evidence from some of the supposedly more peaceful English counties. Likewise, in the justiciar's bench in four terms, 1306-7, of ninety-six cases pending, the death sentence was pronounced in four of them.⁶⁴

In general, the criminal law was far from being a dead letter, but breaches were punished principally through the purse. Perhaps in Ireland offenders sometimes resorted to bribing the jury as an alternative to purchasing a pardon; certainly juries were particularly amenable to outside influences. Alongside the crop of malicious indictments which were quashed in parliament may be placed Lord Chancellor Gerrard's report that

> if a fellonye were committed, the partie comonlye in a piece of paper delivered to the justice the name of the fellone, the goodes stollen, the daye, tyme and place, written in Englishe, and that then the justice used to examin the witnesses uppon the proufe, and after subscribe his name under that paper and deliver this to the jurye, and that without more enquirie the jurye wold then wryte *billa vera;* so as the justice and not the jurye ever indicted the fellon.⁶⁵

Juries were of course more willing to bring in guilty verdicts for non-capital offences – this is clear from the number of king's bench defendants electing to make fine rather than stand trial for trespass in Michaelmas 1485.⁶⁶ Nevertheless, felons and traitors were executed from time to time, and the governor's prerogative of pardon was clearly an essential instrument in the administration of the lordship, as well as being a useful source of revenue.⁶⁷ Even the surviving extracts

---

⁶³P.R.O.I., RC 8/43, pp 1-47, Ferguson coll., iii, ff 312-15v. Cf. Blatcher, *King's bench,* pp. 53-4: in Michaelmas 1488, 27 defendants made fine in the English court, but the fines were usually rather larger.

⁶⁴Hand, *Eng. law in Ire.,* pp. 235-7.

⁶⁵*Anal. Hib.,* ii, 114.

⁶⁶Cf. Bellamy, *Crime and public order,* pp. 151-9.

⁶⁷See especially, S.G. Ellis, 'Henry VIII, rebellion and the rule of law', *Hist. Jn.,* xxiv (1981), 513-31. Cf. Otway-Ruthven, *Med. Ire.,* p. 146.

from patent rolls, scanty as they are, include a substantial number of pardons enrolled, and not only for Palesmen: pardons for merchants of Cork, Galway and Waterford, a miller and a butcher of Limerick, the archdeacon of Cork, the abbess of Kilculliheen, Co. Waterford and men of Co. Carlow, Co. Kilkenny and the liberty of Wexford were among those enrolled, despite the fact that commissioners visiting these districts were normally empowered to grant pardons under their own seals.[68] There were complaints that those 'indytede of felonies and treison, yf they be pore wrachys not havyng landes ne goodes ne frendes, then shall they have the extremetyss of justice', whereas richer men had their pardons, 'so as there ys noun ensample yeven of amendment by the execution of anye grete man'.[69] In fact by no means all the indictments reviewed by parliament were malicious, some petitioners were pardoned for good service, and others were required to sue their pardons under the great seal, malicious indictment notwithstanding.[70] Normally, however, pardons of treasons and felonies might be purchased for a fine of between 6s. 8d. and 20s., although this was sometimes remitted; but in addition the clerks might charge 2s. and 6s. respectively for writing the fiant and the actual pardon, the fee for the great seal was 20s., and the offender had then to appear in king's bench in person and pay the clerk of the crown there 12d. to have the pardon allowed.[71]

Even great men were unlikely to throw this sort of money away on unnecessary pardons. Clearly they were bought only because, inefficient as the operation of the law was, there was a fair chance that otherwise criminals might be brought to book.

Though principally a court of audit, the upper exchequer exercised a largely parallel jurisdiction with king's bench in the enforcement of the king's rights, particularly, as in England, with the enforcement of penal law. It proceeded upon information laid before the barons, by the king's ministers and others, and also by inquisition. Normal practice was to summon juries up to Dublin and to charge them to answer questions concerning the king's rights.[72] In this way, the courts

---

[68]*Rot. pat. Hib.*, pp. 270-3; *Cal. pat. rolls Ire., Hen. VIII-Eliz.*, pp. 1-10; see also below, p. 136.

[69]*S.P. Hen. VIII*, ii, 192. Cf. *ibid.*, ii, 116.

[70]E.g. Parliament roll, 19 & 20 Edward IV cc 13, 44 (*Stat. Ire., Edw. IV*, ii, 716-18, 796-800).

[71]*Ibid., Cal. pat. rolls Ire., Hen. VIII-Eliz.*, pp. 41-3; *Fiants Ire., Hen. VIII*, nos 286, 301; Statute roll, 28 & 29 Henry VIII c. 20 (P.R.O.I., CH 1/1); *Registrum Johannis Mey*, no. 360. Cf. Blatcher, *King's bench*, p. 84.

[72]E.g. Memoranda rolls, 14 Henry VII m. 24, 15 Henry VII mm 5, 7d (P.R.O.I., RC 8/43, pp. 144-5, 168-70, 173-4); Exch. Inq., Co. Dublin (P.R.O.I., RC 9/3, ii, 69, iii,

could also keep an eye on local officials. The deputy was however empowered by a statute of 1467 to remove the exchequer and common pleas from Dublin as he pleased, although outside Dublin such work was more normally done by commissions under the great or exchequer seals. Exchequer itinerations finally ceased *c.* 1534,[73] but *c.* 1511 a sheriff of Meath noted that 'their is but fowre placis by the statute þ^t the exchekour may sit in mey3th þ^t shall take effect, that is to saye, Dwleke, Scrine and Nowane & Kenlis', and at least twice under Henry VIII the barons sat at Drogheda, in 1514 and 1528.[74] During FitzEustace's treasurership down to 1492 a few patents attested by him under the exchequer seal were at places outside Dublin.[75] Whether this implies that the whole court was on the move or merely that the treasurer was attending to his duties outside the city and had sent a warrant to the chancellor of the exchequer to seal such letters is obscure, for there is no evidence about the diplomatic of the exchequer seal in this period.[76]

More commonly, the escheator would be commissioned to take the necessary inquisitions and proceedings would be initiated on their return. The Record Commissioners' calendars suggest that such inquisitions normally related to one or two items of business, but in the later 1530s the exchequer was clearly stretched to extract the maximum profit from the lands of traitors, dissolved monasteries and those resumed from absentees. At the same time, the new English administrators were trying to do the same with the king's prerogative rights. Thus in county after county, juries were asked the same questions about lands in the king's hands in a bid to discover their full extent and value, and the inquisitions at times read almost like jury presentments. For example, an inquisition by the escheator of Meath late in 1535 concerned the lands of Kildare and another rebel, the circumstances of the death of two tenants-in-chief, a breach of the Statute of Absentees and three breaches of an otherwise unknown statute of 22 Henry VI (1443-4) requiring clerks to be resident in their benefices.[77]

7-11), Exch. Inq., Co. Meath (*ibid.,* RC 9/8, iii, 23, 28, 41, 45); L.P. Murray (ed.), 'A calendar of the register of Primate George Dowdall', *Louth Arch. Soc. Jn.,* vii (1929-32), 270.

[73]E.g. Memoranda roll, 11 Edward IV m. 23 (P.R.O.I., Ferguson coll., iii, f. 230); Exch. Inq., Co. Meath (P.R.O.I., RC 9/8, iii, 52, 55, 59).

[74]T.C.D., MS 594, f. 32; Memoranda rolls, 4-5 Henry VIII m. 34, 20 Henry VIII m. 19 (P.R.O.I., Ferguson coll., iv, ff 20, 139).

[75]E.g. Memoranda rolls, 2 Henry VII m. 6 (B.L., Add. MS 4793, f. 149v), 6-7 Henry VII m. 3 (R.I.A., MS 24 H 17, p. 223).

[76]Cf. Memoranda roll, 2 Richard III m. 9d (P.R.O.I., RC 8/33, pp. 411-12).

[77]Exch. Inq., Co. Meath (P.R.O.I., RC 9/8, i, 110-21).

Process by the exchequer upon informations, inquisitions or their own work was normally recorded under the heading *communia* on the late medieval memoranda rolls, although the older heading, *placita dominum regem tangencia* was occasionally substituted.[78] The membranes of *attornati* calendared from the roll for 6 Edward IV (1466-7) suggest that the exchequer dealt with at least thirty-six cases per annum properly relating to the king, but that common pleas by writ of *quo minus* were much more numerous.[79] Unfortunately, however, the remembrancers apparently enrolled proceedings on crown cases somewhat erratically, usually only when they reached judgement: the calendar of five rolls from the middle of the period, those for 1484-5, 1493-4, 1498-9, 1499-1500 and 1507-8, suggests that twenty-one cases were recorded at least as far as the defendant's appearance, plus memoranda of information laid in eight more cases. These twenty-nine cases, therefore, were not the full total for five years and probably also reflect to some degree the eccentricities of the calendaring which cannot be checked on this point. They do, however, give some indication not otherwise available of the range and relative frequency of proceedings in the exchequer and can be supplemented from other memoranda roll extracts and calendars of the period. Seventeen of the twenty-nine cases were commenced by information laid, eight by the king's attorney and the remainder mostly by accountants or the king's serjeant. Ten of them concerned intrusions onto lands in the king's hand or other infringements of the king's seigneurial rights. Very often the heir of a deceased tenant-in-chief was exonerated after exhibiting a grant of livery, although occasionally he was forced to purchase a pardon of intrusion.[80] The king's bench roll for 1485-6 also included one long pleading arising out of a suit for livery of lands in the king's hands.[81] Some military tenants evaded the exchequer's efforts by enfeoffments to use but as a deliberate attempt to avoid feudal incidents this device was seemingly not widely employed before the 1530s, and in 1466 the crown had apparently lost three test cases after a feoffee had intruded upon lands farmed by the treasurer on the death of a tenant-in-chief.[82] One tenant summoned to do homage and fealty in Mary's reign on the basis of an early-fifteenth-century roll of knights fees replied that he held in common socage, and another summoned

---

[78]E.g. Memoranda roll, 23 Henry VII m. 5 (P.R.O.I., RC 8/43, pp. 213-14).

[79]P.R.O.I., RC 8/41, pp. 156-300 (mm 16-19).

[80]Memoranda rolls, 7-9 Edward IV m. 15 (P.R.O.I., Ferguson coll., iii, f. 226v), 7-8 Henry VIII m. 29 (P.R.O.I., Ferguson repertory, iv, 130-31; B.L., Add. MS 4791, ff 197v-8; R.I.A., MS 24 H 17, p. 243).

[81]Coram Rege roll, 1 Henry VII mm 8-9d (P.R.O.I., RC 8/43, pp. 35-43).

[82]Memoranda roll, 6 Edward IV m. 8 (P.R.O.I., RC 8/41, pp. 40-51).

on the basis of an inquisition of 1536 queried whether he was bound to do so outside Ireland since the king and queen were not present there:[83] generally the exchequer had neither the time nor the manpower to pry so deeply into past sins before 1534, although in 1496-7 when the court demanded arrears of 6s. 8d. per annum for lands found by inquisition of 1461 to have been alienated without licence in 1452, the tenant managed to obtain a writ of *supersedeas*.[84]

Alienations without licence contributed only one case in the sample, for which the tenant pleaded a pardon, but it was evidently a common offence: a fine of £80 made for pardon of an alienation discovered in 1495 suggests that contemporary English practice applied in calculating fines payable for licences and pardons.[85] There were also occasional proceedings against widows of tenants-in-chief who remarried without licence: in one case detected by inquisition before the barons in 1531-2 and pleaded in Easter term 1533, the widow and her third husband pleaded a pardon which had been purchased in the interim.[86] The deforcement of collectors of subsidies and customs was a frequent offence (five cases in the sample): even under Edward IV the exchequer proceeded against deforciants of subsidy collectors as a contempt of the king, although subsidies were until 1494 granted to the governor, and commonly an exemption by act of parliament was pleaded.[87]

Strangely, only one case relating to the customs occurs in the sample, in which the defendant was driven to purchase a pardon for his deforcement,[88] but other evidence suggests that the exchequer was particularly keen to enforce the king's rights concerning customs, especially under Poynings when a total of £15 9s. was entered in the journal as accruing from customs offences.[89] In 1480 a merchant

---

[83]Memoranda rolls, 1-2 Philip & Mary m. 22, 2-3 Philip & Mary m. 16 (P.R.O.I., Ferguson coll., v, ff 10, 26).

[84]Memoranda roll, 12 Henry VII mm 2, 40-0d (S.P.W., Hore MS I, pp. 1148-50).

[85]Memoranda rolls, 15 Henry VII m. 19 (P.R.O.I., RC 8/43, pp. 190-1), 19 Henry VII mm 5, 22, 24 Henry VII m. 7 (P.R.O.I., Ferguson repertory, iv, 60, 70-71, 77), 4-5 Henry VIII m. 34 (P.R.O.I., Ferguson coll., iv, f. 20); B.L., Royal MS 18C, XIV, f. 45; *L. & P. Hen. VIII*, xii (ii), no. 963; *Rot. pat. Hib.*, p. 272b no. 8. Cf. Bean, *Decline of English feudalism*, p. 101 n. 1.

[86]Memoranda roll, 25 Henry VIII m. 9 (P.R.O.I., Ferguson coll., iv, f. 176). Cf. Memoranda roll, 4-5 Henry VIII m. 38 (*ibid.*, iv, f. 21).

[87]E.g. Memoranda rolls, 11 Edward IV m. 14 (S.P.W., Hore MS I, pp. 1113-27), 2 Richard III m. 18, 14 Henry VII m. 7 (P.R.O.I., RC 8/33, pp. 517-18, RC 8/43, pp. 106-11).

[88]Memoranda roll, 23 Henry VII m. 15 (P.R.O.I., RC 8/43, pp. 242-3).

[89]See esp., *L. & P. Ric. III & Hen. VII,* ii, 68-9.

forfeited goods worth £80 for refusing to pay poundage on them.[90] Usually the offence was concealment of dutiable goods,[91] but it sometimes concerned the export of prohibited goods, such as horses in contravention of a statute of Poynings's parliament, or wool forbidden by an act of Surrey's parliament.[92] In 1527 a number of Dublin merchants were presented for exporting wool: this apparently led to a test case in which one merchant pleaded not guilty but was found guilty and eventually fined after the court had taken time to be advised about the case. Subsequently process issued against another merchant on the same charge, but he produced a pardon dated 11 January 1528 granted to the whole city.[93] Probably a less usual offence concerned a customer who kept a tavern contrary to an English statute of 20 Henry VI: he likewise was forced to buy a pardon.[94] And in 1478 when distraining for rent, the treasurer was threatened: 'quam cito hoc fecerit, tam cito decapitus erit'.[95]

In regulating imports into the lordship, the exchequer frequently proceeded against merchants who failed to comply with the 1472 Statute of Archers which required them to bring longbows to the value of 100s. for every £100 worth of merchandise imported from England: four merchants made fines of 20d. each in Easter 1508 for this offence.[96] The statute was also enrolled on the king's bench roll for 13 Edward IV (1473-4).[97] And with regard to internal trade, the commonest offences were forms of regrating the market or making excessive profits, such as buying a cow for 10s. and selling the four tanned hides from it at between 2s. 8d. and 3s. 4d. each, for which fines of 20d. and 40d. were made.[98] Much less usual were the

[90] Memoranda roll, 20 Edward IV m. 10 (P.R.O.I., Ferguson coll., iii, ff 298, 301).

[91] E.g. Memoranda rolls, 11-12 Henry VIII m. 19 (fined £7), 19 Henry VIII m. 16d, 36 Henry VIII no. 1 m. 69 (P.R.O.I., Ferguson coll., iv, ff 60, 126, 304; R.I.A., MS 24 H 17, p. 251).

[92] Memoranda rolls, 8-9 Henry VIII m. 8, 20 Henry VIII m. 19, 24 Henry VIII m. 10 (P.R.O.I., Ferguson coll., iv, ff 39, 139, 167).

[93] Memoranda roll, 19 Henry VIII mm 21, 22 (P.R.O.I., Ferguson coll., iv, f. 129).

[94] Memoranda roll, 17 Henry VIII m. 19 (P.R.O.I., Ferguson coll., iv, f. 106).

[95] Memoranda roll, 18 Edward IV m. 26 (P.R.O.I., Ferguson coll., iii, f. 221v).

[96] Memoranda roll, 23 Henry VII m. 17 (P.R.O.I., RC 8/43, pp. 245-6); Parliament roll, 12 & 13 Edward IV c. 45 (*Stat. Ire., Edw. IV,* ii, 98-100). Cf. Memoranda roll, 19 Henry VIII m. 16d (P.R.O.I., Ferguson coll., iv, f. 126).

[97] Coram Rege roll, 13 Edward IV (T.C.D., MS 1731, p. 6). Cf. Parliament roll, 12 & 13 Edward IV c. 45 (*Stat. Ire., Edw. IV.,* ii, 98-100). This and the ordinances in note 41 above do not accord with claims that chancery clerks did not communicate to the courts such statutes as they were required to enforce: cf. Richardson & Sayles, *Ir. parl. in middle ages,* p. 224.

[98] Five fines were made for this offence in Hilary 1499, fourteen for not carrying bows

proceedings against the former provost of Athboy in 1507-8 for levying 'throwtoll' or 'thorrogh toll' without authority from those passing through the town, an offence also presented against the constables of Leighlinbridge and Athy in 1537,[99] though the exchequer periodically required accounts from inland towns of the Pale which had been granted customs for expenditure on murage and pavage, from Navan in 1466, Fore in 1470 and Kells in 1523.[100]

Proceedings on the Statute of Absentees were also common. An interesting case pleaded in 1524 concerned the rector of Wicklow found by inquisition to have been absent without licence for 3½ years to 1520. He pleaded that one William O'Byrne, clerk, a rebel, had entered and taken all the profits until 1518 but that thereafter he had provided an acceptable substitute as required by law. The court reserved judgement and unfortunately the outcome is unknown.[101] Breaches of most other statutes seem only rarely to have been detected. Process was made in 1467 on a statute of 1456 imposing a duty of 40d. per pound of silver exported, in 1486 on a disseisin by main force contrary to an otherwise unknown statute of 11 Henry IV (1409-10), and in 1508 on a similar case probably under the same statute.[102] These cases, however, warn against accepting too readily reiterated complaints that 'the law and statutes made in this lond are not observed ne kept after the making of theme eight days'.[103] Rivalry between the common law and church courts also generated business for the exchequer, although king's bench and general commissions beyond the Pale were also active in defence of the common law. In 1466, for example, the archbishop of Dublin's ordinary made fine for contempt in ignoring a writ of prohibition against proceedings in his court, and the precentor of St. Patrick's was similarly fined for

---

and ten for breaches of a statute regulating the sale of tanned hides: Memoranda roll, 14 Henry VII mm 8-9 (P.R.O.I., RC 8/43, pp. 111-18). Cf. Memoranda roll, 17-18 Henry VIII m. 19 (P.R.O.I., Ferguson coll., iv, f. 112).

[99]Memoranda roll, 23 Henry VII m. ? (P.R.O.I., Ferguson coll., iii, f. 364); Hore & Graves, *Southern & eastern counties*, p. 131.

[100]Memoranda rolls, 6 Edward IV mm 22, 26, 10 Edward IV m. ?, 15 Henry VIII m. ? (P.R.O.I., RC 8/41, pp. 151, 169; Ferguson coll., iii, f. 253, iv, note on slip bound between ff 77-8).

[101]Memoranda roll, 15 Henry VIII m. 11 (P.R.O.I., Ferguson coll., iv, ff 80-2).

[102]Memoranda rolls, 7 Edward IV pt. i m. 2 (P.R.O.I., Ferguson coll., iii, f. 225), 1 Henry VII m. 23d (R.I.A., MS 24 H 17, 221-3), 23 Henry VII m. 15 (P.R.O.I., RC 8/43, pp 242-3).

[103]Finglas C.B., *c.* 1528, in Walter Harris (ed.), *Hibernica: or some ancient pieces relating to Ireland* (Dublin, 1777), p.99. Cf. Richardson & Sayles, *Ir. parl. in middle ages*, pp. 224-6.

assaulting and detaining the king's messenger who delivered a writ of prohibition.[104]

The other cases frequently pleaded concerned the account (three cases in the sample), and statutes concerning the Gaelic Irish (six cases) which were also enforced in king's bench.[105] Inquisitions frequently presented 'quod Willelmus Obeghan, clericus, Hibernicus [est], de Hibernice sanguine & nacione, videlicet de lez Obeghnez, Hibernicis inimicis dicti domini regis'.[106] If, as was usually the case, the Irishman had been presented to an ecclesiastical benefice within the Pale, the jury would be asked the value of the benefice (normally it was small, often under £5 a year) and who had presented and inducted him. The incumbent would then be distrained to show cause why the temporalities should not be taken into the king's hand. Cases concerning laymen holding land in freehold occasionally occur, and it appears that the exchequer was especially interested in Irishmen in positions of some status, for though grants of English liberty to Irish merchants and traders were frequently enrolled on the memoranda rolls,[107] proceedings against them are rare. Exceptionally lands might be forfeit to the crown, such as those in Swords worth 10s., granted in 1458 to William Obelan, clerk, discovered by inquisition in 1471,[108] but in the vast majority of cases the defendant had previously armed himself with a charter of English liberty and freedom from Irish servitude, and often such charters were of long standing.[109] An alternative plea was that the defendant was an Englishman: in one case the prior of St. John's, Kells, protested 'quod suum nomen baptismi est Cornelius McGilduff & non Cowconnagh prout suppositum

---

[104]Memoranda roll, 6 Edward IV mm 10, 21d-22 (P.R.O.I., RC 8/41, pp. 59, 148-9); see also below, ch.5.

[105]E.g. Memoranda roll, 3 Henry VIII m. 9 (P.R.O.I., Ferguson coll., iv, ff 9-10): enrolment of exemplification of proceedings on information by the king's serjeant in king's bench, 1506, against Thomas Ryan of Dunboyne, husbandman, in possession of land without the king's licence. A jury found that he was an Englishman.

[106]Memoranda roll, 12 Henry VII m. ? (P.R.O.I., Ferguson coll., iii, f. 345). The formula is strikingly similar to that employed of Welshmen in the marcher lordships of Wales, but Welsh law was accorded some official standing in the courts of the lordship, unlike Gaelic law, and the privileges of Englishmen vis-à-vis the native population were less extensive: see R.R. Davies, 'The twilight of Welsh law, 1284-1536', *History*, li (1966), 143-64.

[107]E.g. Memoranda rolls, 14 Henry VII m. 10, 24 Henry VII m. 8 (P.R.O.I., RC 8/43, pp. 119, 281).

[108]Memoranda roll, 2 Richard III m. 17 (P.R.O.I., RC 8/33, pp. 515-17). Cf. B.L., Royal MS 18C, XIV, f. 119.

[109]E.g. Memoranda rolls, 14 Henry VII m. 24 (pleaded charter of 1423), 15 Henry VII m. 28 (pleaded charter of 1456) (P.R.O.I., RC 8/43, pp. 144-5, 200-1).

est per dictam inquisicionem' and pleaded that he was presented on 3 July 1522, not on 10 September 1520 as was stated, that 'Patrick McGilduff alias Duff de ffygarth, husbandman' and his issue had been granted English liberty by charter of 25 May 1522, and that he was Patrick's son.[110] Evidently for those Irish with property the threat of forfeiture or a large fine was normally too great in comparison with the much lesser fine – usually between 6s. 8d. and £1 –[111] for a charter of denization which also covered the petitioner's descendants.

Closely related were the proceedings sometimes initiated for marrying an Irish wife or husband,[112] though again the purchase of a charter was usually preferred to buying a pardon later.[113] In the Pale, therefore, and at least fitfully in the Ormond lordship and Co. Wexford,[114] the legislation against Irishmen continued to be enforced, but charters of English liberty were easily purchased. In Meath in the mid-1460s, ten per cent of plaintiffs in the central courts, eight per cent of defendants and a much higher proportion of the jurors had recognizably Gaelic names and were clearly substantial peasants, husbandmen and yeomen, who could afford the costs of denization and litigation as well as being sufficiently anglicized to use the king's courts.[115] On the other hand, there is a marked absence of evidence which would suggest continuing large-scale emigration from the Pale into England as in the Lancastrian period – only one fine in Michaelmas 1476 for carrying two labourers from Malahide port and a few unsupported complaints in the state papers from the 1520s.[116] The Dublin administration continued to enforce the Statute of Absentees of course, and licences of absence frequently occur in the records,[117] but these cases all concerned men of substance, not the

---

[110]Memoranda roll, 17 Henry no. 1 m. 10 (P.R.O.I., Ferguson coll., iv, f. 105). Cf. Memoranda rolls, 23 Henry VII m. 5 (P.R.O.I., RC 8/43 pp. 213-14), 28 Henry VIII m. 14, 30 Henry VIII m. 7 (P.R.O.I., Ferguson repertory, iv, 146).

[111]*Rot. pat. Hib.*, pp. 266; *Fiants, Ire., Hen. VIII,* nos. 188, 200, 302-3; *Cal. pat. rolls Ire., Hen. VIII-Eliz.,* p. 40.

[112]E.g. Memoranda rolls, 20 Edward IV m. 23, 4-5 Henry VIII m. 38 (P.R.O.I., Ferguson coll., iii, f. 238, iv, f. 16, repertory, iv, 91).

[113]E.g. *Rot. pat. Hib.,* p. 272b no. 12; Memoranda roll, 5 Edward VI m. 11 (P.R.O.I., Ferguson repertory, iv, 91).

[114]Cf. Hore & Graves, *Southern & eastern counties, passim; Rot. pat. Hib.,* p. 270a no. 2.

[115]P.R.O.I., EX 3/1.

[116]Receipt roll, 14-18 Edward IV (R.I.A., MS 12 D 19, p. 175); *S.P. Hen. VIII,* ii, 12, 74; *L. & P. Hen. VIII,* iv (ii), nos. 2405, 4485. Cf. Otway-Ruthven, *Med. Ire.,* pp. 344, 351, 365, 368-9.

[117]E.g. Memoranda rolls, 15 Henry VII m. 22 (S.P.W., Hore MS I, pp. 1152-3), 23

English husbandry whom the Lancastrian government had been so anxious to keep in Ireland.[118] Clearly the Dublin administration had been able to establish a new equilibrium in Yorkist Ireland. The conditions which had earlier attracted the English husbandry back to England, underpopulation in England and political instability in the lordship, were changing while the acceptance of Irishmen of low status who were amenable to control and English influence alleviated somewhat the shortage of tenants and permitted expansion in the border districts. The legislation against consorting with the Irish was used to regulate this process, while providing a useful additional source of revenue for the crown,[119] and to exclude intransigent wild Irishmen well connected with the Gaelic nobility.

Extant cases give the impression that once initiated process in the exchequer, and no doubt the other courts, was normally speedy, but to a large extent this may reflect the enrolment practices of the remembrancers. In 1524, a Meath gentleman, Gerald Fleming of Newcastle, with others deforced a subsidy collector, beating and wounding him, for which he was committed to the Marshalsea. He pleaded not guilty, but later departed without licence, and the case was adjourned successively from term to term until Michaelmas 1525 when he was condemned in 6s. 8d. for contempt. Evidently he had gone to ground and there is no evidence that he was ever brought to justice.[120] In similar cases, however, the exchequer dealt briskly with such contempt. In June 1460, for example, the mayor of Drogheda made fine in 10s., assessed by the lieutenant, for threatening an exchequer messenger the previous July, 'ʒif þou loove thy hele, serewe no more such writts nethir such commaundements': and when the unfortunate messenger returned with more writs a few days later, he was greeted with, 'Þou falsharlot! What dosthou here? I ha bade þe thou scholdist cum nomore here wᵗ such writts ne warantys', words which cost the mayor a further 10s.[121] Similarly, in Michaelmas 1465, William Starkey made fine of 2s. for contempt the previous March

> eo quod. . . venit apud Leyton & insultum fecit in Johannem White, clericum Edwardi Plunket de Balrath, armigeri, vicecomitis

Henry VII m. 22 (P.R.O.I., Ferguson coll., iv, f. 157); *Rot. pat. Hib.,* pp. 270b no. 8, 271 no. 24, 272b no. 3, 273 no. 17.

[118]See esp., J.F. Lydon, 'The problem of the frontier in medieval Ireland', *Topic: a journal of the liberal arts,* xiii (Washington, 1967), 14-15.

[119]The fine for a charter of English liberty was commonly 6s. 8d. or 13s. 4d. at this period, depending on status: *Rot. pat. Hib.,* p. 266; *Cal. pat. rolls Ire., Hen. VIII-Eliz.,* pp. 39, 40; *Fiants Ire., Hen. VIII,* nos. 188, 200, 271, 284, 302, 303, 333.

[120]Memoranda roll, 16 Henry VIII m. 23 (P.R.O.I., Ferguson coll., iv, f. 98).

[121]Memoranda roll, 38 Henry VI m. 39 (P.R.O.I., Ferguson coll., iii, f. 214).

Midensis & ipsum verberauit & eum non permisit execucionem brevis domini regis exequi nec facere.[122]

Obstruction of a different kind was encountered in 1527 when Patrick Clinton was charged with carrying away three hogsheads of wine, sea-wreck, value 16s.: his attorney denied that they were of such value and pleaded that on the acre of land on which they were found Clinton and his ancestors had always enjoyed sea-wreck. To try this question a jury was summoned but, suspiciously, the whole jury defaulted. After distraint they appeared and found that Clinton was not seized in fee of the acre and did not have 'wreccum maris'. He was therefore fined two marks, which he paid.[123] And in 1470 when William Butler called the treasurer a traitor he was imprisoned and his goods seized: Butler was later attainted of treason in 'Edward VI's' parliament in 1487 for adhering to Henry Tudor.[124] Perhaps the most outrageous contempt was committed by James Keating, the unruly prior of Kilmainham, then head constable of Dublin castle, who entered the castle 'vi et armis, videlicet gladiis & cuttellis' in May 1480 and took away one Robert Keating of Chapelizod, a prisoner in the Marshalsea. He admitted the offence before the barons in June but escaped the same day by force: the outcome of the suit is unknown.[125] More normally, however, the exchequer was allowed to complete its investigations without hindrance, perhaps because in most cases they merely disclosed that, despite appearances, the law was in fact being observed. In those cases where a genuine offence was discovered, the defendant nearly always chose to buy a pardon, and only rarely was judgement given against him.

Jurisdiction in review

The court of king's bench also had a jurisdiction in review of cases pleaded in inferior courts. Although this was the most imporant of the court's functions, it took up only a small portion of its time. In the roll of 1485-6 there was just one case in which the defendant in a plea of trespass in common pleas, which had been remitted to the county court for process of outlawry in Michaelmas 1465, sued out a writ of

---

[122]P.R.O.I., EX 3/1 m. 35; Memoranda roll, 6 Edward IV m. 23 (P.R.O.I., RC 8/41, p. 152).

[123]Memoranda roll, 19 Henry VIII m. 26 (P.R.O.I., Ferguson coll., iv, f. 130). Cf. Memoranda roll, 17-18 Henry VIII m. 34 (P.R.O.I., Ferguson coll., iv, f. 114: a second case concerning sea-wreck).

[124]Memoranda roll, 10 Edward IV m. 8 (P.R.O.I., Ferguson coll., iii, f. 221); Ellis, 'Parliaments and great councils', p. 103.

[125]Memoranda roll, 20 Edward IV mm 8d, 31d (S.P.W., Hore MS I, pp. 1137, 1138-9). Cf. Bryan, *Great Earl of Kildare,* pp. 17, 33, 53, 104, 124, 141.

error in April 1485 and had the outlawry quashed the following year. Clearly outlawry was no more effective a weapon for securing appearance than in England although the case seems to be an early instance of an alternative method of reversing an outlawry which became common in sixteenth-century England, the discovery of more or less frivolous errors in the process as issued instead of the fictitious surrender and pardon usual in the fifteenth century (unless, that is, the error was genuine).[126] In the common plea roll of 1479-80, three cases were transferred into king's bench by writ of error, and the court was also in this period profitably engaged in issuing writs of prohibition to prevent ecclesiastical courts from proceeding in cases of which the cognizance belonged to the common law.[127]

Proceedings in king's bench or other common law courts in Ireland were subject to review in the English king's bench. The only case for the period 1470-1534 which has so far come to light is an assize of fresh force originating in the Dublin city court which was reviewed in the Irish king's bench in 1526 and called to the English king's bench by writ of error in June 1532.[128] In Edward I's reign a dozen or so Irish cases per annum had been called up, and down to 1441 at least, an intermittent trickle of such cases continued, but a sampling of controlment rolls of the Yorkist and early Tudor period failed to yield any example.[129] In the later fifteenth century, however, the Irish parliament frequently reviewed process in king's bench and elsewhere: for example, in 1484 process and judgement upon a plaint of debt of two marks in king's bench were reviewed by the deputy and lords of parliament by writ of error.[130] Moreover, a case in 1428 had established that the English king's bench had no authority to review the acts of the Irish parliament, and since under the Yorkists and down to 1494 sessions of parliament or great council were held on average

---

[126]Coram Rege roll, 1 Henry VII m. 10 (P.R.O.I., RC 8/43, pp. 44-7). Cf. Hastings, *Common pleas,* pp. 179-81; J.H. Baker (ed.), *The reports of Sir John Spelman,* ii (Selden Soc., 94; London, 1978), 90-1, 121.

[127]*Registrum Iohannis Mey,* pp. 7, 242, 254, 329, 352: five cases, 1443 x 1456. Thereafter practice in compiling the registers apparently changed, but cf. Octavian's register, copy in T.C.D., MS 557, ix, 362-3, x, 797; *Alen's reg.,* p. 290.

[128]P.R.O., K.B. 27/1085 m. 82. See now Baker (ed.), *Spelman's reports,* ii, 119 n.6, which also notes two cases of 1539 and 1545.

[129]P.R.O., K.B. 29/101, 102, 105, 116, 150, 161, 162, 171 (rolls of 11, 12, 15 Edward IV, 1 Henry VII, 10, 23, 24, 30 Henry VIII); Hand, *Eng. law in Ire.,* pp. 140-3; 'Eng. law in Ire.', pp. 411-12; Richardson & Sayles, *Ir. parl. in middle ages,* pp. 252, 254-5, 257.

[130]Parliament roll, 1 Richard III c. 16 (P.R.O.I., RC 13/8). Cf Parliament rolls, 11 & 12 Edward IV c. 78, 15 & 16 Edward IV c. 37 (*Stat. Ire., Edw. IV,* i, 868-70, ii, 338-40).

about three times a year,[131] parliament probably took from the English king's bench as a court of review until 1494, being no doubt cheaper and speedier to Irish litigants.

One court whose proceedings were not normally subject to review by king's bench was the exchequer. Following attempts by king's bench in England to establish a jurisdiction in error, on the grounds that the exchequer there was a court of common law entertaining civil suits, a statute of 1357-8 established a court of exchequer chamber to review such cases. This statute was promulgated in Ireland, for a copy was entered in the Irish Red Book of the Exchequer: in 1450 an exchequer case was removed to exchequer chamber by writ of error with *supersedeas*.[132] Nevertheless, Irish exchequer proceedings had earlier been reviewed by the English king's bench, and in 1508 a common plea determined in the exchequer was removed to the Irish chancery by the (admittedly different) writ of *certiorari*: it may be, therefore, that practice was not entirely fixed at the end of the middle ages.[133]

In England, the exchequer chamber was frequently used as a *place* of meeting for an entirely distinct consultative assembly of all the justices to debate difficult points of law, effect to decisions reached there being given in the court which had cognizance of the case. In Ireland, the justices apparently met for a similar purpose in 1527 'in quadam camera iuxta scaccarium'.[134] In extreme cases, doubtful points might be referred for an opinion to the king's judges in England.[135]

Judicial commissions

By virtue of various commissions under the great seal, cases which would otherwise have come before the justices of the central courts were regularly heard in the localities. Until the later fourteenth

---

[131] Calculated from *New hist. Ire.,* ix, 600-2; Mac Niocaill, *Na Buirgéisí* ii, 583. On the 1428 case, see Richardson & Sayles, *Ir. parl. in middle ages,* pp. 254-5.

[132] Parliament roll, 38 Henry VI c. 27 (*Stat. Ire., Hen. VI,* pp. 704-6); J.F. Ferguson, 'A calendar of the contents of the Red Book of the Irish exchequer', *Transactions of the Kilkenny Archaeological Society,* iii (1854-5), 41; Holdsworth, *Hist. Eng. law,* i, 41*, 243.

[133] Hand, *Eng. law in Ire.,* pp. 16, 127-9, 142, 146, 147, 149, 151, 162; Memoranda roll, 23 Henry VII m. 16 (P.R.O.I., RC 8/43, pp. 241-2). Wood, *Public records of Ireland,* p. 60 states that exchequer proceedings were reviewed by king's bench.

[134] N.L.I., D. 1820, 2149 (*Ormond deeds, 1413-1509,* no. 243, *1509-47,* no. 133).

[135] N.L.I., D. 2096 (*Ormond deeds, 1509-47,* no. 93).

century, this aspect of royal justice developed on the same lines as in England. Under Edward I, commissions of oyer and terminer, of gaol delivery and of assize were issued, regular circuits of assize were organized, and under Edward II the general eyre disappeared.[136] In the Lancastrian period, however, this system broke down and the lordship effectively became divided into two zones – the Pale which suffered from too much 'justice', and the outlying counties which petitioned for more.[137] Within the Pale, after one or two earlier attempts, a statute was passed in 1449 that, excepting commissions of the peace, no commission of oyer and terminer or of oyer and certifier was to sit unless one of the king's principal legal officers were included in the *quorum* and present at the session. These commissions were otherwise apt to be vexatious, because issued to unsuitable persons, and unnecessary because of the proximity of the central courts. Probably the statute brought practice into line with that in England where such commissions were employed primarily to deal with serious disturbances.[138] At any rate the complaints ceased and in the following period surviving instances of the use of commissions of oyer and terminer in the Pale resembled practice in England – a commission for Co. Dublin headed by the chief justice in 1475 at which the archbishop of Dublin was indicted of treason and others in 1535 in the aftermath of the Kildare rebellion, also headed by the king's justices.[139] Similarly, commissions of assize were not normally issued for the Pale, although special commissions, of assize or of oyer and terminer, at the suit of a private party could be had upon payment of a fine in chancery. In 1537, Luttrell C.J.C.P. urged 'all maters, except urgent causeis, to be tryed by *nisi prius*, except maters within the same shyres where the courtes doo sytte', but there is at this date no evidence of regular circuits of assize on the English model. The effect of this, therefore, was that within the Pale justice was highly centralized, particularly after king's bench had become sedentary: freeholders, it was claimed, were 'moche troblid in ofte comeing to

---

[136] Hand, *Eng. law in Ire.*, pp. 99, 104-12; 'Eng. law in Ire.', pp. 396, 413-14; Otway-Ruthven, *Med. Ire.*, p. 160.

[137] E.g. Frame, 'Med. Ir. keepers', pp. 319-20, 324-5; Richardson & Sayes, *Ir. parl. in middle ages*, pp. 175-6.

[138] Parliament rolls, 10 Henry VI c. 4, 27 Henry VI cc 4, 8, 28 Henry VI c. 8 (*Stat. Ire., Hen. VI*, pp. 42, 112, 116, 188-90); *Proceedings and ordinances of the privy council of England*, ii, 43-6. Cf. J.G. Bellamy, 'Justice under the Yorkist kings', *American Journal of Legal History*, ix (1965), 147-8.

[139] Parliament roll, 16 & 17 Edward IV c. 27 (*Stat. Ire., Edw. IV*, ii, 500-4); Ellis, 'Henry VIII, rebellion and the rule of law', pp. 517-19.

Dublin'. By Elizabeth's reign, however, justices had begun to go on circuit round the Pale as in England.[140]

Beyond the Pale, the system eventually adopted was the periodic appointment of general commissions with wide powers to inquire into most aspects of local administration as well as to do justice, and their supplementation by special *ad hoc* commissions. Three original, general commissions survive, dated 1519, 1522 and 1523, although this form of commission had clearly evolved much earlier, probably in the fourteenth century, and many other examples of its use can be identified. The main provisions of the three commissions are the same, despite minor variations: they covered the counties and crosses of Carlow, Cork, Kerry, Kilkenny, Limerick, Tipperary, Waterford and Wexford, appointing during pleasure between five and nine commissioners of oyer and terminer, gaol delivery and assize. Additionally, the commissioners were empowered to inquire concerning royal rights and their evasion and generally to exercise the office of escheator, and also to admit delinquents to fine. The commissioners normally included a chancery clerk to draw up original and judicial writs and pardons which were to have the same force as if under the great seal, the profits being reserved to the hanaper. In most respects the commissions were phrased in the same manner, conferring the same powers as their English equivalents, where similar general commissions of inquiry were also developed by Henry VII as a considered policy. Their purpose was, however, more openly fiscal than the Irish commissions which apparently concentrated on the dispensing of justice. The section relating to assizes seems to exclude proceedings on writs of right, which were of course notoriously dilatory. Moreover, a clue to their origin is provided by the wide powers conferred as justices of oyer and terminer, approximating to commissions of trailbaston in fourteenth-century England, but adapted to Irish conditions. The commissioners were to inquire concerning breaches of the Statute of Provisors, the pleading of cases which pertained to the common law in church courts, and breaches of the Statutes of Kilkenny and of Dublin.[141]

---

[140]*S.P. Hen. VIII,* ii, 501, 508, 509; Close roll, 19 Edward IV m. 7d (Gilbert, *Viceroys,* pp. 595-6); Wood, *Public records of Ireland,* pp. 61-3; Davies, *Discovery,* p. 267; *Anal. Hib.,* ii, 183-5. Cf. *Cal. pat. rolls Ire., Hen. VIII-Eliz.,* p. 34; *Stat. Ire., Hen. VII & VIII,* pp. 117-18, 131, 165.

[141]N.L.I., D. 2043, 2080, 2091 (*Ormond deeds, 1509-47,* nos. 52, 81, 89). Cf. Holdsworth, *Hist. Eng. law,* i, 45-7*, 273-4, 668-70; Jewell, *English local administration,* pp. 142, 208; W.C. Richardson, 'The surveyor of the king's prerogative', *E.H.R.,* lvi (1941), 54-7.

These general commissions appear to be descended from the general eyre, a response to like problems. The eyre indeed survived in an attenuated form – two writs are extant for eyres in the palatinate of Tipperary in 1432 and 1509.[142] Until 1922 there survived a roll of sessions held in Co. Cork, Co. Limerick and the cross of Kerry in February-March 1382, which was classified by the Public Record Office of Ireland with the rolls of justices itinerant, a series which otherwise ended in 1307.[143] A commission of 1400 for the same three counties empowered the commissioners to act as keepers of the peace, as justices of assize, oyer and terminer and gaol delivery, to superintend coroners and to inquire concerning the king's feudal rights.[144] Commissioners of this period were sometimes resident and combined their duties with those of keepers of the peace, but in May-June 1438 the second justice of king's bench and the king's serjeant itinerated in Cos. Kerry, Kilkenny, Limerick, Tipperary, Waterford and Wexford.[145] Further research is needed, but it appears that the eyre was gradually transformed into the general commission by diminishing certain of its powers, extending its authority to a group of counties and by appointing commissioners for six to ten weeks, generally out of term, instead of on a semi-permanent basis. Even in the 1530s, however, some of its powers still resembled those of the eyre. The commissioners were empowered to sit within liberties and, besides determining the four pleas always reserved to the crown in the Irish palatinates, to determine other pleas and to inquire concerning and to correct abuses of the liberty's jurisdiction and of its officers. The *Ordinances* of 1534 required towns and cities to assist the king's justices, who were not to infringe their liberties, 'except the justice of oyer determyner commeth and awardeth a wrytte of *quo warranto*', when 'theyr lyberties [should] cesse for that season accordynge to the lawe'.[146] In the early sixteenth century, these commissions normally issued once a year, although this may have been more frequently than before: such commissioners can also be identified as itinerating (with the counties certainly included in brackets) in June 1500 (Kilkenny, Tipperary, Waterford), Shrovetide ?1518 (Waterford, Wexford), and January-April 1532 (Cork, Kilkenny, Tipperary, Waterford,

---

[142]*Ormond deeds, 1413-1509,* nos. 102, 337.

[143]*P.R.I., rep. D.K., 26,* p. 63, *28,* p. 47. Another roll of sessions at Trim in 1412 survived, but the liberty was then in the king's hands.

[144]Frame, 'Med. Ir. keepers', p. 319.

[145]*Rot. pat. Hib.,* pp. 262 no. 24, 263 no. 24.

[146]*S.P. Hen. VIII,* ii, 210; N.L.I., D. 2349 (*Ormond deeds, 1509-47,* no. 261); *L. & P. Hen. VIII,* ii, no. 3853, xi, no. 200. Cf. Ball, *Judges,* i, 112-13.

Wexford).[147] These five counties plus Carlow were evidently visited annually, as was the case in the three northern counties of England, but Kerry and Limerick were included less regularly, and Connaught and Ulster very seldom if at all. This pattern continued after 1534, although remote counties like Limerick and Connaught began to be visited more frequently.[148]

References to the work of special commissioners are scarce, but two assizes of novel disseisin in Co. Kilkenny in 1499 were specifically remitted to justices assigned and apparently two more in Co. Tipperary and Co. Kilkenny in 1464 and 1474 respectively, although the latter were possibly actions at *nisi prius* remitted from the Dublin courts. In 1501 a recurrence of the Waterford-New Ross dispute concerning prisage led to the issue of a commission of oyer and certifier; in 1521 the lieutenant asked for a special commission of oyer and terminer to try some pirates; and in 1531 title to a house in Limerick was apparently determined by special commissioners. Exceptionally, in 1493 the chief baron received a general commission for life to execute the law in Co. Kilkenny and Co. Waterford at the special request of the lords and commons there in parliament, though by 1498 Sir Piers Butler and James Sherlock were commissioners in Co. Kilkenny.[149]

The actual work of the general commissioners is very poorly documented, but jury presentments survive, plus a few indictments, taken before commissioners in late 1537, and are illustrative of conditions in the southern counties at the end of the middle ages. Exceptional features were the presence of high-ranking commissioners from England, and the commissioners' interest in excesses of the clergy and crown rights arising from the Reformation legislation: the itineration took less time than usual, probably four weeks, and was especially concerned with general conditions, extortion of the lords and gaelicization – some juries were encouraged to suggest remedies.[150]

---

[147]*Liber primus Kilkenn.*, pp. 156-8; *L. & P. Hen. VIII*, ii, no. 3853; *Ormond deeds, 1509-47*, nos. 177-81.

[148]E.g. *Cal. pat. rolls Ire., Hen. VIII-Eliz.*, pp. 77-8, 112, 133; P.R.O., S.P. 65/1/2; M.J. Blake, *Blake family records 1300 to 1600* (London, 1902), nos. 100, 104, 121; Hore & Graves, *Southern & eastern counties, passim;* B.L., Add. MS 19865, ff 68v-72v. Cf. C.A.F. Meekings, 'King's Bench files', in J.H. Baker (ed.), *Legal records and the historian* (London, 1978), p. 108.

[149]Parliament rolls, 5 Edward IV c. 72 (*Stat. Ire., Edw. IV*, i, 412), 8 Henry VII c. 10 (P.R.O.I., RC 13/9); N.L.I., D. 1813, 1890-94 (inaccurately calendared in *Ormond deeds, 1413-1509*, nos. 239, 301); *Rot. pat. Hib.*, p. 272 no. 16; *Cal. pat. rolls Ire., Hen. VIII-Eliz.*, p. 10; *S.P. Hen. VIII*, ii, 76-7; *Liber primus Kilkenn.*, p. 103.

[150]Hore & Graves, *Southern & eastern counties, passim. Cf. L. & P. Hen. VIII*, xii (ii), nos. 762, 786, 837, 859, 943; D.B. Quinn, 'Parliaments and great councils in

The juries varied in size from eleven to twenty, usually fifteen to eighteen, and their fourteen sets of presentments (those of other juries are now missing) were in English, probably still the dominant language of the region, and cover the liberty, cross and town of Wexford; the gentry of Kilkenny, the commonalty of that shire, the corporation and the commonalty of the town of Kilkenny, the towns of Irishtown and Gowran, and the town of New Ross; Waterford city, the commonalty of the shire, and the lordship of Dungarvan; and two juries for the gentry and commonalty of Tipperary and the town of Clonmel which effectively represented the southern part of the county. Generally, English administrative forms were better preserved in the towns than in the surrounding countryside and, despite suggestions to the contrary, a substantial English yeomanry clearly survived.[151] In Co. Kilkenny and Co. Waterford Gaelic law frequently replaced criminal and personal actions, but English forms of land tenure were universal despite a Kilkenny presentment that the common law there was 'clerly voide and frustrate'. In fact its position was by no means as weak as juries wished the commissioners to believe. The Tipperary presentments may be compared with more normal ones by a jury at sessions of the liberty in 1514: thirteen offences were presented – five murders and three robberies, harbouring felons, receiving stolen goods, pleading title to land in a church court, the purchase of lands by an Irishman, and the breach of a statute restraining landless men from keeping hunting dogs.[152] In 1537, the jurors were charged principally to present breaches of the Statutes of Kilkenny – taking coign and livery without consent, consorting with the Gaelic Irish and the spread of Irish law and customs – but in Wexford the presentment of felonies, breaches of the Statute of Provisors and the king's feudal rights predominated, and in Tipperary the abuse of the liberty was a grievance. Problems which emerged only incidentally were the encroachment of seigneurial jurisdiction on matters pertaining to the royal courts and the excesses of serjeants appointed by the magnates. The towns provided information concerning customs tolls and their expenditure and the forestalling and

Ireland, 1461-1586', *I.H.S.*, iii (1942-3), 75 n. 11; R.D. Edwards, 'The Irish Reformation Parliament of Henry VIII, 1536-7', *Historical Studies*, vi (London, 1968), 78-9.

[151]Cf. *Cal. pat. rolls Ire., Hen. VIII-Eliz.*, p. 22; *Ormond deeds, 1509-47*, no. 1; Canny, *Elizabethan conquest*, pp. 17, 19-20 and my review in *Studia Hibernica* xix (1979), 174-7. Ormond had likewise agreed c. 1448 that the liberty sessions of Tipperary should be held at least once a year, but by 1508 they were being held more regularly: Empey & Simms, 'Ordinances of the White Earl', pp. 169, 171-2, 174-5; *Ormond deeds, 1413-1509*, nos. 331, 332, 337; Quinn, 'Anglo-Irish local government', pp. 372-3.

[152]N.L.I., D. 2007 (*Ormond deeds, 1509-47*, no. 23).

regrating at markets and impeding river navigation with weirs, matters which elicited legislation in parliament two months later.[153]

Perhaps more typical of the activities of these commissions was that itinerating in 1532. It issued on 26 January 1532 and the commissioners were additionally empowered to determine a dispute referred by the council between the earls of Desmond and Ossory about lands and prise wines. By 2 February, they had reached Waterford and remained in the vicinity for about four weeks awaiting Desmond's appearance. In the interim they journeyed to Carrick-on-Suir, just beyond Co. Waterford in the liberty of Tipperary, where they took depositions on a bill of complaint by Ossory and no doubt held a session, plus another at Knockgowne, Co. Waterford. The two commissioners of the *quorum* then travelled to Dungarvan to hear evidence on Desmond's behalf, remaining two days, and a decree was finally given in Ossory's favour at Waterford on 26 March.[154] At least one of the commissioners then returned to Dublin, but the others held a session in Co. Kilkenny where a decree by the chancellor in 1528 concerning lands in Thomastown was reaffirmed on 9 April against a different disseisor. Finally, the commissioners apparently held a session in the cross of Wexford and found one Philip Sompter guilty of treason. An inquisition *post mortem* was also returned concerning the lands of Walter Synnot of Ballybrenan, and on 8 April the exchequer sold Sompter's goods for forty marks.[155] This was a small commission but when, as in 1523, as many as six commissioners were of the *quorum*, the opportunities for independent action by different groups of commissioners must have been greatly increased.

To an extent, therefore, these commissions were both effective and profitable although, naturally, they were less successful against the magnates. An earlier commission in Co. Wexford apparently took into the king's hand the castle and lordship of Durbard's Island on the Barrow, and this was committed by the exchequer in February 1531 to the custody of the seneschal of Wexford. By April, however, Ossory had forcibly taken possession and he retained it, though at least three commissions itinerated there, until the king granted it to him as a reward in October 1537.[156] Moreover, in July 1531 the

[153]Cf. Edwards, 'Irish Reformation Parliament', pp. 78-9.

[154]N.L.I., D. 2207; *Ormond deeds, 1509-47,* nos. 177, 181

[155]Memoranda roll, 24 Henry VIII mm 2, 4 (S.P.W., Hore MS I, pp. 1174-6; P.R.O.I., Ferguson coll., iv, ff 162, 163); *Cal. pat. rolls Ire., Hen., VIII-Eliz.,* p. 10; T.C.D., MS 569, f. 20v.

[156]Memoranda roll, 22 Henry VIII m. 19 (S.P.W., Hore MS I, pp. 1172-3); Hore & Graves, *Southern & eastern counties,* pp. 39, 42; P.R.O., S.P. 65/1/2; *Ormond deeds, 1509-47,* no. 218; *L. & P. Hen. VIII,* xii (ii), no. 1008 (35).

bishop and dean of Ferns gave recognizances in 200 marks each in the exchequer, probably to keep the peace. They were committed to the Marshalsea in September, but were later presented for consorting with Irishmen from May 1532.[157] It is, nevertheless, unlikely that the Dublin administration would have gone to the expense of appointing commissioners to tour the outlying shires for up to ten weeks each year unless they were both popular, and therefore effective, and profitable.

A more general statement concerning the operation of the royal courts in Ireland is reserved for the close of the next chapter, but some more particular remarks about the common law courts are called for. Though a sustained effort was made to ensure that royal justice was freely available throughout the lordship, the area of effective jurisdiction of the traditional courts had narrowed alarmingly between 1300 and, at the latest, 1450, leaving a dangerous preponderance of debt and trespass actions. Yet this collapse had not been matched by a comparable decline in the numbers of cases commenced there. Certainly, the business of the Dublin bench had fallen off dramatically, to perhaps a fifth of what it had been: it had not only lost its earlier monopoly of real actions but was also losing out elsewhere to the speedier and cheaper process available in king's bench and the exchequer. But even common pleas recovered in the following half-century, and by Henry VIII's reign judicial reforms had gone some way towards restoring the traditional balance between king's bench and common pleas, as well as bringing the Irish legal system more into line with that in England.

Nevertheless, the traditional courts had even before this seemingly been able to compensate both for the narrowing of the range of cases pleaded there and the overall contraction of the lordship in the period 1300-1460, so that, overall, the number of cases coming before them in the 1460s was substantially more than it had been under Edward I and apparently continued to grow during the following half-century. How this paradoxical result was achieved is not entirely clear, but three likely causes may be advanced. First, the abandonment of ordinary judicial commissions for the Pale drove many actions back to the central court, and it is unlikely that there was in fact an overall increase in the amount of litigation throughout the lordship. Second, the later medieval recovery was probably based in part on the courts' willingness to entertain actions for debt of less than 40s. This in turn suggests a third, more general point, that the central courts had in fact

---

[157] Memoranda roll, 23 Henry VIII mm 8-8d, 10 (S.P.W., Hore MS I, p. 1174; B.L., Add. MS 4791, f. 203v); Hore & Graves, *Southern & eastern counties*, pp. 48-9.

attracted business from the local courts and, certainly in Co. Meath, from franchisal courts too.[158]

Thus it would be wrong to regard the traditional courts as totally hamstrung by the inadequacies of their mesne process: evidence concerning the exchequer suggests that that court, and probably also king's bench, were capable of brisk action to protect the interests of the crown and, on occasion, of its subjects. Nevertheless, the major changes in the lordship's legal system at this time took place elsewhere, with the establishment of new courts, and it was on these developments that the recovery of royal justice was chiefly based.

---

[158] It is worth noting in this context that municipal authorities frequently attempted to proscribe resort to the central courts in cases cognizable in the city courts: Mac Niocaill, *Na Buirgéisí,* ii, 411-14.

5

LEGISLATION AND THE PREROGATIVE COURTS

In terms of legal administration, the principal departure of the late middle ages was, as in England, the development of an alternative curial system based on the council and chancery, and the shift in business and areas of jurisdiction of the courts which this entailed. Nevertheless, these changes were not slavishly modelled on developments in England and in particular the development of parliament suggests that Irish institutions were being adapted rather in response to similar needs within the lordship than to some ideal of uniformity throughout the area of the common law.

Parliament

Medieval Irish parliaments were chiefly remembered in a more democratic age for their intermittent support for two basic principles of constitutional monarchy, that of consent to taxation and the idea that legislative power should rest with the king, lords and commons of Ireland in parliament there. In practice, however, the king's high court of parliament came nearer after 1460 to realising that other misleading claim of medieval parliaments, to be a court, although it was never a court in the full sense.

Even a cursory glance at the parliament rolls discloses that parliament's legislative role was not very important. The reason for this was simple. The medieval lordship was considered to be a dependency of the realm of England and legislation of the English parliament was applicable to Ireland.[1] This left the Irish parliament the minor role of enacting statutes of purely local concern. Thus the pressures which led in England to the primacy of the legislative aspect of parliament, and the rerouting of administrative and judicial matters back to the ordinary sessions of the council, probably operated the other way in Ireland. Scrutinizing the fifteenth-century parliament rolls, Sir John Davies remarked on the 'extraordinary number of private bills and petitions answered and ordered in parliament, containing such mean and ordinary matters as, but for want of other business, were not fit to be handled in so high a court'.[2]

Parliament was of course the highest court in the land, superior to

---

[1]Richardson & Sayles, *Ir. parl. in middle ages,* pp. 61-2, 248-51, 260.
[2]Sir John Davies, *Historical tracts* (Dublin, 1787), pp. 297-8.

both king's bench in Ireland and England, and this partly accounts for its importance in administration, but in fact the years from 1460 saw a great expansion of its role in government. Under Henry VI parliaments had usually met annually but there was rarely more than one sitting or session of each parliament and in the last fourteen years of the reign the tally of acts passed varied between twenty and forty.[3] Then in 1460 the parliament held by Richard duke of York ran to six sessions between February and July and passed sixty-three statutes. This set the pattern for Edward IV's reign. By custom confirmed by statute, the governor was restrained from summoning parliaments more frequently than once a year,[4] but four or five sessions were frequently held, evenly scattered over ten or eleven months, and the number of acts passed normally reached about eighty or ninety. Precise information about parliamentary sessions is usually lacking but in 1463-4, when the earl of Desmond took parliament with him on a progress through the south-east, the four sessions lasted twenty-three days and no less than 106 acts were passed; in 1467-8 there were ten sessions lasting sixty-five days or more in which eighty-four acts were passed; and in 1471-2 five sessions lasted altogether thirty-eight days during which ninety-one acts were passed.[5] Thus not only were parliaments convoked much more often than in England, where in the fifteenth century their frequency was decreasing, but under Edward IV they each sat for approximately the same number of weeks. It is true that some parliaments were dissolved after only one session with few acts passed, but in every case these early dissolutions can be linked to a change of governor or dynasty.[6] In 1476 an act limited the number of sessions to three, but its impact on parliamentary litigation can only have been temporary since the limit was exceeded in the parliaments of 1479-81 and 1485 and later ignored.[7]

Parliament's increasing role in government at this time stemmed entirely from the bulk of administrative and judicial matters which came before it. Much of this litigation might have been tried at

---

[3]No meaningful distinction was made in the Irish parliaments of this period between sittings after an adjournment and after a prorogation: see Quinn, 'Parliaments and great councils', p. 62. Only three parliament rolls from before 1447 were extant in 1922 and these did not include private bills which had been recorded among the chancery warrants: Richardson & Sayles, *Ir. parl. in middle ages,* pp. 198-9.

[4]Parliament rolls, 29 Henry VI c. 5, 34 Henry VI c. 6 (*Stat. Ire., Hen. VI,* pp. 258, 354).

[5]*Stat. Ire., Hen. VI, passim; Stat. Ire., Edw. IV,* i, ii, *passim.*

[6]*New hist. Ire.,* ix, 600-2; *Handbook Brit. chron.,* pp. 532-4.

[7]*Stat. Ire., Edw. IV,* ii, 904; Richardson & Sayles, *Ir. parl. in middle ages,* pp. 181, 187.

common law and it has been well described by Mr Richardson and Professor Sayles in their book on the medieval Irish parliament.[8] Nevertheless, this upsurge in business was more than just a consequence of the decline of the common law courts brought about by the collapse of the lordship: rather the dwindling length of the fifteenth-century plea rolls of the traditional courts to a large extent reflected changing patterns of litigation. From c.1450, to judge from its rolls, parliament began to supply the need for a court with power to override the form of the law in favour of justice, and within a decade it had become a sort of clearing house for disputes about land, many of which would under the three Edwards have come directly before the common law courts.[9] The normal remedy was to appoint a day in one of the common law courts for the determination of title, thus circumventing the weakness of mesne process at common law. Between 1470 and 1480, for example, the surviving parliament rolls alone record thirty-six such cases, seventeen of them from beyond the Pale.[10] And, as Richardson and Sayles have shown, almost any other matter in which the traditional courts offered no remedy or were powerless to enforce it might come before parliament.[11]

These facts, however, do not explain why in Ireland parliament became involved in the transformation of the legal system when in England similar difficulties had led to the development of chancery, nor why this occurred only after 1450. One minor consideration is that with the increased frequency of its sessions under Edward IV the Irish parliament almost ousted the English king's bench as a court of review;[12] but more generally, much of this new parliamentary litigation had apparently been determined by the council under the Lancastrians, although further research is needed to establish this point with certainty.[13] Yet the Lancastrian council in Ireland was notoriously faction-ridden,[14] and it may be that parliament was felt by litigants – highly placed ones at first but very soon the nobility and gentry at large – to offer a more impartial and of course more

---

[8]*Ir. parl. in middle ages*, ch. 14.

[9]Cf. *ibid*., pp. 174-5, 196-7.

[10]*Stat. Ire., Edw. IV*, i, 650ff, ii,*passim*. Cf. Richardson & Sayles, *Ir. parl. in middle ages* pp. 215-21.

[11]*Ir. parl. in middle ages*, pp. 215-24.

[12]Above, pp. 133-4.

[13]Richardson & Sayles, *Ir. parl. in middle ages*, p. 199.

[14]See especially, Griffith, 'The Talbot-Ormond struggle', pp. 376-97. Cf. Richardson & Sayles, *Ir. parl. in middle ages*, pp. 171-2.

prestigious tribunal for the settlement of private disputes. Parliament therefore became an instrument in the revival of crown government under Edward IV.

Excluding duplicates, fourteen parliament rolls of Edward IV's reign survived until 1922, including all but one of the rolls for the twenty years 1462-81, plus the roll of the 1462 great council. Although some were then incomplete, they recorded a total of 809 acts, of which the overwhelming majority apparently arose from private petitions.[15] In fact only 155 acts related to the lordship as a whole, and they included few which were in any sense important alterations of the law. Although a number of acts attempted to fix prices or to regulate the coinage,[16] and though a very few like the Statute of Archers remained in force until well into the sixteenth century,[17] it was not to legislate that parliaments were called. Nor, until the reforms of the parliamentary subsidy from 1477 onwards, was it the need for taxation, since until then the government could in practice obtain more worthwhile sums by local taxation or a scutage, neither of which strictly required parliamentary consent.[18] Moreover, taxation might even act as an incentive to absent oneself from parliament, for silence by no means implied consent. As late as 1479 it was found necessary to enact that communities which sent no representatives to parliament should nonetheless be bound by its legislation.[19]

In practice the governor probably permitted such frequent sessions of parliament because they were a useful means of strengthening the Dublin administration's feeble control beyond the Pale and of dealing with disorders. Although parliament's work was at times hasty and perfunctory, the increased weight of business under the Yorkists suggests that it was on the whole relatively effective and popular. This suggestion receives some corroboration from the occasional practice of clerks of parliament who subsequently entered the word *vacatum* in the margin against certain acts to denote that they had achieved the

---

[15] Calculated from *Stat. Ire. Edw. IV*, i, ii.

[16] Parliament rolls, 10 Edward IV c. 10, 11 & 12 Edward IV c. 17 (*Stat. Ire., Edw. IV*, i, 656-60, 746-50); Ellis, 'Struggle for control of the Irish mint', pp. 17-36.

[17] Parliament roll, 12 & 13 Edward IV c. 45 (*Stat. Ire., Edw. IV*, ii, 98-100); *Stat. Ire., Hen. VII & VIII*, pp. 113, 115. For examples of prosecutions under the statute, see above, p 127.

[18] Above, p 67-72.

[19] Parliament roll, 19 & 20 Edward IV c. 20 (*Stat. Ire., Edw. IV*, ii, 728-30).

desired effect or had been repealed.[20] No doubt the outlying communities continued to be represented, occasionally at least, because of the comparative effectiveness of parliamentary arbitration. It comes as no surprise to learn that 604 of the 886 acts on the eighteen rolls which survived for the period 1462-93 arose out of particular interests of the Palesmen, but a further 112 acts, or 12½ per cent of the total, chiefly relate to the various communities beyond the Pale. All the late medieval counties except Kerry are included and all the major towns and cities from Carrickfergus round to Galway, although nearly 65 per cent relate chiefly to Cos. Wexford (twenty-eight acts), Kilkenny, Waterford and Limerick and the cities of Waterford and Limerick.[21] While it has long been recognized that representation in the Irish parliament was never confined entirely to the Pale,[22] this evidence of legislation in favour of particular interests suggests that, overall, outside representation was in fact quite substantial even if, individually, only the shire of Wexford and the city of Waterford were regularly represented. It can be supported by evidence concerning the practice in Ireland of amercing those who absented themselves from parliament. This practice had been common in the fourteenth century, and was resumed under Henry VI, presumably in a bid to strengthen the Dublin administration's control over the outlying shires at a time when it seemed in danger of collapsing. The practice apparently continued until 1450 and the last recorded instance occurred in 1499.[23] This gap, however, seems to be more than just a quirk of the evidence. In 1494 Lord Deputy Poynings was for the first time explicitly empowered by his commission of appointment to amerce those absent from parliament. His successor, the earl of Kildare, received the same powers, and for the first time amercements were inflicted in 1499 on temporal lords and proctors of the clergy as well as on the commonalty and the lords spiritual.[24] It looks therefore as if the practice had been allowed to lapse after 1450 and was deliberately revived, a suggestion which accords well with the evidence outlined above, that under Edward IV representation in parliament was fairly wide because parliament's judicial role had expanded.

[20]The rolls of 3, 11 & 12, and 18 (I) Edward IV were frequently so marked: *Stat. Ire., Edw. IV*, i, ii, *passim*.

[21]Calculated from *Stat. Ire., Edw. IV*, i, ii; Parliament rolls, 1, and 2 & 3 Richard III (P.R.O.I., RC 13/8; P.R.O.I., transcript), 8 Henry VII (P.R.O.I., RC 13/9).

[22]For example, H.G. Richardson, 'The Irish parliament rolls of the fifteenth century', *E.H.R.*, lviii (1943), 457; Richardson & Sayles, *Ir. parl. in middle ages*, pp. 179-81.

[23]Richardson & Sayles, *Ir. parl. in middle ages*, ch. 10.

[24]Close roll, 10-15 Henry VII art. 46 (B.L., Add. MS 4797, ff 109v-10, printed with commentary in *Galvia*, xiii (1985), 56-62); *Cal. pat. rolls, 1494-1509*, pp. 12, 62; Richardson & Sayles, *Ir. parl. in middle ages*, ch. 10, esp. pp. 143-4 and note 50.

The surviving list of amercements inflicted for non-return of writs and absence from the 1499 parliament offers almost the only precise evidence concerning the level of representation in the late medieval period, and there is no reason to believe that it distorts the picture. In the fifteenth century representation in the three houses of the Irish parliament was fairly fixed and by correlation with earlier evidence the list indicates that in the first session at Dublin thirty-two out of a maximum of forty-six members were present in the commons, falling to twenty-seven for the second session at Castledermot, and that in the lords attendance was twenty-nine at the first session out of thirty-four and twenty-four at the second session. The level of attendance by the clerical proctors is less clear because representation of some dioceses was increased from two to four proctors during the fifteenth century, and there is no evidence about how Cork and Cloyne were represented after the amalgamation of these dioceses in 1429.[25] The proctors' interests in parliament were in any case limited and in most cases their consent to legislation was unnecessary; but at the Dublin session eleven dioceses were apparently represented, falling to eight for the Castledermot session, and the total number of proctors present must have been at least twenty-seven at the first session and twenty at the second.[26] By comparison we know that attendance in the convocation house in 1450 was twenty-seven, and in the 1491 parliament eight prelates plus ten temporal peers attended.[27]

In view of this relatively high level of attendance in parliaments of the later fifteenth century, it is unlikely that the preponderance of acts relating primarily to the Pale reflects no more than the ability of the Palesmen to secure their own interests at the expense of the outlying shires. Certainly the Pale was comparatively overrepresented in parliament, and in the lords Palesmen must normally have been in a majority, but in 1499 in both convocation and the commons the representatives of the outlying communities apparently had a comfortable majority. Only when attendance was exceptionally low can the Palesmen have been preponderant in all three houses. The implication, therefore, is that the enactments of the Irish parliament in the later fifteenth century reflected the interests of the political nation of the lordship as a whole and not merely those of the Palesmen.

The diverging functions of parliament in kingdom and lordship in the fifteenth century probably had no direct influence on the passage

---

[25] *Handbook Brit. chron.*, p. 326.
[26] Cf. Richardson & Sayles, *Ir. parl. in middle ages*, pp. 183-6.
[27] *Rot. pat. Hib.*, p. 265 no. 13; *L. & P. Ric. III & Hen. VII*, i, 377-82.

of Poynings' Law, if indeed the king was conscious of this divergence. Poynings' Law was rather part of a reforming legislative programme of political and constitutional import and was designed to strengthen royal control over the Irish parliament as a legislature.[28] The weakness of this control had recently been highlighted by the activities of Yorkist pretenders. Nevertheless, though conservative in aim, the Law was revolutionary in application and brought the Irish parliament much more closely into line with its English counterpart. Whereas a parliament had met almost every year down to 1494, over the next forty years there were only seven parliaments, and only five more to the end of Elizabeth's reign.[29] Moreover in 1494 the medieval parliament rolls, which had recorded, in Norman-French, the results of parliamentary action, were replaced by statute rolls in English, recording only enactments which had previously been approved by the governor and council in Ireland and by the king and council in England.[30] This poses a problem for the historian because it is not entirely clear how far the role of parliament was changing and how far merely the character of its principal record. There is in fact some evidence that, initially at least, Poynings' Law was interpreted as not precluding parliament from determining minor administrative matters as before, even though these matters were no longer recorded on the roll. A licence of 1532 to found a chantry was granted 'on the requisition and assent of both houses of parliament, and at the solicitation of certain persons therein'; and in 1541 the lords granted letters of protection to a man attainted of treason for complicity in the Kildare rebellion and a petition against an indictment for larceny in king's bench by a gypsy resident in Dublin was referred to the council. Arbitration in various disputes among the magnates also took place in that parliament.[31] Indeed, unless parliament were regularly so employed, it is hard to see why, for example, in 1508-9 parliament required four sessions to pass three bills and reject three more, or why in 1521-2 seven sessions totalling about twenty days were necessary to debate nine bills.[32] Nevertheless, the relative infrequency

---

[28] Richardson & Sayles, *Ir. parl. in middle ages*, ch. 17.

[29] See the table in *New hist. Ire.*, ix, 599-604.

[30] Cf. Richardson, 'Irish parliament rolls', pp. 448-50; *Stat. Ire., Hen. VII & VIII*, pp. 73-4.

[31] J. D'Alton, *The history of the county of Dublin* (Dublin, 1838), p. 577 (quoting an inquisition of 1613); *Cal. pat. rolls Ire., Hen. VIII-Eliz.*, pp. 71-2; N.L.I., D.2349 (*Ormond deeds, 1509-47*, no. 261); *Fiants Ire., Hen. VIII*, no. 264; Bradshaw, *Irish constitutional revolution*, pp. 238-42. Cf. Quinn, 'Early interpretation of Poynings' Law', pp. 252-3.

[32] *Stat. Ire., Hen. VII & VIII*, pp. 104, 108, 116, 123.

of parliaments after 1494 and, for most purposes, the need to obtain in advance the king's licence for each bill effectively deprived the institution of much of its value as a court and administrative board. Parliament in Ireland therefore became primarily a legislature, convened every five or six years mainly for a grant of taxation or in connection with the sporadic attempts at governmental reform through an English-born governor. The judicial and administrative duties of parliament largely devolved on the council aided by the development of chancery,[33] although not all the private bills considered by parliament were susceptible of remedy in this way.

Nevertheless, parliament's role in lawmaking was not quite so clearly defined as in England, and was in fact under attack from two different quarters. Within the lordship, many local ordinances were approved by local assemblies, often the county court or an afforced council of the magnates and gentry of a particular locality, while general ordinances continued until 1494 to be enacted in great councils. Irish great councils of the fifteenth century cannot in fact be distinguished either in composition or function from parliaments, and have been fully discussed by Richardson and Sayles.[34] Afforced councils were readily distinguishable by the fact that they did not contain elected representatives and were summoned, not under the great seal of Ireland, but under the governor's privy seal.[35] After 1494, great councils in their traditional form ceased to be summoned. Probably they could not have been summoned for legislative purposes without following the procedure laid down by Poynings' Law and their chief advantage over parliaments had earlier been the shorter period of summons necessary. Nevertheless, afforced councils which had not strictly been classed as great councils continued to be convoked and soon acquired such status. In 1520 a proposed council was unofficially so styled and by Elizabeth's reign the earlier distinction had been forgotten and the work of the medieval great council was being cited misleadingly as a precedent for granting what was effectively a form of taxation in the mid-Tudor 'graund counsell'.[36] The confusion is readily explained: the composition of the late medieval great council in England approximated to that of an afforced council in Ireland. It was attended by parliamentary peers and knights who were personally summoned, but after 1353 at least it contained

[33] Below, pp. 154-63; Ellis, 'Henry VII and Ireland', pp. 248-9.

[34] *Ir. parl. in middle ages*, pp. 160-1, 187-8.

[35] *Ibid.*, pp. 188-9.

[36] *L. & P. Hen. VIII*, iv, no. 80; *Anal. Hib.*, ii, 104-5; *Cal. Carew MSS, 1575-88*, pp. 424-5, 479.

no elected representatives and could not legislate nor grant taxation.³⁷ Thus the Irish body would probably have been mistaken by Englishmen for a great council, and once representative great councils had fallen into disuetude in Ireland, the pressure to rename the former would gradually have become irresistible.

Evidence of two such councils held at different locations in Dublin in 1488 and at Trim in 1493 survive from the pre-Poynings period. In both cases parliamentary peers attended, but neither assembly included elected representatives. Both were summoned to debate important matters of policy in conjunction with royal commissioners sent from England, although in 1488 Sir Richard Edgecumbe who had come to negotiate terms of pardons after the Simnel conspiracy was excluded from certain sessions. Significantly, Edgecumbe referred to the assembly as a great council.³⁸ The 1493 council drew up a set of ordinances for the restoration of peace throughout the Pale and its proceedings were recorded, unlike those of a parliament or great council, on the close roll in English.³⁹ The ordinances made no alteration in the law but rather confirmed existing law with a view to its enforcement.

After 1494 such councils continued to be called, although it is seldom that we have sufficient information to distinguish between them and less formal assemblies. Extracts of concern to the borough of Kilkenny were later entered in the corporation book from the ordinances of a council held there before the deputy in 1500.⁴⁰ The council's purpose was 'the reformation of the contres of Kilkenny and Typerary', which was again to be achieved by the enforcement of the common law. The ordinances were drawn up 'by thassent of the hoole clergy, gentilmen and comens of the said shire and towne', on the advice of the king's council, the bishops of Ossory and Leighlin, the sovereign and council of Kilkenny, and the recorder and council of Waterford, and it may be that further sessions were planned for Co. Tipperary and Co. Waterford. What is apparently the work of another local assembly, concerned with the defence of Co. Meath, was entered on the patent roll immediately after a commission of the peace for the barony of Slane in 1499.⁴¹ In this case nothing is known of the

---

³⁷E.g. G.O. Sayles, *The king's parliament of England* (London, 1975), pp. 132-5.

³⁸Harris, *Hibernica* (1st ed.), pp. 64-73.

³⁹Close roll, 9 Henry VII (*Stat. Ire., Hen. VII & VIII*, pp. 88-91). Cf. *Proc. king's council, Ire., 1392-3,* pp. 305, 311.

⁴⁰*Liber primus Kilkenn.*, pp. 156-8.

⁴¹Patent roll, 14 Henry VII art. 15 (P.R.O.I., Lodge MS 'Articles', i, f. 221; *Rot. pat. Hib.*, p. 272).

actual council, although its ordinances are an early example of the sort of measures for the promotion of English weapons which were suggested to the king in reform tracts which survive from 1515 onwards. Thus afforced councils continued to be summoned for quasi-legislative purposes, although they apparently adhered to the spirit of Poynings' Law by confining themselves to measures designed to promote the observance of existing law rather than to the creation of strictly new law.

The more serious threat to parliament's legislative role concerned the English parliament's claim to legislate for Ireland. In the fourteenth century it had sometimes legislated specifically for Ireland and much general legislation was also applied.[42] This in theory remained the position in the following century, but the issue was confused by the fact that English statutes were now usually proclaimed in the Irish parliament before enforcement, that in 1460 the Irish parliament had explicitly denied the principle that English legislation was applicable in Ireland, and that thereafter some English legislation was confirmed by the Irish parliament.[43] On the other hand, when the issue was raised in court in England, in 1441 and 1485, the judges eventually ruled that statutes made in England bound those in Ireland.[44] And that in general the lordship stood in an inferior relationship to the realm of England was seemingly acknowledged by the Irish parliament itself in 1474. In a neat attempt to turn the tables, parliament then argued that 'of very ryght the realme of England is bound to the defense of [the king's] land of Irland by resoun that it ys oon of the membres of his moost noble corone and eldest membre therof'.[45]

It has been argued that doubts about the validity of English legislation were resolved by an act of Poynings's parliament which allegedly declared 'that the statute law of England should be deemed good and effectual in law "and over that be accepted, used and executed within this land of Ireland"'.[46] In fact it is so ambiguously worded that its intention and effect are unclear, which is probably why the controversy surfaced again in the seventeenth century.[47] In its

---

[42]Richardson & Sayles, *Ir. parl. in middle ages,* pp. 92-3, ch. 16.

[43]Lydon, *Lordship,* pp. 263-5. Cf. William Molyneux, *The case of Ireland stated* (ed. J.G. Simms, Dublin, 1977), pp. 62-7.

[44]E.g. Lydon, *Lordship,* pp. 263-5.

[45]P.R.O., C.47/10/29 (printed in Bryan, *Great Earl of Kildare,* p. 22).

[46]Statute roll, 10 Henry VII cc 7, 39 (*Stat. Ire.,* i, 43-4, 56-7); Richardson & Sayles, *Ir. parl. in middle ages,* pp. 266, 273-4 (quotation at p. 273); Lydon, *Lordship,* p. 265.

[47]See Molyneux, *Case of Ireland,* pp. 7-14.

preamble the statute observed that 'many and diverse good and profitable statutes late made within the realm of England' had brought that realm 'to great wealth and prosperity, and by all likelyhood so would this land, if the said estatutes were used and executed in the same'. It enacted

> that all estatutes late made within the said realm of England concerning or belonging to the common and publique weal of the same from henceforth be deemed good and effectuall in the law, and over that be acceptyd used and executed within this land of Ireland in all points at all times requisite according to the tenor and effect of the same; and over that by authority aforesaid, that they be and every of them be authorized, proved and confirmed in this said land of Ireland.[48]

The context seems to fit a particular application of English legislation to Ireland better than a general one. Although stress has been laid on the clause 'from henceforth' to suggest that English statutes should in future apply, the sense is rather that certain statutes for the common good *late made*, not all statutes past and future, should *from henceforth* apply, even though they had not hitherto been executed in Ireland. This did not necessarily raise the general issue, which the king no doubt regarded as settled by the judges' decision of 1485, if not before, for it had long been accepted that only statutes deemed suitable should be applied to Ireland. Moreover, the suggestion here advanced, that this was a particular measure which accorded with the general constitutional position as understood by the king and his advisers, gains support from evidence of user. Within a few years actions in the Irish exchequer were being brought on foot of English statutes applied to Ireland by virtue of the act of 1494 – for example a statute of 1442 restraining customs officials from keeping taverns, and one of 1490 permitting royal tenants who went on military service to convey their lands to feoffees without payment of fines – but there is apparently no instance of a later statute being so applied.[49] Nevertheless, precisely because it did not address itself to the general issue, the effect of the act was to reinforce rather than resolve existing doubts. If certain English acts were now in force because the Irish parliament had confirmed them, did not this imply that English legislation not so confirmed was inapplicable to Ireland? In fact, the English parliament

---

[48] The quotation in Lydon, *Lordship,* p. 265 is in fact from Edmund Curtis, 'The acts of the Drogheda parliament, 1494-5, or "Poynings' Laws"' in Conway, *Henry VII's relations with Scotland and Ireland, 1485-98* (Cambridge, 1932), p. 129 and not from the statute.

[49] Memoranda rolls, 17 Henry VIII m. 19, 23 Henry VIII m. 26 (P.R.O.I., Ferguson coll., iv, ff 106, 158). Cf. Bean, *Decline of English feudalism,* p. 146 and note.

still legislated occasionally for Ireland. In 1495 it reversed the attainder of the eighth earl of Kildare by Poynings's parliament, in 1534 it attainted the tenth earl of Kildare, and in 1536 it attainted two of the tenth earl's uncles.[50]

In 1534, therefore, the general issue was still unresolved, with important consequences for the future, but in the late medieval period this issue was more a minor irritant in Anglo-Irish relations than a source of deep resentment to the political community of the lordship. This was partly because the king rarely chose to legislate for Ireland through the English parliament. Although in the fifteenth century a weak king might have difficulty in preventing a governor from using parliament for his own ends, the king's overall control of parliament, when asserted, was never seriously questioned.[51] More especially, however, the interests of the Old English political community, including legislative ones, were remarkably similar to those of the political nation in England, of which they were generally accepted as a part. Thus although in the modern context a greater significance has been attributed to the occasional conflicts between king and governor or community, the existence of a separate parliament which offered mainly administrative solutions to particular problems within the framework of the common law did not necessarily promote separatist tendencies in the lordship.[52]

The council

In England, Henry VIII's reign saw the differentiation of the administrative and judicial functions of the council – between the council as a court, the embryonic court of Star Chamber, and an administrative board, from which the privy council was created in the mid-1530s. In Ireland, a distinct privy council had been established rather earlier, but this did not apparently lead to a full differentiation of conciliar business. From 1562 certain exclusively judicial sessions of the council were indeed authorized and termed the court of Castle Chamber after the English model, but the privy council continued to hear suits and reserved the right to review cases in Castle Chamber. And as late as 1622, James I issued directions restraining the

---

[50] *Rotuli parliamentorum* (6 vols., London, 1761-83), vi, 481-2; *The statutes of the realm,* 26 Henry VIII c. 25, 28 Henry VIII c. 18. See also Ellis, 'Henry VIII, rebellion and the rule of law', pp. 516-24.

[51] Richardson & Sayles, *Ir. parl. in middle ages,* pp. 263-8.

[52] Cf. Lydon, *Ireland in the later middle ages,* chs. 5-6.

council's judicial activity.⁵³ In fact in the late medieval period, council sessions probably determined both administrative and legal matters as the need and opportunity arose. The 1534 *Ordinances* required

> that the chancler, calling to him a juge of every of the kinges courtes & such other of the lordes & counsayle as shalbe present in terme tyme, shal syt twies every weke during terme season in the counsayle chamber, there to receyue and here such compleyntes as the kynges subiectes shal exhibite and take order therin accordyngly.

Although this ordinance is of some value concerning Cromwell's establishment of a privy council in England, in Ireland it was ignored, and in 1537 more formal arrangements were suggested for the automatic issue of process by the clerk of the council for petitions to the deputy to be determined by the chancellor and council.⁵⁴

As in England, the council's judicial business seems primarily to have been in civil suits. Many suits of course would earlier have been determined in parliament, but this business was not entirely new in the sixteenth century.⁵⁵ Much of the scanty surviving evidence relates to cases in which title to land or other rights was tried, thus ignoring as in England a statute of Edward III's reign which had sought to prevent this.⁵⁶ In 1494-5 the deputy and council found in favour of the earl of Kildare, defendant in a suit concerning title to the manor of Moynalvy, Co. Meath. In 1501 the council remitted the examination of title in the prisage dispute between Waterford and New Ross to commissioners, and similar actions about title which were determined by the council in 1516, 1521, 1524 and 1527 involving the archbishop of Dublin were entered in Archbishop Alen's register.⁵⁷ More generally, the council intervened in a dispute in 1516 about a ship taken as a prize by the inhabitants of Drogheda, in 1524 in the town's dispute with Lord Howth about a rent of 40*s*. there, in two disputes about customs involving Dublin city, in a dispute between a

---

⁵³Herbert Wood, 'The court of Castle Chamber or Star Chamber in Ireland', *R.I.A. Proc.*, xxxii (1914), sect. C, 153-5; Quinn, 'Cal. Ir. council bk.', pp. 98, 103-5; G.J. Hand & V.W. Treadwell, 'His majesty's directions for ordering and settling the courts within his kingdom of Ireland, 1622', *Anal. Hib.*, xxvi (1970), 90.

⁵⁴*S.P. Hen. VIII*, ii, 209, 501.

⁵⁵Cf. Parliament rolls, 28 Henry VI c. 6, 36 Henry VI c. 27 (*Stat. Ire., Hen. VI*, pp. 169, 548); Richardson & Sayles, *Ir. parl. in middle ages,* p. 199.

⁵⁶Guy, *Cardinal's court,* pp. 15, 17.

⁵⁷*L. & P. Hen. VIII,* Add. no. 297; *Ormond deeds, 1413-1509,* no. 301 (2); *Alen's reg.*, pp. 262, 271-2. Cf. Parliament roll, 19 & 20 Edward IV c. 18 (*Stat. Ire., Edw. IV*, ii, 724-6).

Youghal merchant and the earl of Desmond in 1529, and in another between citizens of Limerick concerning a house there in 1531-2.[58] In addition, many cases which were determined by individual councillors or local gentlemen must have been referred by the council. As in England, the council probably relied heavily on delegation – a bill of 1539 seemingly anticipated the council's usual response by petitioning for a commission of *dedimus potestatem* – but specific examples are difficult to prove.[59]

Other references to assemblies of justices occur, but many are to cases in which the king's councillors were called in as private arbitrators. These were not courts of course, but it is difficult at times to draw a meaningful distinction in Ireland between extracurial arbitration, jurisdiction in review and other cases which posed legal difficulties. While judges and legally trained councillors were, as in England, in demand as arbitrators, some of these disputes were effectively brought back within the purview of the courts by the taking of bonds to abide by arbitrators' opinions. For example, in an attempt in 1531 to end a long-running dispute in the exchequer concerning the manor of Rathwire, resumed to the king by statute of 1494, the two parties entered into recognizances of £40 payable to the king and recorded on the memoranda roll to abide by the arbitration of the four judges and two barons concerning their respective claims and those of the king to the manor.[60] In this case the king had an interest, but in other instances of arbitration backed by bonds this was clearly not so.[61] Effectively therefore a series of *ad hoc* courts had been erected which recall the origins of conciliar jurisdiction in England, and there are signs that after 1534 private arbitration by councillors backed by bonds began to be regarded as a form of delegation of business by the council.[62]

Petitions to the council regularly alleged riot, trespass or forcible entry and were frequently found on examination to be primarily civil suits not involving a serious threat to the king's peace. But the Irish

---

[58]*Cal. pat. rolls Ire., Hen. VIII-Eliz.*, pp. 1, 10, 76; B.L., Add. MS 19865, ff 58v-9; J.T. Gilbert (ed), *Calendar of ancient records of Dublin*, i (Dublin, 1889), pp. 176-83; *Ormond deeds, 1509-47*, no. 150.

[59]*Christ Church deeds*, nos. 401, 426, 436; Parliament roll, 8 Henry VII c. 9 (P.R.O.I., RC 13/9); *Alen's reg.*, p. 262. Cf. Guy, *Cardinal's court*, p. 39.

[60]Memoranda roll, 23 Henry VIII m. 8d (P.R.O.I., Ferguson coll., iv, f. 154); B.L., Add. MS 4763, ff 126-7 (*L. & P. Hen. VIII*, v, app. no. 20). Cf. P.R.O.I., Ferguson coll., ii, f. 16v, iii, ff. 336, 356; Baker (ed.), *Spelman's reports*, ii, 92.

[61]E.g. *Christ Church deeds*, nos. 405, 1055, 1130.

[62]*Ibid.*, nos. 426, 433.

council was certainly active in trying to compose disputes which threatened more serious consequences, even though there is no direct evidence of official prosecutions. In 1519 a papal provisor to the priory of Selskar, Co. Wexford ignored writs of *sub poena* to answer for his breach of the Statute of Provisors, and at the chancellor's motion the deputy eventually appeared with an army to enforce the statute. About 1525 the mayor and bailiffs of Dublin, riding their franchise, entered the archbishop's liberty of St. Sepulchre, upon which a riot ensued: the council referred the archbishop's bill to the three senior judges who found in his favour. Between 1529 and 1532 the council was active in composing disputes between the earls of Ossory and Desmond and between Ossory and Kildare.[63]

Finally, one important case, in which the king intervened directly, concerned the disputed succession to the earldom of Ormond in 1515, in which a conflict arose between the custom of Ireland and the law of England. In Edward III's reign, it was settled that tenure by barony in Ireland involved liability to attend parliament: it followed, if peerages were linked to baronies, that in an entail of the peer's lands the peerage devolved with the barony, whether or not its heir were heir to the whole estate. Thus Piers Butler of Carrick claimed the earldom as cousin and heir male on the grounds that its lands were so entailed. This claim was accepted by Lord Deputy Kildare and the council, and Butler was granted livery of the lands (in Ireland only no doubt) under the Irish great seal in April 1516, notwithstanding livery of all the lands of the earldom in England, Wales and Ireland granted to the heirs general, Anne St. Leger and Margaret Boleyn, under the English great seal the previous December. And in a case brought by the king's attorney in the Irish exchequer, Butler was exonerated for intruding into four manors parcel of the earldom. In July, however, the king ordered Kildare to give his lawful assistance to the heirs general in prosecuting their claim by the common law, or 'with assistence of your counsail and chancellor here' to examine title 'and to set suche fynall ende and determinacion therein as shuld be consonant with equetie and justice if I might'. And if 'thrugh thobstynacy of any of the parties' he were unable to proceed, he should command them upon their allegiances to appear in person before the council in England.[64]

---

[63]*L. & P. Hen. VIII,* ii, no. 3853; *Alen's reg.,* pp. 272-3; N.L.I., D. 2096, 2207; *Ormond deeds, 1509-47,* nos. 93, 149, 162, 181; *S.P. Hen. VIII,* ii, 148, 160.

[64]*Facs. nat. MSS Ire.,* pt. iii, no. 62; *L. & P. Hen. VIII,* ii, nos. 1230, 1269, 1277; *Ormond deeds, 1509-47,* no. 33; Memoranda roll, 7 & 8 Henry VIII m. 29d (B.L., Add. MS 4791, ff 197v, 198; P.R.O.I., Ferguson repertory, iv, 130-1). Cf. William Lynch, *A view of the legal institutions ... established in Ireland* (London, 1830), pp. 132-8, ch. 8.

The Irish council heard the case in Michaelmas term, accepting the claim of the heirs-general that no fair trial could be had at common law because of the 'great aliaunce' of Butler, but was obstructed by Butler who asked that the case be remitted to the common law and claimed that 'great warres' with the king's Irish enemies prevented him from attending. In reply, the ladies' counsel exhibited evidence – principally the creation patent of the earldom with a grant of £10 in support of the dignity, and some entailments to the heirs-general of lands in Co. Dublin and Co. Meath – which suggests that they were arguing that the earldom did not subsume a tenurial barony but was a new creation. At this stage, the council respited the case pending instructions from the king, though their interim arrangements suggest that they considered Butler had the better title except to those lands specifically entailed to the heirs-general. Political considerations seem to have influenced the eventual determination of the case: the king refused to recognise Butler as earl, but letters under the great seals of England and Ireland styled him as such. The case was resumed in Star Chamber about 1526 and in 1528 a temporary settlement was effected whereby Sir Thomas Boleyn, son of Margaret and father of Henry VIII's future queen, was created earl of Ormond and Butler became earl of Ossory, but after the Boleyns' fall Butler became earl of Ormond as well in 1537.[65]

After 1494 the king's council in England gained ground as a court for the trial of cases which presented political or legal difficulties.[66] In 1516 a statute enacted that persons suing privy seals to bring Irish suits before the king and council should give recognizances in the Irish chancery to pay defendants' costs and damages should they be acquitted, it being alleged that legal remedy was available in Ireland and that many suits were malicious, designed to put defendants to costs.[67] In 1519, when the age-old dispute over prisage between Waterford and New Ross broke out once again, the city chose to petition the king instead of bringing an action in the Irish courts as previously. This and three cases involving the earl of Ormond in 1526-7 were remitted to the council in Star Chamber for determination.[68]

[65] *Ormond deeds, 1413-1509,* no. 320, *1509-47,* nos. 33, 64, 80-1, 89, 100-1, 115, 136; *L. & P. Hen. VIII,* xii (ii), no. 963; Ellis, 'Tudor policy and Kildare ascendancy', pp. 236, 240; Quinn, 'Henry VIII and Ireland', pp. 322, 334. Cf. Richardson & Sayles, *Ir. parl. in middle ages,* pp. 119-20, 134-5.

[66] *L. & P. Hen. VIII,* Add. no. 297 (two actions against the ninth earl of Kildare: n.d., ?1515).

[67] Statute roll, 7 & 8 Henry VIII c. 5 (*Stat. Ire.*, i, 59-60).

[68] *L. & P. Hen. VIII,* iii, no. 356; *Cal. anc. rec. Dublin,* i, 177-8; *Ormond deeds, 1509-47,* nos. 115, 136; J. Hardiman, *History of the town and county of Galway*

Chancery

Although there is no hard evidence concerning the weight of business in council at this time, surviving references suggest that it was important, probably increasingly so under the early Tudors, as a court of law. Nevertheless, the most significant legal development at this time was the growth of chancery. The Latin, or common law, jurisdiction of chancery had developed in the fourteenth century when cases, chiefly of replevin, were enrolled on the patent roll. In the later fifteenth century, parliamentary petitions were sometimes referred to chancery and there are occasional references to other suits there, for example an action for the king in 1479 following a fraudulent suit of livery; but such business as there was was clearly inconsiderable before 1494.[69]

Of more consequence for the future, however, were the origins of the chancellor's equitable jurisdiction. In England this can be traced to the early fifteenth century, but under the Yorkists chancery was transformed from an administrative department with some judicial business into one of the four central courts of the realm.[70] In Ireland, as Richardson and Sayles have shown, cases in which the common law afforded no remedy or where 'lack of governance' inhibited its execution were early considered in parliament.[71] Even before 1494, however, the association of the chancery with equity had begun, although the stimulus for its further development was provided by Poynings' Law. In a case before parliament in 1460, the plaintiff in an ecclesiastical suit was authorised, if she wished, to proceed by bill in chancery and writ of *sub poena* because judgement could not be enforced at common law. This, it has been argued, shows 'that the Irish chancellor did not claim equitable jurisdiction and that he required the authority of parliament, not only to adjudicate in equity, but also to issue the characteristic writ of an English court of equity, the *sub poena*'.[72] A careful examination suggests, however, that the

(Dublin, 1820), p. 83; Guy, *Cardinal's court*, p. 67. Cf. *L. & P. Hen. VIII*, Add. no. 666.

[69]Parliament rolls, 38 Henry VI c. 24 (*Stat. Ire., Hen. VI*, p. 698), 18 Edward IV (I) c. 14 (*ibid., Edw. IV*, ii, 602: entry of default in margin of parliament roll, suggesting that separate rolls for this business were not normally kept by chancery), 19 & 20 Edward IV c. 42 (*ibid.*, ii, 786-94); A.J. Otway-Ruthven, 'The mediaeval Irish chancery' in *Album Helen Maud Cam* (Louvain, 1961), p.130.

[70]Nicholas Pronay, 'The chancellor, the chancery and the council at the end of the fifteenth century' in H. Hearder & H.R. Loyn (eds.), *British government and administration: studies presented to S.B. Chrimes* (Cardiff, 1974), pp. 87-103.

[71]*Ir. parl. in middle ages*, pp. 215-21.

[72]*Ibid.*, p. 219; Parliament roll, 38 Henry VI cc 25, 51 (*Stat. Ire., Hen. VI*, pp. 698-700, 772-8).

case proves no more than that an exceptional expedient was being employed: and in fact what was considered exceptional was probably not the *sub poena* itself but the method of its employment. The penalty in the writ, £40 in this case, was not normally leviable, and the term set for defendant's appearance would normally be from four to twelve weeks: but in this case, a term of six days was set and the penalty for non-appearance was leviable, half to be paid to the plaintiff in lieu of a debt of £20 as determined in the ecclesiastical court, and half to the king.[73] On the other hand, a chancery case of 1480 which has been cited as an early instance of the chancellor's equitable jurisdiction is in fact inconclusive. This was certainly a case in equity, involving an enfeoffment to use, but in the previous year depositions in the case had been taken by the governor and other senior ministers which suggests that the case had been transferred from the council, perhaps returning for judgement.[74]

Nevertheless, more conclusive evidence does survive for the later fifteenth century. As early as 1449, a great council provided that petitions to the lieutenent should be remitted to the chancery 'si il soit mater de consciens'.[75] In 1472 a civil action commenced by *sub poena* sued from chancery was continued in parliament after the writ had been ignored, whereupon parliament remitted the trial of the action itself to the justices of common pleas 'come il fuit vne accion. commense al comune ley', providing that if the defendant did not appear he should be outlawed and should forfeit £40, half to the plaintiff and half to the king.[76] Other occasional references to *sub poenas* survive, and in 1493 when justice was denied by the municipal authorities in Kilkenny, parliament provided that the defendants should surrender 'sour pein en la bill comprise' to answer 'sicom le courte du roy du chauncery voet agarder' or otherwise that the resident justice for Co. Kilkenny should hear and determine the case 'sicom il fuit determine en le dit courte du chauncery' or elsewhere by the common law.[77]

It is unlikely that Henry VII foresaw the consequences of Poynings' Law for the development of chancery, but even so the appointment of English lawyers to the Irish bench for two years from 1494 would have given some impetus towards the standardization of

[73] Cf. Guy, *Cardinal's court*, p. 83.

[74] *Christ Church deeds*, nos. 326, 1014-19, 1021. Cf. *New hist. Ire.*, iii, 23.

[75] Parliament roll, 28 Henry VI c. 6 (*Stat. Ire., Hen, VI*, p. 169).

[76] Parliament roll, 11 & 12 Edward IV c. 85 (*ibid., Edw. IV*, i, 882-4).

[77] Parliament rolls, 16 & 17 Edward IV c. 55 (*ibid.*, ii, 582), 8 Henry VII cc 1, 28 (P.R.O.I., RC 13/9).

legal forms and procedures on the English model. More specifically, on the appointment as chancellor of Henry Deane, councillor and bishop-elect of Bangor, his patent specifically empowered him to determine plaints (*lites*) moved in chancery. At the same time, two prominent Old English ecclesiastics were appointed by English patent to the Irish council and to the hitherto obscure office of master in chancery. And when we learn that in January 1496 the chancellor received 50*s*. 9*d*. for green cloth 'pro loco sessionis suo pro cancellaria ac tabula eiusdem infra castrum Dublin.', it is evident that some reorganization was proceeding.[78] The comparatively plentiful references, direct and indirect, to chancery business in the years following strongly suggest that chancery was by then established as a principal court, but it is not until 1520 that direct evidence survives. Chancery was then keeping regular terms, and profits of £55 for the two years to Easter 1522 were recorded from four cases from Co. Meath, New Ross and Kilkenny, in which defendants forfeited recognizances for default after an initial appearance and, in the New Ross case, a subsequent amercement of the sovereign and portreeves for not returning a writ of attachment.[79] Again, in Michaelmas 1534 when rebellion was raging throughout the Pale, Lord Chancellor Cromer recorded in his archiepiscopal register the appearance of four Palesmen before him in chancery at Termonfeckin on 14-16 October in response to *sub poenas*.[80]

Early chancery proceedings frequently dealt with cases which were also determinable by the council – maintenance, embracery and title to land – suggesting that there was as yet no real distinction between what was properly matter for chancery or for the council.[81] Moreover, if circumstances were unusual, litigants might be told to sue before the council if they wished: in 1502, a master in chancery, retained by Ormond in a suit for debt against the abbot of St. Mary's, reported that he had

---

[78]*Cal. pat. rolls, 1485-94*, p. 473 *1494-1509*, pp.7, 15; B.L., Royal MS 18C, XIV, f. 33v.

[79]P.R.O., E.101/248/21, S.P.1/67, f. 33v (*L. & P. Hen. VIII*, v, no. 398); *Christ Church deeds*, nos. 375, 377, 378; *Cal. anc. rec. Dublin*, i, 394, 441-2; *H.M.C. rep. 10*, app. v, p. 328; *Cal. anc. deeds, Pembroke Estate Office*, no. 202; T.C.D., MS 594, f. 6v; *Ormond deeds, 1509-47*, app. no. 66; *Cal. pat. rolls Ire., Hen. VIII-Eliz.*, p. 10; *S.P. Hen. VIII*, ii, 40n.

[80]Cromer's register, copy in T.C.D., MS 557, xii, 556-7. Cf. Ellis, 'Tudor policy and Kildare ascendancy', pp. 260-3.

[81]Parliament roll, 8 Henry VII c. 28 (P.R.O.I., RC 13/9); *Christ Church deeds*, nos. 375, 377-8; *Cal. pat. rolls Ire., Hen. VIII-Eliz.*, p. 10; P.R.O.I., RC 6/1. Cf. Elton, *Tudor constitution*, pp. 150-1.

sued the saide abbot in the chauncery and courte of conscience in your behalfe vnto a iugement and, because I myght haue no iugement [there], ... befor my lorde the kinges depute of this land and the kinges counsell of the same in the mooste effectuous maner by thaduice of the best larned counsell in the kinges lawe that I moght get here.[82]

By the later 1530s, however, chancery was already showing signs of that capacity for extending its jurisdiction which characterized the expansion of English law in the Elizabethan conquest. A *sub poena* was served on Rory O'More, captain of Leix, who 'not regardeing it, toke it unreverently and threwe it in the myre', for which he was presented by a Co. Kilkenny jury in 1537. And in 1538, a Galway merchant recovered possession of lands in Co. Connaught near Galway, let by lease to the ancestors of the lord of Clanrickard. The decree was in Latin, not the usual English, and the defendant, having contested the action, permitted its execution, and later made suit concerning a castle built by his ancestors on the lands.[83]

Once chancery had become established as one of the central courts of the lordship, the question arose of a deputy in the chancellor's absence. Later practice was for the master of the rolls to determine suits, but in the fifteenth century neither this officer, though of the council, nor the other chancery clerks had authority *ex officio* to act in a judicial capacity. Nevertheless, the keeper of the rolls was normally commissioned, as keeper of the great seal, to preside over the Latin jurisdiction of chancery in the chancellor's absence.[84] Under the early Tudors, one of the first indications of the new status of this officer is the change in his official title from *clericus sive custos rotulorum* to *magister rotulorum*, but the earliest examples of the new style – dating from 1494 and 1521-2 – probably reflect the new English usage and are not warranted by patent.[85] From 1523, however, when John Ricard, an Englishman, was appointed master by English patent, this style became normal, though as late as 1532 a

---

[82] *Ormond deeds, 1509-47,* app. no. 66.

[83] Hore & Graves, *Southern & eastern counties,* p. 104; Blake, *Blake family records,* nos. 90, 100, 104, 108, 121; *Rec. comm. Ire. rep., 1811-15,* p. 79.

[84] Gen. Off., MS 22, p. 45. Cf. Otway-Ruthven, 'Med. Ir. chancery', p. 129.

[85] Statute roll, 10 Henry VII c. 2 (*Stat. Ire.*, i, 42, which includes the master of the rolls among the judges); P.R.O., E.101/248/21; Patent roll, 7 Henry VII (B.L., Add. MS 4787, f. 53); Memoranda roll, 13 Henry VIII m. 15 (P.R.O.I., Ferguson coll., iv, f. 63; B.L., Add. MS 4791, f. 199).

conservative clerk in the Irish chancery could use the old style in a patent.[86]

From the early 1530s, evidence survives of the master acting as a judge in chancery, and by 1537 he was accounted one of the judges of the four courts. John Alen, appointed master in 1533, was explicitly granted by patent the same powers as his English counterpart, including the determination of suits in the chancellor's absence: these powers he exercised in Michaelmas and Hilary terms 1533-4, later claiming (when he had his eye on the chancellorship) that 'thextreaties of the corte, no man injured, surmounteth 200 markis and mo causes spedd ther thois 2 termes than was 2 yeres before'.[87] As early as January 1532, however, Alen's predecessor heard a case because the chancellor was personally involved.[88]

Until 1494 and probably after on a lesser scale, the Irish parliament was an important instrument in the efforts of the lordship's government to secure unity and cooperation among the king's subjects there. Its development under the Yorkists demonstrates that despite a weaker central authority and the correspondingly stronger local traditions of self-reliance, the lordship remained in a very real sense a political entity apart from Gaelic Ireland, closely linked to England and with many similar interests and problems. As a lawcourt, parliament had not really begun before 1494 to rival the traditional courts in the number of suits which it entertained, although in the range and gravity of cases pleaded there it was far more important. It is unfortunate that there is no hard evidence about the comparative weight of business in chancery and the council or their development after 1494, but by 1534 the indications are that the two courts had attracted most of the sort of litigation earlier coming before parliament and rather more besides. Probably the proportion of parliamentary litigation originating in the counties outside the Pale under the Yorkists, about 15½ per cent of all private petitions, was somewhat higher than the overall proportion of cases from these shires reaching the central courts as a whole. This was because the commoner sort of suits would largely be dealt with by itinerant commissioners, but since there was really no

---

[86]*L. & P. Hen. VIII*, iii, no. 3188; Memoranda rolls, 15 Henry VIII m. 25 (B.L., Add. MS 4791, f. 201), 21 Henry VIII m. 4 (P.R.O.I., Ferguson coll., iv, f. 144); N.L.I., D.2146 (calendared inaccurately in *Ormond deeds, 1509-47*, no. 130); *Cal. pat. rolls Ire., Hen, VIII-Eliz.*, p. 6.

[87]*S.P. Hen. VIII*, ii, 269, 498.

[88]*Alen's reg.*, pp. 280-1.

alternative to parliament for certain types of litigation before 1494, this evidence suggests that the weight of business before the royal courts operating outside the Pale must have been reasonably substantial.

Thus despite some contradictions, the Yorkist and early Tudor period saw a perceptible recovery in the common law in Ireland. The decline of the traditional courts was more than offset by the development of new courts in response to the changing needs of society in the lordship; and the evident flexibility of the new courts, in contrast with the cumbersome process of the traditional courts, enabled the common law system as a whole both to benefit from and to assist in the revival of government there. And while the central courts probably prospered in part at the expense of local or seigneurial courts, it may be that by 1500 a more vigorous system overall coupled with more settled conditions and stronger government was beginning as in England to wean the magnates and gentry away from violence to the pursuit of their interests through the courts. In any event, the evidence suggests that under the early Tudors the availability or otherwise of justice in the Pale was much as it was within the more settled shires of England and, less clearly, that the outlying counties were in no worse situation than the other borderlands of the Tudor state.

6

THE SEALS AND SECRETARIAT

In previous chapters, the emphasis has been on the revival in the powers of the Dublin government by the initiation of administrative reform. The organization and operation of the seals and secretariat were less immediately important in this context, but more clearly than for other aspects of administration they illustrate the efforts to maintain effective government with the limited resources available. The lordship's chief writing office, the chancery, was organized broadly on the English model but it was less elaborate and an earlier tendency towards specialization in the duties of clerical staff was being reversed. The period saw the continued decline of the great seal as an original instrument and chancery's eclipse as the central writing office in favour of the governor's privy seal and its keeper who was probably also clerk of the council for much of the time. After 1534 the Irish chancery was reorganized on more strictly English lines, the office of keeper of the privy seal and clerk of the council were more firmly separated, and in 1560 the official use of the governor's seal was curbed by the provision of a royal privy seal kept by the clerk of the council who was renamed the secretary.[1]

The chief chancery officers were, in order of importance, the chancellor himself, the keeper of the rolls, and the clerks of the hanaper and the crown. Excepting masters in chancery from 1494, there were no other patentee officers at this time, and the other clerks, who received occasional rewards but no regular salary, were maintained by the chancellor out of his diets, by the keeper of the rolls or survived on the perquisites of office.[2] The chancellor's salary was £40, but until 1395 he had also received the issues of the seal. These were reserved to the king for most of the fifteenth century, as in England, and instead he received diets which varied from 5s. to 10s. but were increasingly fixed at 6s. 8d. down to 1479.[3] In 1479, however, Edward IV found it necessary to issue instructions that the keeper of the rolls 'see and write at every sele what profite growith on to the kyng therof, and the specialtees of the same, so that his boke so made may be a controllement uppon thaccompts of p^e clerc of the hanaper'. Out

---

[1] See S.G. Ellis, 'Privy seals of chief governors in Ireland, 1392-1560', *I.H.R. Bull.,* li (1978), 187-94.
[2] E.g. B.L., Royal MS 18C, XIV, ff 43, 63v; P.R.O., E.101/248/21, S.P. 65/1/2.
[3] Otway-Ruthven, 'Med. Ir. chancery', pp. 124-5; B.L., Add. MS 4787, ff 55v-56.

of the profits and fines of chancery the latter was required to 'pay the chaunsellor his fees, wages and rewards accustomed and delivre the remnant unto the kyngs exchequer upon his accomptes which he shall make yerly therof'.[4] Treasurer's accounts and extents suggest that in practice the chancellor's diets were paid directly by the clerk of the hanaper and that the exchequer was responsible only for the salaries of the chancellor and his clerks. Moreover, apart from Poynings's deputyship when they were increased to 10s. and paid by the exchequer, there was apparently a partial reversion to fourteenth-century practice with regard to the chancellor's diets.[5] At c.£40 per annum, hanaper profits paid into the exchequer were suspiciously low – for ten months in 1427 assignments of £269 17s. 3d. had been made on this source[6] – and after 1534 search had to be made to discover what diets were properly payable to the chancellor. In 1537 the master of the rolls reported that the chancellor and his clerks 'receyve to ther owne use the fines of writes of entres in le post and all other fynes of wrytes fynable whiche be paide to the kinges use', and requested an order 'howe the clerke of the hanaper shalbe chargeid to accompte for the fees of thinges that passe the greate sealle'. This practice no doubt encouraged the granting of pardons and exemplifications without fine but for a fee of 20s. for the great seal.[7] At a later date, the chancellor was entitled to half the receipts of the hanaper and could order expenditure for the upkeep of the court from the other half.[8]

Nevertheless, the chancellor was more important as a councillor and the second officer in the administration than as head of chancery, and with its development as a court of equity from 1494 his duties there became primarily judicial. To a lesser extent, this was also true of the keeper of the rolls, whose salary of £20 a year placed him on a par with the puisne judges, but as will appear the keeper also retained important responsibilities on the administrative side of chancery as well as custody of the rolls and records. These included the patent, close, parliament (to 1494) and (from 1494) statute rolls, files of fiants under the governor's or the English seals as warrants to the great seal, files of inquisitions and other returns to chancery commissions and, from the end of the period, chancery decrees together with the bills,

---

[4]Close roll, 19 Edward IV m. 7d (Gilbert, *Viceroys,* pp. 594-6).
[5]P.R.O., E. 101/248, nos. 17, 21, S.P. 65/1/2; B.L., Royal MS 18C, XIV, ff 148-51.
[6]P.R.O., E. 101/248/1.
[7]*S.P. Hen. VIII,* ii, 500; B.L., Add. MS 4787, ff 55v-56; *Stat. Ire., Edw. IV, passim.*
[8]Wood, *Public records of Ireland,* pp. 45, 132.

answers, replications and rejoinders relating to them.⁹ As with the exchequer, however, there was never the elaborate subdivision of rolls which occurred in England. It appeared to the Irish Record Commissioners that a new class of recognizance rolls had commenced with one of 21-27 Henry VIII, but it seems more likely that recognizances merely came to form the principal entry on existing close rolls, as had sometimes ocurred with pleas and fines at an earlier date: from the later Tudor period only two close rolls proper survived, although beginning with a roll of 27-33 Henry VIII several more were styled 'Rotulus clausus recognitionum . . .'[10]

The rolls were very badly kept both at the time and subsequently. Some patent rolls extant in Stuart times had disappeared before the last century: the patent roll of 14 Henry VII which comprised three membranes with sixteen articles in 1819 had had at least seven more articles in the seventeenth century. A slip of parchment used to append the great seal to a pardon of 1519 had evidently been cut from the record of a recent inquisition, and even plea rolls were cannibalized for parchment.[11] From 1494 the patent rolls probably averaged about six membranes a year, and a close roll of 10-15 Henry VII was at least fifty-five membranes long,[12] but many grants, commissions and pardons were in fact not enrolled and down to 1534 the deputy made grants under his privy seal which should have been made under the great seal.[13] The instructions of 1479 required that 'the clerc of the rolles do enroll all patents under the kyngs gret seall befor that they be deliveret to the parties and kepe so the kyngs recordes that none of them be rased ne besoiled'.[14]

After the chancellor and keeper, the clerks of the hanaper and crown were the only ones of importance. Although the hanaper office had originally paid less, only £5 a year, this clerkship was the more

---

[9]*Ibid.*, pp. 9-58, 72; *S.P. Hen. VIII*, ii, 499-501; *Ormond deeds, 1413-1509*, no. 301 (4).

[10]*Rec. comm. Ire. rep., 1816-20*, pp. 390-2, 431. Cf. Wood, *Public records of Ireland*, p. 14; *S.P. Hen. VIII*, ii, 500; Otway-Ruthven, 'Med. Ir. chancery', pp. 129-30.

[11]*Rec. comm. Ire. rep. 1816-20*, pp. 389-90; *Rot. pat. Hib.*, pp. 271-2; B.L., Add. MSS 4787, ff 52v-53, 4797, ff 109v-10; T.C.D., MSS 1731, pp. 75, 78, 1739, p. 2, 1740, p. xiv; N.L.I., D. 2055 (*Ormond deeds, 1509-47*, no. 61); Exch. Inq., Co. Dublin, P.R.O.I., RC 9/3, pp. 271-3; P.R.O.I., CB 1/9.

[12]*Rot. pat. Hib.*, p. [xvi]; *Cal. pat. rolls Ire., Hen. VIII-Eliz.*, pp. 1-21; T.C.D., MS 1739, p. 2.

[13]E.g. *S.P. Hen. VIII*, ii, 166.

[14]Close roll, 19 Edward IV m. 7d (Gilbert, *Viceroys*, p. 594). Cf. *S.P. Hen. VIII*, ii, 500.

important and by 1470 the clerk received ten marks rising to £10 by 1520, while the clerk of the crown's salary remained ten marks.[15] Under Poynings, the two offices were temporarily combined and an English-born clerk appointed with a salary of twenty marks plus robes, and eventually under Charles I the offices were amalgamated.[16] Moreover, in practice, though the clerk of the crown's duties were to 'make and enroll commissions and all thinges that twiche the king', these and other sorts of writs were frequently countersigned by the clerk of the hanaper.[17] The latter was responsible for collecting fines and fees payable to the hanaper and accounting for them annually in the exchequer. In practice, the clerk did not account so frequently before 1534 and standard fines were sometimes reduced. In 1479, 'to thentent that noone ignoreunce may be pretendit what fines ben to be made within the kyngs chaunsery', Edward IV had a list of standard fines sent over, but this was not fully enforced: the fine for respite of homage remained at 20d. or 40d. instead of the 6s. 8d. prescribed.[18] Sometime between 1413 and 1444 the courts of king's bench and common pleas received separate great seals for the issue of judicial writs, where before the judges had been authorized to issue them without the seal if the chancellor had been unable to be present at sessions – for some years under Henry VIII, common pleas made do with Richard III's great seal.[19] The clerk of the hanaper appointed deputies to receive the fees and fines in these courts, but they were apparently subject to defalcations similar to chancery fines and amounted to £9 17s. 8d. and £1 8s. 1d. only in king's bench and common pleas respectively in 1483-4, assigned for the payment of the justices' salaries.[20]

Although the duties of the senior clerks were not so well defined as in England, an ordered hierarchy of first and second grade clerks certainly existed, and only the senior clerks were entitled to write to the seal in their own names. For example, two surviving commissions

---

[15] P.R.O., E. 101/248, nos. 17, 21; Otway-Ruthven, 'Med. Ir. chancery', p. 127.

[16] *Cal. pat. rolls, 1494-1509,* p. 6; B.L., Royal MS 18C, XIV, f. 147; Wood, *Public records of Ireland,* p. 45.

[17] *S.P. Hen. VIII,* ii, 500; N.L.I., D. 2080, 2091 (*Ormond deeds, 1509-47,* nos. 81, 89); P.R.O., E. 101/248/21. Cf. Elton, *Tudor revolution in government,* p. 130.

[18] Close roll, 19 Edward IV m. 7d (Gilbert, *Viceroys,* pp. 594-6); Memoranda roll, 23 Edward IV m. 1 (P.R.O.I., Delafield MSS M. 2675, p. 73); Pipe roll, 18 Henry VII (N.L.I., MS 761, p. 332); P.R.O., S.P. 65/1/2.

[19] *Ormond deeds, 1413-1509,* nos. 83, 135, 243, *1509-47,* no. 133; Otway-Ruthven, 'Med. Ir. chancery', p. 128 and the references there cited.

[20] Close roll, 19 Edward IV m. 7d (Gilbert, *Viceroys,* p. 596); P.R.O., E. 101/248/17.

of the early 1520s were countersigned 'Wycombe', the clerk of the hanaper, though clearly in different hands.[21] Under Edward III there had usually been four senior clerks in office at any one time, although evidence about the distinct clerkships of the crown and the hanaper does not survive until later.[22] From 1494, however, patentee masters in chancery were appointed, apparently two at a time until 1534 and three or four later.[23] It seems that their duties were mainly administrative at first, but by 1533 one of the masters was a bachelor of civil law and they soon became associated with the judicial work of chancery – in 1547, for example, a master was commissioned to hear an appeal from the archbishop of Armagh to the king. It may be conjectured that what occurred in 1494 was rather the application of an English title to recognized senior clerkships than the creation of a new office. Ostensibly the masters were appointed by the deputy, but the fact that the archdeacon of Armagh was appointed master shortly after the archbishop of Armagh took office as chancellor suggests that the office was really in the chancellor's gift.[24]

To test this conjecture about the masters' origins, a total of seventy-three chancery writs – originals, transcripts and calendars – has been assembled for the period 1470-1534, on which appear the names of the clerks responsible for their drafting, plus a further twenty-six for Henry VIII's later years. No original chancery rolls now survive, and the sample includes few writs of course and many grants and exemplifications, but it suffices as a guide to which clerks were entitled to write to the great seal. Of these seventy-three writs, forty-two and probably forty-three carried the name of the clerk of the hanaper, seven and probably fourteen that of the clerk of the crown, and eight and probably nine the keeper of the rolls. Although a fair sample would no doubt disclose a preponderance of writs in the keeper's name, as in the period to 1450,[25] there appear to be only seven writs in the sample not made out in the name of these three clerks. These comprise a pardon of 1519 countersigned 'Golding', who may have been clerk of the crown then, an exemplification in

---

[21] N.L.I., D. 2080, 2091 (*Ormond deeds, 1509-47*, nos. 81, 89). Cf. Elton, *Tudor revolution in government*, pp. 130-1; Otway-Ruthven, 'Med. Ir. chancery', p. 124.

[22] Richardson & Sayles, *Admin. Ire.*, pp. 16-21; Otway-Ruthven, 'Med. Ir. chancery', pp. 122-4.

[23] *Cal. pat. rolls, 1485-94*, p. 473, *1494-1509*, p. 7; Wood, *Public records of Ireland*, pp. 24-5; the references cited in note 24.

[24] *Cal. pat. rolls Ire., Hen. VIII-Eliz.*, pp. 3, 4; P.R.O., S.P. 65/1/2; *Christ Church deeds*, no. 438; O'Flanagan, *Lives of the lord chancellors*, i, 164-5.

[25] Cf. Otway-Ruthven, 'Med. Ir. chancery', p. 124.

1499 of a statute and a pardon in 1507 for the clerk of the hanaper with the names appended of the two clerks appointed masters in 1494, and four more exemplifications of statutes. Exemplifications had additionally to be examined by two senior clerks, resulting in the names of two or three appended; and since Patrick Cogley, appointed clerk of the crown and of all parliaments and great councils for life in 1461, was responsible for those in the Yorkist period, usually with one Stephen Roche, the clerk of the parliament evidently attended to these. Likewise, exemplifications of acts of 1489 and 1491 and a writ of summons to the 1491 parliament were in the name of William Candell with William Kyltale associated; exemplifications of acts in 1493 were in the name of James Prendregast, probably a relation of the James Prendregast who served as clerk of the council, of the hanaper, and J.C.P. in the 1450s and 1460s, with Robert Lynn associated; and exemplifications of 1499 and 1508 were examined by Thomas Rochfort, king's serjeant 1511-13 and keeper of the rolls 1513-21.[26] Thus there were apparently at least two other senior clerks throughout this period who were entitled to write to the seal.

Even among the senior clerks there were prospects of promotion, and no doubt from among the lesser clerks too: Patrick Cogley was temporarily keeper of the rolls for two months in 1461 and had also been clerk of the hanaper, 1459-61; Nicholas Wycombe was promoted to keeper, 1532-3, as was Robert Cowley, clerk of the crown, 1535-9.[27] But by then the development of the judicial duties of the office must have hindered the promotion of those without legal training. Of the more junior clerks, the keeper of the rolls had two or three clerks of his own, the predecessors of the Six Clerks, who normally wrote in the keeper's name. This no doubt explains the preponderance of writs bearing his name down to 1450.[28] From 1534, however, they apparently began to write to the seal in their own names, contrary to practice in England: of twenty-six writs for the period 1535-47, sixteen were supervised by five otherwise unknown

[26] *Ormond deeds, 1413-1509*, nos. 261, 298, 301 (4); N.L.I., D. 2055 (ibid., *1509-47*, no. 61); *Stat. Ire., Hen. VII & VIII*, p. 103; *Rot. pat. Hib.*, p. 268 no. 42; Parliament roll, 7 & 8 Edward IV c. 48 (*Stat. Ire., Edw. IV*, i, 538); Memoranda rolls, 9 Henry VII mm 6, 10, 23 Henry VII m. 15 (P.R.O.I., RC 8/43, pp. 59, 70, 241), 15 Henry VIII m. 20 (P.R.O.I., Ferguson coll., iv, ff 78-9); Octavian's register, copy in T.C.D., MS 557, xi, 1290; H.J. Lawlor, 'A calendar of the Liber Niger and Liber Albus of Christ Church, Dublin', *R.I.A. Proc.*, xxvii (1908-9), sect. C, 20; *Alen's reg.*, p. 247.

[27] Ball, *Judges*, i, 180, 203; *Cal. pat. rolls Ire., Hen. VIII-Eliz.*, p. 6; Otway-Ruthven, 'Med. Ir. chancery', p. 138.

[28] *S.P. Hen. VIII*, ii, 499-500; Wood, *Public records of Ireland*, p. 42; Otway-Ruthven, 'Med. Ir. chancery', p. 124; Elton, *Tudor revolution in government*, p. 130.

clerks who were evidently kinsmen of the three masters of the rolls acting in this period, S. Alen 1536-7, S. Cowley 1539 (two original writs in the same hand),[29] J. Cowley 1540-1, J. Cusack 1543, and S. Cusack 1543-4. There were probably two acting at any one time and the office was clearly in the master's gift. Not long after, a copy made of a statute was signed, 'examinata per me Iacob. Newman, clericum in officio magistri rotulorum', and by 1578 there were specific cursitors charged with the writing of writs *de cursu*.[30] Throughout the medieval period, however, there was a distinct shortage of skilled clerks, and senior clerks must often have had to do their own copying: Richard Nangle, clerk of the hanaper 1470-94 and 1497-?1514, was rewarded in 1496 'pro factura ac scriptura diuersorum commissionum pro constablis pacis'.[31] This shortage was commented on by English-born administrators, and in 1536 Undertreasurer Brabazon asked for his kinsmen and two or three other clerks to be sent over.[32] Nevertheless, junior clerks were occasionally rewarded for their labours in chancery, for example Robert Isam received 12*s.* 6*d.* for writing statutes sent to England, and in 1462 John Power was appointed as sealer of writs of chancery.[33]

No doubt because of the shortage of clerks, a feature of clerical careers in the Dublin administration was the extent of mobility between the courts, even though the exchequer and chancery had earlier evolved separate bodies of clerks.[34] Patrick Cogley was also chief chamberlain in 1463-4, Thomas Alen was appointed both joint clerk of the hanaper and second chamberlain in 1535, and even John Alen, master of the rolls 1533-8, admitted to some exchequer experience.[35] Robert Lynn, a chancery clerk in 1493, was in 1494-5 writing rolls of subsidy assessment for the treasurer, and by 1498 he was acting second remembrancer.[36] Richard Anyden, rewarded with Philip Flatesbury for writing indentures for the council in 1496, was then

---

[29] N.L.I., D. 2318-19 (*Ormond deeds, 1509-47*, nos. 241-2).

[30] T.C.D., MS 581, f. 16; Wood, *Public records of Ireland*, p. 23.

[31] B.L., Royal MS 18C, XIV, f. 64; Otway-Ruthven, 'Med. Ir. chancery', pp. 121-2.

[32] *S.P. Hen. VIII*, ii, 86; *L. & P. Hen. VIII*, xi, no. 521.

[33] P.R.O., E. 101/248/21; *Rot. pat. Hib.*, p. 268 nos. 25-6. Cf. Otway-Ruthven, 'Med. Ir. chancery', p. 124.

[34] Cf. Otway-Ruthven, 'Med. Ir. chancery', p. 121.

[35] Ball, *Judges*, i, 180; Parliament roll, 3 Edward IV c. 31 (*Stat. Ire., Edw. IV*, i, 110); *Cal. pat. rolls Ire., Hen. VIII-Eliz.*, p. 16; *Fiants Ire., Hen. VIII*, nos. 40, 42; *S.P. Hen. VIII*, ii, 499.

[36] B.L., Royal MS 18C, XIV, f. 138v; Memoranda roll, 14 Henry VIII m. 6, 15 Henry VII m. 11 (P.R.O.I., RC 8/43, pp. 105, 177).

clerk of the customs in Dublin port and controller there in 1499.[37] Flatesbury is now best known for his historical interests, especially as the compiler of the 'Annales Phil. Flatesburii' and as the scribe of the Red Book of the Earls of Kildare, for which he had access to the records of chancery and the exchequer, and for which he was rewarded by an appointment as treasurer's clerk to Kildare's son in November 1507.[38] The most versatile was apparently Richard Nangle, temporarily displaced from the hanaper, who was clerk of the works in Dublin castle in 1495-6, treasurer's clerk, and controller of the mint, yet still at times employed in chancery.[39]

Nor were king's bench and common pleas entirely distinct. There were only three patentee offices in the two courts, the chief clerk of king's bench and the prothonotary and chirographer of common pleas. They and other clerks also acted as attorneys in the courts. The chief clerk received £5 a year, rising to £10 between 1496 and 1520, a salary which was no doubt for his services on the crown side of the court as in England, although he also acted on the civil side and presumably got the bulk of his income from fees paid by civil suitors.[40] The offices of prothonotary (or chief clerk and keeper of the writs) and chirographer of common pleas were more often than not combined, as had been the case in the fourteenth century, and paid ten marks a year, rising to £10 under Henry VIII. When the offices were held separately, however, as in 1520-2 and from 1534, each clerk received £5, no doubt to compensate the chirographer for the decline in his fees as common recoveries replaced fines in conveyances of land, for in England only the prothonotary was salaried.[41] Nevertheless, when the offices were combined they were usually held jointly, as was the chief clerkship of king's bench which was at times held by three clerks.[42] Other clerks who appear from time to time were also senior

---

[37] B.L., Royal MS 18C XIV, ff 63v, 67v; Memoranda roll, 14 Henry VII m. 10 (P.R.O.I., RC 8/43, p. 118).

[38] *Red Bk Kildare*, p. vi; Robin Flower, 'Manuscripts of Irish interest in the British Museum', *Anal. Hib.*, ii (1931), 325-9; above, ch. 3, p. 98.

[39] B.L., Royal MS 18C, XIV, ff 64, 66, 71, 135v; above, p. 171.

[40] Coram Rege roll, 1 Henry VII m. 5d (P.R.O.I., RC 8/43, pp. 29-30; Ferguson coll., iii, f. 314); B.L., Royal MS 18C, XIV, f. 148; P.R.O., E.101/248/21. Cf. Blatcher, *King's bench*, pp. 40-1; Baker, 'English legal profession', p. 24.

[41] De Banco roll, 19 Edward IV m. 6 (P.R.O.I., CB 1/10); P.R.O., E.101/248, nos. 17, 21, S.P. 65/1/2; *Cal. pat. rolls Ire., Hen. VIII-Eliz.*, p. 4; *Fiants Ire., Hen. VIII*, no. 36. Cf. Richardson & Sayles, *Admin. Ire.*, pp. 39-40; Hastings, *Common pleas*, pp. 137-9; Blatcher, *King's bench*, p. 41.

[42] E.g. De Banco roll, 19 Edward IV m. 6 (P.R.O.I., CB 1/10); Coram Rege roll, 1 Henry VII m. 5d (P.R.O.I., Ferguson coll., iii, f. 314).

and sat on the bench or examined exemplifications.[43] There were apparently at least four senior clerks in each court at any one time: in 1466, John Kiltale, 'un[us] clericorum communis banci', was rewarded 'scribendo ibidem recorda & billa pro proficuo nostro'. Yet in 1477 the keeper of the rolls of chancery was recording *attornamenta* in king's bench at Trim. In 1484 the prothonotary of common pleas was also transcriptor of the exchequer and between 1514 and 1520 another prothonotary was also clerk of common pleas in the exchequer.[44]

Although in the later fifteenth century the chancery was more often than not in Dublin, this was probably because the governor spent more of his time there than previously, as did the other central courts. From 1458 chancery letters were attested from the place at which the court was then kept, even though the fiant, the governor's privy seal warrant for its issue, might have been attested elsewhere.[45] Down to 1494 the chancery frequently itinerated about the Pale, and was evidently in regular attendance on the governor, for when the earls of Kildare were in office chancery letters attested at Maynooth, Naas or Kildare were common, and from Viscount Gormanston's deputyship, 1493-4, letters survive attested at Navan, Rathmore and Gormanston.[46] The fact that the other central courts did not venture beyond the Pale in the later fifteenth century was of less significance in this respect than that few governors spent much time beyond: during Desmond's deputyship, chancery was at Cork on 5 September 1466, at Killussy (?) on the 28th, and at Dungarvan on 7 October.[47] From 1494, however, chancery effectively became sedentary at Dublin, although the disturbed conditions throughout the Tudor period meant that the chancellor had occasionally to leave Dublin: chancery was at Kilkenny in 1540 for example, and in 1553 the chancellor gave

---

[43]*Christ Church deeds,* nos. 326, 1014, 1021, 1029; N.L.I., D. 1820, 2149 (*Ormond deeds, 1413-1509,* no. 243, *1509-47,* no. 133); Memoranda roll, 3 Henry VIII m. 9 (P.R.O.I., Ferguson coll., iv, ff 9-10).

[44]Parliament roll, 18 Edward IV (I) c. 3 (*Stat. Ire., Edw. IV,* ii, 632); Memoranda rolls, 6 Edward IV m. 13, 2 Richard III m. 31 (P.R.O.I., RC 8/41, p. 86, 8/33, p. 547), 4-5 Henry VIII m. 24 (P.R.O.I., Ferguson coll., iv, f. 17); T.C.D., MS 1747, pp. 12-13.

[45]Ellis, 'Privy seals', pp. 188-9.

[46]*Rot. pat. Hib.,* pp. 269-70; Memoranda rolls, 21 Edward IV m. 8d, 9 Henry VII mm 8, 20, 10 Henry VII m. ?, 12 Henry VII m. 35 (S.P.W., Hore MS I, pp. 1141-2; B.L., Add. MS 4793, ff 150, 151; P.R.O.I., Delafield MSS M. 2675, p. 75, Ferguson coll., iii, f. 335).

[47]Memoranda roll, 6 Edward IV mm 4, 6, 14 (B.L., Add. MS 4793, f. 155v; P.R.O.I., RC 8/41, pp. 91-2). Cf. Otway-Ruthven, 'Med. Ir. chancery', p. 128.

judgement in a case at Galway.[48] Between 1494 and 1534, however, only five writs attested at places other than Dublin have so far come to light – Maynooth in 1497, Castledermot in 1499, Tallaght in 1514 (two on the same day) and Navan in 1520[49] – and chancery itinerations were by then evidently abnormal. Once chancery began to develop as a law court, from 1494, itinerations must have become increasingly inconvenient and this is no doubt the principal reason for the change. In June 1496, when the chancellor and acting governor held a council at Drogheda immediately before his departure for England, a messenger had to be sent to the keeper of the rolls in Dublin with a commission and indenture for the seal: two years earlier chancery would most probably have been in attendance on the governor.[50] The problem was not a new one. In 1479 Edward IV had given instructions that 'the chaunseller in person shall in term tyme make his abidyng in the place wher the kyngs courts be kept, unlesse ther be a grete and urgent cause by the deputé, wyth the advice of the more part of ye kyngs consele, it be thought his absence to be allowed'. The idea of leaving the court in one place while the chancellor departed elsewhere with the great seal had apparently also been tried to the detriment of the king's records and evidence. The chancellor was ordered to 'sete alweyes in suche place and tymes as the clerc of the rolles, the clerc of the hanaper and other ministres of ye chaunsery may be ther and then present', and to deliver all warrants to the keeper who should 'enroll all patents under the kyngs gret seall befor that they be deliveret to the parties'.[51]

A second factor influencing the permanent location of chancery in Dublin from 1494 was the gradual eclipse of the great seal by the governor's privy seal as an original instrument of government.[52] Fiants had long been used by the governor in the same way as English privy seal warrants to activate the great seal when it was not to hand, but this practice had apparently been a convenience and notes of

---

[48]Memoranda roll, 32 Henry VIII m. 22 (B.L., Add. MS 4791, f. 207); Blake, *Blake family records,* no. 121.

[49]Patent roll, 14 Henry VII (P.R.O.I., Lodge MS 'Articles', f. 221); Memoranda rolls, 13 Henry VII m. 5, 4-5 Henry VIII m. 24, 12 Henry VIII m. 6 (B.L., Add. MS 4793, f. 151v; P.R.O.I., Ferguson coll., iv, f. 18; B.L., Add. MS 4791, f. 199); T.C.D., MS 1207, no. 207.

[50]Patent roll, 11 Henry VIII (B.L., Add. MS 4787, f. 53); B.L., Royal MS 18C, XIV, ff 63v, 64.

[51]Close roll, 19 Edward IV m. 7d (Gilbert, *Viceroys,* p. 594; *P.R.I., rep. D.K. 57,* p. 569).

[52]The following paragraphs, except where otherwise indicated, are based on Ellis, 'Privy seals', pp. 187-94.

warranty appended by clerks to chancery letters suggest that the governor, or occasionally the council, frequently bye-passed the privy seal. Thus in the fifteenth century, although the great seal had lost much of its original force, it was by no means exclusively confined to the formal authentication of decisions conveyed to it by privy seal. In 1560, however, the chancellor was forbidden to seal letters without a warrant under the privy seal, but since already in 1534 the Irish chancery had discontinued the practice of appending notes of warranty, except for warrants from England, this order evidently related only to the use of the new royal privy seal in preference to the governor's: soon after 1494 privy seal warrants probably became mandatory to activate the great seal. Moreover, by the late fourteenth century, the governor's privy seal had ousted the great seal in the authentication of conciliar warrants and was being used for original instruments, warrants for arrest for example, as well as for warrants to the great seal. This was so even if, for some reason, the council met in the governor's absence. And in the fifteenth century, there was a gradual extension in the use of the privy seal. By 1444 privy seals were being used to convoke the council and thereafter their use spread to other matters for which the great seal would not have been required in England, an order that the court of common pleas be held outside Dublin castle, directions concerning the payment of prisage, and instructions to the exchequer about ecclesiastical temporalities.

Under the Yorkists and Henry VII, however, privy seals also began to be used as original instruments in matters which more properly required the great seal. Already in 1459-60, Richard duke of York had directed privy seals to the barons after receiving homage of tenants, whereas customarily they were directed to chancery for a writ to exchequer. These privy seals were ratified by act of parliament in 1465 and by 1495 privy seal warrants to the exchequer were accepted in place of chancery warrants. Licences of absence and safe conduct from Ireland, freedoms from coign and livery and commissions of inquiry also issued under the governor's privy seal during Henry VII's reign. In 1476 and 1485 parliament empowered the governor to appoint a deputy by privy seal to continue parliament in his absence, and in 1519 the governor was commissioned under the English great seal so to appoint a deputy during his absence in England. Thus by 1494 the chancellor's attendance on the governor in order to seal instructions was unnecessary because the governor's privy seal sufficed in almost all circumstances either for original instruments or for warrants to chancery. For other reasons, the chancellor's attendance was of course still desirable, but in 1494 the Dublin administration recognized that, although formally indispensable, the great seal and with it the chancery had been ousted from the centre of government in the lordship by the governor's privy seal, now accepted as the Irish equivalent of the king's privy seal.

Nevertheless, because this privy seal was a private seal in the literal sense, changing with each governor, the development of its official role in government was not altogether in the king's interests and perhaps an indication of how little was known in England about certain aspects of the lordship's government. In 1534, Cromwell had instructions drawn up that the king's ministers 'have their patentes out of the chauncery, and recordes made there as is used in the chauncery of Englande', and likewise that 'the deputie do not let nor sette any manours, londes, tenementes, or other revenues of the kinges but by letters patentes under the kynges seale'.[53] Moreover, by the Tudor period a distinctive form for royal warrants was emerging which was followed by the governor's privy seal warrants issued in his own name: in 1487 Kildare as lieutenant to 'Edward VI' had issued a privy seal for the arrest, on charges of treason, of one of Henry VII's supporters; and during the 1534 revolt, Lord Offaly continued to issue warrants in the same style as he had used as acting governor. Steps were taken after 1534 to see that the governor followed the standing instruction to act only with the advice of the council, but in fact the rise of the privy seal had earlier assisted the governor in acting without the council, though in Lancastrian England the association of the king's privy seal with the council had arguably produced a different outcome.[54]

The development of the privy seal also enhanced the importance of its keeper, the governor's secretary. In 1455, when the archbishop of Armagh required a pardon of debts, he hoped it would 'pas by fiat under my sayd loord deputy his privy seale . . . saunce fyne or fe yf hit mowe so be . . . or els to passe thoruȝ lyȝt fyne yf ȝe seme so best, and we shull content the privy seale ii*s*. or sumwhat more as ye asserte us ther for of for his wrytyng'. By then, evidently, the keeper was in a stronger position than the clerk of the hanaper whose job it was to determine chancery fees and fines, and the keeper's own fees were clearly lucrative. In fact, for most of Edward IV's reign successive clerks of the council were also clerks of the hanaper and the clerk of the crown was clerk of parliaments and great councils. But thereafter the connection between chancery and the council was replaced by one between the offices of clerk of the council and keeper of the privy seal.

---

[53] *S.P. Hen. VIII*, ii, 209.
[54] Cf. Elton, *Tudor revolution in government*, pp. 14-17.

From c.1520 clerks of the council again had experience in chancery.[55] And although under the early Tudors the offices of keeper and clerk of the council were sometimes distinct, as in 1495,[56] the fact that at other times they were combined, that the governor's privy seal was the one used by the council, and that as late as 1537 administrators failed to 'make a dystinction betwyxt the secretaries office and the clerkes of the counsaill', these points strongly suggest that by the late fifteenth century a writing office separate from chancery had been created which was the mainspring of government in the lordship.[57] So far as the custody of the king's records was concerned, this change was initially disadvantageous: the clerk of the council complained in 1537 that whereas formerly important matters relating to the governor and council had been 'inrollyd by the clerke of the crowne on the backe of the open rolle in the chauncery', some had more recently been lost and others were unavailable because 'the deputys or the kinges chauncelours as chief of the counsaylle kepe the same, whiche upon ther deathe or admocion from ther rome shalle never be hadde'.[58] Nevertheless, this defect was amply offset by the greater flexibility which the establishment of another writing office gave to government and was after 1534 soon rectified by the more systematic preservation of records in the council registers.

At times in the fourteenth century, the exchequer seal had threatened to rival the great seal in sealing judicial writs for other courts, but by the late middle ages it was firmly confined to exchequer business.[59] The other seals which were in common use in the lordship were the great seal of England, the privy seal and the signet, notwithstanding their statutory proscription for political reasons in 1460.[60] The great seal was commonly used in appointments to Irish offices of which the nomination was reserved to the king, and after 1494 for transmisses of bills and licences to hold parliament; though its function in authenticating letters and directives from the king and

[55] *Rot. pat. Hib.*, p. 268 nos. 38-9, 51-2; P.R.O., E. 101/248, nos. 17, 21, S.P. 65/1/2; Parliament rolls, 7 & 8 Edward IV c. 48, 12 & 13 Edward IV c. 28 (*Stat. Ire., Edw. IV*, i, 540, ii, 56); Memoranda roll, 3-4 Henry VIII m. 23 (P.R.O.I., Ferguson repertory, iv, 97); *S.P. Hen. VIII*, ii, 44; *Ormond deeds, 1509-47*, nos. 81, 89.

[56] B.L., Royal MS 18C, XIV, ff 25v, 52v.

[57] *S.P., Hen. VIII*, ii, 497; above, ch. 1 p. 37.

[58] *S.P. Hen. VIII*, ii, 494. Similar developments occurred in England under the Yorkists: Lander, *Crown and nobility*, ch. 7.

[59] Cf. Otway-Ruthven, 'Med. Ir. chancery', pp. 128-9.

[60] See Richardson & Sayles, *Ir. parl. in middle ages*, ch. 16; Otway-Ruthven, *Med. Ire.*, pp. 154-5, 190, 370, 387.

council in England had long since been usurped by the privy seal and latterly the signet. Such instructions were under the Yorkists sent both under the privy seal and the signet,[61] but the use of the privy seal for this purpose appears to have diminished thereafter and under Henry VIII letters from Wolsey and Cromwell were more frequent than signet letters. By 1537, Cromwell was even writing to the Irish exchequer directly, ordering it to suspend the levy of debts on Limerick city.[62] Letters of the governor and council to England were normally just signed, though the Irish great seal was appended to addresses of parliament and after 1494 to bills devised by the government for parliament and sent for the approval of the king and council.[63]

As the control exercised by the king over the Irish administration increased after 1460, this must have further circumscribed the role of the Irish great seal. A draft grant of Irish prise wines notwithstanding Poynings's act of resumption was endorsed, 'M[emoran]d[um] p^t if ther be non officez founde, this graunt is voide if office be founde herafter; also hit is a dowte wheder this graunt of the profittes be goode vnder the pryvey seale & not vnder the grete seale in Irland': notwithstanding the grant issued under the privy seal.[64] By Henry VIII's reign, the privy seal was in danger of being ousted for warrants to the Irish great seal.[65] Though commissions and grants under the English great seal were perfectly acceptable in Ireland and normal for certain purposes, practice was seemingly determined by convenience and custom and the two seals were constitutionally almost interchangeable in Ireland.[66] The king sometimes preferred to direct a warrant to the Irish chancery for the issue of letters which could have issued under the English great seal, but the choice often appears arbitrary. In 1535, when there was question of Lord Deputy Skeffington's supersession by Lord Grey, Lord Keeper Alen offered to seal a patent in accordance with Skeffington's patent to save time; and in 1536 Lord

---

[61] E.g. P.R.O., E. 28/91 no. 35, E. 28/92 nos. 1-2, P.S.O., 1/31/1626, 1/40/2082, 1/42/2192, 1/43/2210, 1/44/2269; *L & P. Ric. III & Hen. VII*, ii, 286; Memoranda roll, 2 Richard III m. 8d (Gilbert, *Viceroys*, p. 602; P.R.O.I., RC 8/33, p. 406); *Ormond deeds, 1413-1509*, no. 288.

[62] Memoranda roll, 29 Henry VIII m. 29d (P.R.O.I., Ferguson coll., iv, f. 205).

[63] E.g. *L. & P. Ric. III & Hen. VII*, i, 377-8; *S.P. Hen. VIII*, ii, *passim*, Cf. *Stat. Ire., Hen. VII & VIII*, p. 75; Richardson & Sayles, *Ir. parl. in middle ages*, esp. p. 172.

[64] P.R.O., S.C. 1/58/56; *Ormond deeds, 1413-1509*, no. 288.

[65] Cf. Elton, *Tudor revolution in government*, pp. 270-80.

[66] By the early fourteenth century, it had been established that writs *de cursu* for the lordship and a few others should be under the great seal of Ireland: Hand, *Eng. law in Ire.*, pp. 27-9.

Chancellor Audley consulted the Irish clerk of the crown, then at court, as to whether creation patents of Irish peers were properly issued under the great seal of England or of Ireland.[67] For such purposes, the English great seal was more normal: its letters were certainly held in higher estimation in Ireland, but this was because Irish letters might convey only the deputy's pleasure, and officers so appointed could often be removed by him.[68]

So far as this affected the Irish chancery, English chancery letters relating to Ireland would usually be enrolled on the Irish patent or close rolls.[69] Royal warrants to the Irish chancery were treated, down to 1534, in exactly the same way as fiants under the governor's privy seal; that is, the date of their delivery into chancery was noted on them for the purpose of dating the letters and these were nominally attested by the governor at Dublin, or wherever the chancery happened to be, though it is a moot point whether the governor was necessarily informed.[70] Thus the only (not altogether reliable) means of distinguishing between Irish chancery letters pursuant to fiants and royal warrants was the clause of warranty;

> per billam per ipsum deputatum concessum & signo suo manuali consignato ac de data predicta auctoritate parliamenti ac priuato sigillo suo similiter consignato,
>
> per billam ipsius domini regis manu sua propria signata & cancellario suo Hibernie directa de data predicta auctoritate parliamenti,

or more usually some shorter variant of these two forms. 'Per breve de privato sigillo' on its own referred to the governor's seal.[71] Unfortunately no example of these warrants appears now to survive in an Irish context, but the wording of warranty clauses suggests that signed petitions and signet warrants were more common than privy seals.[72] Signed bills were evidently as acceptable in the Irish as the English

---

[67]*S.P. Hen. VIII*, ii, 271; *L. & P. Hen. VIII*, ix, no. 358.

[68]E.g. *S.P. Hen. VIII*, ii, 222. See also above, ch. 1, p. 17.

[69]E.g. *Rot. pat. Hib.*, pp. 267 nos. 35-6, 272b no. 3; *Ormond deeds, 1509-47*, nos. 100, 136 (2); *Cal. pat. rolls Ire., Hen. VIII-Eliz.*, passim.

[70]N.L.I., D. 2103, 2146 (*Ormond deeds, 1509-47*, nos. 100 (inadequately calendared), 130); N.B. White (ed.), *The 'Dignitas decani of St. Patrick's Cathedral, Dublin* (Dublin, 1957), no. 141. Cf. Herbert Wood in *I.H.S.*, i (1938-9), 410.

[71]Memoranda roll, 9 Edward IV m. ? (P.R.O.I., Ferguson coll., iii, f. 245); *Ormond deeds, 1413-1509*, no. 295; Ellis, 'Privy seals', p. 189. Cf. Lander, *Crown and nobility*, ch. 7.

[72]See *Fiants Ire., Hen. VIII*, pp. 27-8. Cf. Elton. *Tudor revolution in government*, pp. 276, 285-8.

chancery. From mid-1534 chancery practice concerning letters pursuant to warrants from England was altered so that they ended somewhat incongruously, 'Teste me ipso apud Dublin.'[73] Thus, even when entered on the chancery rolls without the clause of warranty, as was sometimes the case, they were readily distinguishable both from letters ordered by the governor and enrolments of letters under the great seal of England.

In the period 1470-1534 continuity rather than change was apparent in the organization of the seals, but behind this facade there occurred important but predictable changes which eliminated the original force of the great seal of Ireland and consolidated the role of the governor's privy seal. By 1534 the chancery clerks, *as chancery clerks,* wrote mainly documents copied from warrants under the privy seal, although the scarcity of clerks meant that many of them found more stimulating work elsewhere, and to a lesser extent continued to do so after 1534.[74] The need for a second royal seal in the lordship was forcibly driven home to the king on more than one occasion, but it was not in fact provided until 1560. This was arguably the real reason behind the decline in record keeping during the period, and it is hard to avoid the conclusion that in this case the Dublin administration was behind necessary reforms which could not be properly implemented because the king did not fully understand the need for them.

---

[73] Ellis, 'Privy seals', p. 188 n. 4.

[74] For example, Patrick Dowdall, a chancery clerk, was in 1547 appointed second engrosser of the exchequer: *Cal. pat. rolls. Ire., Hen. VIII-Eliz.,* p. 144.

7

LOCAL GOVERNMENT

In recent years historians have again become interested in the extent to which the common law and English administration were undermined by the Gaelic resurgence.[1] Forty years ago, David B. Quinn issued a timely warning against the uncritical acceptance of exaggerated claims about degeneracy and imminent collapse in the lordship. This took the form of a description of local government, based mainly on surviving court records, in which the survival of English forms was stressed.[2] Since then, however, the pendulum has swung back as attention has been concentrated on the more accessible state papers and other printed sources, although these frequently originated in efforts to goad the king into remedial action. There have been serious suggestions that by the mid-sixteenth century royal justices had long since ceased to sit in Munster and that even within the Pale 'the whole structure of English local government had fallen into abeyance'.[3] The reader might in fact be pardoned for believing that by 1534 residual English forms were rapidly being overwhelmed in a sea of Gaelic culture.

This belief is nonetheless false. The paucity of evidence concerning local government should not be taken as implying its collapse, and it is in fact questionable whether the stranglehold of the magnates on government in many parts of the lordship differed markedly from the position in certain areas of England. Undoubtedly the Dublin administration was less vigorous than the Westminster government in the repression of serious internal disorder, but then it was much less adequately financed and more dependant on the cooperation of the nobles in the defence of the marches. This was the key to the problem: it could and did intervene in the outlying localities from time to time, but its resources did not extend to the exercise of continuous control there. In fact by the late middle ages this difficulty was fully recognized. Beyond the Pale the governor now aimed to supervise rather than closely control shire government which was, more openly

---

[1] See especially, Nicholls, *Gaelic and gaelicised Ireland;* Canny, *Elizabethan conquest,* ch. 1; Bradshaw, *Dissolution of the religious orders,* pp. 40-6.

[2] Quinn, 'Anglo-Irish local government', pp. 354-81.

[3] Canny, *Elizabethan conquest,* p. 18; Nicholls, *Gaelic and gaelicised Ireland,* p. 19.

than in England, entrusted to the local magnates. The support of the magnates and towns in these areas was essential to defence and good government, and this support, it would appear, was deliberately bought by their appointment to local government offices and the consolidation of local privileges.

Under the Yorkists and Henry VII successive royal charters extended the self-government of the major towns and cities. Youghal received powers to determine a fairly wide range of civil pleas within the town in 1462, as did Cashel in 1484, and to exercise the offices of escheator, clerk of the market and admiral. In 1485 these were extended to all pleas real and personal, the town receiving all fines and amercements arising, and the courts there were allowed to proceed in civil actions by bill without writ from chancery. Charters to Waterford granted power in certain circumstances to deliver its own gaol in 1462, in 1487 to appoint its own coroners and to be sole justices of gaol delivery without further royal commission, and in 1488 to be justices of oyer and terminer there; Dublin had received the latter power in 1485 and in 1484 Galway received a charter excluding the lord of Clanrickard from interfering in its government.[4] By the late fifteenth century, therefore, Dublin, Drogheda, Wexford, Waterford, New Ross, Youghal, Cork, Limerick and Galway were to a large extent self-governing and independent of the normal county officials. This did not, however, make of them city-states on the German model: even the most isolated of them was subject to control by the Dublin administration, although they also petitioned the king directly concerning alterations to their charters which were *ultra vires* in Dublin.[5] Cork's charter was forfeited for complicity in the Warbeck conspiracy, and in 1498 the citizens, with the burgesses of Kinsale, took their oaths of allegiance before the deputy, who appointed four citizens to govern the city and to collect the king's rents there, before Henry VII issued a new charter in 1500.[6] At Easter 1499, the bailiffs of Cork and Limerick proffered 20*s.* each at the exchequer, and a Limerick case was pleaded before the king's council in 1531-2.[7] Pardons of citizens of Cork, Limerick and Galway were enrolled on

---

[4]Mac Niocaill, *Na Buirgéisí.*, i, *passim*, ii, 414-15; *Cal. pat. rolls, 1485-94*, pp. 176, 224; *New hist. Ire.*, ii, (forthcoming: for Cashets 1484 charter).

[5]E.g. *Cal. pat. rolls, 1476-85*, pp. 390, 536, 537, *1485-94*, p. 176, *1494-1509*, pp. 71, 204-5.

[6]Close roll, 10-15 Henry VII (B.L., Add. MS 4787, f. 52v); *Rot. pat. Hib.*, pp. 272a no. 13, 272b nos. 1, 4, 16; *Cal. pat. rolls, 1494-1509*, pp. 204-5; Ware, *Antiquities and history of Ireland*, p. 22.

[7]Memoranda roll, 14 Henry VII m. 14 (P.R.O.I., RC 8/43, p. 124); *Cal. pat. rolls Ire., Hen. VIII-Eliz.*, p. 10; B.L., Add. MS 19865, ff 58v-9.

the patent roll of 21 Henry VII (1505-6).[8] Even for Galway, recently described as 'possibly the most completely detached from the care of either the Dublin or the London administrations', a town in which Roman law had allegedly ousted the common law, substantial evidence survives of continued supervision.[9] Three petitions against process in the mayoralty court, by civil law or otherwise than by the common law, were referred by parliament in 1472 (two) and 1477 to the central courts, and in two of these the Galway officials were evidently amenable for the acts were later marked 'vacatur' on the roll: civil law was in any case applicable in certain matters involving foreigners and foreign goods.[10] And in 1484 and 1491 parliament reviewed cases in which the course of the common law had certainly been observed: the return of the mayor and bailiffs to the writ shows that in 1491 at least its judgement was also executed.[11] At the other end of the period, the mayor's return survives to a writ of 1533 directed to him.[12] And by 1525 the exchequer was collecting some revenue from the town, for licences to have salmon nets there, to repair a mill and to build a bakehouse there. These licences were reviewed in 1532 after an inquisition was taken into the king's rights in Galway.[13]

Significant evidence of the crown's more positive attitude towards private jurisdictions in Ireland also survives for the seigneurial franchises.[14] In England proper and the marches of Wales a plausible case can be made for the view that the statutes of 1536 and 1540 which enforced the common law and royal writs throughout the realm marked a more vigorous and systematic resumption of an attack on the liberties which had previously been pursued piecemeal as the opportunity arose. The argument is supported by reference to the crown's gradual acquisition of the Welsh marcher lordships during the fifteenth century, to Henry VII's moves against ecclesiastical

---

[8]*Rot. pat. Hib.*, pp. 272-3.

[9]*New hist. Ire.*, iii, 13.

[10]Parliament rolls, 11 & 12 Edward IV cc 56, 86, 16 & 17 Edward IV c. 53 (*Stat. Ire., Edw. IV*, i, 818-24, 886-8, ii, 570-76). Cf. Elton, *Tudor constitution*, pp. 152-3.

[11]Parliament roll, 1 Richard III c. 22 (P.R.O.I., RC 13/8); Blake, *Blake family records*, no. 68a.

[12]E. MacLysaght, 'Report on documents relating to the wardenship of Galway', *Anal. Hib.*, xiv (1944), 11.

[13]Memoranda roll, 22 Henry VIII m. 13 (P.R.O.I., Ferguson coll., iv, f. 146); T.C.D., MS 569, f. 13; *Cal. pat. rolls Ire., Hen. VIII-Eliz.*, p. 5; P.R.O., S.P. 65/1/2.

[14]See S.G. Ellis, 'The destruction of the liberties: some further evidence', *I.H.R. Bull.*, liv (1981) on which the following paragraphs are based.

sanctuaries, the liberties of Tynedale and Redesdale and his narrow interpretation of the law of Quo Warranto. Even from the mainland, however, there is some evidence that before the 1530s kings of England were more concerned with the reliability and cooperation of the magnates and with the provision of cheap and effective government in border areas than with the circumscription of royal government by franchisal jurisdictions. And in the lordship, the government was much more tolerant. Between 1312 and 1331 the king had indulged in 'a new wave of liberty creation' in order to ensure the cooperation of the magnates and better government in border districts which the Dublin administration found difficult to govern directly.[15] Although in 1399 the governor and council complained that the proliferation of palatinates was a 'prejudice et destruccion al corone et al terre' because 'pluseurs contees que sont obeiantz a le ley ne sont my en les maines du roy', under the Lancastrians it was clear that English law and administrative forms survived in many parts precisely because this was so.[16] With Edward IV's accession, the liberties of Meath and Ulster reverted to the crown, and through the attainder of the earls of Ormond (Wiltshire in England) and Desmond in 1462 and 1468 and a long minority in the Talbot family after the death of the sixth earl of Shrewsbury in 1473, the liberties of Tipperary, Kerry and Wexford came into the king's hand. Edward thus gained an opportunity to sweep away these ancient limitations on royal authority, for the archbishop of Dublin who held the only other Irish palatinate, the territorially small liberty of St. Sepulchre, had his temporalities withheld for much of the early 1470s.[17]

Far from wishing to extend royal control more permanently into these border areas, however, most of which were worth little beyond the costs of their own defence, the king seemed more concerned to restore the traditional arrangements as quickly as possible. Although the earl of Ormond was not restored until 1475, the liberty of Tipperary apparently continued to operate throughout the period, and Desmond's attainder was reversed almost immediately. In 1476 the liberty of Wexford was restored as necessary to the good government of the region, to be operated during the earl's minority by one of his kinsmen as seneschal, and in 1480 Edward issued directions about that liberty's administration. The liberties of Meath and Ulster posed different problems beause there were no obvious candidates from

---

[15] Otway-Ruthven, *Med. Ire.*, pp. 174-5.

[16] *Proc. king's council, Ire., 1392-3*, pp. 265-6.

[17] *Handbook Brit. chron.* p. 337.

among the nobility to administer them. The lack of a resident peer had been largely responsible for the collapse of English law and administration in east Ulster in the fourteenth and fifteenth centuries and the mere continuance of existing arrangements with the head of the local Savage family as seneschal did nothing to reverse the colony's fortunes there. In 1464 or soon after, the liberty was abolished, but in 1468 the king ordered its restoration to facilitate the maintenance of law and order there, and in 1473 after further setbacks Edward tried a different strategy, granting the lands and rights of the earldom of Ulster for forty years to Lord Grey of Codnor, with the intention of so creating a resident magnate. Apart from an unhappy few months spent as deputy-lieutenant in 1478-9, however, there is no evidence that Grey took up residence in Ireland, and it was left to the earls of Kildare under the early Tudors to make a reality of crown claims in the area.

Meath was in many ways a much easier task for the government because there were no geographical barriers, nor military obstacles posed by the Irish, to its administration from Dublin. Initially, however, the government attempted to compensate for the liberty's suppression by arranging for sessions of king's bench to be held there, for some time from Easter 1461 and again between Michaelmas 1466 and Easter 1468 when the court spent most of its time at Trim. These measures were not altogether satisfactory and in 1468 a seneschal with the customary powers was appointed, and briefly in 1472 and 1478 Edward ordered the full restoration of the liberty despite opposition from Dublin. Thereafter, however, Meath was administered in the same way as other royal shires in the Pale.

A more remarkable instance of the delegation of royal authority in this manner was Henry VIII's restoration of the liberty of Kildare about 1514, although this liberty had been suppressed as long ago as 1345. The precise circumstances and date of the restoration are not entirely clear, and all crown pleas were reserved to the king, so that in its revived form the liberty did not amount to a palatinate; but it is evident that the grant was a recognition of successful efforts by the earls of Kildare over the previous half-century to strengthen the English interest in a key area on the southern borders of the Pale, and also a bid to facilitate the administration of the region.[18] By 1519, the earl's justices were itinerating round the liberty, even holding pleas at Carbury castle in a region which had earlier constituted an almost independent marcher lordship.

---

[18] See also above, pp. 59-60.

Thus, far from trying to destroy private jurisdictions as anachronistic and obstacles to law and order, successive kings of England realised their value and promoted them in the lordship as a cheap and effective method of extending the normal reach of the Dublin administration. It was only with the advent of Thomas Cromwell that a settled policy of opposition to the liberties emerged, and this in the changed circumstances of the Reformation period which saw a vast extension in the claims of government on individuals and a new policy of consolidating outlying regions of the Tudor state more closely into the realm of England. The first real indication of the direction in which royal policy was moving was the suppression of the liberty of Kildare in 1534, on the alleged grounds that it had no warrant in law, but after the rebellion and the ensuing problems of direct rule and its financing, the government wisely decided against suppressing the Irish palatinates. Unless crown lands and patronage beyond the Pale were greatly increased and provincial councils introduced in line with the reorganized councils in the north and the marches of Wales, as in fact were provided for Connaught and Munster under Elizabeth, the retention of the liberties and the cooperation of the magnates were essential to good government. And Henry VIII baulked at the cost of the alternative.

Nor was the confidence of the Yorkists and early Tudors in the traditional expedient entirely misplaced. In the liberty of Wexford, English law and administration were fully maintained and there was little infiltration of Gaelic law and customs. Though the 1537 presentments and other reports about that time disclosed a good deal of violence and disorder, its level was unexceptional by English standards and it has been fairly claimed that 'the English settlement was more substantially based than anywhere else in the island except within a twenty-mile radius of Dublin itself'.[19] The liberty of Tipperary was also tolerably well administered, particularly after 1491 when the absentee earl began to appoint a deputy with extensive powers, so curbing the feuding between the junior branches of the Butler family, and even more so with the accession of a resident earl in 1515. It was of course part of a larger territory, the Barrow-Nore-Suir basin, 'the distinctive Anglo-Norman character' of which had been preserved, thanks largely to the efforts of the Butlers, even though the region was much less easily defended than south Wexford. Nevertheless, the existence of a palatinate in the western part which was less

---

[19] Quinn, 'Anglo-Irish local government', pp. 375-7 (quotation at p. 377).

accessible to the Dublin administration played a large role in the establishment of this 'second pale', as it has been described.[20]

Tipperary and Wexford were palatinates which are comparatively well-documented for this period, in the records of the central courts, the Ormond deeds and the 1537 presentments. The same is true of St. Sepulchre,[21] but then the archbishop's liberty could well have been incorporated into the royal shire of Dublin and was in any case closely supervised by the central government. There is, however, a minimum of evidence about Desmond's liberty of Kerry, but again what there is suggests that it continued as an effective unit of government throughout this period, although the Dublin administration can scarcely have exercised any effective supervision. The well-known copy of an assize of novel disseisin held at Dingle in the liberty in 1485 was very probably transcribed from proceedings on a writ of error returned into king's bench – the record discloses at least one error – and the seneschal sometimes made proffers in the exchequer.[22] Moreover, the powers of the Irish palatinates were all inferior to their English and Welsh counterparts, admitting of closer supervision, by law at least. Four pleas were invariably reserved to the crown, the liberties were represented and, in theory, subject to general taxation in parliament; and like the English counties palatine, they were also subject to the royal writ of error, so preventing the conflict between the common law and the law and custom of the liberty which occurred in the Welsh marcher lordships. The administration of the liberties has been well described elsewhere,[23] and few changes were made under the Yorkists and early Tudors.

Altogether, about a quarter of the late medieval lordship was withdrawn from the direct control of the Dublin administration by the grant of private jurisdictions, mainly outside the Pale; and this was clearly deliberate policy by successive kings. It has come in for criticism from both contemporaries and modern historians alike and was of course an admission of the weakness of royal government in

---

[20] See especially, Empey, 'Butler lordship', pp. 174-87 (quotations at p. 185); Empey and Simms, 'Ordinances of the White Earl', pp. 161-87; Quinn, 'Anglo-Irish local government', pp. 369-75.

[21] *Alen's reg.* contains much information about the liberty organization.

[22] Quinn, 'Anglo-Irish local government', pp. 366-8.

[23] Otway-Ruthven, *Med. Ire.,* pp. 174-5, 181-7. The four pleas were arson, rape, treasure trove and forestall. Except in the small liberty of St. Sepulchre, the chief liberty officers, where they can be traced, were of a pattern — seneschal, chief justice, treasurer, attorney, plus the normal local government officials whose powers were usually the same as their counterparts in the royal shires.

Ireland; but in the circumstances the policy was a realistic one and a cheap method of reducing the burden on the central government.

For both the liberties and royal shires beyond the Pale, the chief means of controlling local government were the annual general commissions, described in an earlier chapter,[24] which had powers to enter and review the workings of all the franchises throughout the counties for which they were commissioned. After these, the central government relied especially on the sheriff who, to an extent which was no longer true in England, remained the principal royal officer in the counties – outside the liberties where this position belonged to the seneschal to whom he was a subordinate seigneurial officer. For administrative, military and judicial work, the sheriff remained the normal link with the machinery of local government, although in England sheriffs were rapidly being overtaken in importance by the justices of the peace.

It was not until the mid-Tudor period that the medieval Irish keepers of the peace developed into judicial officers along the lines of their English counterparts.[25] Though in Ireland officers styled justices and supervisors of the peace were appointed for each shire, and keepers or wardens for the baronies (the equivalent of the hundred or wapentake in England), their powers were broadly the same. They were primarily military, and even in this sphere they were overshadowed by the sheriff, whose military duties were the more important because of the proximity and disorders of the marches. A set of ordinances enrolled with a commission of the peace for the barony of Slane, Co. Meath in 1499 illustrates well the relationship between the two:

> Also that all lords, knights, squyers, gentlemen & all others so horsed & harneysed at every great nede, when any of the king's enemies shall enter or invade the [cou]ntre, upon reasonable warninge shall yive their attendance upon the shirreff of the shire & the wardeyns of the peace when any nede shall be, in the absence of my lord deputy, & to accept the said shereff & wardeyns of the peace for their capteyns, and that upon pain of 20*s*. & so higher, every man after his degree, & the wardeyns of the peace make musters in their baronies every 21 days, upon pain of 10 *libri*.[26]

---

[24] Chapter 4.

[25] See, in general, Frame, 'Medieval Irish keepers', pp. 308-26 for the following.

[26] Patent roll, 14 Henry VII (P.R.O.I., Lodge MS 'Articles', i, f. 221; *Rot. pat. Hib.*, p. 272 nos. 14-15). Cf. *S.P. Hen. VIII,* ii, 19-20.

189

Throughout the Lancastrian period, the keepers might or might not be granted power to determine indictments, though they were empowered to inquire of treasons, felonies and trespasses; and since in 1496 the guardians and keepers of the peace in the barony of Skreen, Co. Meath were appointed justices there, this flexibility was evidently maintained.[27] Keepers appointed in Meath and Louth in 1410 and 1412 had however no judicial powers and it may be that under the Yorkists and early Tudors purely military keepers became more normal. Outside the major franchises, there is no reliable evidence of the keepers acting in a judicial role.[28] It is true that under Henry VIII governors were from time to time enjoined, 'to cause justices of the pease to be made ... and to cause thaym to kepe quarter sessyons yerely and to here and determyne all cawses and matters at their sessyons accordyng to the lawes',[29] but this was evidently not normally the case. No county commission rolls survived earlier than Edward VI's reign, and there are no references to fines and amercements imposed by J.P.s being estreated into the exchequer.[30] Evidence about the activities of king's bench and the failure of the *nisi prius* system to develop in Ireland points to the same conclusion. And though in 1529 the earl of Ossory was appointed with others as justice of the peace in the Ormond territories and ordered to keep sessions quarterly, a jury of Kilkenny town presented in 1537 that sessions there were held only at need, 'but in the countrey they saye there is none kepte as farre as they here, but that the sheref sytteth 2 tymes a yere, but they thinke it be no session for there be no justices'.[31] Very probably, part of the difficulty was that outside the Pale there was a scarcity of trustworthy magnates and gentlemen with the necessary knowledge of the law, whereas within the Pale they were the less necessary because of the continued itinerations of king's bench.

Nevertheless, for the Pale, the palatinates, and some of the outlying towns and cities, commissions of the peace continued to be issued. In no case are the terms of the commissions extant,[32] but

[27] *Rot. pat. Hib.*, p. 271 no. 28.

[28] Of the palatinates, however, only Wexford seems to have had true justices of the peace: see especially, Hore, *Wexford town*, i, 145.

[29] *S.P. Hen. VIII*, ii, 116.

[30] *P.R.I., rep. D.K. 28*, p. 47. Cf. *L. & P. Ric. III & Hen. VII*, ii, 65.

[31] Hore & Graves, *Southern & eastern counties*, p. 126; *Ormond deeds, 1509-47*, no. 149.

[32] Patent roll, 1 Edward IV (P.R.O.I., Lodge MS 'Articles', i, f. 221: patents not calendared in *Rot. pat. Hib.*); *Rot. pat. Hib.*, pp. 271 no. 28, 272 nos. 12, 14. Cf. B.L., Royal MS 18C, XIV, f. 64.

surviving extracts show that keepers were commonly appointed commissioners of array at the same time, and the commissions were kept small and aristocratic, approximating to English commissions of an earlier date.[33] The statutes of Kilkenny had laid down that 'en chescun countie soient ordynez quatre de melth vauetz du counte pur estre gardeyns de la peez'.[34] Numbers had however expanded somewhat since then, although only ten were commissioned for Co. Dublin in 1461, seven for Kilkenny and Irishtown in 1499, and five for the barony of Slane in the same year; apparently all from the chief men of their localities.[35] For the reformation of Meath in 1515, it was recommended that the deputy and council 'ordayne certen persons of the noble folke of the sayd countye', Lords Gormanston, Slane, Delvin and Trimbleston, 'to be iustices of pease allwaye within the sayde countye' with '2 wardens of peace assygned in every barony'.[36] Nevertheless, although the keepers were charged with fresh duties by parliament from time to time, they were far from prominent in shire government: in 1524, royal commissioners took recognizances from the marcher lords of the Pale that they would maintain the king's officers 'as shryffes, eschetors, coroners and other officers as be requisid for the order and ministration of justice'.[37]

After 1534, *custodes pacis* as opposed to true J.P.s continued to be commissioned: in 1540 such a commission was issued for Meath, though the numbers were increased to twenty-one and included all the king's judges and legal counsel plus the bishops, lords, knights and squirearchy of the shire. By 1550, however, when eighteen were commissioned, they were appointed 'custodes pacis, justices of the peace and commissioners to preserve the peace within the county of Kildare & commissioners of oyer & terminer & gaol delivery in ye said county', and a commission of twenty-four covering all the counties beyond the Pale conferred the same powers.[38] It looks therefore as if, by Edward VI's reign, commissions of the peace were being assimilated to those in England, although until well into the seventeenth century the disturbed state of Ireland must have made complete assimilation impossible.

---

[33] Jewell, *English local administration*, p. 146; Elton, *Tudor constitution*, pp. 453, 457.

[34] Parliament roll, 40 Edward III c. 24 (*Stat. Ire., John-Hen. V*, p. 454).

[35] The references in note 32.

[36] *S.P. Hen. VIII*, ii, 19.

[37] *Ibid.*, ii, 112, 116.

[38] P.R.O.I., Lodge MS 'Articles', i, ff 82, 87.

The military functions of the keepers seem to have been closely related to the captainries and governorships met with from time to time and, if the ordinances for Meath in 1499 were typical,[39] the keepers were *ex officio* captains of the shire, assisting the sheriff with the leading of the *posse comitatus,* the making of 'roads' on the Irish and organizing resistance to counter-raids. Nevertheless, the burden of preparations for offensive action against the king's enemies and rebels fell principally upon the sheriff. It was to the sheriff that the writ ordering the proclamation of a general hosting was directed: he was to have the *posse comitatus* ready to appear at six days' notice with victuals and carts sufficient 'ad proficiscendum . . . pro resistencia malicio inimicorum & rebellorum nostrorum'.[40] For the purpose of computing cartage or the collection of local subsidies for which he was responsible, the sheriff kept extents of the number of ploughlands in each barony throughout his bailiwick. He also compiled a list of the county gentry to be summoned to do military service – in Meath, a total of 162 temporal lords and gentlemen, nineteen clerics and fifteen portreeves and sovereigns of small towns throughout the shire.[41] All this required careful organization by the sheriff if the mishap which befell the archbishop of Armagh's contingent on one occasion were to be avoided: the archbishop wrote to the deputy, then awaiting assembly of the king's host at Carlow castle, that the carts of Drogheda had been arrested by the mayor of Dublin for the city's use and that none were to be had elsewhere in Louth, and inquired whether they were to set out without victuals.[42] Sheriffs had powers of purveyance, no doubt principally exercised in connection with hostings, and probably received allowance for the cost of cartage, shared between the exchequer and the local community, on their accounts.[43] Manifestly, the problem of defence accounted for the differences between the sheriff's duties in England and the lordship.

In England the justices of the peace had practically reached the extent of their influence under the Tudors by the late fourteenth century, and in 1461, in a further attempt to curb corruption in local government, a statute required sheriffs to send indictments from their tourns to them. This underlined the sheriff's subordination in this

---

[39] See above, pp. 151-2.

[40] Bodl., Rawl. MS C. 168, f. 110: the only known example of what was no doubt a standard writ. Cf. T.C.D., MS 594, f. 9.

[41] T.C.D., MS 594, ff 2-2v, 5v, 11, 14-15, 19-20, 20v-22, 25-9v, 38-40v.

[42] Octavian's register, T.C.D., MS 557, xi, 1339-40.

[43] P.R.O., S.P. 1/67, f. 35v (*L. & P. Hen. VIII,* v, no. 398).

sphere to the justices and effectively marked the end of his judicial powers.[44] In Ireland, however, where a similar problem existed, this statute was not promulgated and the sheriff was still active in his tourn in Elizabeth's reign.[45] In the Ormond districts, an ordinance of 1500 attempted to curb abuses by laying down that 'wheras the shireff and undyr shireff use to endicte the pore comen people and to put them to affynaunns, that non from hensforth be endicted but in presens of a learned mane'.[46] Five indictments for felonies before the sheriff of Kildare in 1468 and 1470 were sent up to king's bench for determination and later quashed by parliament;[47] and in 1495 cases were removed *coram rege* by writs of *certiorari* directed to the sheriffs of Dublin and Louth.[48] In the liberty of Tipperary, the only region from which records of tourns survive for this period, they continued to be held twice a year in each barony. In 1527 'the rolls of the shiriffs tournes yerely' were offered to the king's council in England as evidence of the liberty's jurisdiction.[49] Records of two tourns held at Easter 1465 and Michaelmas 1476 comprised four and eight cases respectively. In the earlier tourn, the cases were all of trespass. Three defendants were amerced – one for deforcing the serjeant and failing to appear after an adjournment – and the plaintiffs were awarded damages with costs of court. In the fourth case, the defendant received a day to reply and a jury was summoned. At the second tourn, there were six presentments, mainly by serjeants and subserjeants of baronies, concerning effusions of blood, some with hue and cry, and causing an affray, plus two pleas of trespass. Of those presented, one was found guilty, two were acquitted and three were found guilty of causing affrays of whom one was amerced. Two cases were merely continued. The plaintiff in one trespass case was amerced for failure to prosecute, and in the second the defendant received a day and a jury was summoned.[50] Together with the proceedings extant for four tourns in 1457-8, these records show that the sheriff's tourn remained an important element in law enforcement, particularly since these records survive for a period in which the liberty administration fell prey to faction: thereafter law enforcement might be expected to have

---

[44] Jewell, *English local administration,* pp. 132-3, 145-6.

[45] *New hist. Ire.,* iii, 23.

[46] *Liber primus Kilkenn.,* p. 157.

[47] Parliament roll, 12 & 13 Edward IV c. 78 (*Stat. Ire., Edw. IV,* ii, 172-8).

[48] B.L., Royal MS 18C, XIV, f. 27.

[49] N.L.I., D. 1793 (calendared inadequately in *Ormond deeds, 1413-1509,* no. 224); *Ormond deeds, 1413-1509,* no. 200, *1509-47,* app. iii.

[50] N.L.I., D. 1793 (*Ormond deeds, 1413-1509,* no. 224).

improved. Nearly half the litigants had Gaelic surnames, although they or their ancestors must have received grants of English law. Probably most of them were copyholders and lesser manorial tenants of free status, often descendants of betaghs, but clearly the use of the common law by peasants of Gaelic origin was not peculiar to Meath.[51] Moreover, though Tipperary was somewhat exceptional in that by reason of the liberty it was relatively unaffected by the weakness of the central government, these differences did not extend to the sheriff's tourn, where his powers were the same as a royal sheriff.

Undoubtedly, the machinery of government in the royal shires beyond the Pale laboured under two related disadvantages, the problem of communications and the Dublin administration's difficulty in enforcing unpopular aspects of the common law. The major reason why there was little resort to the central courts from these shires was that Dublin

> where your lawes are executid, standith soo farr from sume parties there whiche wolde be obedyent ynogh to your gracis lawes, soo that they coulde reasorte thidther without daungier, as the inhabitauntes of the counties of Kilkeny, Tipperarie, Waterford, Corke and Lymeryk; and daily when they reasort thidther are robbyd, takyn prysoners and others slayne by the Irishrie.[52]

This problem was not new in 1533 and had long been recognised by the Dublin administration. In 1480, the new bishop of Ferns received restitution of his temporalities *in absentia*,

> eo quod idem episcopus propter immensa pericula & insulta hibernicorum inimicorum nostrorum ac anglicorum rebellorum ac guerrarum turbines dictum [sic!] insurgentes necnon quamplurima alia viarum discrimina tam per terram quam per mare indiesque eminencia personaliter coram nobis in cancellaria nostra Hibernie ad prosequenda in forma juris pro temporalibus predictis cum pertinenciis adesse non potuit.[53]

In consequence the administration of the law tended to suffer in so far as litigants had to resort to Dublin to prosecute their claims. Conditions in the royal counties of south Leinster and Munster were probably worse than in the liberties of Wexford and Tipperary: when about 1536 there was question of suppressing the liberty of Wexford

---

[51] See above, p. 130. Cf. T.C.D., MS 1207 no. 209: plea of debt in the Dublin county court between a labourer and a husbandman.

[52] *S.P. Hen. VIII*, ii, 172.

[53] Memoranda roll, 21 Edward IV m. 8d (S.P.W., Hore MS I, pp. 1141-2).

the community was vehement against the proposal.[54] A by-product of this was the tendency for the magnates to use Gaelic or Brehon law in criminal cases, although compositions for murder were not unknown in England,[55] and significantly the magnates were much more conservative concerning real actions. Amercements and damages for trespass were barely distinguishable from the pecuniary penalties usually prescribed by Brehon law. Thus the widespread reluctance of common law juries to convict for capital offences may well have combined with the preference of the magnates for the financial advantages accruing from the use of Brehon law in criminal matters to produce the characteristic mixture of English and Brehon law exemplified in the mysterious Statutes of Kilcash.[56] It was claimed of the earl of Kildare in 1537 that

> he used two lawes, our princes lawes and brehens lawes, which he thought most beneficiall as the case did require. Brehennes lawe is for stealing of a shepe or like thing v marks *tociens quociens* and not to be hanged ... & all the forsaid forfaitures to come to the forsaid erle & nothing to the partie, wherby ther fell many gentylmens lands to hym.[57]

Likewise in Co. Kilkenny, tourns were held twice a year, but 'divers of the bookes of the same statutes [of Kilcash] ar in the keping of the shiref of the shire' for use by Ossory and his Gaelic judges.[58] The use of Brehon law is an indication of the weakness of central government control in the localities, but it occurred primarily in connection with a notoriously weak aspect of common law enforcement; and its use was perhaps a more satisfactory alternative to the refusal of juries to present or convict their neighbours which was the usual outcome of criminal law cases in England.[59] Ironically, in the marches of Wales where, because of the additional profit and control which they brought, the English lords continued for their Welsh tenants much Welsh law, procedural, civil and tenurial, and many dues inherited from the native princes, they faced an uphill struggle to enforce these customs on a native population which was increasingly anxious to abandon them.[60]

---

[54] *L. & P. Hen. VIII,* xi, no. 200.

[55] Cf. W.H. Dunham Jr., *Lord Hastings' Indentured Retainers, 1461-83* (Connecticut, 1970), p. 20.

[56] N.L.I., MS 2551, f. 2v. See *New hist. Ire.,* iii, 8-9.

[57] Hore & Graves, *Southern & eastern counties,* pp. 162-3.

[58] *Ibid.,* pp. 112, 126.

[59] Bellamy, *Crime and public order,* ch. 5.

[60] Davies, *Lordship and society in the March of Wales,* esp. chs. 7. 8, 18.

Clearly, in the outlying shires at least, the sheriff's tourn dealt with the bulk of such offences as were not reserved to itinerant justices, though in Connaught, for which general commissions were rarely issued, the sheriff was styled the king's justice there in 1464 and had presumably been empowered to determine pleas of the crown in the county also.[61] In addition to the tourn, the sheriff was responsible for the conduct of business in the county court, which in the Pale at least met once a month as in England,[62] though here he was only the president, and the court's administrative functions had long since become more important than its judicial ones. Proceedings of seven county courts of the liberty of Tipperary in 1457-8 show, however, that there were usually three or four items of judicial business,[63] and elsewhere also considerable business was transacted. In 1463, when the undersheriff of Louth was murdered while keeping the court, £5 of the king's money plus the records were stolen; and in 1466 information was laid against a former undersheriff of Dublin for embezzling 20s. of the issues and profits at each court session, amounting to £10 in all, during the sheriff's year of office.[64] In 1515 a record was made, probably to allow the case to be reviewed in a higher court, of a plea of debt in the Dublin county court before the sheriff, in which a jury of twelve found for the defendant: Luttrell C.J.C.P. observed in 1537 'that in the countie courtes, for lak of knowlege of the lawe, maters under 40s. be not determyned as the lawe wolde', which probably explains the use of a jury instead of suitors in this case.[65] Outlawries could of course only be pronounced by the county court and, within the Pale at least, statutes, ordinances and proclamations were also read there, the sheriff being responsible for this task.[66] In the outlying royal shires they must also have been kept periodically, for knights of the shire were elected in them and on occasion until 1494 sheriffs also.[67]

Within the Pale, the office of sheriff was by the late medieval

---

[61] Blake, *Blake family records,* no. 57; Memoranda roll, 6 Edward IV mm 1, 2, 5 (P.R.O.I., RC 8/41, pp. 23, 25, 31).

[62] E.g. Coram Rege roll, 1 Henry VII mm 10-10d (P.R.O.I., RC 8/43, pp. 44-7).

[63] *Ormond deeds, 1413-1509,* no. 200.

[64] Parliament roll, 3 Edward IV c. 61 (*Stat. Edw. IV,* i, 164-6); Memoranda roll, 6 Edward IV m. 10 (P.R.O.I., RC 8/41, pp. 59-60).

[65] T.C.D., MS 1207 no. 209; *S.P. Hen. VIII,* ii, 509. Cf. Holdsworth, *Hist. Eng. law,* i, 74.

[66] Reference in note 62; *Stat. Ire.,* i, 58. Cf. Otway-Ruthven, 'Anglo-Irish shire government', p. 20.

[67] Cf. Parliament roll, 16 & 17 Edward IV c. 48 (*Stat. Ire., Edw. IV,* ii, 558-62).

period considered a burden,[68] no doubt because the duties were heavy and the financial risks far outweighed the possibilities of profit. It was sometimes possible to purchase charters of exemption from this and other offices, but in 1475 they were statutorily resumed because so many had been granted and few men of substance were available for office or to take inquisitions.[69] Thereafter charters were granted more sparingly, or perhaps enrolled less frequently, but even so the sheriffs of Dublin and Meath had to be granted £10 and twenty marks respectively to offset the charges of the office, rewards which, though customary and far larger in England, the Irish exchequer could ill afford.[70] And if they could find an excuse, those appointed refused to serve.[71] The sheriff's oath of Mary's reign, an abbreviated version *mutatis mutandis* of the oath administered in England c. 1460, enjoined on him not to allow the withdrawal or concealment of royal rights, 'nother for gyft nor favour respyte their debtes where thei maye be without greatt grevaunce of the debtor be levyed', to do justice 'indifferently' 'aswell to poore as to ryche', to receive, serve and return in due manner all the king's writs, precepts and commands, and to account 'truely and rightously' at the exchequer.[72] These duties had changed little since the thirteenth century. Formerly sheriffs had spent considerable sums on the king's business in the localities, in purchasing supplies and making repairs, but apart from assignments for ministers' fees and rewards, apparently very little money was now so spent.[73] Nevertheless, collection of the revenues was no easier and many sheriffs found themselves owing considerable sums on their accounts. Successive sheriffs were also responsible for the arrears which accumulated, and until 1472 they were opposed on ancient debts going back to Edward III's reign. Even after, the sheriff of Kildare was pardoned £33 16s. 8d. arrears in 1472, and on their accounts in 1495-6 the sheriffs of Kildare, Meath and Louth owed

---

[68] Cf. Otway-Ruthven, 'Anglo-Irish local government', p. 11.

[69] Parliament roll, 15 & 16 Edward IV c. 6 (*Stat. Ire., Edw. IV,* ii, 256).

[70] Parliament rolls, 10 Edward IV cc 15, 16, 12 & 13 Edward IV c. 5 (*Stat. Ire., Edw. IV,* i, 674-6, ii, 4-8); P.R.O., E. 101/248/17, S.P. 65/1/2; B.L., Royal MS 18C, XIV, f. 148. Cf. Dunham, *Hastings' Indentured Retainers,* p. 37; Wolffe, *Crown lands,* p. 95.

[71] E.g. Memoranda roll, 10 Edward IV m. 10 (P.R.O.I., RC 8/41, pp. 236-7: the baron of Skreen was exonerated from service as sheriff of Co. Dublin because a citizen of Dublin).

[72] T.C.D., MS 588, f. 187v. Cf. *English Historical Documents,* iv (ed. A.R. Myers, London, 1969), 555-6.

[73] Cf. Otway-Ruthven, 'Anglo-Irish shire government', p. 15.

£52 6s. 8d., £20 10s. and £28 1s. 10d. respectively.[74] Very often former sheriffs had to petition for a commission to allow them to collect the arrears for which they remained liable.[75]

Sheriffs frequently risked amercement for inadequate performance of their duties, often in circumstances over which they had little control.[76] The memoranda roll calendars for the regnal years 14, 15, 23 and 24 Henry VII contain eleven examples, usually for non-return of writs, though two sheriffs had no attorney to receive writs and another had refused a royal command.[77] In Trinity 1465, the exchequer amerced the sheriff of Meath nine times in sums ranging from 12d. to 40d. for not having the defendant in court as he had returned, and rarely a term passed without two or three amercements inflicted for this offence, although the sheriff was no doubt well rewarded by defendants for his laxity.[78] Sheriff Cusack thought it advisable to keep a record of the correct returns to the commonest writs with which he dealt, and he also recorded some of the actual returns he made for reference;[79] but one of his successors who was less fortunate or prudent ran up arrears of £4 in 1521-2 in amercements imposed in king's bench and common pleas for insufficient returns of writs.[80]

A less common aspect of the sheriffs' duties related to escheats. Until Henry VI's reign, the usual arrangement had been to appoint a separate escheator for the whole lordship with subescheators under him; but by 1399 the value of escheats had fallen drastically, although the escheator still received an annual salary of £42.[81] Under the

---

[74]Parliament roll, 12 & 13 Edward IV c. 9 (*Stat. Ire., Edw.* IV, ii, 14-16); Memoranda rolls, 12 Edward IV m. 22 (P.R.O.I., RC 8/41, pp. 394-5), 2 Henry VII m. 15 (P.R.O.I., Delafield MSS, M. 2675, pp. 73-4); Pipe roll, 11 Henry VII (B.L., Royal MS 18C, XIV, ff 151v-2).

[75]E.g. Memoranda rolls, 2 Richard III mm 3d, 4, 15 Henry VII m. 9, 24 Henry VII m. 5 (P.R.O.I., RC 8/33, pp. 397-8, RC 8/43, pp. 168, 228-9, 273); *Dowdall deeds*, no. 490.

[76]*L. & P. Ric. III & Hen. VII*, ii, 65. Cf. Memoranda roll, 23 Henry VII m. 19 (P.R.O.I., RC 8/43, p. 248).

[77]Memoranda rolls, 14 Henry VII mm 12, 17, 21, 15 Henry VII m. 7, 23 Henry VII mm 7, 19, 24 Henry VII m. 7 (P.R.O.I., RC 8/43, pp. 121, 133, 142, 221, 223-5, 248, 280). Commonly the sheriff arranged for the court clerks to receive his writs.

[78]P.R.O.I., EX 3/1.

[79]T.C.D., MS 594, ff 6-7.

[80]P.R.O., E. 101/248/21.

[81]*Ormond deeds, 1413-1509*, no. 101; *Proc. king's council, Ire., 1392-3*, p. 268; Otway-Ruthven, *Med. Ire.*, p. 162.

Yorkists, therefore, individual unpaid escheators were appointed for single counties and, as earlier, the office was very often combined with that of clerk of the market and measures. In Mary's reign, escheators swore that 'ye shall in your proper person make the extentes of landes after the veray value and enquestes' and to 'take your enquestes in open places'.[82] In 1496, Undertreasurer Hattecliffe urged that they 'duly enquere upon the writtes of *diem clausit extremum* and suche other writtes of *mandamus*' so that 'true extentes' were made, and that any escheator thought to be 'favourable to the partie, or insuffisiant or indescrete' be superseded by commissioners.[83] Even so, there were no regular appointments of escheators beyond the Pale before 1534. Here, the itinerant justices exercised the office and presumably sheriffs were then charged with the sums due.[84] Exceptionally, on the death of the seventh earl of Ormond, an escheator and clerk of the market was appointed for Kilkenny.[85]

Within the Pale, escheators were seemingly appointed to take charge of any sizeable amount of land in the king's hand, regularly so in Henry VII's reign, but less frequently under the ninth earl of Kildare. There was apparently no escheator active in Meath between 1510 and 1521, although exceptionally a separate clerk of the market was appointed in 1517, and in 1518 the undertreasurer himself took some inquisitions *post mortem*. Thereafter the new escheator seized the lands of one gentleman found to have been absent without licence from Ireland since 1519 and took five inquisitions *post mortem* concerning tenants who had died in 1511, 1514, 1518 and 1522 (two cases).[86] Presumably the sheriff had been responsible for the profits in the interim and in 1510 Sheriff Cusack had taken at least one inquisition.[87] Sheriffs must have discharged the bulk of these duties when no escheator was in office: in 1495-6 the sheriff of Meath was charged with £5 6s. 8d. for the office of clerk of the market and

---

[82] T.C.D., MS 588, f. 187. The oath follows almost *verbatim* that of English escheators of the fifteenth century: cf. E.C. Lodge & G.A. Thornton (eds.), *English constitutional documents, 1307-1485* (Cambridge, 1935), pp. 357-8.

[83] *L. & P. Ric. III & Hen. VII*, ii, 65-6.

[84] See above, p. 136. Cf. Jewell, *English local administration*, p. 95.

[85] N.L.I., D. 2022 (calendared inaccurately in *Ormond deeds, 1413-1509*, no. 35). Similar appointments were made for Cos. Carlow, Cork, Kilkenny and the cross of Tipperary, Wexford, and Waterford in 1535-7: *Cal. pat. rolls Ire., Hen. VIII-Eliz.*, pp. 17, 23, 31, 52; Memoranda rolls, 28 Henry VIII m 34, 29 Henry VIII m. 22d (S.P.W., Hore MS I, pp. 1183, 1190).

[86] Exch. Inq., Co. Meath (P.R.O.I., RC 9/8, i, 3, 12-14, 33ff); Memoranda roll, 8 Henry VIII m. 10d (B.L., Add. MS 4791, f. 197v).

[87] T.C.D., MS 594, ff 30v-31.

measures then in the king's hand.[88] By itinerations and commissions of inquiry appointed from time to time the exchequer supervised and supplemented this work. A commission headed by the king's serjeant was inquiring into the king's feudal rights at Trim in 1532 and in 1538 another headed by the chief justice of common pleas and the keeper of the great seal was empowered 'to inquire as to forfeited and other lands belonging to the king in Co. Meath and of other things concerning the office of escheator, or which are usually enquired of by the barons of the exchequer'.[89] In 1466, the bailiffs of Dundalk made fine in the exchequer for contemptuously throwing away a royal warrant issued by the escheator and clerk of Louth and refusing to bring their measures for testing or to empanel a jury 'ad inquirendum super quibusdam articulis regem tangentibus'; and the escheator of Kildare did likewise for taking 20*d*. of the townsmen of Leixlip as clerk 'pro officio suo eis relaxando'.[90] Additionally, sheriffs were occasionally commissioned to take assizes: the sheriff of Meath took an assize of novel disseisin in 1510-11.[91]

Because the sheriffs of the outlying shires were altered so infrequently, the surviving evidence from the memoranda rolls, despite gaps, may be regarded as fairly complete. As in England, the government had to defer to the dominant local interest in the appointment of sheriffs and such other officers as it made,[92] but the balance between the spheres of influence of the magnates and the central administration was probably more favourable to the magnates in Ireland than in lowland England because their landholdings were, as in the north of England and the Welsh marches, generally more compact: in the fifteenth century the king's lordship was effectively organized into a patchwork of lordships each under the control of one magnate, an arrangement which was prompted by the comparative weakness of the central government, the incessant border warfare, and the necessity the local communities were under of obtaining some form of protection from the Irish.[93] Thus successive de Burgh lords of Clanrickard were quasi-hereditary sheriffs of Connaught in the Yorkist period and down to the early years of Henry VIII's reign;

[88] B.L., Royal MS 18C, XIV, ff 117v-18, 119.

[89] *Cal. pat. rolls Ire., Hen. VIII-Eliz.*, p. 53; Exch. Inq., Co. Meath (P.R.O.I., RC 9/8, i, 90).

[90] Memoranda roll, 6 Edward IV mm 10, 25 (P.R.O.I., RC 8/41, pp. 60-1, 362).

[91] T.C.D., MS 594, f. 7.

[92] Cf. Lander, *Crown and nobility,* pp. 13, 16-17, 30, 35-6.

[93] See especially, Frame, 'Power and society in the lordship of Ireland', pp. 3-33 *passim.*

throughout Henry VII's reign, William Hussey was sheriff of the cross of Kerry, Richard Vale, followed by his son, Thomas, was sheriff of Carlow, and John FitzDavy sheriff of Limerick; and for most of the early Tudor period the heads of the Fitzgeralds of Dromana and the Powers of Waterford were sheriffs of Cork and Waterford respectively. Elsewhere, however, and at other times, the choice was not quite so limited. No doubt the popularity of the office in the outlying counties explains the willingness of the magnates to serve and the government's ability to maintain royal sheriffs for eight or nine shires there.[94] The lack of control and the large possibilities for extortion may account for this, giving the government some leverage and explaining the comparative frequency with which proffers were made – even the sheriff of Connaught made at least four proffers between 1493 and 1511, and the sheriff of Kilkenny proffered at least once a year between 1523 and 1528. And under Henry VIII, the sheriffs of Kilkenny and the cross of Tipperary were changed sufficiently frequently to suggest that the government had a reasonable choice. Even elsewhere alternatives could be found. For Cork, Lord Roche was appointed by the king in 1488; and John Fitzgerald of Dromana was sheriff of Waterford in 1498 and Peter Butler of Potlerrath in 1517, although also sheriffs of Cork and Kilkenny respectively. Early in Henry VIII's reign, Edmund FitzJames Butler, sheriff of the cross of Tipperary, was intruded as sheriff of the cross of Wexford while, more understandably, the heads of a pro-Kildare Keating family were switched from sheriff of the cross of Wexford until 1505 to sheriff of Carlow in the 1520s; and Gerald Aylmer, a future chief justice, must have been fairly reliable as sheriff of Limerick in the 1520s. Thus, although no attempt was made to appoint sheriffs annually, as in the Pale and parts of England, separate sheriffs were normally appointed for each county during pleasure. Government control was greater in this respect than in the far north of England where sheriffs were frequently appointed for life, if at all, or even Worcestershire where from 1497 the office was held in fee.[95]

Control over the outlying shires, therefore, was by no means as negligible and residual as has been alleged. To the evidence of proffers and appointments to shrievalties may be added the exchequer assignments on sheriffs, judicial commissions and the grants of pardons to

---

[94]Except where otherwise stated, this paragraph is based on a study of the surviving extracts from the Irish memoranda rolls, particularly evidence of sheriffs' proffers. Cf. Dunham, *Hastings' Indentured Retainers*, pp. 36-9.

[95]Reid, *King's council in the north*, pp. 41n, 42, 59, 60, 93; Guy, *Cardinal's court*, p. 33.

offenders living in these areas. Moreover, though Richard III's circular to magnates in Munster, Connaught and Ulster, and the pardons issued and oaths of allegiance exacted by Henry VII from the Munster magnates after the Simnel and Warbeck conspiracies were perhaps exceptional,[96] a recent study of Anglo-papal relations has suggested that under the early Tudors royal nominations to vacant bishoprics were usually decisive in Old English areas, though the king had to compromise with local interests in this, and that his influence increased throughout the period.[97] The evidence on which this study is based is supported by the regular grants of episcopal temporalities recorded on the memoranda rolls – Armagh 1470-6, Kildare 1475-6, Waterford and Lismore 1480, Ossory 1487 and notably in 1490 when custodiams of temporalities were granted for the archbishopric of Cashel, and the bishoprics of Waterford and Lismore, Ossory, Leighlin, Limerick, and Cork and Cloyne, seized into the king's hand for reasons now obscure.[98]

Within the Pale at least, the sheriff's duties were obviously very heavy and he needed a sizeable staff to assist in their performance. Each county had a chief serjeant to serve and execute writs and for other routine duties, but very often he was a chief serjeant of fee, over whom the sheriff had little control. The chief serjeants appointed serjeants for each barony, the equivalent of the English hundred bailiffs, and they might in turn appoint their own deputies or subserjeants.[99] In 1465, the sheriff of Meath had the satisfaction of levying 6s. 8d. from the hereditary chief serjeant, Thomas Bermingham, an amercement imposed in common pleas for a false return, but this was exceptional. In 1493 his son feared forfeiture of office but got the office confirmed by act of parliament.[100] The following year it was resumed to the king and was valued at £9 13s. 4d. It was later restored but seized again in 1498 when John Roche was appointed chief

---

[96]*Cal. pat. rolls, 1485-94,* pp. 227, 229, *1494-1509,* p. 76; Conway, *Henry VII's relations,* pp. 221-5; Harris, *Hibernica,* pp. 59-77; Memoranda roll, 12 Henry VII m. ? (P.R.O.I., Ferguson coll., iii, f. 347).

[97]W.E. Wilkie, *The Cardinal Protectors of England* (Cambridge, 1974), pp. 63-73, 79-80, 161-8. Cf Katherine Walsh, 'The beginnings of a national protectorate', *Arch. Hib.,* xxxii (1974), 72-80.

[98]Memoranda rolls, 10 Edward IV m. ?, 12 Edward IV m. 2, 14-15 Edward IV m. 17, 15 Edward IV m. ?, 16 Edward IV m. ?, 20 Edward IV m. 7, 2 Henry VII m. 6, 6-7 Henry VII m. 18 (B.L., Add. MS 4793, ff 149v-50, 157, 157v, 159; P.R.O.I., Ferguson coll., iii, ff 232, 238v, 303).

[99]Cf. Otway-Ruthven, 'Anglo-Irish shire government', pp. 21-3.

[100]P.R.O.I., EX 3/1; Parliament roll, 9 Henry VII c. 12 (P.R.O.I., RC 13/9).

serjeant.[101] In Co. Dublin, the office had been held since the thirteenth century by the Cruise family, but the king made a series of appointments to the office in the early 1530s after which it was restored.[102] There was traditionally also a separate chief serjeant for the barony of Newcastle, where the king's demesne manors lay: he probably doubled as second serjeant-at-arms which may explain the salary of £5 per annum attached.[103] In Kildare, there had originally been chief serjeants of fee in each barony, an arrangement which can be traced to the thirteenth-century liberty, but by 1461 there was a chief serjeant for the whole county and after the suppression of the revived liberty, the king regranted the office in 1535.[104] For the cross of Wexford the appointment of a chief serjeant in 1466 is recorded; and the chief serjeant of Carlow appears in 1495, then also constable of the castle. Much evidence about their activities in the liberty of Tipperary survives among the Ormond deeds.[105]

The offices of chief serjeant and serjeant were seemingly popular and profitable – in 1495 the serjeanty of Offaly, in the king's hand, was valued at a mark.[106] The real work was done by the subserjeants who appear occasionally. For example the subserjeant of the barony of Salt, Kildare was sworn before the barons in 1499. In 1484, the subserjeant of Coolock, Co. Dublin made fine in 20d. before the barons for contempt. Four men were appealed in king's bench in 1486 of ?assault against the subserjeant of Duleek, Co. Meath after he had gone to arrest them on a plea of debt, and in 1485 the subserjeant of Naas, Co. Kildare laid information in exchequer that in a similar case the defendant broke arrest.[107]

---

[101] Statute roll, 10 Henry VII c.11 (Conway, *Henry VII's relations*, pp. 204-9); B.L., Royal MS 18C, XIV, f. 118v; Memoranda rolls, 13 Henry VII m. 19 (P.R.O.I., Ferguson repertory, iv, 55), 14 Henry VII m. 10 (P.R.O.I., RC 8/43, p. 118).

[102] *Cal. pat. rolls Ire., Hen. VIII-Eliz.*, pp. 4, 25, 31; Memoranda roll, 28 Henry VIII m. 21d (P.R.O.I., Ferguson coll., iv, f. 200); Lynch, *Legal instit. Ire.*, pp. 105-6.

[103] P.R.O., E. 101/248/17, S.P. 65/1/2; Memoranda rolls, 2 Richard III m. 3 (P.R.O.I., RC 8/33, p. 395), 16 Henry VIII m. 7, 28 Henry VIII m. 21d (P.R.O.I., Ferguson coll., iv, ff 91, 200); *Cal. pat. rolls Ire., Hen. VIII-Eliz.*, p. 25 (where the salary is incorrectly given as £10). When the office was combined with that of chief serjeant of the county in 1536, the salary was increased to £6 15s.

[104] *Cal. pat. rolls. Ire., Hen. VIII-Eliz.*, pp. 15, 29; *Rot. pat. Hib.*, p. 269 no. 63; A.J. Otway-Ruthven, 'The Medieval County of Kildare', *I.H.S.*, xi (1958-9), 193-4.

[105] B.L., Royal MS 18C, XIV, f. 45; Memoranda roll, 6 Edward IV m. 3 (S.P.W., Hore MS I, p. 1106).

[106] B.L., Royal MS 18C, XIV, f. 117v.

[107] Memoranda rolls, 2 Richard III mm 21d., 23d, 14 Henry VII m. 17 (P.R.O.I., RC 8/33, pp. 530, 535, RC 8/43, p. 133); Coram Rege roll, 1 Henry VII m. 6d (P.R.O.I., RC 8/43, p. 33).

Besides the serjeants who served under him without ever being entirely amenable to his wishes, the sheriff generally had a sizeable staff of his own, appointed and maintained by him. Usually the sheriff nominated a subsheriff to serve under him, who was occasionally sworn before the barons at the same time as the sheriff,[108] but this was probably the practice only if the sheriff did not wish to serve in person. The sheriff's oath under Mary enjoined on him to 'do your vndersherif, clerkes & baylles to do suche othe as longeth to them', implying that undersheriffs were not necessarily sworn before the barons.[109] No doubt sheriffs usually appointed undersheriffs on an *ad hoc* basis, delegating only a portion of their duties. Exceptionally in 1470 a new sheriff of Kildare was elected, appointed and sworn before the barons on 28 June, and on 12 July his two deputies were likewise sworn.[110] The sheriff had a writing office staffed by his clerks who received and filed the king's writs, had custody of the county rolls and moneys collected by the serjeants, and generally assisted the sheriff with correspondence relating to his office. In December 1495, the exchequer disbursed 20*d*. in expenses to a messenger 'deferenti brevia domini regis de serchearare [*certiorari*] Petro Cabbot & Philipi Garnon clericis in officiis vice-comituum Dublinensis & Vrielliis'.[111], The sheriff also appointed a number of deputies, probably itinerant bailiffs who are certainly encountered in Meath in 1540-1, to execute process or serve writs in cases where he felt he could not rely on the sergeants; for example a writ of replevin directed by the sheriff of Meath 'Willemo Murrey seruienti baronie de Scrine, Nicholao Cusak et Richardo Cusake, meis deputatis in hac parte'. Sheriff Cusack had at least three such deputies in 1510-11.[112] A second writ was sent by Thomas Cusack 'vicecomes comitatus Midensis', who was probably the sheriff's son and himself sheriff in 1536: in 1510 he must have been subsheriff. Similar confusion existed in England between sheriffs and subsheriffs.[113]

Little is known for this period about the activities of the coroners, though the king's bench rolls recorded *inter alia* their election in the

---

[108]Memoranda rolls, 2 Richard III m. 3, 9 Henry VII m. 3, 23 Henry VII m. 9 (P.R.O.I., RC 8/33, p. 395, RC 8/43, pp. 53, 228).

[109]T.C.D., MS 588, f. 187v.

[110]Memoranda roll, 10 Edward VI m. 3 (P.R.O.I., RC 8/41, pp. 207-8).

[111]B.L., Royal MS 18C, XIV, f. 27. Cf. Otway-Ruthven, 'Anglo-Irish shire government', p. 21; Jewell, *English local administration,* pp. 197-9.

[112]T.C.D., MS 594, ff 7, 25; White, *Extents of Irish monastic possessions,* pt. 8.

[113]Jewell, *English local administration,* p. 197.

county courts and their swearing-in before the justices.[114] The sheriff supervised their election and saw that they took office, but otherwise they acted independently and as a check on his activities. If the sheriff failed to act, or was himself involved in a case, the coroners were ordered to act in his stead. They frequently levied amercements inflicted on the sheriffs, often two or three times a term, and were occasionally themselves amerced, usually in 40d., for failing to return a writ against the sheriff.[115] Although earlier there had apparently been coroners for each barony, in the late middle ages two coroners were elected for each county,[116] though their duties were unchanged. A record survives of an outlawry before the sheriff and themselves in the county court of Meath in 1466.[117] A jury summoned by the admiralty court in Louth in 1490 stated that the coroner had held an inquest and viewed 'unum [blank in MS] Omulcrewe' overturned in the water of Drumdugne and found on the sea-shore and removed by Roger Gernon of Gernonstown without licence of the admiral, of which offence he stood indicted.[118] In 1503, when John Plate drowned after falling from Dublin bridge into the Liffey, the city bailiffs who acted as the king's coroners there held an inquest upon view of his body.[119] In the liberty of Tipperary in 1508-9, the sheriff summoned the two coroners to be present with their rolls for the start of an eyre.[120] And when the constables of the township of Ballybough in Coolock barony were ordered to arrest two men indicted of various felonies, the men apparently sought sanctuary in St. Mary's abbey and the coroner came to hear their abjurations.[121]

Lastly there were innumerable private courts within the shire, held by lords of manors for their tenants. For the Pale, a large number are noticed in the 1540-1 extents of lands then in the king's hand. In most cases, the profits merely offset the seneschal's expenses in holding court. Some showed net profits, but rarely more than half a mark per

---

[114]Coram Rege roll, 1 Henry VII m. 1d (P.R.O.I., RC 8/43, pp. 8-9; Ferguson coll., iii, f. 312v).

[115]P.R.O.I., EX 3/1; Memoranda roll, 18 Edward IV m. 21 (P.R.O.I., Delafield MSS M. 2675, p. 73).

[116]References in notes 114-15. Cf. Otway-Ruthven, 'Anglo-Irish shire government', p. 26; Jewell, *English local administration,* p. 154.

[117]Coram Rege roll, 1 Henry VII m. 10 (P.R.O.I., RC 8/43, pp. 44-7).

[118]Octavian's register in T.C.D., MS 557, ix, 30.

[119]*Cal. anc. rec. Dublin,* i, 390.

[120]*Ormond deeds, 1413-1509,* no. 337.

[121]D'Alton, *Hist. Co. Dublin,* p. 59.

annum.¹²² Twenty-three tenants owing suit of court to the Holy Trinity manor of Grangegorman, Co. Dublin attended a session c.1496-7 at which they presented six minor matters and offences pertaining to the lord and returned *ignoramus* to a complaint of an affray within the lordship.¹²³ The record of two sessions of the court baron of Knockgraffon, Co. Tipperary, held in November 1491 and September 1500 also survives: in the first, the baron of Knockgraffon complained that the burgesses there had withheld rent and the suitors declared that he could distrain for it. In the second, held before Philip Roche who was probably the baron's steward, a case of distraint was pleaded between the baron and the lord of Geraldstown, one of his tenants, as to a stray or escheat found at Geraldstown. The baron produced ancient court rolls and rentals to prove that the latter was his tenant and a jury of seven of the 'ancienty' declared that the custom was that the value of strays be divided between lord and tenant.¹²⁴

In the later middle ages, local government in the lordship continued to develop along broadly the same lines as in England, although the disturbed conditions in many parts, the scarcity of reliable gentlemen and the need for economy were sometimes responsible for significant departures from the English pattern. Within the Pale, the surviving records suggest that shire government was as effective as in many parts of England: there is no reliable evidence that landowners 'allowed the local courts, where the husbandmen might have voiced their grievances, to lapse'.¹²⁵ Outside, the dearth of evidence leaves many areas under something of a cloud, but undoubtedly the essential minimum for the administration of the common law survived throughout almost all the traditional English areas, and in some parts very much more than the minimum. This is not to say that local government in the more distant shires was necessarily very efficient, or that Gaelic law presented no major problem, but equally it will not do to talk about a collapse of local government there. The ability of the Dublin administration to intervene in these shires as and when it chose ought not to be underestimated, nor should the historian mistake the significance of the government's conscious decision to strengthen private jurisdictions and switch from close control to general supervision. The resources of government were limited, but they were generally well used.

---

[122] White, *Extents of Irish monastic possessions, passim;* P.R.O., S.C. 11/934-5, S.P. 65/3/2.

[123] *Christ Church deeds,* no. 1105.

[124] N.L.I., D. 1866 (*Ormond deeds, 1413-1509,* no. 281).

[125] Canny, *Elizabethan conquest,* p. 18.

CONCLUSION

What then were the essential characteristics of English government in Ireland? The lordship was by no means ill-governed, especially when compared with the north of England — a more appropriate comparison than that implicitly made with the Home Counties, since Scottish raids and extended lines of communication created similar problems. The principal defects of government, it appears, arose from the permanent absence of the king, which in the long term accounted for the exiguity of his revenues there, and the feebleness of the central government against overmighty subjects and Gaelic Ireland. Although the king's institutional control over the Dublin administration was stepped up during this period, in medieval terms the problem was ultimately insoluble since the king could not be in two places at once. It was, however, exacerbated by the crown's general neglect of the lordship for much of the period and, when neglect proved impossible, feverish but short-term and often misguided activity.[1] In these circumstances, it says a lot for the resilience of English institutions that the lordship survived at all into the sixteenth century as a meaningful political entity. In fact it not only survived but, within the limits set by royal policy, it actually prospered.

Precipitated by the crown's refusal to subsidize the lordship, the Yorkist and early Tudor period witnessed a modest reform of government aimed at exploiting internal resources more efficiently to meet economically as many of its commitments as possible. In a negative sense, this entailed acceptance of a *fait accompli* of the Lancastrian period, that resources did not extend to the government of the entire lordship: in consequence resources were regrouped to administer the Pale efficiently, and from this base the government strove to exercise a general oversight over the outlying English districts. Though taken in the first instance for reasons of economy, the crown's decision to rule as far as possible through a local magnate with a social standing and extensive resources of his own in the Pale was the key to this success. The standard of government there appears to have improved steadily under Edward IV and Henry VII. Royal justice was readily available, generally speedy and, though manipulated by local magnates, probably rather less corrupt after 1494 than it had been before that date. The military defence of the area was reorganized to rely more heavily on an unpaid militia and the deputy's household troops. The ensuing stability and relative prosperity, coupled with effective if unambitious tax reforms, produced a moderate increase in

---

[1] See, for example, Ellis, 'Tudor policy and Kildare ascendancy', pp. 235-71.

the revenue which could in turn be used to extend government control on the borders of and beyond the Pale. One result was the tolerably well-documented efforts at expansion by the earls of Kildare in the marchlands of Wexford, Carlow, Kildare, Westmeath and Ulster.[2] This had some direct impact on the revenue before 1534, though rather more after the Kildare inheritance had fallen to the crown,[3] and greatly facilitated the defence of the Pale. By 1500 the Pale was by standards in England usually well-governed.

Beyond the Pale the position is less clear. As is suggested by the government's failure to levy subsidy and scutage there, the daily defence and administration of the outlying English districts had to be delegated to the local magnates, towns and cities. The Dublin administration did however try to ensure that some effective supervision was maintained and that English institutions and law were preserved. In fact the towns and cities remained entirely English, and in the palatinates of Wexford and Tipperary at least, common law institutions were also well preserved. By continuing the policy of decentralization begun in the fourteenth century through the creation of extensive liberties and franchises, the government was able to purchase renewed support against the Irish, and in this way to redirect its efforts to the supervision of duties which it had earlier performed directly but ineffectively. In the counties directly under crown control, the position was less satisfactory, partly because royal rights and justice sometimes cut across the interests of local magnates, encouraging the toleration of certain Gaelic customs which the government alone was too weak to prevent. Nevertheless, sheriffs and other local officials were maintained and, as is shown in particular by the sheriffs' proffers and the activities of the general commissioners, these remained to a degree responsive to control from Dublin and ensured that throughout Munster and south Leinster the common law was available to the king's subjects there. The revenue generated in this area was probably not very substantial, perhaps averaging $c.£150$ a year, though the quasi-permanent assignment of customs and feefarms for the payment of royal officials, the constables of Carrickfergus and Limerick for example, was an additional benefit.

The precise position in each locality must have depended on a number of factors — particularly the military situation there, relations between the local magnate and the governor and the ability of the

---

[2] Above, ch. 2. See also, B..L., Harleian MS 3756; P.R.O.N.I., Kildare deeds; *Red Bk Kildare*.

[3] Ellis, 'Cromwell and Ireland', nn. 61, 112, 119, 124.

government to intervene — but perhaps a suggestion of a general pattern may be made. English institutions were apparently best preserved in Co. Wexford, Co. Kilkenny and parts of Waterford and Tipperary, and it may be that a continuing decline in Munster and Connaught was offset by a recovery in those areas more easily supervised from the Pale. Moreover, only on the assumption that the survival of English institutions was appreciably more widespread than had once seemed the case is it possible to explain the direction of royal policy after 1534. According to the conventional wisdom that the late medieval lordship was confined to the Pale and a few walled towns and cities, its 'recovery' down to 1547 in the traditional Anglo-Norman areas would seem astonishing. And in general, the traditional distinction between the English and Gaelic areas of the country continued: Gaelic Ireland was eventually remodelled by military conquest, garrisons and plantation, whereas in the former Anglo-Norman districts the accent was on curbing the power of the magnates and the alleged degeneracy of the inhabitants from English civility. In turn, the typical Old English and Gaelic responses to centralization differed: for control of Gaelic Ireland wars of independence were fought, whereas Old English resistance was generally constitutional followed, as in England, by demonstrations of dissent within a context of overall obedience.[4] At any rate, despite the problems of distance from England and coexistence with an unconquered Celtic society, the hard-line strategy pursued in the lordship of proscribing or ignoring native customs as far as possible, was not altogether unsuccessful and made for administrative and social structures in much of Ireland which must have appeared far more familiar to contemporary Englishmen than those in the Welsh marches.

Financially, government in the lordship was placed on a sounder footing. Although there was a modest increase in revenue accounted for at the exchequer, this was mainly achieved by tailoring costs to the moneys available, as is clear from the smooth operation of the system of assignment in contrast with the Lancastrian period. The more intensive use of unpaid militia service and coign and livery allowed a sharp reduction in military expenditure, the principal economy effected, though the resumptions of 1493 and 1494 appear to have saved about £400 a year. Moreover, except in periods of direct rule, the costs of the establishment were also gradually reduced by eliminating superfluous offices, keeping salaries low and the flexible use of

---

[4]See Bradshaw, *Irish constitutional revolution,* pts. ii-iii *passim;* Canny, *Elizabethan conquest,* chs. 3-7 *passim.*

available manpower through combining offices and transferring clerks from court to court. Clearly this meant that bureaucratic standards were much lower in Dublin than at Westminster, but in contrast with the periods before and after, the lordship generally ceased to be a financial liability to the crown and this of itself was a considerable achievement. When, occasionally, deputies supported by English troops and money were sent over, it became apparent that the king's feudal rights had not been efficiently exploited, but such slackness was inevitable under a deputy reliant on local support and was more than offset by the increased costs which direct rule entailed.

The period also saw important developments in the law courts and the use of the seals. Under the early Tudors, king's bench, chancery, the exchequer and even to an extent the deputy and council gradually ceased to itinerate and the position of Dublin as the administrative centre of the lordship was consolidated. A substantial recovery took place in the business of the king's courts, and following the curtailment of parliament's judicial functions with the passage of Poynings' Law, a stimulus was given to the development of chancery and the council as courts: a shift in business occurred from the traditional common law courts to the new courts, making for a more flexible curial system overall. Parliament went through a period of eclipse after 1495 but an overall increase in the resort to law apparently prevented an absolute decline in the business of the common law courts. Concerning chancery and the great seal, developments in Ireland again followed those in England: chancery ceased to be the mainspring of government in the lordship and the original force of the great seal was eliminated, being replaced by the resourceful improvisation of the governor's seal in default of a second royal seal.

If, in an administrative context, there is any truth at all in the assertion that 'Poynings' acts mark a clear watershed between medieval Ireland and the Tudor period',[5] it would appear that the long-term impact of Poynings on government was by no means what had originally been intended or has since been surmised. The principal reforms in finance and taxation were largely completed under Edward IV, and Poynings's régime appears generally to have aimed at consolidating previous gains, for example by reestablishing exchequer control over local government officials and taxation, rather than finding new solutions to traditional problems. Even so novel an instrument as Poynings' Law aimed at recovering for the king the control over parliament which he had exercised at the beginning of the

[5] Otway-Ruthven, *Med. Ire.,* p. 408.

century by less formal means. In this context the remodelling of the roles of parliament, chancery and the council on contemporary English lines were unexpected bonuses rather than integral parts of the programme.[6]

No doubt to contemporary Englishmen, trained in the elaborate bureaucracy developed at Westminster, the Dublin administration appeared feeble, corrupt and old-fashioned. Nevertheless, it is at the least misleading to claim that 'it had remained structurally unchanged since the early fourteenth century, and contained a number of institutions and offices which by 1534 were purely nominal'.[7] The administration was certainly less developed than its English counterpart, but in the circumstances it was reasonably well-adapted to the needs of the lordship. This emerges especially from the similarities and differences between the institutions of the lordship and kingdom and the reasons for them, illustrating the continued vitality of the lordship. In general, its institutions developed along the same lines as their English counterparts, if a generation or so later, and this was not necessarily the result of reforming English-born administrators during periods of direct rule. For example, the innovations in the use of actions at common law or of the governor's seal, and the development of equity in parliament were Irish adaptations of English developments. Those 'archaicisms' which did survive usually did so because they were better suited to Irish conditions: thus the general commissions beyond the Pale, the absence of the *nisi prius* system within, and the different functions and powers of sheriffs and keepers of the peace. Even the system of taxation can partly be explained in this way, as a response to the problem of defence, though here innate conservatism and the sensitive issues of parliamentary representation and consent were also important. Significantly, the English system of taxation was not introduced until James I's reign. Nevertheless, the direct impact of Gaelic Ireland on the lordship was small: adaptations of English institutions in the lordship seldom reflected borrowings from Gaelic lordships — English administration had little if anything to learn in this context — but rather the problems created by the survival of a backward, highly militarized and decentralized form of society in about half the island and the efforts of the colony to meet them. In this context 'gaelicization' is a misnomer: even the borrowings from Gaelic law to produce the so-called 'march law' — probably the only significant, direct contribution of Gaelic Ireland to the later medieval administrative history of the lordship — arose principally out of

[6] See also Ellis, 'Henry VII and Ireland', pp. 237-54 for this paragraph.
[7] *New hist. Ire.*, iii, 21.

inherent general weaknesses in the common law system and can be paralleled in other areas where royal government was weak.[8]

Had the Dublin government been ossified in routine, one would have expected more archaisms and the restriction of reform to periods of direct rule. Clearly, however, Irish-born administrators were in many ways better qualified to deal with Irish problems than English-born officials introduced periodically at short notice. Of course the injections of money and a standing army made up for this, but arguably the most successful combination for dealing with traditional problems, and the least easily arranged, was when the two groups cooperated effectively, as occurred only briefly under Poynings and, in the 1540s, under Sir Anthony St. Leger. The comparatively large number of schemes for reformation which the age threw up — chiefly surviving in the form of addresses to the king from parliaments and great councils in the fifteenth century, and from less formal sources after 1494 — shows that Irish-born officials were not without ideas for overcoming the problems which faced them, rather they usually lacked the resources for dealing with them. Some problems, such as underpopulation and emigration to England, could only be rectified by natural means, and the Tudors were more fortunate in this respect than their predecessors, but periods of direct rule increased the resources available, though it often deprived the Old English of the control necessary to carry them out. Even the best-known of the reform tracts, Cromwell's *Ordinances for the government of Ireland,* contains no proposals which had not been made in the previous half-century, and sometimes reproduced sections of them almost verbatim,[9] and the king's absence from Ireland meant that in some respects the Irish government was more acutely aware of administrative problems tackled by Cromwell: as is most strikingly illustrated by the creation of a privy council and the redistribution of the balance of executive power between governor and council, developments in Ireland occasionally preceded, and even influenced, those in England.[10] Once the dust had settled after the Kildare rebellion and the Irish Reformation Parliament, the resources were more forthcoming to put some of the ideas into practice, but much of the criticism then levelled

---

[8]See, for example, Frame, 'Power and society in the lordship of Ireland', esp. pp. 24-8; Denys Hay, 'England, Scotland and Europe: the problem of the frontier', *R. Hist. Soc. Trans.,* 5th ser., xxv (1975), 77-91; R.R. Davies, 'The law of the march', *Welsh History Review,* v (1970-1), 1-30.

[9]See Ellis, 'Cromwell and Ireland', pp. 502-4.

[10]Other instances are the making of murder upon malice aforethought treason by statute in 1494-5 to limit benefit of clergy, and the debasement of the coinage from 1536: Baker (ed.), *Spelman's reports,* ii, 305 n. 6, 333; *New hist. Ire.,* iii, 408-10.

at the Dublin government was ill-founded since its detractors had frequently little grasp of the disabilities under which it had operated. The real difficulties were only gradually identified, and because the Dublin administration was also continually responding to changes in England and Gaelic Ireland as well as within the lordship, administrative reform down to the 1540s tended to be piecemeal. In general, continuity rather than revolution is more apparent.[11]

In terms of the political history of the late medieval lordship, the picture of overall stability and vitality which the surviving court rolls present is in marked contrast to the traditional emphasis on 'Anglo-Irish separatism', decline and degeneracy and the notion of 'mortal crisis'[12] which can be culled out of the state papers. Admittedly, the nature of the court rolls is such that exceptional sequences of events are sometimes reduced by the clerks compiling them to situations of normality in line with preconceived notions of how things ought to be. Yet the idea of a lordship snatched from extinction by Henry VIII's interventionist policies of the 1530s does seem to owe rather too much to an understandable preoccupation with charting the origins of the modern Irish nation at the expense of developments which in this context are of lesser significance. Manifestations of particularist sentiments among the colonists and their adoption of certain Gaelic customs have achieved a prominence out of all proportion to their impact on contemporary politics, and are chiefly viewed as laying the foundations of modern Irish nationalism instead of in connection with contemporary movements on the Anglo-Scottish border or in the marches of Wales. The lordship is too readily treated as a special case, when parallels for some of its supposed peculiarities can in fact be found elsewhere.[13]

This nationalist interpretation has in turn been too easily accepted by English historians, glad to be discharged from responsibility for charting developments in yet another borderland where conditions apparently diverged markedly from those in the Home Counties. Thus the significance in an English context of Irish evidence about the

---

[11] Ellis, 'Cromwell and Ireland' pp. 507-11. For a more optimistic view of the achievements of the 1530s, see Bradshaw, *Irish constitutional revolution,* pt. ii.

[12] The comment by Robin Frame ('Power and society in the lordship of Ireland', p. 33) on the conventional view as expounded in Bradshaw, *Dissolution of the religious orders,* pp. 40-1.

[13] In the Welsh marches, for example, it would seem that native customs and law were much more widely and openly adopted by the settler population, but these developments were not generally regarded as undermining English rule: Davies, *Lordship and society in the March of Wales,* chs. 7-8, 17-18.

planning, enforcement and reaction to government policy (frequently more explicit because of the need to work through a subordinate administration in Dublin) has not been appreciated, perhaps because the independence of the present Dublin government has been allowed to detract from the position of the lordship within the English state. The traditional interpretation, it might appear, has also been bolstered at times by a less than critical evaluation of the Irish state papers, particularly for those periods when more sober sources of evidence are scarce. Fortunately, for the early Tudor period the tales of woe, disseminated by ambitious officials who eagerly petitioned for a reformation in government in the expectation of personal political advancement, can be checked against the court rolls. And although these are far less numerous than for the fourteenth century, when employed in conjunction with the state papers, they make it possible to recreate a much more balanced picture of the workings of government than for any other period down to the seventeenth century.

* * * * *

Taken in conjunction with recent work on the lordship under the three Edwards,[14] the conclusions drawn from this study suggest a new framework for the general history of the medieval lordship. Even before 1300 the medieval lordship it has been convincingly argued, had been 'a highly regional land, of many marches, in which government always had a slender direct hold and fairly limited potential'.[15] And although by about 1500 English government had collapsed in many of those areas which had not been heavily colonized, the overall position was not disastrously worse. Decline was less precipitous or continuous and more localized than has been imagined. More work needs to be done on the Lancastrian lordship, but it is becoming apparent that the fabric of Old English society and government was more resilient than was formerly supposed. The lack of any effective supervision by Henry VI, coupled with the sharp reduction in English subventions, certainly reduced still further even the limited hold which the Dublin administration had previously had outside the Pale; but under more competent kings this control revived. Not that Edward IV or Henry VII were very interested in or conscious of presiding over governmental reform and the reduction of the

---

[14]Especially, Frame, 'Power and society in the lordship of Ireland', pp. 3-33; 'English officials and Irish chiefs', pp. 748-77.

[15]Frame, 'Power and society in the lordship of Ireland', p. 32.

lordship to comparative peace and prosperity: in fact they were probably unaware of many of the changes taking place, but they did see the need to appoint a strong magnate willing and able to protect their comparatively limited interests there so that they could turn their attention to more important matters elsewhere. And in fact the stability of the lordship depended in large measure on the king's ability to find an effective substitute for himself rather than on mere administrative reform. A weak deputy was worse than a weak king. In the late 1520s, when the Dublin administration was temporarily in difficulties, these were brought about solely by Henry VIII's unrealistic refusal either to allow the Fitzgeralds to govern as had his father or to provide an adequate replacement; and the problem was quickly solved with the despatch of a little money, a few troops and the return of Kildare.[16]

The crisis of 1534 arose not out of long-term processes of decay in the lordship but from the changing fortunes of faction at the court of Henry VIII.[17] It brought in its train fundamental changes in the function and powers of the Dublin government. The claims of government on the people of Ireland were greatly increased by the legislation of the Irish Reformation Parliament and the parliament of 1541-3. The Irish administration was now headed by an English-born governor working with a reconstituted Irish council, backed by a small English garrison, and, especially since it was no longer financially self-sufficient, controlled more firmly from London. Thus the crown's Irish problem was both transformed and exacerbated. In part this was because the king required the comparatively weak Dublin government to implement in Ireland the revolutionary changes of the 1530s which had taxed so heavily the much greater capacity of the Westminster government. The resources available in Dublin did not extend to the task which the government there was expected to perform, and the king was more concerned to limit the costs of intervention in Ireland and to prune the deficit on the Irish establishment than to provide for good government whereby his Irish problem might have been solved.[18] In dealing with this problem, however, a more fundamental defect of government after 1534 was the lack of any consistent policy followed for more than two or three years at a time. Thus by the mid-1560s the stability and prosperity of the late medieval lordship had

---

[16] Ellis, 'Tudor policy and Kildare ascendancy', pp. 238-46.

[17] *Ibid.,* pp. 250-60; 'Cromwell and Ireland', pp. 500-2.

[18] See Bradshaw, *Irish constitutional revolution,* pts. ii-iii *passim,* and the alternative interpretation suggested in Ellis, 'Cromwell and Ireland', pp. 497-519.

been thoroughly undermined and English government in Ireland was beginning to look like a military occupation of the country without any real support from its inhabitants.[19] But this sequel to the changes of the 1530s should not blind us to the very real achievements of government in the preceding period: by 1500 the Gaelic tide had long since turned and was on the ebb.

* * * * *

In approaching the history of the later medieval lordship, I intended to investigate its relationship with other areas of English rule rather than to consider its contribution to the making of modern Ireland. The lordship's history is of course part of the history of Ireland, but recent work on the subject has perhaps neglected the fact that in a wider sense it is also a part of English history. I am not suggesting that the lordship was a little England across the Irish sea. Nevertheless, there is a strong case for seeing it as another region of the English state, with its own peculiar problems certainly, but also with many problems common to other areas of English rule, particularly outlying areas. I rather suspect that in the late middle ages the real contrast is more often (though not invariably) between the border areas of the lordship and the Home Counties of England than between the Pale and the rest of England. And if in the long run these ties were insufficient to maintain the constitutional link between lordship and kingdom, they do deserve more careful consideration than they have usually received. In this way the essential characteristics of the history of both regions are more readily appreciated.

---

[19]Canny, *Elizabethan conquest*, chs. 1-2; Ellis, 'Parliament and community in Yorkist and Tudor Ireland', pp. 54-63; 'Cromwell and Ireland', pp. 517-19.

APPENDIX

Tables of the principal officers of the Dublin administration

The following tables are based on Ellis, 'Admin. Ire.', app. i, where full references are cited. Dates entered in brackets are those on which officers are first found acting, otherwise those of first appointment. In the list of chief governors, the following abbreviations have been used: L. lieutenant, D.L. deputy lieutenant, D. deputy, J. justiciar.

Chief governors

	date of appointment	period of office
Thomas, e of Kildare, J.	p. 31 Dec. 1460 confirmed 30 Apr. 1461	Jan. 1461 – ? June 1462
George, d. of Clarence, L.	28 Feb. 1462	12 June 1462 – Apr. 1463
Roland FitzEustace, 1d. Portlester, D.L.	16 May 1462	? Apr. 1463 – p. 13 Oct. 1467
Thomas, e. of Desmond, D.L.	1 Apr. 1463	p. 24 June 1464 – late summer 1464
Thomas, e. of Kildare, D. to Desmond (John, e. of Worcester, D.L.)		
John, e. of Worcester, D.L.	May 1465	a. 31 Oct. 1467 – p. 9 Jan. 1470
John, e. of Worcester, L.	spring 1467	
Edmund Dudley, D.L.	23 May 1470	spring – summer 1470
Thomas, e. of Kildare, J.		a. 13 Oct. 1470 – p. 3 Dec. 1470 (appointed by Henry VI)
George, d. of Clarence, L.		a. 7 Feb 1471 – ? Apr. 1471
Thomas, e. of Kildare, D.L.		(appointed for Edward IV)
Thomas, e. of Kildare, J.	18 Feb. 1471	a. 12 May 1471 – 22 x 28 Dec. 1471

	date of appointment	period of office
George, d. of Clarence, L.	16 Mar. 1472	22 x 28 Dec. 1471 – ? May 1475
Thomas, e. of Kildare, D.L.		? May 1475 – Feb. 1478
William Sherwood, bp. of Meath, D.L.	*a.* 18 Apr. 1475	
Robert Preston, 1d. Gormanston, D. to Sherwood		1477
Thomas, e. of Kildare, J.	10 Mar. 1478	Feb. 1478 – 25 Mar. 1478
(John, d. of Suffolk, L.)		
Gerald, e. of Kildare, J.		*c.* 25 Mar. 1478 – *a.* 15 Sept. 1478
George, son of Edward IV, L.	6 July 1478	
Henry, 1d. Grey, D.L.		*a.* 15 Sept. 1478 – *p.* 15 Dec. 1478
Robert Preston, visct. Gormanston, D. to Grey		*a.* 14 Jan 1479 – *p.* Mar. 1479
Richard, d. of York, L.	5 May 1479	
Robert Preston, visct. Gormanston, D.L.	7 May 1479	?1 June 1479 – *p.* 18 Oct. 1479
Gerald, e. of Kildare, D.L.	*a.* 5 Oct. 1479	*p.* 18 Oct. 1479 – *p.* 9 Apr. 1483
Gerald, e. of Kildare, J.		*p.* 9 Apr. 1483 – 31 Aug. 1483
Edward, son of Richard III, L.	19 July 1483	
Gerald, e. of Kildare, D.L.	31 Aug. 1483	31 Aug. 1483 – ? Mar. 1484
Gerald, e. of Kildare, J.		? Mar. 1484 – *p.* 15 Oct. 1484
John, e. of Lincoln, L.	21 Aug. 1484	
Gerald, e. of Kildare, D.L.	*c.* 22 Sept. 1484	*p.* 22 Oct. 1484 – ? 24 Oct. 1485
Gerald, e. of Kildare, J.		*a.* 18 Dec. 1484 – ? Mar. 1486
Jasper, d. of Bedford, L.	11 Mar. 1486	
Gerald, e. of Kildare, D.L.		? Mar. 1486 – 20 May 1492
(Gerald, e. of Kildare, L.)	appointed by 'Edward VI'	*a.* 24 May 1487 – *p.* 13 Aug. 1487
Walter FitzSimons, abp. of Dublin, D.L.	20 May 1492	20 May 1492 – *p.* 3 Sept. 1493
James Ormond, governor		*a.* 6 July 1492 – *p.* 3 Sept. 1493

	date of appointment	period of office
Robert Preston, visct. Gormanston, D.L.	*a.* 12 Sept. 1493	*a.* 12 Sept. 1493 – *a.* 12 Oct. 1494
William Preston, D. to Gormanston		*c.* Nov. 1493 – *a.* 20 Feb. 1494
Henry, d. of York, L.	12 Sept. 1494	
Edward Poynings, D.	13 Sept. 1494	*a.* 12 Oct. 1494 – *p.* 20 Dec. 1495
Henry Deane, bp. of Bangor, J.	1 Jan. 1496	1 Jan 1496 – *p.* 4 July 1496
Gilbert Nugent, ld. Delvin, commr.		6 July 1496 – 21 Sept. 1496
Gerald, e. of Kildare, D.	6 Aug. 1496	21 Sept. 1496 – *p.* 21 Apr. 1509
Walter FitzSimons, abp. of Dublin, D. to Kildare		Apr. 1503 – Aug. 1503
Gerald, e. of Kildare, J.	8 Nov. 1510	*a.* 1 June 1509 – Nov. 1510
Gerald, e. of Kildare, D.		Nov. 1510 – 3 Sept. 1513
Gerald, e. of Kildare, J.	4 Sept. 1513	4 Sept. 1513 – *p.* 26 Nov. 1513
Gerald, e. of Kildare, D.	26 Nov. 1513	*a.* 13 Jan. 1514 – *p.* 5 May 1515
William Preston, visct. Gormanston, J.	13 Apr. 1515	*a.* 14 May 1515 – *a.* 20 Sept. 1515
Gerald, e. of Kildare, D.		*a.* 20 Sept. 1515 – *p.* 10 Sept. 1519
Maurice FitzGerald, D. to Kildare		*a.* 20 Dec. 1519 – 23 May 1520
Thomas, e. of Surrey, L.	10 Mar. 1520	24 May 1520 – *p.* 21 Mar. 1522
Peter, e. of Ormond, D.L.		*p.* 21 Dec. 1521 – *a.* 9 Mar. 1522
Peter, e. of Ormond, D.	6 Mar. 1522	6 Mar. 1522 – 4 Aug. 1524
Gerald, e. of Kildare, D.	13 May 1524	4 Aug. 1524 – *p.* 20 Dec. 1526
Thomas FitzGerald, D. to Kildare		*p.* 20 Dec. 1526 – ? *a.* 14 Sept. 1527
Richard Nugent, ld. Delvin, D. to Kildare		? *p.* 14 Sept. 1527 – *p.* 10 June 1528
Thomas FitzGerald, captain	15 May 1528	15 May 1528 – *a.* 14 Oct. 1528
Peter, e. of Ossory, D.	4 Aug. 1528	*a.* 14 Oct. 1528 – *a.* 4 Sept. 1529
Henry, d. of Richmond, L.	22 June 1529	

	date of appointment	period of office
John Alen, abp. of Dublin	secret council as D.	a. 4 Sept. 1529 – 24 Aug. 1530
Patrick Bermingham		
John Rawson		
William Skeffington, D.	22 June 1530	24 Aug. 1530 – 18 Aug. 1532
Gerald e. of Kildare, D.	5 July 1532	18 Aug. 1532 – 11 June 1534
Thomas Fitzgerald, ld. Offaly, D. to Kildare		mid-Feb. 1532 – 11 June 1534
Richard Nugent, ld, Delvin governor		? 11 June 1534 – ? early Aug. 1534
John Barnewall, ld. Trimbleston, ? governor		? early Aug. 1534 – 24 Oct. 1534

CHANCERY

Chancellors

18 July 1461	William Welles
?	Walter Devereux
25 Jan. 1464	Thomas e. of Kildare
31 Jan. 1464	John e. of Worcester
?	Edmund Dudley
16 Apr. 1472	Roland FitzEustace, ld. Portlester & John Tapton
5 Aug. 1474	Gilbert Debenham
15 Feb. 1478	Richard Martyn
5 Oct. 1479	William Sherwood bp. of Meath
1482	Walter Champfleur abb. of St. Mary's, Dublin (keeper)
25 Aug. 1482	William Sherwood bp. of Meath
11 Jan. 1483	Robert St. Lawrence, ld. Howth
1482/3	Thomas Fitzgerald
1486/7	Roland FitzEustace ld. Portlester
11 June 1492	Alexander Plunket
13 Sept. 1494	Henry Deane bp. of Bangor
6 Aug. 1496	Walter FitzSimons, abp. of Dublin
(16 Apr. 1505)	John Payne bp. of Meath (keeper)
21 May 1512	William Rokeby abp. of Dublin
6 Nov. 1513	William Compton
8 Feb. 1522	Hugh Inge bp. of Meath
19 Sept. 1528	John Alen abp. of Dublin
5 July 1532	George Cromer abp. of Armagh
16 Aug. 1534	John Barnewall ld. Trimbleston
?11 June 1534 – ?early Aug. 1534	
?early Aug. 1534 9 – 24 Oct. 1534	

Keepers of the rolls

15 Jan. 1461	Amaury de St. Lawrence
2 May 1461	Patrick Cogley
4 Aug. 1461	Peter Trevers
10 Sept. 1464	Thomas Colt
7 Sept. 1467	William Norys
10 Sept. 1471	Thomas Dovedall
1479	Thomas Archbold (deputy)
10 July 1492	Thomas Butler
3 Oct. 1496	John Payne bp. of Meath
1513	Thomas Rochfort
12 June 1521	Walter Wellesley pr. of Conall
7 July 1522	Thomas Darcy
17 July 1523	John Ricard
1528	Thomas Darcy
19 Sept. 1530	Anthony Skeffington
25 Sept. 1532	Nicholas Wycombe
9 July 1533	John Alen

Clerks of the hanaper

1 Dec. 1461	John Prendregast alias Collyn
mid-1470	Richard Nangle
22 Sept. 1494	John Forster
1 Sept. 1495	William Shragger
(1496-7)	Richard Nangle
16 Jan. 1514	Thomas Nangle
(Mich. 1521)	Nicholas Wycombe
26 Aug. 1532	William Fitzwilliam
11 Aug. 1535	Nicholas Stanyhurst & Thomas Alen

Clerks of the crown in chancery

2 May 1461	Patrick Cogley
22 Sept. 1494	John Forster
(1520-22)	Peter Travers
24 Aug. 1532	Nicholas Stanyhurst
(East. 1535)	Robert Cowley
11 Jan. 1536	Robert & Walter Cowley

KING'S BENCH

Chief justices of king's bench

May 1461	Thomas Plunket
14 Apr. 1462	Nicholas Barnewall
(Nov. 1463 × Feb. 1464)	Thomas Plunket
(June 1468)	John Chevir
25 June 1474	Philip Bermingham
26 Feb. 1490	Thomas Cusack
1 Aug. 1494	Thomas Bowring
1496/7	John Topcliffe
2 Dec. 1513	Patrick Bermingham
15 Jan. 1533	Bartholomew Dillon
8 May 1534	Patrick Finglas
11 Aug. 1535	Gerald Aylmer

Second justices of king's bench

20 May 1461	Barnaby Barnewall
(c. 1511)	John Barnewall
(East. 1520)	Patrick Finglas
Mich. 1520	Bartholomew Dillon
1 Apr. 1533	Christopher Delahide
(Mich. 1534)	Patrick White
12 Aug. 1535	Thomas St. Lawrence

Justices of king's bench

21 May 1461	John Beg
(14 Jan. 1479)	John Danston
(6 June 1506)	Christopher Taylor

Chief clerks of king's bench

23 Sept. 1461	James Acton
8 May 1464	James Acton & John Danston
3 Dec. 1486	idem et Richard Danston
(East. 1520)	James Cusack

COMMON PLEAS

Chief justices of common pleas

1438	Robert Dovedall
Nov. 1471	idem et Robert FitzRery
(1 Mar. 1479)	Robert Dovedall
1482	Thomas Plunket
10 July 1492	Nicholas Turner
1 Aug. 1494	John Topcliffe
1496	Thomas Bowring
28 May 1498	Thomas Plunket
16 Jan. 1514	Thomas Plunket & Richard Delahide
26 Jan. 1515	Richard Delahide
Mich. 1534	Thomas Luttrell

Second justices of common pleas

1479	Henry Duffe
30 May 1494	Nicholas Turner
4 June 1516	Patrick Finglas
East. 1520	Thomas Netterville
Sept. 1528	Gerald Aylmer
24 May 1534	Thomas Cusack
12 Aug. 1535	Walter Kerdiff

Justices of common pleas

(Trin. 1463)	James Power
(a. 1465)	John Blakeney
(1466)	John Cornewalshe
(Dec. 1467)	James Prendregast
1472	Thomas Talbot

Prothonotaries of common pleas

14 Jan. 1514	Gerald Dillon
(1520-22)	John Gefferey
28 Sept. 1532	Gerald Dillon
2 June 1534	Thomas Finglas

Chirographers of common pleas

(Nov. 1471	Thomas Walker
1479	idem et Edward Tankard
(1520-22)	Gerald Dillon
12 Sept. 1532	Robert Barnewall
2 June 1534	Thomas Finglas

EXCHEQUER

Chief barons

1441	John Cornewalshe
1473	Thomas Bathe
1478	Henry Duff
(May 1480)	Thomas Plunket
25 Oct. 1482	Oliver FitzEustace
	John Burnell (deputy)
12 Mar. 1485	John Estrete (deputy)
(1490-91)	John Burnell
10 July 1492	John Wise
(20 Nov. 1493)	Clement FitzLyons (deputy)
1 Aug. 1494	Walter Yvers
(10 May 1496)	John Topcliffe
(Jan. 1497)	Walter St. Lawrence
(1503-4)	Thomas Kent
26 Apr. 1511	Richard Goulding
(8 May 1514)	Bartholomew Dillon
(1515)	Richard Goulding
2 July 1516	Bartholomew Dillon
(17 Dec. 1520)	Patrick Finglas
25 June 1534	Gerald Aylmer
(East. 1535)	Patrick Finglas

Second barons

1443	John Gogh
12 Oct. 1472	Nicholas Sutton
(July 1477)	John Archbold
(1478)	Nicholas Sutton
4 Aug. 1478	Thomas Archbold
(1478-9)	John Burnell
(July 1480)	Thomas Archbold
8 Apr. 1499	James Dillon
14 Jan. 1500	Thomas Strangeways
27 Sept. 1515	Nicholas FitzSimon
(Mich. 1520)	Patrick White
27 Mar. 1535	Walter Golding

Third barons

1445	William Sutton
24 Mar. 1469	Nicholas White
1514	Nicholas FitzSimon

Fourth barons

(Mar. 1469)	William Sutton

Barons

(Nov. 1463 × Feb. 1464)	Thomas Baryngton
(10 Dec. 1484)	Patrick Burnell
(Trin. 1485)	William Sutton
1491	Edward Golding
1495	Nicholas White
1505	Richard Nangle
20 Nov. 1507	Bartholomew Dillon
c.1535	Walter Hussey

Treasurers

1 May 1461	Roland FitzEustace
21 Dec. 1461	Idem et John 1d. Wenlock
(Dec. 1479)	Roland FitzEustace
(14 Jan. 1484)	Robert Dovedall (deputy)
11 June 1492	Thomas e. of Ormond
15 June 1492	James Ormond
(10 Mar. 1494)	William Preston (deputy)
13 Sept. 1494	Hugh Conway
28 Feb. 1504	Gerald Fitzgerald
(25 Nov. 1505)	William Darcy (deputy)
13 Jan. 1514	Christopher Fleming 1d. Slane
(11 Feb. 1516)	Bartholomew Dillon (deputy)
8 Feb. 1522	John Rawson
13 May 1524	Peter e. of Ormond
19 Sept. 1528	John Rawson
5 July 1532	James 1d. Butler

Undertreasurers

26 Apr. 1495	William Hattecliffe
2 July 1516	Bartholomew Dillon
11 Mar. 1520	John Stile
(13 Oct. 1523)	William Darcy
3 Sept. 1524	John Barnewall 1d. Trimbleston
(East. 1529)	Bartholomew Dillon
11 Sept. 1532	William Bath
26 Aug. 1534	William Brabazon

Receivers-general

(1495-6)	James Dillon
(18 Nov. 1501)	William Darcy

223

Chief remembrancers

(Dec. 1467)	John Higham
13 Oct. 1470	Philip Eustace
(26 May 1478)	Henry White (deputy)
(1486-7)	Henry Rowe & Henry White
(mid-1495)	John Bath
(Mich. 1496)	James Dillon
(10 Dec. 1507)	Bartholomew Dillon
(Mich. 1519)	Christopher Delahide
Mich. 1520	William Talbot
	Christopher Delahide
7 Jan. 1524	Bartholomew Dillon
20 Mar. 1524	Thomas Messyngham (deputy)
(East. 1528)	John Ryan
(East. 1534)	Thomas Howth

Second remembrancers

(10 Dec. 1484)	John Fleming
(10 Dec. 1498)	Robert Lynn (acting)
(*c.*1500-03)	John Dexter
20 Sept. 1515	Robert Howth
24 Sept. 1532	John Netterville
(East. 1534)	Patrick Moole

Chief chamberlains

5 Sept. 1461	Nicholas Strangeways
(Nov. 1463 × Feb. 1464)	Patrick Cogley
(1467-8)	Nicholas Strangeways
(p.5 May 1481)	Nicholas Barnewall
13 Apr. 1484	Patrick Burnell
20 June 1495	Hugh Blagg
4 Jan. 1499	John Hattecliffe
14 ? 1501/2	Peter Nangle
(East. 1520)	George Cobham
East. 1521	Edward Foley
Mich. 1521	Edward Iseley
15 Apr. 1524	William Bushe
26 Sept. 1527	idem et Thomas Bath
(East. 1534)	Thomas Bath

Second chamberlains

1 Oct. 1494	Thomas Barnewall
(10 Dec. 1498)	John More
East. 1520	John Wyseman
28 Aug. 1532	Thomas Dillon
10 Mar. 1535	Thomas Cannon
11 Aug. 1535	Thomas Alen

Chief engrossers

5 Mar. 1464	Roger Rochfort
(Dec. 1467)	William Sterling & Thomas Sharpe
(12 May 1471)	Thomas Sharpe
20 June 1495	Hugh Blagg
15 Feb. 1499	Peter Barnewall
(10 Dec. 1499)	James Dillon (deputy)
(*c.*1511)	Walter Hussey

Second engrossers

11 May 1461	Richard Tame
(10 Dec. 1484)	John Tole
(10 Dec. 1499)	Thomas Walshe
24 Jan. 1508	Richard Delahide
31 Aug. 1532	Walter Golding
27 Mar. 1535	Richard Savage
	Thomas Hackett
12 Aug. 1535	Walter Golding

Chancellors of the exchequer

8 July 1461	Robert Norreys
23 Feb. 1468	Robert St. Lawrence 1d. Howth
(24 Mar. 1477)	William Molyneux
p. 24 Mar. 1477	Nicholas Harpisfeld
a. c. 1486	Walter Yvers
1 Oct. 1494	Edward Barnewall
3 Jan. 1497	Nicholas St. Lawrence 1d. Howth
(10 Dec. 1498)	Thomas Sharpe (depty)
1 Mar. 1520	Patrick Bermingham
25 Aug. 1532	Richard Delahide
c. Jan. 1533	Thomas Cusack
12 Aug. 1535	John Alen
10 Mar. 1536	Thomas Cusack

Clerks of common pleas of the exchequer

23 Nov. 1463	Walter Delahide & Janico Dartas
(3 Jan. 1471)	Thomas Sharpe & William Moleynes
(c. May 1476)	Robert St. Lawrence 1d. Howth & ?[William Molyneux]
(Jan. 1481)	Robert St. Lawrence & ?[Nicholas Harpisfeld]
(10 Dec. 1498)	Thomas Walshe
4 Feb. 1508	idem et Thomas Burnell
28 Sept. 1513	Gerald Dillon
East. 1520	Thomas Messyngham
28 Sept. 1531	John Beling
12 Sept. 1532	John Talbot
15 Nov. 1535	John Beling
3 Feb. 1536	Walter Archer

Treasurers' clerks

(1 Oct. 1461)	James Power
(22 Apr. 1471)	John Fleming
(Trin. 1496)	Richard Nangle
12 Nov. 1507	Philip Flatisbury
(20 Jan. 1537)	John Ryan

Summamsters

(Dec. 1467)	Thomas Sharpe
(10 Dec. 1499)	Walter Hussey
4 Apr. 1509	Thomas Bathe
(Mich. 1519)	John Dillon
Mich. 1520	Thomas FitzSimons
16 Mar. 1529	Thomas Hackett
(a. Mich. 1534)	Robert Howth
Mich. 1534	Nicholas Bellew

Transcriptors

(10 Dec. 1484)	Thomas Walker
(10 Dec. 1498)	Robert Luttrell
(a. Mich. 1502)	Walter Golding
Mich. 1520	Thomas FitzSimons
8 May 1535	Walter Golding

Serjeants-at-arms

20 June 1461	Nicholas Dawe
(8 Dec. 1495)	John Berde
6 May 1514	John Dullarde
(East. 1520)	Radi Framynghame
15 July 1524	Lewis Bushe
12 June 1527	Edward Lyence
6 July 1528	John White
(East. 1534)	idem et Owen White

Ushers

(1475-6)	Thomas Pekok
10 Aug. 1484	Philip FitzRobert & Thomas Harrold
(14 Oct. 1527)	Richard Fitzwilliam
30 Sept. 1536	John Clerck

King's serjeants-at-law

(Nov. 1463 × Feb. 1464)	Philip Bermingham
(Dec. 1467)	Thomas Dovedall
(1471)	Henry Duff
(July 1477)	John Estrete
8 Nov. 1496	Thomas Kent
1501-2	John Egyr
(1503-4)	John Barnewall
(1505)	Clement FitzLyons
20 Jan. 1508	Patrick Finglas
?11 Apr. 1516	Thomas Rochfort
(Mich. 1520)	Robert Barnewall
9 Sept. 1532	Thomas Luttrell
17 Oct. 1534	Patrick Barnewall

King's attorneys

(Nov. 1463 × Feb. 1464)	Thomas Dovedall
(Dec. 1467)	Robert FitzRery
22 May 1471	Nicholas Sutton
(1478)	Thomas Archbold
early 1479	Thomas Cusack
(East. 1491)	Walter St. Lawrence
(20 Jan. 1494)	Patrick Barnewall
(East. 1496)	Walter St. Lawrence
2 Nov. 1496	Patrick Barnewall
(1 Oct. 1499)	Clement FitzLyons
(1504)	John Barnewall
4 Mar. 1504	Nicholas FitzSimon
(20 June 1516)	Thomas Netterville
(Mich. 1520)	Christopher Delahide
(10 Nov. 1528)	Walter Cowley
19 Aug. 1532	Thomas St. Lawrence
(Mich. 1534)	Robert Dillon

Clerks of the Council

(Dec.1467)	James Prendregast alias Collyn
1472	Richard Nangle
(22 Nov. 1495)	John Sonnes alias Swvnney
(1512-13)	William Delahide
(East. 1520)	Robert Cowley
(*a*. June 1529)	John Alen
9 July 1533	John Alen

BIBLIOGRAPHY

Of books and manuscripts cited in the text

I   MANUSCRIPTS

British Library, London
Additional MSS 4763, 4784, 4787, 4790, 4791, 4793, 4797, 4801, 19865
Cotton MSS Otho E. IX, Titus B. XI
Harleian MS 3756
Royal MS 18C, XIV

Bodleian Library, Oxford
Laud MS 613
Rawlinson MSS B. 484, C. 168

Genealogical Office, Dublin
MSS 22, 192

National Library of Ireland, Dublin
Dowdall deeds
Ormond deeds
MSS 761, 2551

Public Record Office, London
C. 47   Chancery, Miscellanea
C. 66   Chancery, Patent rolls
E. 28   Exchequer, Treasury of Receipt, Council and Privy Seal
E. 30   Exchequer, Diplomatic documents
E.101   Exchequer, King's Remembrancer, Various Accounts
K.B.27   King's Bench, Plea rolls
K.B.29   King's Bench, Controlment rolls
P.S.O.1   Warrants for the Privy Seal, Series I
S.C.1   Ancient Correspondence
S.C.11   Rentals and Surveys, Rolls
S.P.1   State Papers, Henry VIII
S.P.2   State Papers, Henry VIII, large folios
S.P.60   State Papers, Ireland, Henry VIII
S.P.65   Exchequer Records, Ireland, Henry VIII

Public Record Office of Ireland, Dublin
CB 1   Common Bench rolls
CH 1/1   Statute roll, 28-9 Henry VIII

EX 3/1 Controlment roll, estreats, Co. Meath (EX 3/2 ultra-violet
        photographs of original)
RC   Irish Record Commission papers
RC 6/1   Repertory of chancery decrees
RC 8   Calendar of memoranda rolls
RC 9   Repertory of exchequer inquisitions
RC 13   Transcripts of parliament rolls
Ferguson collection of memoranda roll extracts
Ferguson repertory of memoranda rolls
Lodge MSS 'Acta regia'
        'Articles with Irish chiefs [etc.]'
Transcript of Parliament Roll, 2-3 Richard III
MSS 2675, 3072

Public Record Office of Northern Ireland, Belfast
Kildare deeds

Royal Irish Academy, Dublin
MSS 12 D 10, 12 D 19, 24 H 17

St. Peter's College, Wexford
Hore MS I

Trinity College, Dublin
MSS 543/2, 557, 569, 578, 588, 594, 1207, 1731, 1739, 1740
Liber niger Alani (on loan)

II   SOURCE COMPILATIONS

A calendar of the contents of the Red Book of the Irish exchequer. Ed.
    J.F. Ferguson. In *Transactions of the Kilkenny Archaeological
    Society*, iii (1854-5).
A calendar of the Liber Niger and Liber Albus of Christ Church,
    Dublin. Ed. H.J. Lawlor. In *R.I.A. Proc.*, xxvii (1908-9).
A calendar of the register of Primate George Dowdall. Ed. L.P.
    Murray In *Louth Archaeological Journal*, xii (1929-32).
Acts of the privy council in Ireland, 1556-71. Ed. J.T. Gilbert. In
    H.M.C. rep. 15, app. iii. London, 1897.
Acts of the privy council of England, 1542-7 [etc.]. London, 1890-
Annála Uladh Annals of Ulster. Ed. B. MacCarthy. Vol. iii, Dublin,
    1895.
*A roll of the proceedings of the king's council in Ireland for a portion
    of the sixteenth year of the reign of Richard II, 1392-3.* Ed. J.
    Graves. London, 1877.
Blake family records, 1300 to 1600. Ed. M.J. Blake. London, 1902.

Calendar to Christ Church deeds, 1174-1684. Ed. M.J. McEnery. In *P.R.I. rep. D.K. 20* (1888), *23* (1891), *24* (1892), *27* (1895).

Calendar to fiants of the reign of Henry VIII. In *P.R.I. rep. D.K. 7-22* (1875-90).

Calendar of ancient deeds and muniments preserved in the Pembroke Estate Office, Dublin. Dublin, 1891.

Calendar of ancient records of Dublin. Ed. J.T. Gilbert. Vol. i, Dublin, 1889.

Calendar of Archbishop Alen's register, c. 1172-1534. Ed. C. McNeill. Dublin, 1950.

Calendar of Ormond deeds, 1172-1350 [etc.]. Ed. E. Curtis. 6 vols., Dublin, 1932-43.

Calendar of patent and close rolls of chancery in Ireland, Henry VIII to 18th Elizabeth. Ed. J. Morrin. Dublin, 1861.

Calendar of the Carew manuscripts preserved in the archiepiscopal library at Lambeth, 1515-74 [etc.]. 6 vols., London, 1867-73.

Calendar of the close rolls, 1500-9. London, 1963.

Calendar of the Gormanston register. Ed. J. Mills & M.J. McEnery. Dublin, 1916.

Calendar of the Irish council book, 1581-6. Ed. D.B. Quinn. In *Anal. Hib.*, xxiv (1967).

Calendar of the patent rolls, 1232-47 [etc.]. London, 1906-

Chartularies of St. Mary's Abbey, Dublin. Ed. J.T. Gilbert. 2 vols., London, 1884-6.

Dowdall deeds. Ed. C. McNeill & A.J. Otway-Ruthven. Dublin, 1960.

English constitutional documents, 1307-1485. Ed. E.C. Lodge & G.A. Thornton. Cambridge, 1935.

English Historical Documents. Vol. iv, ed. A.R. Myers. London, 1969.

Extents of Irish monastic possessions, 1540-41. Ed. N.B. White. Dublin, 1943.

Facsimiles of the national manuscripts of Ireland. Ed. J.T. Gilbert. 4 vols., Dublin, 1874-84.

Foedera, conventiones, litterae et cujuscunque generis acta publica. Ed. T. Rymer. London, 1740-1.

Guide to English financial records for Irish history, 1461-1558 with illustrative extracts, 1461-1509. Ed. D.B. Quinn. In *Anal. Hib.,* x (1941).

Hibernica: or some ancient pieces relating to Ireland. Ed. W. Harris. 1st ed., Dublin, 1747.

Kilkenny city records; Liber primus Kilkenniensis. Ed. C. McNeill. Dublin, 1931.

Letters and papers, foreign and domestic, Henry VIII. 21 vols., London, 1862-1932.
Letters and papers illustrative of the reigns of Richard III and Henry VIII. Ed. J. Gairdner. 2 vols., London, 1861-3.
Liber munerum publicorum Hiberniae. Ed. R. Lascelles. 2 vols., London, 1852.
Lord Chancellor Gerrard's notes of his report on Ireland, 1577-8. Ed. C. McNeill. In *Anal. Hib.*, ii (1931).
Parliaments and councils of mediaeval Ireland. Ed. H.G. Richardson & G.O. Sayles. Vol. i, Dublin, 1947.
Parliaments and great councils, 1483-99: addenda et corrigenda. Ed. S.G. Ellis. In *Anal. Hib.*, xxix (1980).
Proceedings and ordinances of the privy council of England, 1386-1410 [etc.]. 7 vols., London, 1834-7.
Registrum Iohannis Mey The register of John Mey Archbishop of Armagh 1443-1456. Ed. W.G.H. Quigley & E.F.D. Roberts. Belfast, 1972.
Report of the Deputy Keeper of the Public Records in Ireland. Dublin, 1869-
Reports of the commissioners appointed . . . respecting the public records of Ireland. 3 vols., [London, 1815-25].
Rotuli parliamentorum. 6 vols., London, 1761-83.
Rotulorum patentium et clausorum cancellariae Hiberniae calendarium. Dublin, 1828.
Select cases in the council of Henry VII. Ed. C.G. Bayne & W.H. Dunham Jr. London, 1968.
Select cases in the court of king's bench under Richard II, Henry IV and Henry V. Ed. G.O. Sayles. London, 1971.
State papers, Henry VIII. 11 vols., London, 1830-52.
Statutes and ordinances, and acts of the parliament of Ireland, King John to Henry V. Ed. H.F. Berry. Dublin, 1907.
Statute rolls of the parliament of Ireland . . . reign of King Edward IV. Ed. H.F. Berry & J.F. Morrissey. 2 vols., Dublin, 1914-39.
Statute rolls of the parliament of Ireland, reign of King Henry VI. Ed. H.F. Berry. Dublin, 1910.
The annals of Ireland. Ed. R. Butler. Dublin, 1849.
The bills and statutes of the Irish parliaments of Henry VII and Henry VIII. Ed. D.B. Quinn. In *Anal. Hib.*, x (1941).
The . . . chronicles of England, Scotlande and Irelande. Raphael Holinshed. Ed. H. Ellis. 6 vols., London, 1807-8.
The 'Dignitas decani' of St. Patrick's Cathedral, Dublin. Ed. N.B. White. Dublin, 1957.
The Marcher Lordships of South Wales 1415-1536. Ed. T.B. Pugh. Cardiff, 1963.

The Red Book of the earls of Kildare. Ed. G. Mac Niocaill. Dublin, 1964.
The reports of Sir John Spelman. Ed. J.H. Baker. 2 vols., London, 1977-8.
The register of Primate John Swayne. Ed. D.A. Chart. Belfast, 1935.
The social state of the southern and eastern counties of Ireland in the sixteenth century. Ed. H.F. Hore & J. Graves. Dublin, 1870.
The statutes at large passed in the parliaments held in Ireland. 20 vols., Dublin, 1786-1801.
The statutes of the realm. 12 vols., London, 1810-28.

III SECONDARY WORKS

Baker, J.H., 'The English legal profession, 1450-1550' in W. Prest (ed.), *Lawyers in early modern Europe and America* (London, 1981).

Ball, F.E., *The judges in Ireland, 1221-1921* (2 vols., London, 1926).

Bean, J.M.W., *The decline of English feudalism, 1215-1540* (Manchester, 1968).

Bellamy, J.G., *Crime and public order in England in the later middle ages* (London, 1973).

―――― 'Justice under the Yorkist kings', *American Journal of Legal History,* ix (1965).

Berry, H.F., 'Sheriffs of the county Cork — Henry III to 1660', *R.S.A.I. Jn.,* xxxv (1905).

Betham, Sir William, *The origin and history of the constitution of England and early parliaments of Ireland* (Dublin, 1834).

Blatcher, M., *The court of king's bench 1450-1550 a study in self-help* (London, 1978).

Bradshaw, B., *The dissolution of the religious orders in Ireland under Henry VIII* (Cambridge, 1974).

―――― *The Irish constitutional revolution of the sixteenth century* (Cambridge, 1979).

Bryan, D., *Gerald FitzGerald, the Great Earl of Kildare, 1456-1513* (Dublin, 1933).

Bush, M.L., 'The problem of the far north: a study of the crisis of 1537 and its consequences', *Northern History,* vi (1971).

Butlin, R.A. (ed.), *The development of the Irish town* (London, 1977).

Canny, N.P., *The Elizabethan conquest of Ireland: a pattern established 1565-76* (Hassocks, 1976).

―――― *The formation of the Old English Elite in Ireland* (Dublin, 1975).

Cheney, C.R. (ed.), *Handbook of dates for students of English history* (London, 1970).
Chrimes, S.B., *Henry VII* (London, 1972).
Conway, A., *Henry VII's relations with Scotland and Ireland, 1485-98* (Cambridge, 1932).
Cosgrove, A., 'Irish episcopal temperalities in the thirteenth century', *Archivium Hibernicum,* xxxii (1974).
────── 'The execution of the earl of Desmond, 1468', *Journal of the Kerry Archaeological and Historical Society,* viii (1975).
Curtis, E., 'The acts of the Drogheda parliament, 1494-5, or "Poynings' Laws" ' in A. Conway, *Henry VII's relations with Scotland and Ireland, 1485-98* (Cambridge, 1932), ch. 7.
D'Alton, J., *The history of the county of Dublin* (Dublin, 1838).
Davies, Sir John, A discovery of the true causes why Ireland was not entirely subdued (Shannon, 1969).
────── *Historical tracts* (Dublin, 1787).
Davies, R.R., *Lordship and Society in the March of Wales 1282-1400* (Oxford, 1978).
────── 'The law of the march', *Welsh History Review,* v (1970-1), 1-30.
────── 'The twilight of Welsh law, 1284-1536', *History,* li (1966), 143-64.
Dunham, W.H., Jr., *Lord Hastings' Indentured Retainers, 1461-83* (Connecticut, 1970).
Edwards, R.D., *Ireland in the age of the Tudors: the destruction of Hiberno-Norman civilization* (London, 1977).
────── 'The Irish Reformation Parliament of Henry VIII, 1536-7', *Historical Studies*, vi (London, 1968).
Ellis, S.G., 'An indenture concerning the king's munitions in Ireland, 1532', *Irish Sword,* xiv (1980-1).
────── 'Henry VII and Ireland, 1491-6' in J.F. Lydon (ed.), *Anglo-Irish relations in the later middle ages* (Dublin, 1981).
────── 'Henry VIII, rebellion and the rule of law', *Hist. Jn.,* xxiv (1981).
────── 'Ionadaíocht i bparlaimint na hÉireann i ndeireadh na meán-aoise', *Galvia,* xiii (1985).
────── 'Ioncam na hÉireann, 1384-1534', *Studia Hibernica,* xxi (1985).
────── 'Parliament and community in Yorkist and Tudor Ireland' in A. Cosgrove & J.I. McGuire (eds.), *Parliament and community: Historical Studies XIV* (Belfast, 1983).
────── 'Privy seals of chief governors in Ireland, 1392-1560', *I.H.R. Bull.,* li (1978).

───── 'Taxation and defence in late medieval Ireland: the survival of scutage', *R.S.A.I. Jn.,* cvii (1977).
───── 'The administration of the lordship of Ireland under the early Tudors' (Ph.D. thesis, Belfast, 1979).
───── 'The destruction of the liberties: some further evidence', *I.H.R. Bull.,* liv (1981).
───── 'The Irish customs administration under the early Tudors', *I.H.S.,* xx (1980-1).
───── 'The Kildare rebellion and the early Henrician Reformation', *Hist. Jn.,* xix (1976).
───── 'The Kildare rebellion, 1534' (M.A. thesis, Manchester, 1974).
───── 'The struggle for control of the Irish mint, 1460-c. 1506', *R.I.A. Proc.,* lxxviii (1978).
───── 'Thomas Cromwell and Ireland, 1532-40', *Hist. Jn.,* xxiii (1980).
───── 'Tudor policy and the Kildare ascendancy in the lordship of Ireland, 1496-1534', *I.H.S.,* xx (1976-7).
Elton, G.R., *Reform and Reformation: England 1509-58* (London, 1977).
───── *Studies in Tudor and Stuart politics and government* (2 vols., Cambridge, 1974).
───── *The Tudor revolution in government* (Cambridge, 1953).
───── 'Tudor government: the points of contact. II. The council' *R. Hist. Soc. Trans.,* 5th ser., xxv (1975).
Empey, C.A., 'The Butler lordship', *Journal of the Butler society,* i (1970-1).
───── & Simms, K., 'The ordinances of the White Earl and the problem of coign in the later middle ages', *R.I.A. Proc.,* lxxv (1975).
Falls, C., *Elizabeth's Irish wars* (London, 1950).
Flower, R., 'Manuscripts of Irish interest in the British Museum', *Anal. Hib.,* ii (1931).
Frame, R.F., 'English officials and Irish chiefs in the fourteenth century', *E.H.R,* xc (1976).
───── 'Power and society in the lordship of Ireland, 1272-1377', *Past & Present,* no. 76 (Aug. 1977).
───── 'The judicial powers of the medieval Irish keepers of the peace', *Irish Jurist,* n.s., ii (1967).
Gilbert, J.T., *History of the viceroys of Ireland* (Dublin, 1865).
Griffith, M.C., 'The Talbot-Ormond struggle for control of the Anglo-Irish government, 1414-47', *I.H.S.,* ii (1940-1).
Guy, J.A, *The Cardinal's court* (Hassocks, 1977).

Gwynn, A., *The medieval province of Armagh, 1470-1545* (Dundalk, 1946).
Hand, G.J., *English law in Ireland, 1290-1324* (Cambridge, 1967).
_____ 'English law in Ireland, 1172-1351', *Northern Ireland Legal Quarterly,* xxiii (1972).
_____ & Treadwell, V.W., 'His majesty's directions for ordering and settling the courts within his kingdom of Ireland, 1622', *Anal. Hib.,* xxvi (1970).
Hardiman, J., *History of the town and county of Galway* (Dublin, 1820).
Hastings, M., *The court of common pleas in fifteenth-century England: a study of legal administration and procedure* (Cornell, 1947).
Hay, D., 'England, Scotland and Europe: the problem of the frontier', *R. Hist. Soc. Trans.,* 5th ser., xxv (1975).
Hayes-McCoy, G.A., 'The early history of guns in Ireland', *Journal of the Galway Archaeological and Historical Society,* xviii (1938-9).
Holdsworth, Sir William, *A history of English law* (7th ed., 13 vols., London, 1922-52).
Hore, P.H., *History of the town and county of Wexford* (6 vols., London, 1900-11).
Hoskins, W.G., *The age of plunder: the England of Henry VIII, 1500-47* (London, 1976).
Ives, E.W., 'The common lawyers in Pre-Reformation England', *R. Hist. Soc. Trans.,* 5th ser., xviii (1968).
Jacob, E.F., *The fifteenth century* (Oxford, 1961).
Jewell, H.M., *English local administration in the middle ages* (Newton Abbot, 1972).
Kirby, J.L., 'The rise of the under-treasurer of the exchequer', *E.H.R.,* lxxii (1957).
Lander, J.R., *Crown and nobility, 1450-1509* (London, 1976).
_____ *Government and community: England 1450-1509* (London, 1980).
Lydon, J.F., 'A survey of the memoranda rolls of the Irish exchequer, 1294-1509', *Anal. Hib.,* xxiii (1966).
_____ *Ireland in the later middle ages* (Dublin, 1972).
_____ *The lordship of Ireland in the middle ages* (Dublin, 1972).
_____ 'The problem of the frontier in medieval Ireland', *Topic: a journal of the liberal arts,* xiii (Washington, 1967).
Lynch, W., *A view of the legal institutions... established in Ireland* (London, 1830).

MacLysaght, E., 'Report on documents relating to the wardenship of Galway', *Anal. Hib.*, xiv (1944).

MacNiocaill, G., *Na Buirgéisí* (2 vols., Dublin, 1964).

―――― 'Socio-economic problems of the late medieval Irish town' in D.W. Harkness & M. O'Dowd (eds.), *The town in Ireland: Historical Studies XIII* (Belfast, 1981).

Maitland, F.W., *The forms of action at common law* (ed. Cambridge, 1965).

Meekings, C.A.F., 'King's Bench files' in J.H. Baker (ed.), *Legal records and the historian* (London, 1978).

Mills, M.H., '"Adventus vicecomitum", 1272-1307', *E.H.R.*, xxxviii (1923).

Molyneux, W., *The case of Ireland stated* (ed. J.G. Simms, Dublin, 1977).

Moody, T.W., Martin F.X., & Byrne F.J., (eds.), *A new history of Ireland*, ii (Oxford, forthcoming), iii (Oxford, 1976), ix (Oxford, 1984).

Nicholls, K.W., *Gaelic and gaelicised Ireland in the middle ages* (Dublin, 1972).

O'Flanagan, J.R., *The lives of the lord chancellors and keepers of the great seal of Ireland* (2 vols., London, 1870).

Otway-Ruthven, A.J., *A history of medieval Ireland* (London, 1968).

―――― 'Anglo-Irish shire government in the thirteenth century', *I.H.S.*, v (1946-7).

―――― 'The chief governors of mediaeval Ireland', *R.S.A.I. Jn.*, xcv (1965).

―――― 'The medieval county of Kildare' *I.H.S.*, xi (1958-9).

―――― 'The medieval Irish chancery' in *Album Helen Maud Cam* (Louvain, 1961).

―――― 'The organization of Anglo-Irish agriculture in the middle ages' *R.S.A.I. Jn.*, lxxxi (1951).

Powicke F.M., & Fryde E.B., (eds.), *Handbook of British chronology* (2nd ed., London, 1961).

Price, L., 'Armed forces of the Irish chiefs in the early sixteenth century', *R.S.A.I. Jn.*, lxii (1932).

Pronay, N., 'The chancellor, the chancery and the council at the end of the fifteenth century' in H. Hearder & H.R. Loyn (eds.), *British government and administration: studies presented to S.B. Chrimes* (Cardiff, 1974).

Pugh, T.B., *The Marcher Lordships of South Wales 1415-1536* (Cardiff, 1963).

Quinn, D.B., 'Agenda for Irish history. II. Ireland from 1461 to 1603', *I.H.S.*, iv (1944-5).

―――― 'Anglo-Irish local government, 1485-1534', *I.H.S.*, i 1938-9).
―――― 'Anglo-Irish Ulster in the early sixteenth century', *Proceedings and Reports of the Belfast Natural History and Philosophical Society* (1934).
―――― 'Henry Fitzroy, duke of Richmond, and his connexion with Ireland, 1529-30', *I.H.R. Bull.*, xii (1934-5).
―――― 'Henry VIII and Ireland, 1509-34', *I.H.S.*, xii (1960-1).
―――― 'Parliaments and great councils in Ireland, 1461-1586', *I.H.S.*, iii (1942-3).
―――― 'The early interpretation of Poynings' Law, 1494-1534', *I.H.S.*, ii (1940-1).
―――― 'The Irish parliamentary subsidy in the fifteenth and sixteenth centuries', *R.I.A. Proc.*, xliii (1935).
Rawcliffe, C., *The Staffords, earls of Stafford and dukes of Buckingham, 1394-1521* (Cambridge, 1978).
Reid, R.R., *The king's council in the north* (London, 1921).
Richardson, H.G., 'The Irish parliament rolls of the fifteenth century', *E.H.R.*, lviii (1943).
―――― & Sayles G.O., 'Irish revenue, 1278-1384', *R.I.A. Proc.*, lxii (1962).
―――― *The administration of Ireland, 1172-1377* (Dublin, 1963).
―――― *The Irish parliament in the middle ages* (Philadelphia, 1952).
Richardson, W.C., 'The surveyor of the king's prerogrative', *E.H.R.*, lvi (1941).
Ross, C., *Edward IV* (London, 1974).
Sayles, G.O., *The king's parliament of England* (London, 1975).
Simms, K., 'Warfare in the medieval Gaelic lordships', *Irish Sword*, xii (1976).
Steel, A., *The receipt of the exchequer, 1377-1485* (Cambridge, 1954).
Storey, R.L., 'The wardens of the marches of England towards Scotland, 1377-1485', *E.H.R.*, lxxii (1957).
Treadwell, V.W., 'The Irish parliament of 1569-71', *R.I.A. Proc.*, lxv (1966).
Walsh, K., 'The beginnings of a national protectorate', *Archivium Hibernicum*, xxxii (1974).
Ware, Sir James, *The antiquities and history of Ireland* (ed. R. Ware, Dublin, 1705).
Wilkie, W.E., *The Cardinal Protectors of England* (Cambridge, 1974).
Williams, P., *The council in the marches of Wales under Elizabeth I* (Cardiff, 1958).
―――― *The Tudor regime* (Oxford, 1979).

Wolffe, B.P., *The crown lands, 1461-1536* (London, 1970).
Wood H., *A guide to the records deposited in the Public Record Office of Ireland* (Dublin, 1919).
———— 'The court of Castle Chamber or Star Chamber in Ireland', *R.I.A. Proc.*, xxxii (1914).
———— 'The office of chief governor of Ireland, 1172-1509', *R.I.A. Proc.*, xxxv (1923).

INDEX

(The index excludes the names of officials appearing only in the appendix.)

absentee landowners, 8, 79-80, 83, 84, 124, 198; licences of absence, 80, 83, 85, 130, 175
account, action of, 116, 118, 119
admiral, jurisdiction of, 182, 204
Alen, John, archbishop of Dublin, 33, 37, 38-9, 85, 155, 218, 220
Alen, John, clerk of the council and master of the rolls, 37, 38-9, 163, 171, 178, 220, 223, 225
Alen, S., 171
Alen, Thomas, 171, 220, 223
Alleyn, James, C.J.K.B., 107
'Anglo-Irish separatism', 2, 8, 154, 212
Annall, le, 77
Anyden, Richard, 171-2
appeals, 32, 119, 121, 202
Ardee, barony of, 103
Ardglass, 72, 74
Arklow, 60
Armagh: archbishop of, 79, 107, 169, 176, 191. *See also* Cromer; archbishopric of, 201; archdeacon of, 169; clergy of, 107
Armies, English, in Ireland, 3, 4, 26-8, 49-50, 52, 53, 81, 84, 211. *See also* subventions
Arteboye, 63
assizes, 109, 117, 199. *See also* commissions; of novel disseisin, 118, 138, 187, 199; of mort d'ancestor, 118; of fresh force, 133; circuits of, 134-5
Athboy, 31, 128
Athenry, 9, 57
Athlone, 86
Athy, 59, 60, 128
attorneys, 113, 132, 172, 197. *See also* king's attorney; warrants of, 114, 117, 119, 122, 125
Audley, Thomas, lord chancellor of England, 179
Aylmer, Gerald, C.J.K.B., 200, 221, 222

Ballybough, 204
Ballymore Eustace, 6
Baltimore, 74
Baltinglass, 59

Bann, river, 85
Barnewall, Barnaby, J.K.B., 107, 221
Barnwall, John, baron of Trimbleston, 34, 40, 45, 101, 190, 219, 220, 221, 222, 224
Barrow valley, 58-60, 186
Bath, William, undertreasurer, 16, 101-2, 222
Beg, Roger, 110
Bellew, Patrick, 80
Bermingham, family, 59
Bermingham, Patrick, C.J.K.B., 34, 39, 45, 218, 221, 223
Bermingham, Thomas, 201
Betham, Sir William, 113
Bishops, royal nomination of, 15-16, 201; temporalities, 14, 30, 78-9, 175, 193, 201
Boleyn, Margaret, 157-8
Boleyn, Thomas, earl of Wiltshire and Ormond, 17, 42, 158
Bordeaux, 113
Brabazon, William, undertreasurer, 75, 85, 99, 102, 171, 222
Bray, Stephen, C.J.K.B., 102
Brotherhood of Arms, 52-3
Browne, George, archbishop of Dublin, 37
Butler, family, 40, 59, 60, 61, 186
Butler, James, 4th earl of Ormond (1411-52), 3, 12, 139
Butler, James, 5th earl of Ormond (1452-61), and 2nd earl of Wiltshire (1449-61), 184
Butler, John, 6th earl of Ormond (1470-1, 1475-7), 184
Butler, Thomas, 7th earl of Ormond (1477-1515), 28, 77, 107, 157, 161, 186, 198, 222
Butler, Piers (Peter), 8th earl of Ormond (1515-28, 1537-9), and 1st earl of Ossory (1528-39), 40, 42, 43, 45, 140, 157-8, 186, 189, 194, 222; earlier career, 60, 61, 138, 157-8; chief governor (1521-4, 1528-9), 15, 16, 20, 21, 23, 28, 29, 34, 43, 44, 54, 60, 101, 218; feud with Kildare, 16, 19, 33-4, 35, 40, 42, 44, 60, 85, 101
Butler, James, lord Butler, 10th earl of Ormond, and 2nd earl of Ossory (1539-46), 23, 40, 101-2, 222
Butler, James Ormond, chief governor (1492-3), 28, 76, 217, 222
Butler, Edmund FitzJames, 200
Butler, Peter (of Potlerrath), 200
Butler, William, 132

Cabbot, Peter, 203
Calais, 48
Calverstown, 59
Candell, William, 170

Cantwell, James, 110
Carbury, 59, 185
Carlingford: castle, 62; lordship, 85; town, 62, 74
Carlow: shire, 54, 56, 58, 59, 60, 89, 91, 123, 136, 138, 198, 200, 202, 207; town and castle, 57, 59, 60, 62, 191, 202
Carrickfergus: castle, 62, 72, 207; town and port, 5, 57, 72, 74, 147
Carrick-on-Suir, 140
Cartmel Priory, 80
Cashel: archbishop, 38, 113; archbishopric, 201; town, 182
Castle Chamber, court of, 154
Castledermot, 59, 60, 148, 174
Castlekevin, 60
Chancellor, 15, 16, 32, 37, 38, 112, 122, 162, 163, 167; administrative duties, 33, 107, 166, 168, 169, 173, 174, 175, 199; judicial duties, 106, 140, 155, 159, 160, 173-4; president of the council and residual head, 20, 22, 42, 43, 47, 155, 174, 177; councillor, 22, 24, 36, 40, 43, 44, 45, 155, 157, 166; salary and perquisites, 80, 85, 107, 165-6 training, 109
Chancery (of England), 114, 145, 159, 165, 170, 176, 179. *See also* seals
Chancery (of Ireland), 85, 90, 92, 135, 144, 158, 175, 182
    administrative organization and practices of, 165-71, 173, 174, 175, 176-7, 179-80, 193, 209, 210
    as a law court, 134, 143, 150, 163, 169, 174, 209; Latin jurisdiction, 159, 162, 167; equitable jurisdiction, 159-62, 166
    hanaper of, 79-80, 136, 165-6, 172
    itineration of, 43, 173-4, 179, 209
    rolls of, 22, 38, 39, 102, 123, 151, 159, 166-7, 169, 172, 177, 179, 180, 183
    officers of: chancellor, q.v;
        clerk, keeper, or master of the rolls, administrative duties, 165, 166, 167, 169, 171, 172, 174, judicial duties, 106, 162-3, 166, 170, as councillor, 22, 36, 162, salary of, 166, training of, 109, 171, clerks of, 170-1, also mentioned, 16, 34, 37, 108, 170; clerk of the crown, 165, 167, 168, 169, 170, 176, 177, 179, salary of, 168; clerk of the hanaper, 30, 94, 165-71 *passim*, 174, 176, salary of, 167-8; clerks of, 37, 38, 109, 110, 123, 127, 136, 162, 163, 165, 166, 167, 169-72, 175, 180; masters in, 46, 161, 165, 169, 170. *See also*, seals
Charles I, king of England, 168
Chevir, William, J.K.B., 107
Chief governor:
    as justiciar, 14, 138, 155, 157, 160, 181; as military commander, 9, 10, 14, 25-9, 32, 49-57, 62-3, 68, 104, 188, 191, 206
    household and private council of, 37, 41, 42, 80, 176

inauguration of, 22, 39

itineration of, 43, 173-4, 209

powers of, 12-21, 30, 93, 107, 124, 131, 151, 167, 174, 175, 176, 177, 180, 182, 189, 190, 211; appointment of officers, 14-17, 62, 87, 95, 97, 101, 169, 179; deputation, 13, 18-20, 175; knighthood, 13; parliament, 14, 15, 17-18, 19, 144, 146, 147, 149, 150, 154, 175; pardon, 14, 17, 21, 30, 31, 35, 40, 41, 44, 122; purveyance, 14, 20, 31, 43, 54. *See also* coign and livery

royal control over, 12, 32, 47, 91, 154, 178, 206, 214

salary and perquisites of, 25-7, 29-31, 49-50, 78, 80-1, 83, 87, 101, 126

titles of, 12-13, 19-20, 23, 28

also mentioned, 184. *See also* seals, council

Chiefs in Gaelic Ireland, 3, 9, 10, 29, 38, 39, 55, 58, 61, 62, 63, 65, 66; blackrents of, 63-4

Clanrickard, lord of, *see* de Burgh

Clinton, Patrick, 131-2

Cloncurry, 64

Clonmel, 44, 139

Clonmore, 60

Clonogan, 60

Cogley, Patrick, 170, 171, 220, 223

coign and livery, 20-1, 35, 51, 52, 53-4, 55, 57, 58, 64, 65, 70, 139, 175, 208

commissioners, English, in Ireland, 6, 28, 40, 52, 138-9, 151, 190

commissions of justice, 109-10, 114, 124, 134-41, 156, 168, 175, 200; of assize, 109, 110, 134, 135, 136, 137; of gaol delivery, 134, 136, 137, 182, 190; of oyer and certifier, 135, 138, 155; of oyer and terminer, 110, 134, 135, 136, 137, 138, 182, 190; of the peace, 135, 137, 151, 171, 188, 189-90; general, 110, 123, 128, 137, 163, 188, 195, 198, 207, 210

common bench, court of (in England), 111, 112, 114, 116, 117,

common bench (*alias* common place/pleas, Dublin bench), court of (in Ireland): estreats of, 111, 113, 115, 116, 197; itineration of, 112, 124, 175; jurisdiction of, 112, 117-21, 132-3, 141, 201; privilege in, 108, 119, 120-21; profits of, 111, 168; rolls of, 111-15 *passim*, 117, 118, 120, 133, 145; seal of, 168; standards of justice in, 107-8, 112; weight of business in, 111-17, 119-21, 141, 145; *officers of*: chief justice, duties of, 42, 106, 195, 199, as councillor, 34, 36, 39, 42, 45, legal training, 108, misconduct, 107-8 salary, 106; justices, 16, 34, 36, 106, 107-8, 117, 156, 160, 170, salary, 106, 108; clerks, 108, 120, 172-3; chirographer, 172; prothonotary, 172, 173

compurgation, 119-20

Connaught, shire of, 5, 9, 89, 91, 137, 138, 162, 195, 199, 200, 201, 208

Conway, Hugh, treasurer, 92, 100, 222
Coolock, barony of, 202, 204
Cork: archdeacon of, 123; city of, 5, 13, 57, 74, 77-8, 89, 90, 110, 123, 173, 182; shire of, 58, 86, 88, 89, 91, 136, 137, 193, 198, 200
Cork and Cloyne: bishopric of, 201; diocese of, 148
Cornewalshe, John, chief baron of the exchequer, 32, 221
coroners, 137, 182, 190, 203-4; duties of, 203-4
council of England, 35, 37, 39, 46, 47, 114, 143, 154, 155, 156, 176; Irish business in, 14, 21, 32, 33, 48, 149, 157, 158, 177-8, 192; great councils, 150-1. *See also* Star Chamber
council of Ireland:
  clerk of, 37-9, 155, 165, 170, 176-7
  administrative duties, 17, 20, 22, 23, 24, 31, 32, 34-6, 38, 40, 42-3, 46-8, 51, 56, 62, 85, 93, 149, 150, 151, 155, 171, 174, 178, 184, 190
  executive duties, 42-3, 44, 45, 46-7, 48, 175, 211
  judicial duties, 38-9, 42, 43, 44, 140, 143, 145, 149, 150, 154-63 *passim*, 182, 209-10
  faction in, 15, 17, 32-4, 145
  institutional development of, 36-7, 38, 39-42, 44, 46, 154, 209, 211, 214
  membership of, 31-2, 35-7, 40-1, 44-6, 210, 214
  records of, 38-9, 44
  relations with the chief governor, 14, 15, 17, 22, 23, 24, 31, 32-4, 36, 37, 40, 41-4, 45-6, 47-8, 56, 155, 157, 175, 176-7, 211
  afforced and great councils, 17, 36, 39, 43, 56, 71, 133, 146, 150-2, 160, 170, 176, 211
  legal counsel, 13, 106-10
  regional councils, 44, 186. *See also* Castle Chamber
county courts, 88, 132, 150, 193, 195, 204
Cowley, J., 171
Cowley, Robert, 33, 37, 170, 220, 225
Cowley, S., 171
Cromer, George, archbishop of Armagh, 33, 44, 45, 161, 220
Cromwell, Thomas, lord privy seal, 46-7; Irish policy, 17, 29, 40, 44, 47, 48, 176, 178, 186, 211. *See also Ordinances*
crown lands, 67, 74-8, 81, 83-4, 86, 93, 100, 104, 105, 124, 125, 129, 176, 186, 202, 204
Cruise family, 202
Crumlin, 75
Cusack, Christopher (of Gerardstown), 6, 92-4, 197, 198
Cusack, J., 171
Cusack, Nicholas, 203
Cusack, Richard, 203
Cusack, S., 171

Cusack, Thomas, 203, 223
custom of Ireland, 13-14, 15, 111, 157
customs, 30, 53, 62, 67, 72-4, 84, 86, 94, 103, 126-7, 128, 139, 155, 207; great and small customs, 72-4, 82, 83; poundage, 53, 72, 82, 83, 87, 127; officials, 74, 94, 95, 104, 126, 127, 153, 172

Dalkey, 51
Darcy, William, undertreasurer, 32-3, 35, 75, 84, 85, 99, 100, 101, 222
Davies, Sir John, 38, 143
Deane, Henry, bishop of Bangor: chancellor, 15, 161, 220; chief governor, 15, 17, 218
debt, action of, 112, 113, 116-21 *passim*, 133, 141, 193, 195, 202
de Burgh (Burke), lords of Clanrickard, 63, 162, 182, 199
Delahide, Richard, C.J.C.P., 34, 39, 42, 221, 223
Delahide, Walter, 37
Delahide, William, 37, 39, 225
de la Pole, John, earl of Lincoln, 15, 217
Delvin, baron of, *see* Nugent
Desmond, earl of, *see* Fitzgerald; earldom of, 58, 187
detinue, action of, 112, 118, 119
Dexcester, John, 96, 223
Dillon, Bartholomew, C.J.K.B., 33, 34, 95, 96, 101, 108, 221, 222, 223
Dingle, 187
Dowdall, Patrick, 180
Dowdall, Robert, C.J.C.P., 107-8, 221
Down, shire, of, 9, 61
Drogheda: port of, 72-4; town of, 2, 5, 62, 74, 77, 94, 95, 105, 112, 116, 120, 121, 124, 155, 174, 182, 191; mayor of, 131
Drumdugne, water of, 204
Dublin:
  archbishop of, 78-9, 120, 128, 135, 155, 157, 184, 187. *See also* Alen, Browne, FitzSimons; St. Sepulchre
  castle of, 61-2, 63, 85, 103, 110, 112, 132, 161, 175; clerk of the works, 172; constable of, 62, 110, 132
  city of, 2, 58, 74, 77-8, 90, 94, 95, 105, 112, 113, 119, 127, 140, 149, 151, 155, 157, 182, 191, 196, 204; court of, 133, 182; mayor of, 90, 157, 191; population, 5; recorder of, 110; as administrative capital, 43, 44, 107, 112, 123 124, 136, 138, 148, 173, 174, 175, 179, 180, 182, 185, 186, 193, 207, 209, 213, 214
  port of, 72-4, 94, 103, 104, 172
  shire of, 52, 68, 91, 104, 116, 121, 135, 158, 187, 190, 192, 193, 195, 196, 202, 203, 205
  marches of, 55, 60, 63, 75, 76. *See also* common bench
Duffe, Henry, chief baron of the exchequer, 108, 221, 224

Duiske, abbey of, 60
Duleek, barony of, 202; town of, 124
Dunboyne, 129
Dundalk, 51, 72, 73, 74, 83, 199
Dungarvan, 139, 140, 173
Durbard's Island, 140

Edgecumbe, Richard, 151
Edward I, king of England, 72, 79, 98, 106, 113, 133, 135, 141
Edward II, king of England, 96, 111, 135
Edward III, king of England, 94, 155, 157, 169, 196
Edward IV, king of England, and Ireland, 10, 11, 24, 32, 46, 49, 72, 83, 88, 90, 96, 104, 106, 115, 126, 144, 145, 147, 176, 206, 216; and Irish administrative reform, 15, 25, 36, 41, 50, 67, 69-70, 86, 117, 146, 165-6, 168, 174, 184, 209, 213; Irish policy of, 3-4, 14-16, 28, 75, 76, 78, 184-5
Edward VI, king of England, 189, 190
'Edward VI', pretender, *see* Simnel
Elizabeth I, queen of England, 22, 46, 136, 149, 150, 192; Irish policy of, 9, 11, 27, 70, 186
emigration to England, 10-11, 130-1, 211. *See also* absentee landowners
English language in Ireland, 6, 138-9, 149, 151, 162
escheators, 190; account of, 88, 90-5; appointment of, 88-9; duties of, 124, 136, 182, 197-8, 199; exchequer control of, 87, 88-9; oath of, 198
Esker, 75
Estrete, John, 35, 221, 224
Exchequer (of England), 3, 86-7, 92, 94, 96, 99, 103, 104, 105, 114, 117, 134; and Ireland, 49, 68, 95; court of exchequer chamber, 134
Exchequer (of Ireland):
 exchequer of audit, 76, 77, 86-97, 101, 104, 105, 123, 128, 129, 166, 168, 178, 191, 196, 208
 of receipt, 90, 97-9, 102, 104, 105; issues of, 25, 27, 50, 57, 62, 63, 79, 80-1, 84, 87, 103, 166, 191, 196, 203; receipts of, 30, 60, 72, 76, 79-80, 82, 83-6, 87, 102, 103, 140, 166, 183; assignments by, 80-1, 82-3, 86, 87, 89, 92, 98, 99, 102-5, 196, 200, 208. *See also* revenues
 as law court, 108, 134, 141, 197; common pleas in: 87, 111, 114, 116-20 *passim*, 125, 134; profits of, 111; weight of business in, 111, 116-17, 141; crown business in: 123-32, 142, 153, 156, 157, 199; penal law enforcement, 80, 123, 127-8, 142, 153
 control of, 21, 69-70, 72, 78, 82, 87, 89, 91, 123, 140, 175, 183, 187, 199-200, 209

estreats of, 93, 111, 116, 189
itineration of, 112, 123-4, 209
records of, 63, 94, 96-9 *passim*, 102-3, 111, 116, 125, 126, 130, 167, 172; memoranda rolls, 79, 87, 90, 91, 92, 94, 95-6, 99, 101, 111, 117, 119, 124-5, 129, 156, 197, 199, 200, 201; pipe rolls, 85, 94, 95; receipt and issue rolls, 82, 98, 99, 102
Red Book of, plate between pp. 88-9, 134
seal of, 88, 91, 93, 101, 124, 177
officers of: auditors, 45, 98; barons, 16, duties, 88, 90, 92, 94, 95, 101, 123, 126, 132, 156, 175, 199, 202, 203, legal training, 108, numbers, 106, salary, 106; chief baron, 17, 128, duties, 92, 109, 138, as councillor, 15, 32, 34, 36, 39, 42, 45, legal training, 108, salary, 106; chamberlains, 97, 171 chancellor, 17, 97, 124, clerks, 97, 105, 108, 171-2, 197; of common pleas, 97, 173, of estreats, 93, of the receipt, 98; engrossers, 92-3, 94, 97, 180; janitor and crier, 97; messenger, 97, 128, 131, 203; remembrancers, 125, 131, chief remembrancer, 17, 90, 94, 96, 99, second remembrancer, 96, 98, 99, 171, clerks of, 96; summamster, 92-3, 97; transcriptor, 97, 173
court of chequer chamber, 134

Fartullagh, 77
Fassaroe, 60
Fr. John, government spy, 63
Ferns: bishop of, 141, 193; dean of, 141; manor of, 60, 77
feudal incidents, 78-9, 93, 124, 125-6, 136-7, 139, 153, 199, 209. *See also* wardships
fiants, 29, 30, 35, 123, 166, 173, 174-6, 179. *See also* seals
Finglas, Patrick, C.J.K.B., 34, 221, 222, 224
FitzDavy, John, 200
FitzEustace, Roland, lord Portlester, 6, 26, 95, 107, 124, 216, 220, 222
Fitzgerald (of Desmond), Thomas, 7th earl of Desmond (1462-8), 4, 18, 19, 28, 29, 50, 52, 144, 173, 184, 216
Fitzgerald, Thomas, 11th earl of Desmond (1529-34), 140, 156, 157
Fitzgerald (of Dromana) family, 200
Fitzgerald (of Dromana) John, 200
Fitzgerald (of Kildare), family, 40, 58, 59, 60, 61, 65, 77, 172, 173, 185, 207, 214; feud with Butlers, 16, 19, 28, 33-5, 40, 42, 44, 59, 60, 85, 101
Fitzgerald, Thomas, 7th earl of Kildare (1456-78), 28, 59, 220; as chief governor, 15, 25, 36, 50, 52, 53, 216, 217
Fitzgerald, Gerald, 8th earl of Kildare (1478-1513), 59, 62, 64, 65, 155; as chief governor, 12-13, 15, 16, 17, 19, 25, 26, 28, 29, 30, 32, 36, 50, 53, 54-5, 63, 74, 80, 82, 84, 100, 149, 176, 217, 218; restoration (1496), 54, 84, 100, 154

Fitzgerald, Gerald, 9th earl of Kildare (1513-34), 30, 40, 44, 45, 46, 48, 59, 60, 64, 65-6, 100, 124, 157, 158, 172, 194, 222; as chief governor, 15, 16, 17, 19-24 *passim*, 29, 31, 32-4, 35, 37, 41, 42, 43, 54-5, 62, 74, 81, 82, 100, 101-2, 157, 198, 214, 218, 219
Fitzgerald, Thomas, 10th earl of Kildare (1534-6), 154; as baron of Offaly, chief governor, 22, 23, 176, 219
Fitzgerald, James, brother of 9th earl, 42, 154
Fitzgerald, Maurice, brother of 9th earl, 21, 218
Fitzgerald, Thomas, brother of 9th earl, 8, 23, 77, 218
FitzLeones, Patrick, 90
FitzSimons, Thomas, 110, 224
FitzSimons, Walter, archbishop of Dublin, 28, 217, 218, 220
Flatesbury, Philip, 98, 171-2, 224
Fleming, Christopher, baron of Slane, 32, 100-1, 190, 222
Fleming, Gerald, 131
Fleming, John 98
Fore, 74, 128
France, 10
Furness, abbey of, 80

Gaelic (Irish) culture within Englishry: customs, 5, 7, 64, 138-9, 181, 186, 207, 210, 212. *See also* coign and livery; language, 6, 138-9; law (Brehon law), 5, 64, 129, 138-9, 186, 194, 205, 210
Gaelic population in Englishry, 6-7, 55-6, 129-30, 131, 193; anglicization of, 6, 130, 131, 193; status at common law, 129-30, 139, 141
Gaelic revival, 2-3, 7, 10, 75, 181
Galway, 5, 9, 57, 86, 123, 147, 162, 174, 182, 183
Garnon, Philip, 203
Garristown, 112
Gascony, 118
Geraldstown, 205
Gernon, Roger, 204
Gerrard, William, lord chancellor, 107, 122
Golding, clerk of chancery, 169
Gormanston: baron and viscount of, *see* Preston; manor of, 173
Gowran, 58, 139
Grangegorman, 205
Greencastle, 62
Grey, Arthur, lord Grey de Wilton, 22
Grey, Henry, lord Grey of Codnor, 24, 26, 53, 69, 185, 217
Grey, Leonard, lord Grey, 24, 30, 38, 47, 178
Grey, Thomas, marquis of Dorset, 13

Harrold, Edmund, 63
Hattecliffe, William, undertreasurer, 63, 75, 81, 83, 88, 92, 93, 99, 100, 103, 198, 222
Hawkenshaw, Roger, J.K.B., 102
Henry II, king of England, 118
Henry V, king of England, 102
Henry VI, king of England, 3, 4, 10, 213; and Ireland, 68, 74, 82-3, 85, 102, 105, 113, 144, 147, 197, 216; Irish policy, 3, 10, 15, 32
Henry VII, king of England, 10, 16, 38, 49, 68, 96, 104, 108, 132, 175, 183; and Irish administrative reform, 32, 83, 86, 112, 160, 213. *See also* Poynings; Irish policy, 12, 15, 19, 26, 28-9, 46, 67, 75, 77-8, 90-1, 136, 176, 182, 198, 200, 201, 206
Henry VIII, king of England, ix, 2, 111, 124, 154, 168, 169, 172; and 'direct rule' for Ireland, 1, 20, 65-6, 86, 186, 212; as Henry duke of York lieutenant of Ireland, 12, 14-15, 218; Irish policy, 16, 21, 23, 29, 30, 32, 33, 36, 40, 46, 48, 49, 61, 76-7, 78, 85, 108, 141, 158, 178, 185, 186, 189, 199, 200, 214
Holmpatrick, 94
homage, oath of, 14, 125, 175; respite of, 78-9, 168
hostings, 56-7, 60, 71, 191; cartage for, 56, 191
Howard, Thomas, earl of Surrey: as chief governor, 13, 15, 16, 17, 19, 20, 21, 27, 28, 33-4, 35, 37, 41-2, 45, 76, 127, 218; as duke of Norfolk, 43, 80
Howth, baron of, *see* St. Lawrence
Hussey, Walter, 97, 222, 223, 224
Hussey, William, 200

Indians, 9
indictments, 115, 120-3 *passim*, 135, 138, 149, 189, 191-2, 204
Inge, Hugh, bishop of Meath, 42, 220
Inns of Court, 8, 110
Irishtown, 139, 190
Isam, Robert, 171

James I, king of England, 38, 154, 210
juries: grand, 115, 122, 123, 124, 129, 138-9, 162, 189, 194; trial, 121, 122, 129, 132, 192, 194, 195, 205; presentments of, 124, 138-9, 140, 162, 186, 187, 189, 192, 194

Keating, family, 200
Keating, James, prior of Kilmainham, 132
Keating, Robert (of Chapelizod), 132
Kells, 7, 116, 124, 128, 129
Kerdiff, Walter, J.C.P., 108, 221

Kerry: liberty of, 184, 187 and seneschal, 12, 89, 187; shire of, 58, 136, 137, 138, 147; shire of the cross of, 89, 136, 200
Kilcash, Statutes of, 194
Kilcullen, 59
Kilculliheen, abbess of, 123
Kildare: bishop of, *see* Lang; bishopric of, 201; castle and town of, 59, 173; earl of, *see* Fitzgerald; earldom of, 6, 58, 59, 60, 207; liberty of, 44, 116, 185, 186, 202, and court, 108, and justices, 185; shire of, 54, 55, 58, 59, 69, 82, 84, 85, 93, 118, 190, 192, 196, 199, 202, 203, 207
Kildare rebellion (1534-5), 1, 3, 4, 16, 65, 76, 85, 86, 102, 124, 135, 149, 161, 186, 211
Kilkenny: shire of, 6, 57, 61, 71, 84, 88, 89, 91, 109, 110, 113, 123, 136-40 *passim*, 147, 151, 160, 162, 189, 193, 194, 198, 200; town of, 45, 57, 59, 60, 113, 139, 151, 160, 161, 173, 189, 190
Killussy, 173
Kilmainham, prior of, *see* Keating, Rawson
Kiltale, John, 173
king's attorney, 38, 106, 108, 125, 157
king's bench, court of (in England), 111, 112, 114, 117, 120, 121, 122; Irish jurisdiction of, 133-4, 144, 145
king's bench, court of (in Ireland) (justiciar's bench):
    estreats of, 107, 111, 112, 113, 115, 116, 197
    itineration of, 43, 112, 135, 173, 185, 189, 209
    jurisdiction of: 112, 117, 141, 144, 173; civil, 119-20; criminal, 115, 121-3, 128, 129, 142, 149, 189, 192, 202; review, 117, 132-4, 187, 192
    procedure without writ in, 120, 133
    profits of, 111, 168
    seal of, 168
    standards of justice in, 107, 112, 142
    weight of business in, 111-17, 119-21, 141, 145
    officers of: chief justice of, 15, 16, 17, 32, 102, 112, 200, as councillor, 31, 34, 36, 39, 42, 43, 44, 45, duties, 106, 135, legal training, 108, misconduct, 107, salary, 106; justices of, 16, 34, 36, 37, 45, 96, 106, 107, 108, 137, 156, 204, salary, 106, 168; clerks of, 108, 172-3; clerk of the crown, 123, 172
king's serjeant-at-arms, 97; second serjeant, 202
king's serjeant-at-law and solicitor-general, 37, 108, 170; as councillor, 35, 36; duties, 106, 108, 110, 125, 129, 137, 199; salary, 106
Kinsale, 182
Knockgowne, 140
Knockgraffon, 205
Kyltale, William, 170

Lackagh, 59
Lang, Richard, bishop of Kildare, 35, 37
Lea, 59
Leighlin: bishop of, 151; bishopric of, 201; bridge, 59, 60, 128; castle, 59, 60
Leixlip, 77, 199
Liffey, river, 204
Limerick: bishopric of, 201; castle of, 62, 82, 110, 207; city of, 5, 57, 59, 74, 77, 89, 90, 123, 138, 147, 156, 178, 182; shire of, 58, 86, 89, 91, 136, 137, 138, 147, 193, 200
Lismore, bishop of, *see* Waterford and Lismore
Loughsewdy, 77, 86
Louth, shire of, 91, 93, 116, 121, 189, 191, 192, 195, 196, 199, 203, 204
Luttrell, Thomas, C.J.C.P., 135, 195, 221, 224
Lynn, Robert, 170, 171, 223

McGilduff alias Duff (de ffygarth), Cornelius alias Cowconnagh, 129-30
McGilduff, Patrick, 129-30
McMahon, chief of Oriel, 63
McMahon, William, 64
McMurrough Kavanagh, chief of Leinster, 58, 60, 63
McMurrough, Charles, abbot of Duiske, 60
McRoryk, Cormac, 110
MacShane, Gerald, 44
McWilliam, Ulick de Burgh, lord of Clanrickard, 63
Magyn, Arthur, 110
Malahide, 130
manorial system, 6-7
marches, captains and wardens of, 51, 57, 58, 191; customs of, 7, 8, 63-4, 210, 212; law of, 210; Anglo-Scottish borders, 14, 49, 71, 206, 212. *See also* Pale
markets, clerk of, 182, 198-9
marshal of the four courts, 97, 120; Marshalsea of, 117, 131, 132, 141
Mary I, queen of England, 125, 196, 198, 203
Maynooth: castle and town of, 173, 174; manor of, 6, 59
Meath: bishop of, *see* Sherwood, Staples, Inge; shire of, 56, 59, 61, 68, 69, 70, 75, 91, 92, 94, 104, 111, 112, 115-16, 121, 124, 130, 131-2, 142, 151, 155, 158, 161, 185, 188-91 *passim*, 193, 196-204 *passim*. *See also* Westmeath; liberty of, 116, 141, 184, 185, and seneschal, 185
Middlesex, bill of, 120
mint (in Ireland), x, 79-80, 83, 84, 86, 103, 146, 211; controller of, 172; master of, 15, 104; profits of, 79-80, 103, 105
Moret, 59

Mortimer, earls of March, inheritance of, 75, 86
Moynalvy, 155
Murray, William, 203

Naas: barony of, 202; town of, 74, 173
Nangle, Richard, 99, 171, 172, 220, 222, 224, 225
Navan, 124, 128, 173, 174
Nenagh, 61
Netterville, Thomas, J.C.P., 108, 221, 224
Newcastle, barony of, 55, 202
Newcastle (Lyons, Co. Dublin), manor of, 75
Newcastle (Co. Meath), 131
Newman, James, 171
New Ross, 59, 60, 138, 139, 155, 158, 161, 182
nisi prius, trial at, 135, 138, 189, 210
Norman invasion, 1, 5, 8
Norragh, 59
north of England: government of, 4, 11, 14, 49, 71, 138, 184, 199, 200, 206; king's council in, 4, 47, 186; king's lieutenant in, 14; warden of the marches, 14
Nugent, family, 61
Nugent, Richard, baron of Delvin, 21, 23, 35, 40, 42, 43, 54, 190, 218, 219

Obeghan, William, 129
lez Obeghnez, Irish enemies, 129
Obelan, William, 129
O'Brien, chief of Thomond, 63, 84
O'Brien, Turlough, bishop of Killaloe, 63, 64
O'Byrne, chief of Wicklow, 63, 64
O'Byrne, William, 128
O'Carroll, chief of Ely, 63
O'Connor Faly, chief of Offaly 23, 43, 59, 63-4
Offaly: baron of, *see* Fitzgerald; serjeanty of, 202
O'More, Rory, captain of Leix, 162
O'Neill, chief of Clandeboye, 9
O'Neill, chief of Tyrone, 63
O'Nolan, Irish enemy, 58
Ordinances for the government of Ireland (1534), 30, 41, 137, 176, 211
Ormond, earl of, *see* Butler, Boleyn; earldom of, 3, 5, 6, 42, 57-8, 71, 80, 105, 107, 130, 157-8, 189, 192, 202
Ossory: bishop of, 79, 103, 110, 151; bishopric of, 201; earl of, *see* Butler
O'Toole, Arthur, 63
outlawry, 115, 116, 117, 132-3, 160, 195, 204

palatinates, administrative organization of, 187-9 *passim*; central control of, 137, 184, 187, 188, 207; crown's attitude to, 183-6, 187, 207; jurisdiction of, 137, 187, 189, 192. *See also* Kerry, Kildare, Meath, St. Sepulchre, Tipperary, Ulster, Wexford

Pale (English Pale in Ireland), administration of, 50-51, 68, 69, 71, 72, 74, 78, 86, 88-93 *passim*, 95, 103, 105, 121, 123, 128, 129-30, 135, 141, 147, 148, 151, 164, 173, 181, 185, 189, 195, 198, 200, 201, 204-7 *passim*, 215; defence of, 3, 4, 20, 44, 50-7, 61, 63-4, 65-6, 207; extent of, 50-2; maghery, 51-2, 54; marches, 51-2, 54, 58, 61, 190, 207; lords and gentry of, 6, 33, 36, 40, 51, 55-6, 61, 65, 116, 148, 189, 190; manorial system in, 6, 7; 'second pale', 187; also mentioned, 5, 43, 80, 103, 112, 114, 128, 136, 145, 146, 161, 163, 187, 188, 193, 208, 213

Parliament (in England), 79, 143, 144, 148, 149, 150, 179; legislation for Ireland in, 152-4. *See also* statutes: England

Parliament (in Ireland):
    administrative work of, 15, 19, 52, 59, 71, 104, 107, 116, 122, 123, 126, 144, 146-7, 149-50, 152, 154, 163, 175
    judical functions of, 107, 132, 133-4, 143-7, 149-50, 155, 159-60, 163, 164, 183, 192, 209; equitable jurisdiction, 145, 159-60, 210; weight of business in, 143-7, 149, 163
    legislation by, 24, 140, 143, 146, 150-4, 178, 190, 201, 211, 214; frequency of sessions, 133, 144-5, 146, 149-50
    membership: the commons, 143, 147, 148, 149; the clerical proctors, 68, 147, 147, 148; the lords, 41, 133, 143, 147, 148, 149, 157; speaker of the commons, 110; clerks, 146, 170, 176
    opposition in, 54
    petitions to, 32, 107, 123, 138, 143, 144, 146, 149, 150, 159, 183; addresses to the king, 41, 152, 178, 211
    representation in, 68, 146, 147-8, 157, 210; amercement for absence, 147-8
    rolls of, 69, 143-7, 149, 159, 166, 183
    also mentioned, 14, 17-18, 24, 36, 51, 109, 127, 170, 177, 209, 210. *See also* statutes: Ireland, taxation.

peace, guardians, keepers, justices, wardens of, 137, 188, 189, 190-9; 210; constables of, 171, 204; quarter sessions, 189. *See also* commissions, marches

Pelham, William, chief governor, 22

Pilgrimage of Grace, 4

Plantagenet, George, duke of Clarence, lieutenant of Ireland (1462-78), 13, 14, 15, 18, 216, 217

Plantagenet, George, son of Edward IV, lieutenant of Ireland (1478), 15, 217

Plantagenet, Richard, duke of York lieutenant of Ireland (1447-60), 3, 144, 175
Plantagenet, Richard, son of Edward IV, lieutenant of Ireland (1479-83), 15, 18, 217
Plate, John, 204
pleaders (*narratores*), 109, 110
Plunket, Edward, 131
posse comitatus, 57-8, 191
Power, family, 200
Power, James, J.C.P., 107, 221
Power, John, 171
Powerscourt, 60
Poynings, Edward, chief governor, 3, 15, 17, 18, 27, 29, 45, 51, 53, 84, 94, 98, 127, 151, 154, 166, 178, 209, 211, 218; and administrative reform, 16, 53, 70, 74, 78, 81, 95, 97, 100, 109, 126, 147, 149, 168, 209-10
Poynings' Law, *see* statutes: Ireland
Prendregast, James, clerk of the council, 170, 220, 221, 225
Prendregast, James, clerk of parliaments, 170
Preston, Robert, baron of Gormanston, 1st viscount Gormanston, chief governor (1477, 1479, 1493-4), 15, 18, 19, 24, 25, 26, 28, 30, 173, 217
Preston, William, 2nd viscount Gormanston, chief governor (1493-4, 1515), 19, 22, 190, 218, 222
prise wines, 80, 89, 103, 138, 140, 155, 158, 175, 178
Provisors, statutes of, 121, 136, 139, 157
purveyance, 14, 191. *See also* chief governor, coign and livery

Quinn, David B., 181

Rathangan, 59
Rathmore, 59, 118, 173
Rathvilly, 60
Rathwire, 85, 156
Ratoath, 85
Rawson, John, prior of Kilmainham, 46, 101, 219, 222
real actions, 117-19, 141, 145, 155, 161, 162, 172, 194
Reformation, 1, 186; and parliament, 24, 138, 211, 214; and dissolution of the monasteries, 78, 124
reserved appointments, 14-17, 29, 32, 33-4, 36, 46, 47, 101, 102, 177
resumption, acts of, 85-6, 196; 1493 act, 74, 76, 81, 83, 208; 1494 act, 74, 76, 77-8, 81, 83, 156, 178, 201, 208; 1536 act, 78, 124
revenues of the crown (in Ireland), 25-6, 29-30, 67-86, 102, 104, 131, 206-7, 208-9

Ricard, John, 162, 220
Richard II, king of England, 82, 102
Richard III, king of England, 15, 19, 168, 201
Richardson, H.G., 145, 150
Roche, Maurice, lord Roche, 88, 200
Roche, John, 201
Roche, Philip, 205
Roche, Stephen, 170
Roche, townland of, *see* Bellew
Rochfort, Thomas, 170, 220, 224
Ryan, John, 99, 223, 224
Ryan, Thomas, 129

St. John's Kells, prior of, 129
St. John's, Kilmainham, prior of the Hospital of, *see* Keating, Rawson
St. Lawrence, Nicholas, lord Howth, 45, 155, 223
St. Leger, Anne, 157
St. Leger, Anthony, 211
St. Mary's, Dublin, abbey of, 204; abbot of, 161-2
St Patrick's Cathedral, Dublin, precentor of, 128
St. Sepulchre's, Dublin, liberty of, 157, 184, 187
Salt, barony of, 202
Savage, family, 185
Sayles, G.O., *see* Richardson, H.G.
Scotland, 8, 14, 49, 71, 206, 212
seals:
    great seal of England, 175; Irish appointments under, 16, 17, 24, 88, 101, 162, 177, 178, 179; other Irish business, 117, 157, 158, 175, 177-80 *3passim*
    great seal of Ireland, 17, 20, 23, 24, 88, 89, 98, 115, 123, 124, 134, 136, 150, 157, 158, 162, 165-70 *passim*, 174, 176, 178, 179; decline of original force of, 165-8 *passim*, 174-8 *passim*, 180, 209
    privy seal, king's, 166, 175-9 *passim*; warrants of, 18, 24, 42, 158, 174-80
    privy seal, governor's, 18, 24, 36, 37, 42, 57, 150, 165, 166, 167, 173, 174-7, 179-80, 209, 210; keeper of, 37, 176-7. *See also* fiants
    signet, king's, 166, 177-9
    signet, governor's, 18
See also common bench, exchequer, king's bench
sea-wreck, 132
Selskar, priory of, 157
serjeants, 139, 192, 201, 202-3; chief serjeants, 201-2; underserjeants, 121, 192, 201, 202. *See also* king's serjeant, pleaders

Sharpe, Thomas, 97
sheriffs: account of, 88, 90-5, 191, 196-7; appointment of, 88-9, 195, 199, 200; administrative duties, 111-12, 188, 191, 195-7, 198, 201, 203, 204; judicial duties, 115, 117, 188-93 *passim*, 195, 199; sheriff's tourn, 189, 191-3, 194, 195; military duties, 62, 188, 191; exchequer control of, 87, 88-9, 207; oath of, 196, 203; clerks of, 131, 203; undersheriffs, 192, 195, 203
Sherlock, George, 110
Sherlock, James, 109, 138
Sherwood, William, bishop of Meath, 28, 53, 217, 220
Sidney, Henry, chief governor, 38
Simnel, Lambert, 88, 132, 151, 176, 201, 217
Skeffington, William, chief governor, 15, 16, 24, 27-31 *passim*, 43, 47, 85, 178, 219; as commissioner, 28
Skreen, baron of, 196; barony of, 189, 203; town of, 124
Slane, baron of, *see* Fleming; barony of, 151, 188, 190
Sompter, Philip, 140
Stanley, Thomas, chief governor, 83
Staples, Edward, bishop of Meath, 37, 45
Star Chamber, 119, 154; Irish business in, 63, 158
Starkey, William, 131
statutes: England:
   3 Ric. II, Statute of Absentees, 79, 124, 128, 130
   other statutes and Ireland, 14, 127, 134, 152-4, 155, 191-2. *See also* Provisors
statutes: Ireland:
   40 Edw. III, Statutes of Kilkenny, 136, 139, 190
   12 & 13 Edw. IV c. 45, Statute of Archers, 127, 146
   3 Hen. VII c. 1, Act of Marches and Maghery, 51
   10 Hen. VII c. 5, treasurer to exercise his offices as treasurer of England, 21, 89, 95
   10 Hen. VII c. 6 judges and accountants to hold during pleasure, 14, 16. 109
   10 Hen. VII c. 9, Poynings' Law, 18, 47, 148-50, 152, 159, 160, 209
   10 Hen. VII c. 39, statutes late made in England to be executed in Ireland, 152-3
   Statute of Henry FitzEmpress, 20, 21, 25, 36
   other statutes, 36, 108, 112, 119-24 *passim*, 127, 128, 129, 135, 136, 143, 144, 158, 170, 171, 195, 211. *See also* resumption, Provisors
Stile, John, undertreasurer, 75, 81, 84-5, 101, 107, 222
Strangford, 74
subventions from England, financial, 2, 3, 4, 10, 16, 25-9, 49-50, 52, 53, 65, 67-8, 81, 86, 103, 209, 211, 213, 214; military, 2, 3, 10, 26-8, 49-50, 52, 53, 65, 209, 211, 213, 214

Suttell, Robert, 63
Swords, 129
Synnot, Walter (of Ballybrenan), 140

Talbot, John, 6th earl of Shrewsbury (1460-73), 184
Talbot, George, 7th earl of Shrewsbury (1473-1538), 58, 80, 184
Tallaght, 174
taxation, 25, 86, 143, 146, 150, 187, 206, 209, 210. *See also* customs; local taxation, 52, 58, 67, 68, 69, 146, 191; parliamentary subsidy, 50, 52, 53-4, 67-71, 82-7, 94, 97, 103, 126, 131, 146, 150, 171, 207; scutage (royal service), 57, 60, 67, 71-2, 83, 94, 146, 207
Termonfeckin, 161
Thomastown, 140
Tintern abbey, 80
Tipperary: liberty of, 57, 139, 140, 184, 186, 187, 192-3, 195, 202, 204, 207, and courts, 58, 137, 139, 192-3, 195, and justice, 108, 109, and seneschal, 95, 110; shire of, 6, 57, 61, 84, 136-9 *passim*, 151, 193, 205, 208; shire of the cross of, 88-9, 91, 136, 198, 200
Tiptoft, John, earl of Worcester, 4, 35, 52, 216, 220
Topcliffe, John, C.J.K.B., 32, 220, 221
towns in Ireland, 2, 5-6, 139, 141-2, 147, 182, 189, 191, 207
treasurer (of Ireland):
    lord treasurer, 32, 81, 92; duties, 16, 21, 26, 31, 82, 88, 89, 95, 98, 99-102, 103, 124, 125, 127, 171; as councillor, 15, 36, 37, 40, 42, 44, 45; salary, 100
    deputy-treasurer, 33, 91, 95, 100-1
    undertreasurer, 27, 34, 63, 75, 92, 107; duties, 16, 70, 74, 81, 89, 93, 95, 99-102, 171, 198; as councillor, 37; rise of, 16, 99-102; salary, 100
    treasurer-at-war, 27
    receiver-general, 75, 95, 100; salary, 100
    clerk of, 98, 99, 172; salary, 98
    accounts of, 21, 26, 27, 36, 63, 75, 81, 82-5, 88, 93, 166
trespass, action of, 107, 113, 116, 118-22 *passim*, 132, 141, 156, 192, 194; development of in landed litigation, 118
Trim: castle and town of, 39, 43, 62, 74, 112, 116, 137, 151, 173, 185, 199; liberty of, 137; manor of, 75, 105
Trimbleston, *see* Barnewall
Troserd, exchequer accountant, 99
Tudor, Jaspar, duke of Bedford, 15, 18, 19, 26, 217
Tullow, 59, 60
Turner, Nicholas, C.J.C.P., 108, 109, 221

Ulster: earldom and liberty of, 5, 9, 61, 74, 75, 77, 83, 138, 184-5, 201, 207; seneschal of, 95, 185

Vale, Richard, 200
Vale, Thomas, 200

Wales, 8, 157; council in the marches of, 47, 186; government of, 11, 14, 49, 71, 129, 183, 199; marcher lordships of, 58, 129, 183, 187, 194, 199, 208, 212; Welsh law, 5, 129, 194, 212
Warbeck, Perkin, 28, 79, 89, 182, 201
wardship, feudal right of, 30, 78-9, 84, 100. *See also* feudal incidents
Ware, Sir James, 38
Wars of the Roses, impact on Ireland, 3, 10, 12, 28
Waterford: city of, 5, 57, 62, 74, 77, 89, 90, 92, 103, 113, 123, 139, 140, 147, 151, 182, and dispute with New Ross, 138, 155, 158, and mayor, 92, 110, and recorder, 110, 151; shire of, 58, 68, 89, 91, 109, 110, 113, 123, 136-40 *passim*, 147, 151, 193, 198, 200, 208
Waterford and Lismore: bishop of, 110, 113; bishopric of, 201
weapons, of Englishry, 26-7, 51-6, 127, 132, 152; of Irishry, 9, 55-6. *See also* chief governors, subventions from England
Westmeath, 54, 55, 61, 74, 207; shire of, 93
Westminster, 47, 79, 181, 209, 210, 214
Wexford: shire of, 6, 58, 68, 71, 82, 85, 110, 113, 130, 136, 137, 138, 139, 140, 147, 157, 186, 198, 207, 208; shire of the cross of, 88-9, 92, 136, 139, 140, 200, 202; liberty of, 58, 60, 123, 139, 184, 186, 187, 193-4, 207 and justice, 110 and seneschal, 89, 140, 184; town of, 6, 139, 182
White, James, 110
White, John, 131
Wicklow, 62, 63, 128
Wiltshire, earl of, *see* Boleyn, Butler
Wise, John, 109, 221
Wise, William, 110
Wolsey, Thomas, lord chancellor of England, 13, 44, 47; Irish policy, 27, 41, 42, 47, 178
Worcester, earl of, *see* Tiptoft; shire of, 200
writs, 118, 119, 120, 131, 136, 148, 161, 168-72 *passim*, 175, 183, 191, 196, 197, 198, 201, 203, 204; original, 115, 120, 121, 136, 171, 182; judicial, 136, 168, 177; of *certiorari,* 134, 192, 203; of error, 117, 118, 132-3, 134, 187; of prohibition, 107, 129, 133; of *quo minus,* 119, 125; of *quo warranto,* 137, 184; of *sub poena,* 157, 159-60, 161, 162; of *supersedeas,* 126, 134
Wyatt, Henry, 45
Wycombe, Nicholas, 170, 220

Youghal, 74, 156, 182